Rhetoric Revalued

medieval & renaissance texts & studies

VOLUME 19

INTERNATIONAL SOCIETY
FOR THE HISTORY OF RHETORIC

MONOGRAPH NO. I, RHETORIC REVALUED
Edited by Brian Vickers

Rhetoric Revalued

Papers from the International Society
for the History of Rhetoric

EDITED BY

BRIAN VICKERS

medieval & Renaissance texts & studies
Center for Medieval & Early Renaissance Studies
Binghamton, New York
1982

Library of Congress Cataloging in Publication Data

Rhetoric revalued

  Medieval & Renaissance texts & studies; 19)
  English, French, German, and Italian.
  1. Rhetoric—Congresses. I. Vickers, Brian. II. International Society for
the History of Rhetoric. III. Series: Medieval & Renaissance texts &
studies; 19.
DN171.6.R5 1982   808   82–12447
ISBN 0–86698–020–2

Printed in the United States of America

International Society for the History of Rhetoric

Officers 1981–83

PRESIDENT: *Anton D. Leeman*
Universiteit Amsterdam

FIRST VICE-PRESIDENT: *George A. Kennedy*
University of North Carolina

SECOND VICE-PRESIDENT: *Cesare Vasoli*
Università di Firenze

SECRETARY-GENERAL: *Paolo Bagni*
Università di Bologna

TREASURER: *Kathleen Jamieson*
University of Maryland

Council
(with duration of office)

Contents

II. Rhetoric and Literature

III. Rhetoric and Philosophy

Preface

THE IMPULSE to found an International Society for the History of Rhetoric came during the 1976 conference of the society for Neo-Latin studies, held at Tours. It was a large and lively conference, yet—or so it seemed to myself and to the three colleagues to whom this volume is dedicated—among the vast number of papers offered few were concerned with rhetoric or reflected the importance that our discipline held in general education, in literature, in philosophy, and in other subjects during the Middle Ages and the Renaissance. Rhetoric did appear in different areas of that, and other conferences, before and since, but—due to its very flexibility and applicability—it gave the appearance of being fragmented, of having lost its original coherence. We therefore resolved to try to found a society for its study and advancement, and constituted ourselves—with the additional presence of A. D. Leeman and H. F. Plett—a steering committee, with the goal of planning the first conference for the following year.

The society was duly created, and the first meeting took place in Zürich in June, 1977. Having had the good fortune to be in charge of the Centre for Renaissance Studies at my university, the Eidgenössische Technische Hochschule, Zürich (whose nature might best be described as the Swiss national scientific university), I was able to offer our resources for this inaugural conference. That this proved to be such a success is due in the first place to the participants, and to the dedicated assistance of Ilse Fannenböck and Elisabeth Fritzsche; but the conference could not have taken place without the generosity of the university and its enlightened administrators, in particular the President, Professor Heinrich Ursprung, his secretary, Dr. Peter Schindler, and the director of research programmes, Dr. Eduard Freitag, to whom, as to all the other helpers, go our warmest thanks. It is fitting that our society was founded in an institution whose tradition of encouraging the humanities goes back to its foundation in 1855, and whose first-appointed professors included Jacob Burckhardt and Francesco de Sanctis.

The society, once formed, went from strength to strength, and now has over 400 members, scattered all round the world. The strength and variety of its contribution were clearly visible at the second international conference, held at the Vrije Universiteit, Amsterdam in June 1979. Here the Dutch conference committee, led by A. K. Kibédi Varga and ably assisted by Dr. Hugo Verdaasdonk and Marije van Urk, produced a most varied programme, breaking new ground for many of us in its coverage of rhetoric in the Netherlands. The third conference, planned for the University of Madison, Wisconsin, in the spring of 1981, promises to be even richer.

This volume consists of papers selected from the first two conferences. We hope that it will make several types of contribution to the study of a subject that, from the Greeks to the European Romantics, played such a major role in all forms of expression and communication, but has in modern times suffered precisely from its success in penetrating so many disciplines. The fact is that most of those who study and teach rhetoric in Europe are primarily engaged as historians or teachers of Greek, Latin, English, French, German, Italian and other literatures, and who have to "do rhetoric" in their spare time, or as a very minor part of a general course of study. In England, for instance, there is not, so far as I know, a single university post for the teaching of rhetoric, in sharp contrast to the situation in America, where flourish many departments of rhetoric, speech, and drama. One good result of the lack of specialization in Europe, of course, may be that we are in no danger of losing sight of the relations between rhetoric and other disciplines, as has sometimes happened in America; yet, equally, it means that we are all working away in our separate fields, often with no knowledge of important developments elsewhere, or of the strong links between our work, that fundamental unity of our discipline. The main purpose of our society is to re-establish the unity of rhetoric, and to help translate insights and experience from one historical period or country to another, and to move across boundaries of language and discipline. In the introduction that follows I attempt to point out some of the points of contact within rhetoric studies today, first by means of a general survey of what is being done and what ought to be done, then as a summary of the essays collected here, with their interconnections.

In addition to the eternal *envoi* on such an occasion, "Go, little book," I would like to quote a benediction which we owe to the medieval practitioners of this art:

Vivat, crescat, floreat rhetorica et vivant eius amatores!

BRIAN VICKERS

RHETORICA · XXIII ·

C· Z3

Introduction

I

In order to reconstruct the importance of rhetoric in the past a prolonged effort of the historical imagination is necessary. We have to overcome, first, the distrust and opposition to rhetoric that have prevailed in European poetics and aesthetics since the post-Romantic generation. As a historian of the sixteenth century put it,

> Rhetoric is the greatest barrier between us and our ancestors. . . .

Rhetoric began with the Greek sophists, survived the fall of the Roman Empire and penetrated

> far into the eighteenth century; through all these ages not the tyrant, but the darling of humanity, *soavissima*, as Dante says, "the sweetest of all the other sciences." Nearly all our older poetry was written and read by men to whom the distinction between poetry and rhetoric, in its modern form, would have been meaningless.[1]

Rhetoric is a barrier because we have forgotten it; or because we understand it imperfectly. It is still possible to break the barrier, and to re-live something of the sense that writers and educationalists had of rhetoric as being an essential part of all human knowledge, both in its acquisition and transmission. If mankind was defined, and distinguished from the animal world, by its God-given possession of language, then the cultivation of language and eloquence in the widest sense was not only a supremely human but also a divine activity. If we wish to understand European culture from the Sophists to the Romantics then our studies must include rhetoric.

Yet, as the essays collected here will show, the art of language took many forms, and its history has been one of simultaneous understanding and misunderstanding. Throughout the two thousand years of its dominance it was continually mocked, perverted, misrepresented. Several famous disputes have pursued it: Socrates' attempt to split *cor* and *lingua*, which Cicero drew attention to in *de Oratore*; Plato's attack in the *Gorgias* and *Phaedrus*; that phase in Christianity which rejected rhetoric with other pagan learning; the dispute over *res* and *verba* in the seventeenth century, and the fruitless attempts of Hobbes, Wilkins, Locke, and others, to ground a philosophical language free of ambiguity, appeal to the emotions, or use of metaphor; the polemics of Kant and Croce—it is difficult to think of another discipline that has been accompanied throughout its existence by so much negative criticism. Yet rhetoric survived all these attacks, continued to perform an essential function in society, until, for reasons that have not yet been properly investigated, it began to fall away following the publication of the last influential rhetoric textbooks, in the 1820s and 30s.

It may seem a truism, but it needs to be stated, that the history of rhetoric should be written from the accounts given of it by its friends, rather than its enemies. If Plato's attitude were taken as the starting-point, then the enterprise would be pointless, for we would merely reproduce his prejudices. The task of the historian is to describe the systems of rhetoric in their original forms and in their transformations, and to evaluate their wider social and cultural significance. Our study must be at once internal and external. The failure of several recent histories of rhetoric to grapple with both of these goals shows that writing a history of this subject is not without problems. Too many historians have been preoccupied with rhetorical theory, neglecting the practical dimension, in education, public speaking, law, literature, art, and music that was the whole justification for its existence. Rhetoric books are not works of art, complete in themselves, but handbooks towards mastering an art. They cannot be evaluated in a theoretical vacuum, for rhetoric was an art that taught expressiveness, persuasion, successful communication, success indeed as a human being. It follows that the history of rhetoric cannot be written from the texts alone, but must situate rhetoric in its total cultural context.[2]

Historians of rhetorical theory tend to value new contributions, are inclined to discount an on-going tradition as conservative, non-innovatory. Yet reflection will teach us that the continuing functioning of a discipline is the best possible evidence that it is performing whatever roles society requires of it. Our job is to study those roles in an open-minded way. It is pointless, for instance, to reproach a writer of a rhetoric-book for not aspiring to the heights of a Plato or a Cicero, since the ideal orator of Plato's *Phaedrus* never existed, and as for the more elevated schemes of the *de Oratore* and the *Institutiones Oratoriae*, Robert Bolgar has said that they "transport us into a cloud-cuckoo-land of unrealizable ideals.["3] I do not mean to deny rhetoric its highest potential as a philosophical or educational medium: on the contrary; but I would warn historians who criticize their writers for not addressing themselves to "more philosophic and more humane approaches"[4] that history is the account of what was, and is, not of what ought to have been, according to some lights. The fact that several hundred, or thousand—we still lack an adequate estimate of such data—authors of rhetoric-books, and several hundred thousand teachers of rhetoric over two millennia should have lavished so much energy on the detailed instruction in *elocutio* should make it impossible for a historian to throw up his hands in horror and dismiss this "interminable enumeration of stylistic devices" as the last-named author does. Rather, the historian must buckle down to the attempt at understanding what these devices were meant to do, and why it was that to Quintilian as to so many rhetoricians *elocutio*—which included the whole range of human expressiveness—was considered to be the fundamental part of rhetoric, without which all the rest was useless. As Chaim Perelman puts it in his contribution here,

> Les figures de rhétorique ne doivent plus être étudiées isolément, en dehors de leur contexte, en n'examinant que leur structure, mais doivent être envisagées en fonction de leur action sur l'auditoire.

We need more studies of the psychology of persuasion, the effect of specific types of verbal and emotional structures on the reader and listener, and indeed on the poet or orator who conceived them in the first place. If the injunction of Horace be taken seriously,

> *si vis me flere*
> *dolendum est primo ipsi tibi*
>
> [If you would have me weep,
>   you must first feel grief yourself][5]

then we have to conceive of the writer working his rhetoric on himself before he communicates it to others. He has to be persuaded before he can persuade us.

There are other obstacles to the right understanding of the details of rhetoric. As I point out in my essay "On the practicalities of Renaissance rhetoric," the study of rhetoric in this period has been carried out on one side by historians, who have illuminated its role in political and civil life, but have not concerned themselves with the detailed lore; while, on the other side, philologists and literary critics have become knowledgeable about the details while not appreciating rhetoric's over-all cultural function. We urgently need to bridge this gap, for the success of rhetoric in public life depended on its power to persuade, and persuasion derived from a mastery of verbal techniques. It seems timely to stress the functional, performative aspect of rhetoric since its study is still hindered by the false associations now attaching to the concept of ornament. Rhetorical language has been defined, since the Greeks, in distinction to "normal" or "everyday" language, as being more heightened, more intense, more carefully cultivated. In this branch of theory rhetorical devices, especially the tropes, were seen as "foreign," as deviations from some norm, however impossible it is to define "norms" of language. Yet, at the same time, other parts of the theory held that rhetorical figures were the natural language of the passions, and that human feelings would instinctively fall into these moulds.[6]

Here, as on many other occasions, the historian must note that since rhetoric was a discipline that derived from many sources and spread in many directions, and since no writer succeeded in coordinating or systematising it, then it is all too easy to find fundamental contradictions. Rhetorical language cannot be at the same time merely ornamental *and* essentially functional. We may regret that early theorists introduced the concept of ornament, but we should not let it induce a dismissive attitude. Their "ornament" clearly included the idea of "expressiveness," and it then becomes very difficult to imagine an idea or feeling independent of the form in which it was expressed. In his essay below Ian Thomson shows how late eighteenth-century rhetoricians gave serious attention to the role of figures in effecting mental associations, while at the same time unthinkingly reproducing the old

> dictum "language is the dress of thought," with the inevitable suggestion that figures serve to adorn the dress. The notion of figures as ornament, whether the object is pleasure or persuasion, is not compatible with the notion of figures as a natural and sympathetic correlative between transmitted and received trains of ideas.

If the figures can be seen as organic to thought-patterns they can hardly be dispensed with; if they are vital to the expression of the feelings, are our feelings merely ornamental? We need to take rhetoric more seriously yet.

We must first re-think our conception of the relation between language, feelings, and the codes of expression, abandoning post-Romantic ideas of art being necessarily spontaneous, that is, unshaped by training, craftsmanship, and conventions. Then we must follow up the implications of rhetoric's adoption in so many areas of human life. Plato was right in saying that rhetoric does not have a definite subject-matter of its own: but then it offers an infinity of expressive forms. As Sir Ernst Gombrich concluded, "in classical writings on rhetoric we have perhaps the most careful analysis of any expressive medium ever undertaken."[7] Yet rhetoric offered more than an analysis of an existing medium: it was prescriptive as well as descriptive, and the prescriptive tradition became performative, as it had been in its origins, according to Aristotle, when the expulsion of the tyrants in Sicily in the 470s and 460s B.C. led to widespread litigations to establish ownership of property.[8] Fifty years later, when Gorgias came on an embassy to Athens, the relevance of rhetoric to public life was established, and has never been lost. If the Greek practice of the individual involvement of all qualified citizens in face-to-face political activity did not survive transplantation to Rome, then from that time to this the speeches and writings of elected representatives of democracy, just as much as those by self-appointed tyrants or the tools of totalitarian governments, are constructed according to rhetorical principles, whether knowingly or not, and are amenable to rhetorical analysis, as is witnessed by a truly formidable range of recent American doctoral dissertations on individual politicians, election campaigns, or even single speeches. The implications of such studies for the history of decisive periods of history, with their own ideology, is considerable: I recall the studies of rhetoric in Florentine humanist politics by Delia Cantimori and Peter Herde, for instance.[9]

The interplay between rhetoric and the law is equally great, and just as long-lived. Techniques of training lawyers were derived from the rhetoric-schools, in 1st century Rome as in 16th century England; Roman rhetoric derives much from, and is addressed to, specific issues and processes in court-room procedure, in a way which was evidently lost on many compilers of Renaissance rhetoric-books, who either misunderstood or omitted such passages. The role of Roman Law as a channel for the survival and dissemination of classical culture and rhetoric in Italy during the early Middle Ages has been indicated by Helene Wieruszowski, and deserves much more study, as do the forms of argument developed by law in the vernaculars.[10]

In the history of Western education, rhetoric, as part of the *trivium*, together with grammar and logic, played a major role in elementary, intermediate, and advanced education. The *quadrivium* went through many revolutions of importance, but the *trivium* remained an indispensable part of the curriculum for everyone who had an education in Europe between, let us say, 1400 and 1800 (the earlier date could probably be taken back much further). As T. W. Baldwin and others have shown,[11] English education in the sixteenth, seventeenth and eighteenth centuries was fundamentally rhetorical: from King Edward VI down to Shakespeare or Lord Chesterfield's son, students were exercised in grammatical and rhetorical analysis and composition, were drilled in memorizing a hundred or so figures of speech, taught how to compose themes, argue *in utramque partem*, and so on. The same holds for education in France,[12] Italy,[13] Germany,[14] Spain, the Netherlands — indeed, anywhere of which we have good modern histories. Tell me how many people went to school in Europe during this period and I will tell you how many knew rhetoric. In some areas, notably the Catholic countries, we can already tell exactly which rhetoric they knew. The Jesuits' codification of the *Ratio Studiorum* in 1586 and 1599 ensured that several million schoolboys gained their knowledge of rhetoric from the *De Arte Rhetorica* (1568) of Cyprian Soarez, which had at least 134 editions, in 45 different European cities during a period of 173 years, and a total of 207 reprints in all forms, making it the most widely disseminated of all modern rhetorics.[15] One of the most urgent tasks for the history of rhetoric is to encourage, and influence, the history of education: we have some modern classics in this field, but we also have many areas where the only histories are antiquated, and some studies which show little understanding of rhetoric.

If rhetoric influenced the production of literature it certainly influenced its consumption: literary criticism, techniques of reading and judging, were all shaped by the methods and expectations of rhetoric. For much of the Renaissance through the Baroque the key document was the *Ars Poetica*, and Horace's debts to Cicero and the rhetorical tradition are well known.[16] For the early Renaissance, as O. B. Hardison has shown,[17] Aristotle's *Poetics* was influential through Averroes' redaction of it, with its reduction of all literature to the functions of praise and blame, which helps account for the dominance of epideictic rhetoric. With the re-discovery of the 'pure' text of the *Poetics*, that most problematic of all works in literary criticism, and with the dissemination of Latin and Italian commentaries, neo-Aristotelian categories dominated literary critical theory through the mid-eighteenth century and continued to influence it well into the nineteenth. Aristotle became fused with Horace (which he certainly would not have approved of!) and this essentially rhetorical tradition became a component in virtually all thinking about literature. Our knowledge of these things we owe mostly to American scholars. Joel Spingarn, the pioneer in the re-discovery of Renaissance criticism, belonged to the generation of De Sanctis, Croce, and George Saintsbury, who embodied the 19th Century rejection of rhetoric, and was curiously blind to its significance; but the picture has been put right by Marvin Herrick, Allan H. Gilbert, Baxter Hathaway, and above all the late Bernard Weinberg,[18] whose two-volume history and four-volume collection of treatises is essential to anyone who would understand rhetoric in the Renaissance and after.

Through literary criticism and aesthetics rhetoric influenced theories about the other arts, over the same time-scale. Nancy Struever has recently said that "the major, almost exclusive source of knowledge of literary form through the eighteenth century was the classical rhetorical tradition."[19] One could not claim quite so much for the other arts, but in general such concepts as invention, disposition, elocution or expressivity, instruction and delight, imitation, and decorum, had a major influence on painting and music theories. A model investigation was provided by Michael Baxandall's *Giotto and the Orators* (Oxford, 1971), and the areas he opened up need further study.[20]

Parallels between rhetoric and music have a long history. These range from the general shared concern with expressivity, to the appealing to the emotions or affects (*Die Affektenlehre*), in which music draws directly on the goals of rhetoric; to imitations of specific verbal effects. Thus Francis Bacon, in Book 2 of the *Advancement of Learning* (1605), discussing analogies and resemblances between the disciplines, asked

> Is not the precept of a musician, to fall from a discord or harsh accord upon a concord or sweet accord, alike true in affection? Is not the trope of music, to avoid or slide from the close or cadence, common with the trope of rhetoric of deceiving expectation? Is not the delight of the quavering upon a stop in music the same with the playing of light upon the water?
>
> *Splendet tremulo sub limine pontus:*
> [Beneath the trembling light glitters the sea.][21]

Bacon, as so often, was suggestive rather than systematic: that deficiency was soon supplied by Joachim Burmeister in *Musica Poetica* (Rostock, 1600), and by other seventeenth-century writers, especially in Germany, where a particularly strong tradition established itself. Modern discussions have been dominated by German scholars, beginning with Arnold Schering, although work has begun on England and Italy.[22]

Rhetoric, painting, and music are linked as expressive, communicative systems. They are linked, further, by their common interest in representing, and appealing to, the passions and the imagination. They are linked once more, to the surprise of modern students, perhaps, in the extension of both realms to that of ethics. All the arts were thought to have a moral function. Thus Cesare Ripa's famous collection of moral images, the *Iconologia*, described itself as *a description of universal images* which was *no less useful than necessary to poets, painters, and sculptors, in order to represent virtues, vices, and the human affections and passions*.[23] Rhetoric touches simultaneously ethics and psychology, and it is no accident that Aristotle's *Rhetoric* was used during the Middle Ages and Renaissance as a hand-book to the study of ethical and psychological matters.[24] This practical application was in a sense merely repaying an old debt, for one of the three modes of oratory, epideictic, far from being a mere technique of display, was from the beginning linked with serious ethical concerns. The poet or orator was expected to praise virtue and to attack vice. It was just because epideictic could be applied to his own ethical system that Plato, although banishing the poets from his republic, made an exception for the poetry of praise, "hymns to the gods and encomia to good men." In the *Laws* Plato approves of communal celebrations where songs of praise to the gods, and also to "citizens who are departed and have done good and energetic deeds," will have a beneficial effect on virtue, while in *Protagoras* he explicitly links encomium with the incitement to virtue in the young.[25] Isocrates, orator and teacher, provided model orations in the opposed modes of praise (*Encomium on Helen*) and blame (*Against the Sophists*), and in his *Evagoras* expressly formulated the educative function of epideictic, stating that he had created a new kind of oration, "because it attempted 'to eulogize in prose the virtues of a man' in order to stimulate 'emulation for virtue' among the young."[26] In his *Rhetoric* Aristotle gave much space to epideictic, discussing encomium in relation to virtue and vice and listing the virtuous deeds or qualities that are worthy of praise.[27] The humble school rhetorical exercises, or *progymnasmata*, linked epideictic with biography, giving models for the writing of lives according to virtuous deeds.

In Greek and Latin literary criticism many major works of literature were interpreted as models of epideictic: Xenophon's *Cyropaedia*, the poetry of Pindar, Homer, and Virgil. The late classical and medieval commentators on Virgil, from Donatus (who described the *Aeneid* as an epideictic work designed to praise and glorify Aeneas' virtues) to Fulgentius, and on into the Renaissance, encouraged the notion that the epic was fundamentally an epideictic genre, an idea that had some rather unusual consequences.[28] Given the wide dissemination of Averroes' paraphrase of Aristotle's *Poetics*, which begins "Every poem and all poetic discourse is blame or praise," and states that the poet's aim is to impel men to virtuous actions and repel them from vicious ones, it is fully comprehensible that, even after the re-discovery of the authentic text, this conception of poetry should continue to be influential.[29] That poets should exalt virtue and debase vice is an idea common to virtually every rhetorician or poet from Petrarch to Dryden, and here again we can see another debt to classical rhetoric, for those texts abound in statements of the orator's duty to indicate which actions are to be followed, which avoided.[30] The implicit assumption behind all this theory is that praise will lead to emulation: men will be so fired by the eloquent celebration of virtue that they will be moved to act in imitation. Renaissance theorists recognized here, as everywhere else, the practical utility of rhetoric. For Nifo (in 1531) as for Posio (in 1562) rhetoric is "the instrument of moral philosophy," while Zabarella (writing about logic in 1578), classified citizens into two groups: the lower is the moral man, who "does right" in his own person; the higher is "the citizen," who "causes others to do right," using eloquence. "Rhetoric and poetics are thus instrumental faculties which the citizen employs for action, namely, to make his fellow citizens good."[31] The old definition of the orator as "a good man skilled in speaking" was thus carried into modern times by the speaker's role in activating the basic principles of ethics.

As one follows the dissemination of rhetoric through so many channels it seems as if there is no subject which might not in some way have benefited from the art of eloquence—even the history of science.[32] The corollary is that no adequate account of human culture since the Greeks could ever be written without taking account of rhetoric. It becomes a more interesting activity, once one breaks out of the confining frame of the study of rhetoric-textbooks alone; yet it also becomes much more challenging, since to follow it into every area demands a kind of universal competence. Not being so blessed, I have not dared to mention Scandinavian, Old English, Byzantine, Arabic, or Sanskrit rhetoric, but perhaps I have done enough to justify the claim that rhetoric, being such a universal art, especially benefits from co-operative and collaborative study.

II

THE FOLLOWING ESSAYS demonstrate ways in which rhetoric can be extended, and renewed. The first and largest group concerns the rhetorical tradition itself; that is, the internal structure of rhetorical treatises, and the means by which they were disseminated. Anton Leeman's introductory essay establishes the striking variety that soon established itself within rhetoric from the Sophists to Cicero, a tradition that had already flourished and withered, been abandoned and re-claimed. After the fundamental criticisms of Plato and Aristotle, Cicero can be seen re-establishing the position of Isocrates and the Sophists, that language is the fundamental mark of man, and that therefore "eloquence is one, whatever the subject . . . circumstances . . . speaker . . . or audience." This vision of the unity of rhetoric goes along with an apparent scorn for the *minutiae* of the art—which Cicero had so perfectly mastered himself—and a "philosophizing" of rhetoric which seeks to re-establish the original identity of philosophy and eloquence as the constituent parts of *Logos*. Leeman's lucid general picture is developed in one aspect by P. H. Schrÿvers, who studies the link between invention, imagination, and the theory of the emotions in Cicero and Quintilian. In Book Two of *de Oratore* Antonius advises the young orator to feel the emotions of anger or sorrow himself before he attempts to arouse them in others. This idea—which I quoted in Horace's pithy formulation—implies the necessity of self-persuasion, where the orator, using the *loci* offered by *inventio*, has something in common with two widely differing analogues, the actor playing a role, and the poet creating by enthusiasm and inspiration. Quintilian follows Cicero but adds the idea that the emotions are linked to *visiones*, a way of representing to the mind things absent. This essay shows, amongst other things, that the power to move the imagination is an essential criterion for the working of rhetoric.

Michael Winterbottom's paper takes us farther into the practicalities of rhetoric, and into the declamation-schools, so often criticized for training students with unreal exercises, involving rapes and pirates. Incidentally, pirates were not so unreal in the Hellenistic and later periods: as late as the first century

A.D. two senators were kidnapped by pirates as they walked along the Appian Way and had to be ransomed.[33] Winterbottom has no difficulty in showing that these schools were serious and practical places to train public speakers — as he reminds us, the Romans were nothing if not practical. He defends the use of 'unreal' topics as giving more freedom to invention, another practical point, while his account of why Cicero wrote up his *pro Milone* for publication might be taken to heart by historians who study theory without practice: "it was to exemplify in action the rhetorical rules that seem so lifeless when they are merely placed end to end in an *ars rhetorica*." Having already edited the *Controversiae* of Seneca, and being in the course of preparing the *Minor Declamations* attributed to Quintilian, Dr. Winterbottom is in a good position to evaluate the complexities of the extant documents, many of which are fragmentary, collections of phrases, chips from a practising teacher's workshop.

One of the great difficulties with writing the history of rhetoric, after its original unity within Greek and Roman society and education, is that the tradition broke down with the dissolution first of democracy in Rome, and then with the empire itself. The fragmentation of rhetoric in the Middle Ages is partly due to the break-up of a whole cultural tradition; but, as Michael Leff argues, there is evidence that a decisive change of emphasis took place in the Latin handbooks of the fourth century A.D. Earlier historians, such as R. P. McKeon,[34] argued that in this period two traditions of rhetoric still co-existed: the Ciceronian tradition of rhetoric as a civic discipline, which varied in form and method according to the type of civil issue involved; and, in effect opposed to this, a tradition stemming from Hermagoras which made a systematic analysis of discourse according to invariant topics. Leff's analysis, however, shows that these fourth-century rhetoricians adhered to the second tradition, stressing forensic, legal methods, using such technical concepts as *stasis*, and leaving little scope for dispute or discussion: deliberative and epideictic modes sink while forensic rhetoric triumphs. These treatises thus have "a tendency to distort and contract the general design of the art," giving most attention to *inventio*, and allowing the doctrines of *memoria* and *pronuntiatio* to atrophy. Here as so often we see how the nature of rhetoric reflects the wider social and cultural situation. Where democratic speech is no longer possible, dialogue withers, and the concept of persuasion — which depends on the possibility of free and open judgment — begins to disappear. Also, as John Ward has argued,[35] since court procedures in the late Empire changed, with greater use of written materials and less oral argument, then this change was bound to be reflected in rhetoric, which has always existed in a dialectical relationship with society. Leff's conclusion, that we see here the loss of a holistic concept of the art, with a reduction of rhetoric to various specialized functions, does seem to prefigure the situation that prevailed in the Middle Ages.

The contribution by Robert Bolgar, a scholar who has shown so vividly the relevance of the history of education to the study of rhetoric and indeed all Western culture since the Greeks, traces the vicissitudes of the art in the medieval schools. In the seventh century paganism was still rife, and even Bede, who knew Virgil and the elder Pliny at first hand, regarded Latin literature with suspicion and classed rhetoric and dialectic with heresy. It was in the Carolingian age that rhetoric re-established itself, partly due to reforms in education, such as the pioneering work of Alcuin, whose *De rhetorica et virtutibus* even attempted to reconstruct the Ciceronian relationship between rhetoric and public affairs. Given the vastly different social and political situation that attempt could hardly succeed, yet the other main stimulus to rhetoric shows again its flexibility in responding to external demands: since the Church and Carolingian state needed administrators, rhetoric returned as a school subject. The re-development of the art in this period, however, was uneven, and while the tenth century laid the foundation for the flowering of rhetoric and Latin literature in the twelfth century, "during the remaining portions of the Middle Ages the historian of rhetoric is reduced to depicting survivals rather than new developments." The main cause of this static, or declining situation, was again external to rhetoric, a development in society, namely the rise of the universities, in which the professional disciplines of law, medicine, and theology became entrenched. While they retained dialectic as an introduction to the main courses, rhetoric was demoted to the initial stages of the school course. Rhetoric survived in the de-limited, and at times, one must feel, over-specialized areas of the *ars dictaminis* and the sermons.

What did rhetoric consist of in the Middle Ages? The researches of J. J. Murphy[36] and others have brought together much of what is currently known; yet much remains to be done, as the three substantial essays in this volume will show. Margareta Fredborg addresses herself to one of the least-studied areas, yet one of the most important, the commentaries on the classical rhetorical texts. From the late classical pᵉriod, with the commentaries on *de inventione* by Marius Victorinus and Grillius, to the present day, students, whether elementary or advanced, have gained their knowledge of classical rhetoric mostly from commentated editions and translations, so that these become essential material for the historian (a point oddly overlooked in the work of W. S. Howell on rhetoric in England from 1500 to 1800). Of the nearly six hundred commentaries identified by John Ward (ranging from brief notes to 79 complete explications of Ciceronian works), only a fragment of one commentary has so far been edited, and the fundamental work of identifying manuscript traditions has yet to be carried out. The commentaries were primarily teaching texts, yet they evidently left their mark on students, and Dr. Fredborg is able to show that Matthew of Vendôme, author of one of the most important arts of poetry, borrowed from Thierry of Chartres' commentary on *de inventione*. Since the work of Aristotle and Quintilian was not known, and Cicero's *de oratore* was lost, the major topics were *inventio* and *elocutio* (the list of figures in Book 4 of *Ad Herennium* proving its usefulness over a thousand-year period). The biggest development was within *inventio*, especially the topics, which were valued as a means of invention and as a tool for literary analysis, in the description of character and action (see Mariantonia Liborio's paper below). The medieval rhetoricians were dealing with a tradition which was much fragmented, and whose whole rationale was imperfectly understood, as we see from their real difficulty in reconciling different parts of rhetoric, such as the enthymeme, which was recommended by some, rejected by others. The great interest in defining the borderline between rhetoric and other arts of discourse may point to scholastic training, but it may also indicate an uncertainty about rhetoric's scope and function. Much more work is needed in this area, and we await further knowledge of the researches of John Ward and Mary Dickey.

The following two studies complement each other nicely, Paolo Bagni re-evaluating the role of *inventio* in the arts of poetry, and Franz Quadlbauer analysing their teaching on *dispositio*. Bagni performs an extremely searching study of terminology, a necessary task since the functioning of any discipline depends on the clarity of its internal articulation. The great differences that emerge between the treatment of *inventio* in four treatises written within fifty years of each other is further proof of the fragmentary nature of medieval rhetoric; and also, perhaps, of the phenomenon recurrent throughout the history of rhetoric, whereby each compiler of a rhetoric-book strives to be original either in terminology or in organization. *Inventio* is shown to be no longer the most important part of rhetoric; while epideictic, which, as Mr. Leff noted, had disappeared from the fourth century treatises, reappears in John of Garland—as indeed it had, with such striking consequences for Renaissance literary theory, in Averroes' translation of Aristotle's *Poetics*. The influence of grammar is well brought out, in the transformation of *inventio* first to the doctrine of amplifying and varying matter (one recalls Faral's pioneering observations on this issue[37]), and then to the finding of new words, one of the crucial points in this theory of invention, with important consequences for the relationships between *res* and *verba*.

The teaching on *dispositio* in this group of texts reveals less internal disagreement but some striking shifts of emphasis. The basic distinction was between an *ordo naturalis*, where events are narrated in the order in which they happened, and an *ordo artificialis*, where the narration begins later in the time-sequence. The distinction, like the terminology, derives from late classical rhetoric, and everyone will recall the passage in Horace's *Ars poetica* (42–44), which recommends the second method, with all that it implies in terms of inversion and retrospective narration. Lucan was held to be typical of the *ordo naturalis*, Virgil superior with his *ordo artificialis*. The distinction is simple, but is of profound importance for later narrative theory and practice: Sir Philip Sidney first wrote his *Arcadia* with an *ab ovo* structure, but later, influenced by Heliodorus' *Aethiopica*, re-wrote it, beginning *in medias res*. (Unfortunately he died before completing it, so that we cannot know how he would have solved some of the technical problems.) Quadlbauer shows that the *ordo naturalis* was praised in the eleventh and twelfth centuries, but that in the more self-consciously theoretical thirteenth century, when the *artes poetriae* were composed, the *ordo artificialis* came to be preferred as demanding more artistry (in his *Documentum* Geoffrey of Vinsauf dismissed the natural order as suitable for peasants). Here, as so often, since rhetoric was such a richly developed and unsystematised art, "new" developments took the form of a re-arrangement or re-valuation of extant components. Given that one of the oldest concepts of rhetoric elevated the language of art over the language of nature, it is understandable that the poetic theorists of this period should have preferred the order of art; yet, to the "looker-on"—who, in Francis Bacon's words, "seeth more of the game"—it seems typical of medieval rhetoric, which revelled in theory, not having any firm basis for practice, that Geoffrey of Vinsauf should go on to distinguish no less than eight types of *ordo artificialis*, with the beginning appropriate to each. Guido Faba, similarly, devoted four complete works to the subject of "letter openings,"[38] which might be an early proof of Parkinson's law, or suggest that discussion of the theoretical possibilities was not limited by any concern for practicality or usefulness. Readers must make up their own mind on this issue; certainly the meticulous presentation of the evidence here will much aid that judgment.

The remaining three papers in this opening section follow the rhetorical tradition, at more select intervals, down to 1800. In addition to deploring the gap that exists between the studies of rhetoric carried out by historians on the one hand, literary critics on the other, my own paper addresses a number of issues in Renaissance rhetoric. In sharp contrast to the Middle Ages, the re-discovery of all the major rhetorical texts, and the understanding of essential background works such as Cicero's letters, made it possible for the first time since the fall of the Roman empire for rhetoric to be properly understood in its totality. The role of rhetoric in civic society was enthusiastically propagated, and from Bruni's Florence to Francis Bacon's London the orator as culture-hero was celebrated anew. Yet this revived enthusiasm for rhetoric resulted in another Dispute of the Liberal Arts, and the rhetoricians attacked other disciplines excessively: a praiser of the art of eloquence is not always to be trusted. On the credit side the rediscovery of the importance of *elocutio* carried far more significance than a mere concern with the ornate (in the modern sense), and re-established the Isocratean-Ciceronian concept of man as the master of *Logos*, that union of *ratio* and *oratio*. In the sixteenth, and even more in the seventeenth century, rhetoricians took seriously the perennial claim of rhetoric to sway the passions, and embarked on evermore detailed analyses of psychology and emotion under the power of language.

This concern with the passions continued until the end of the eighteenth century, as the papers by Ian Thomson and Don Abbott show. The English philosopher-rhetoricians, who developed the connection between rhetoric and psychology in the doctrine of the association of ideas, tried to distinguish precepts founded on nature, yet only achieved a deadlock. As Thomson points out, some theorists held to the traditional belief that true passion was naturally expressed in the figures and tropes of rhetoric; others, however, held that genuine passion could not be expressed in images (an idea occasionally found in post-Romantic aesthetics, but which would destroy the nature of poetry). The dispute is between two opposed concepts, of spontaneous non-figurative language against spontaneous figurative language. I see no way of resolving this opposition, and agree with Thomson that it derives from the "lack of coherence inherent in rhetorical theory since antiquity." If you cross Aristotle with Horace the result is not guaranteed to be homogeneous, and the incoherence of the tradition effectively blocked further development. A clear shift of emphasis can be traced in Hugh Blair, for instance, from an interest in the author's intentions in affecting the audience to a concern with the psychology of the author himself. Yet this is implicit in the discussion of Cicero, from which Mr. Schrÿvers departed, as in Horace's *si vis me flere*. Where Joseph Priestley differs, in urging that the writer communicate the "strong sensations" he feels "in the very order and connection" in which they present themselves to him, is that he would apparently deny one of Horace's other precepts, the *labor limae*, the need to shape the work of art. The whole discussion was exceptionally theoretical, and Thomson's conclusion that the belle-lettrist rhetoricians left their subject in a void through not giving enough attention to practical purpose and utility, is a fair comment, and one that might be made, it seems to me, about the medieval poetic theorists.

When rhetoric loses touch with social needs and with the practicalities of composition or criticism, the results are almost always a diminution, a loss of substance and purpose. Antonio de Capmany, a Spanish rhetorician of the late eighteenth century, certainly tried to bring rhetoric back to real life, attacking neo-classicism and the use of Latin, calling for the study of rhetoric in the vernacular. Capmany argues that rhetoric must begin with the human mind, thus a knowledge of psychology is essential to the orator, to which he must add wisdom, taste, genius, imagination, and sentiment. Many of his specific points echo the great classical treatises: that the orator must be moved himself before he can move his audience recalls Cicero, Horace, Quintilian.[39] The distinction between invention, which depends on innate genius, and expression, the application of rules, which can be learned, recalls several English theorists of the same period, and accounts for Capmany, like so many rhetoricians before or since, devoting the major part of his text to "A Treatise on Oratorical Elocution," which is divided into sections on diction, on style, and on the "Adornment of Eloquence," a "veritable catalogue of tropes and figures." Mr. Abbott calls this the first attempt at a "psychologically oriented study of oratory in Spain," and it is significant that Capmany gives so much attention to the figures and tropes.

While showing that Capmany is a traditional rhetorician I do not mean to imply that he is inferior. Originality in rhetoric was scarcely possible beyond a certain point, and where we find it in the sixteenth and seventeenth centuries it is sometimes achieved by idiosyncrasy. Rather I mean to underline the coherence of the rhetorical tradition, despite its many vicissitudes. Capmany echoes Quintilian, but so does Vives, or Melanchthon, or Budé, or Peacham, and since what was being communicated was so intelligent then no one should complain. We should not require rhetoric to be new; only that it should function effectively. Mr. Abbott cites an interesting passage from Frances Hutcheson, who expounds the idea that the rhetorical figures are the natural language of the passions:

> The various Figures of Speech are the several Manners which a lively Genius, warm'd with Passions suitable to the Occasion, naturally runs into, only a little diversify'd by Custom.

The expression is easy and natural, typical of its period and author; yet the idea goes back to Aristotle's *Rhetoric*, Quintilian, Longinus, Puttenham, Sidney, Abraham Fraunce, Dumarsais, and Edmé Mallet, to name a few.[40] The rhetorical tradition is the history of an art designed to be used, one that necessarily embraced many different phenomena. We still find discrepancies and contradictions; but we will also find an underlying unity: as Cicero put it, *una est elocutione*.

III

THE SECOND PART of this volume is devoted to the influence of rhetoric on literature, from five different aspects. A. D. Leeman puts in its social context the opening satire of Horace's second book, in which the poet discusses the difficulties of being a satirist with his *persona*, the successful lawyer Trebatius. This fiction enables Horace to announce his resolve to continue writing satire, in order to satisfy a deep personal dedication to this genre, and to escape the threat of public prosecution or the disfavour of the great. The rhetorical background here is that of the *status* or state of a client's case, usually divided into three categories, not guilty, guilty but of a different crime, and guilty but with extenuating circumstances. Leeman shows how subtly Horace builds this doctrine into his poem, even adding a fourth *status*, where the case is dismissed because the court is not competent. This paper is a fascinating display of how literary criticism can be illuminated by a knowledge of the appropriate rhetorical background. To students of classical or Renaissance poetry concerned with the use of a *persona* there is a fruitful passage in *de Oratore* where Cicero's spokesman recommends his practice of first making his client declare his case fully, then arguing the opponent's case so that the client can argue his own more fully. Finally, when the client has gone, in my own person and with perfect impartiality I play three characters, myself, my opponent and the arbitrator. . . . In this way I gain the advantage of reflecting first on what to say and saying it later, two things which most people, trusting in their talent, do simultaneously, though those same individuals would certainly speak rather more successfully, if they thought fit to take one occasion for reflection and another for speaking.[41]

Those lines would be suggestive not only to Horace but to such later poets as Donne, Marvell, and Pope.

By contrast to this closely focussed and detailed analysis Tony Hunt surveys rhetoric and poetics in twelfth-century France, to sketch in a wide range of rhetorical activity with implications for several types of writing. His distinction, a pragmatic one rather than traditional, is into demonstrative, scholastic, and philosophic rhetoric. Under the latter he includes the tradition deriving from Plato and St. Augustine, and resulting in the Neoplatonism of Chartres, in which attention was given to concealed meanings as a way of challenging the reader's skills in interpretation and as a way of communicating deeper truths (in both fields a direct continuity to Renaissance reading methods can be traced).[42] Demonstrative rhetoric derives from a less esoteric context, "the practical exigencies of oral address to a largely illiterate audience," and results in a mode of writing which is both expressive and affective, using the traditional tropes and figures. Less promising for literature, at any rate at first sight, is the third category, scholastic rhetoric, which derived from Aristotle's *Topics* and *Elenchi*, and taught a mode of dialectical argument and confrontation of oppositions, becoming in effect a handbook of debate. While it had the expected consequences for authors of logic, such as Abelard and John of Salisbury, the constant questioning of an issue also had a surprising effect on the structure of the romances of Chrestien and other school-trained poets, ranging from the exploitation of contrast and opposition to the "self-questioning . . . characteristic of many romance characters and of the best romances themselves."

The validity of this analysis is confirmed by Mariantonia Liborio's independent study of Chrestien de Troyes, which shows that the questioning process is extended to the reader, who is given clues to help interpret important knots in the narrative. Thus the rhetorical figure *effictio*, or portrayal (χαρακτηρισμός is the Greek equivalent), which the author of the *Rhetorica ad Herennium* describes as consisting in "representing and depicting in words clearly enough for recognition the bodily form of some person,"[43] is given an incomplete form in *Erec et Enide*, thus unsettling the reader, alerting his attention. Lancelot, an anti-hero whose excessive and adulterous love has destroyed his personality, is given no *effictio* at all (similarly, in his *Faust Symphony* Liszt gave leit-motifs to the main characters but withheld one from Mephistopheles, embodiment of evil). The way moral judgments organize narrative form can be seen in the other topos studied here, the *locus amoenus*, that stereotypical setting for love. In *Erec et Enide* the magic garden is beautiful but sinister, decorated with the heads of previous intruders, a comment on the effect of this form of love that the reader is expected to understand at first glance, as is the case with later evil love-gardens in Ariosto, Tasso, Spenser, and Sidney. This paper illuminates the working of literary convention as a sub-text energised by the poet, a "frame of reference" which the reader is made to re-actualize and thus experience anew.

From the topoi we move to the rhetorical figures in Salomon Hegnauer's account of *systrophe*, a device that has attracted little attention, even though it was used for major poetic effects by Aeschylus, Seneca, Dante, Shakespeare, Sidney, Donne, Crashaw, Cowley, Vaughan, and many other writers. In my contribution to the first part of this collection I suggest that analysis of the figures and tropes should recognize this distinction:

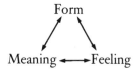

The form remains fixed, but the meaning (semantics) and the feeling (psychology) are probably capable of infinite variation. As we see here, *systrophe*, consisting as it does of definitions heaped up in parallel, usually without connective links, achieves a composite evocation of a term of reference by accumulating a series of individual tropes. The form resembles a list, vertically, but the experience of reading it across the page, horizontally and chronologically, makes it felt, rather, as incremental, adding layers of significance, while perhaps never fully defining its subject. The pull between the vertical and the horizontal planes suggests the curve of an asymptote, always approaching yet never touching the vertical axis. It is also a figure that moves forward yet constantly refers back, and is capable of embracing the most ironic effects, such as Clytemnestra's sickeningly false welcome to her husband, whom she is about to murder:

> I hail this man, the watchdog of the fold and hall . . .
> the running spring a parched wayfarer strays upon . . .[44]

or Macbeth's lament for the sleep that he has destroyed:

> the innocent sleep,
> Sleep that knits up the ravelled sleeve of care,
> The death of each day's life, sore labour's bath,

> Balm of hurt minds, great Nature's second course,
> Chief nourisher in life's feast —

"What do you mean?" Lady Macbeth breaks in, aware that her husband is becoming obsessive, not yet aware what the words will mean to her. This simultaneous forward-and-backward-looking quality of *systrophe* is well brought out here in the analyses of poems by George Herbert and Angelus Silesius. Further study of individual figures is an urgent desideratum.

The last of this group of essays on rhetoric and literature continues the practical analysis of poetry. Marijke Spies begins her study of the seventeenth-century Dutch poet Joost van den Vondel, with the observation that the influence of Heinrich Lausberg's re-codification of rhetoric[45] may not have been beneficial in one particular, since he asserts that epideictic rhetoric was designed mainly for the praise of beauty, and had little importance in argument. But, as we have seen, epideictic was intimately connected with ethics. Scaliger and Vossius, quoted here, extend into the seventeenth century the belief that the poet, like the orator, must praise virtue and attack vice. Vondel, as a conscientous Renaissance poet, not only knew his rhetoric well, but in 1625 — at the age of 38 — took additional lessons in logic "in order to write better poetry," an action that will come as no surprise to anyone who has read Rosemund Tuve's account of the role of logic in Renaissance lyrics.[46] In his own poetry, accordingly, Vondel used the traditional rhetorical techniques of ordering a composition (from *exordium* to *peroratio*), but also employed the tremendously widely-disseminated elementary models of composition in the *Progymnasmata* of Aphthonius and Theon, whose importance has been re-discovered in our time. While showing that Vondel's panegyric to the Amsterdam civic institutions is based on these models, Dr. Spies also shows that Vondel, in his wish to use argument rather than mere amplification, bases his poem — as we now know, like Horace before him — on the technique of *status*. Vondel resembles the medieval writers referred to by Tony Hunt in his way of engaging the reader in a dialogue, raising and answering objections, and he resembles so many poets in making a fruitful use of the rhetorical tradition despite the exhortation of some critics that he should liberate himself from it. That Vossius, a dedicated rhetorician, should have been one of these confirms Lessing's aphorism: "all are not free who mock their chains."

IV

THE SEVEN ESSAYS of the final section confront, in various ways, an issue that has long disturbed the republic of letters, the relationship between rhetoric and philosophy. Alain Michel begins by tracing the debts that each discipline owes to the other. While the sophists developed the art of eloquence for its own sake, Plato's criticisms opposed a philosophical judgment, in the name of truth and reality. Aristotle's development of logic, rhetoric and poetics reconciled the opposition, integrating the arts of language into a total philosophy, a unity developed and extended by Cicero. Yet the unity was not one of equilibrium, for rhetoric has always favoured certain types of philosophy, the dialectical approach rather than the systematic, and here the Ciceronian influence was to become so important in giving the tone and shape to Renaissance philosophy, which is eclectic, pluralistic, anti-dogmatic. Where some philosophers made their discipline superior and rhetoric inferior, Cicero protested in Book 3 of *de Oratore* against the effect of Socrates' splitting *lingua* and *cor*, the tongue and the brain. If the mainstream of Renaissance humanism followed Cicero's call to maintain the unity of language, the Platonic tradition nevertheless persisted, as we can see from the attempts made in the seventeenth century to found a "Real Character," or language of signs in which words would be abolished.

The Ciceronian unity of rhetoric and philosophy covered things as well as words, for the orator was committed to a broad general culture, a knowledge of life that would reconcile theory and practice, action and contemplation. Eugenio Garin's comprehensive discussion of Renaissance humanism stresses the unity of inspiration and expression: man was to be studied in his totality, as expressed in his language. Bartolomeo della Fonte described the speech of eloquent men as providing the basis for society, the structure of law, the cement of culture. To the Florentine humanists, Alberti, Filarete, Brunelleschi's biographer, and others, the correspondences between the arts proved the unity of culture, and their theories of *ut rhetorica pictura* or the identity of rhetoric and architecture recognized the fundamental importance of such concepts as order, invention, ornament, symmetry. Leonard Bruni celebrated Florence as the model of the unity of a city, its arts, architecture, and politics all being based on clarity, order, rationality. Of course we know enough about Florentine history and the bias of panegyric to realize that this was not an open, progressive democracy, and that power was in the hands of a privileged and conservative few. Yet there was more participation in society than previously, and the Ciceronian concept of debate as being basic to the *vita activa* of a civil society had certainly established itself.

This unity of culture and practice, rhetoric and philosophy, affecting every area of life, means that Renaissance humanism cannot be reduced to mere school issues. Professor Garin takes issue with some of the early writings of Paul Oskar Kristeller, which tended to attack Renaissance philosophy for not being truly systematic.[47] Kristeller was using as his standard of philosophy the theoretical systems of Aristotle and Aquinas, and by those criteria could dismiss the rhetorical philosophy of the Renaissance (we come away from these dilettantes "with empty hands"). Garin's answer is that the main issue, first defined by Petrarch, and flourishing by continuous discussion over the next two and a half centuries, was the revaluation of logic, politics, and ethics, from the theoretical place they had held in medieval systems to disciplines that dealt with man in society, and were simultaneously philosophical, psychological, and anthropological. This new orientation towards the human situation, away from once-and-for-all abstract systems, conceived of reality as always changing, always modified by men in a particular society at a particular time. This new direction expressed itself also in the humanists' favourite literary-philosophical forms, the dialogue and the epistle (which is one side of a dialogue), forms that implied two or more speakers. For the humanists truth was not a dogma but a "collective research and a confrontation." Seen in a longer perspective the Renaissance comes between the Middle Ages and the seventeenth century, both periods of great philosophical syntheses and systems. While it produced nothing of comparable elegance or comprehensiveness, it produced not a text-book philosophy but a philosophy from life, from human experience. As such, indeed, it answered one of the fundamental calls made on philosophy, as Isaiah Berlin has defined it, the clarification of basic thought-models by analysis and discussion:

> The goal of philosophy is always the same, to assist men to understand themselves and thus operate in the open, and not wildly, in the dark.[48]

Professor Garin's conclusion is that since philosophy was also seen as a way of forming man, an education for a society in transition, then rhetoric no longer existed in opposition to society but constituted another form of philosophy, equally adapted to man, the world, and to the language with which he apprehends and understands life. That re-statement of the Isocratean and Ciceronian position is delivered with some authority, and holds good for all European cultures in this period. Evidence of its relevance to French humanism in the mid-fifteenth century is provided, *in parvo*, by the unpublished manuscript discussed by Marc-René Jung. The author, Martin Le Franc, used a Latin epistle to pose a rhetorical question: in the art of speaking well, which is the most important, *ars, exercitatio*, or *imitatio*? His answer is that *ars* guarantees order, without which there is no permanence; *exercitatio* is also essential, since there is no skill without practice; while *imitatio* is vital to all creators, who acquire excellence through imitation of the best models. As Garin wrote in his paper, imitation in the Renaissance was not the servile copying of a model but a stimulus to creation, the discovery of new expressive means. While very much a man of his age, Le Franc is obviously drawing on Cicero and Quintilian (also the *ad Herennium*), and his epistle ends with a praise of eloquence which is a summing-up of both classical and Renaissance ideals. Eloquence – in the wider sense of *elocutio*, the power of expressive communication – is important in all areas of life, is indeed the foundation of all civilisation.

But while students of rhetoric will welcome such re-affirmations of the centrality of the arts of language to human society, we must not lose sight of the fact that rhetoric has had, and always will have, its enemies. Roger Moss, in arguing the case for sophistry, challenges Plato's dismissal of the sophists – the most influential judgment ever made about rhetoric – by calling in question its underlying attitudes. The model of a cultural decline or "decadence" applied to rhetoric – in the usual formulation, once *verba* is allowed to triumph over *res* – persists, as he shows, from Dionysius of Halicarnassus to the present day. What strikes anyone interested in the history of human thought-categories is the extent to which this debate has been conducted in terms of simple binary models, of the Right/Wrong type. Thus sophistry was accused of using language for display not for communication, of being the "harlot" of Asiatic oratory ousting the "lawful wife" of Attic oratory, embodying exaggeration not moderation, and so on. Once the subject is split in two by such wedges it is difficult to re-unite it. Yet, as Dr. Moss shows, some of the characteristics attributed to the sophists by their opponents are to be found in Homer, Plato, and Joyce. Not all readers will be convinced by the argument that sophistry produced a sense of language as being complete in itself, self-referential rather than dealing with external reality, but the challenge of received dichotomies, especially in these exclusive forms, is always worth making.

The history of the disputes over rhetoric is often a history of the more or less arbitrary application of dichotomies. Socrates' acceptance of the spoken word while devaluing the written word is one such; Kant's approval of the poet coining new words while denying the orator that right, is another; John Stuart Mill's pat distinction "that eloquence is *heard*, poetry is *overheard*" is yet another. My survey of the territorial disputes over rhetoric begins with Socrates' tactics for repudiating rhetoric, tactics of guilt by association or analogy rather than by rigorous logical argument. One is surprised that for centuries scholars have accepted the *Gorgias* as a work of philosophy, rather than as a piece of rhetoric, brilliantly using eloquence to mock eloquence. Such a great philosopher as Kant, and such a well-read aesthetician as Croce, repeat the process of using rhetoric to reject rhetoric. Yet, while we can see how one-sided that tradition is, study of the rhetoricians' attacks on philosophy, from Quintilian to Melanchthon and Valla, suggests that they are just as one-sided, just as violent. Instead of continuing this *dialogue des sourds* we should teach rhetoric and philosophy what each can gain from the other.

The last pair of papers show two distinguished modern philosophers doing just that. C. S. Peirce, one of the founders of semiotics, wanted to reconstruct the ancient *trivium* in the form of "Speculative Grammar, Critical Logic, and Speculative Rhetoric." The context for the latter would consist of the entire

semiotic milieu within which sign-users operate, and would take notice of the
fact that each sign can be interpreted differently by each interpreter, who has
a different sign-history. While J. R. Lyne links Peirce with Francis Bacon in
recognizing that truth must be presented in different ways to different audiences,
we can cite Aristotle as the precursor of both.[49]

Professor Lyne's analysis of Peirce's concept of the self as existing in a temporal
modality is very fruitful: "the self of one moment must address the self of the
next through the medium of signs," thus necessitating a move from reason to
argument: "the reasoning self . . . becomes an arguing self in order to justify
what it believes." I find that idea extremely applicable to literature (think of
Montaigne's *Essais*, or Hamlet's soliloquies), and to life, since it provides a model
for understanding self-deception and self-ignorance, for if the "person" is seen
as "a plurality of critical and interpretive habits" then we can trace malfunctioning
as taking place between those discrete processes. Peirce's work is full of such
insights: communication is partly a "drawing from" the audience in addition
to a "giving to;" inquiry begins in doubt, "intellectual discomfort or irritation;"
the community is not a finite group but a sign waiting to be interpreted; and
"since 'no mind can take one step without the aid of other minds', the community
is a dialogical collaborator with the individual investigator." The formulation
is modern, but the idea links up with the Renaissance humanists' cultivation
of dialogue, and behind them the medieval dialecticians, and behind them Cicero
and Isocrates.

The last word is given to a jurist, philosopher, and rhetorician who has done
more than anyone in our time to revive and replant rhetoric. Chaim Perelman's
paper begins by observing that the fundamental notions of philosophy are all
confused, since they vary according to the system in which they figure. (We
might add that those critics who find contradictions in rhetoric over the two
thousand years of its history should once try to systematise philosophy!) In
Plato dialectic is a purgative technique, designed to reveal contradictions in
a speaker's argument, force him to withdraw it, and so to prepare the way
for a reminiscence or intuition of truth. To communicate this the philosopher
must then use rhetoric, in the way recommended in the *Phaedrus*. Where Plato's
philosophy is unitary, and dominated by the search for truth, Aristotle's is
pluralist, embracing works of theory, practice (rhetoric, politics, ethics, all
concerned with the action of human beings on each other), and poetry, with
the techniques appropriate to each. For scientific propositions Aristotle
distinguished analytic, demonstrative reasoning, whose conclusions are necessary,
or at least true; for public disputes and controversies Aristotle reserved dialectical
reasoning, whose conclusions are defensible. This distinction between the realm
of science and the realm of opinion was blurred in the Middle Ages and
Renaissance when logic was identified with dialectic, a confusion worst
compounded by Ramus, whose reform of the trivium separated *elocutio* from

inventio and *dispositio* (now assigned to logic) and denied the audience the central place it enjoyed in Aristotle.

Perelman's training, he tells us, was in logic, in the positivist-empiricist tradition, which was irrational in the realm of values since it denied the possibility of practical reason, holding that human beings were dominated by the passions. Perelman's own work has shown that no specific logic existed in the field of values because here, as in all areas involving opinion, one had to use techniques of persuasion deriving from classical rhetoric, and especially the topics. This is why Perelman's "New Rhetoric" — linking up with C. S. Peirce and a tradition back to Cicero and Aristotle — recognises that all argument develops by confrontation with an audience. Dialectic and philosophy, then, are variant forms of argumentation, dialectic involving one listener or speaker in a dialogue, philosophy addressing all men qualified to judge.

This reconciliation between dialectic, rhetoric, and philosophy shows that the rhetorical tradition has learned something from history. In basing his system on argumentation — and seeing the figures of rhetoric as functions of an appeal to the audience — Perelman has returned rhetoric to its original context in society and in interpersonal communication. When rhetoric has declined it has not been because it overcultivated eloquence but because it lost contact with a real and practical social situation. This judgment applies to the overelaborate theoretical treatises of the thirteenth century, as it does to the belle-lettrist criticism of the late eighteenth century (which Ian Thomson describes as being "written in the void," having lost a sense of the practical purpose and utility of rhetoric). The success of Perelman's work shows how far he is from falling into this trap, and many readers will share his belief that rhetoric should once more occupy "a central place in the formation of our thought and our culture." This is not to insist on a hierarchy, merely to say that we cannot afford to ignore rhetoric.

Notes

1. C. S. Lewis, *English Literature in the Sixteenth Century* (Oxford, 1954), p. 61.
2. For further reflections on this topic see Brian Vickers, "Rhetorical and anti-rhetorical tropes: On writing the history of *elocutio*," *Comparative Criticism* 3 (1981), pp. 105–32.
3. *The Classical Heritage and its Beneficiaries* (Cambridge, 1954), pp. 30–31.
4. *Logic and Rhetoric in England, 1500–1700* (Princeton, 1956), pp. 33–34.
5. *Ars Poetica*, 102 f.; tr. H. R. Fairclough (Loeb Library: London, 1970), p. 459.
6. See my essay below, "Territorial disputes," pp. 265 f. and notes.
7. *Art and Illusion* (London, 1960) p. 317.
8. See H. I. Marrou, *Histoire de l'Education dans l'Antiquité*: English translation by

G. Lamb, *A History of Education in Antiquity* (London, 1956); G. Kennedy, *The Art of Persuasion in Greece* (London, 1963).

9. Cantimori, "Rhetoric and Politics in Italian Humanism," *Journal of the Warburg and Courtauld Institutes* 1 (1937–38), 83–102; Herde, "Politik und Rhetorik in Florenz am Vorabend der Renaissance," *Archiv für Kulturgeschichte* 18 (1965), 141–220. See also E. Garin, "I cancellieri umanisti della republica fiorentina da Coluccio Salutati a Bartolomeo Scala," in *La Cultura filosofica del Rinascimento italiano* (Firenze, 1961), 3 ff; English translation in Garin, *Portraits from the Quattrocento*, tr. V. and E. Velen (New York, 1972), pp. 1–29; and *Retorica e Politica*. Atti del II Convegno Italo-Tedesco (Bressanone, 1974), ed. D. Goldin, with a preface by G. Folena (Padua, 1977).

10. Wieruszowski, *Politics and Culture in Medieval Spain and Italy* (Rome, 1971), especially part II, "Italian Culture in the age of Dante," pp. 331–627; R. J. Schoeck, "Rhetoric and law in Sixteenth-Century England," *Studies in Philology* 50 (1953), 110–27; D. S. Bland, "Rhetoric and the Law Student in Sixteenth-Century England," *Studies in Philology* 54 (1957), 498–508; Brian Vickers, *Francis Bacon and Renaissance Prose* (Cambridge, 1968), pp. 30–53, 62–68; A. Kibédi Varga, *Rhétorique et Littérature. Etudes de structures classiques* (Paris, 1970), especially on "Le genre judiciare," pp. 86 ff, with a collection of texts, pp. 143–67.

11. T. W. Baldwin, *Shakespere's 'Small Latine and Lesse Greeke'* 2 vols. (Urbana, Ill., 1944); D. L. Clark, *John Milton at St. Paul's School* (New York, 1948); W. S. Howell, *Logic and Rhetoric in England 1500–1700* (Princeton, 1956); M. H. Curtis, *Oxford and Cambridge in Transition, 1558–1642* (Oxford, 1959); W. T. Costello, *The Scholastic Curriculum at Early Seventeenth-Century Cambridge* (Cambridge, Mass., 1958).

12. On French education see H. Lantoine, *Histoire de l'enseignement secondaire en France au XVIIe et au début du XVIIIe siècles* (Paris, 1874); François de Dainville, *La Naissance de l'humanisme moderne* (Paris, 1940) and "L'evolution de l'enseignement de la rhétorique au XVIIe siècle," in *XVIIe Siècle*, no. 80–81, "Points de vue sur la rhétorique" (1968), pp. 19–43; George Snyders, *La pédagogie en France aux XVIIe et XVIIIe siècles* (Paris, 1965); and Alex Gordon, *Ronsard et la Rhétorique* (Geneva, 1970), pp. 22–27.

13. On rhetoric and education in Italy see Wieruszowski, op. cit., pp. 589–627, "Rhetoric and the Classics in Italian Education of the Thirteenth Century"; E. Garin, *L'Educazione in Europa, 1400–1600* (Bari, 1957², 1966) and (ed. Garin) *Il pensiero pedagogico del Rinascimento* (Florence, 1958); the old studies by W. H. Woodward; and R. R. Bolgar, *The Classical Heritage and its Beneficiaries* (Cambridge, 1954).

14. On rhetoric in German education the indispensable work is still Friedrich Paulsen, *Geschichte des gelehrten Unterrichts*, 2 vols. (3rd, rev. ed., Leipzig, 1919), even though it suffers from a rather antiquated conception of rhetoric. More enlightened, although not so wide-ranging, is Wilfried Barner, *Barock-Rhetorik* (Tübingen, 1970), especially part 3, "Die Verankerung der Rhetorik im Bildungswesen des 17. Jahrhunderts," pp. 241–447, with a bibliography, pp. 456–87. A larger, but still preliminary and incomplete bibliography, is given by Dieter Breuer and Günther Kopsch, "Rhetorik-lehrbücher des 16. bis 20. Jahrhunderts," in *Rhetorik. Beiträge zu ihrer Geschichte in Deutschland vom 16.–20. Jahrhundert*, ed. H. Schanze (Frankfurt, 1974), pp. 217–355.

15. See the exemplary edition, "The *De Arte Rhetorica* (1568) by Cyprian Soarez, S.J.: a translation with introduction and notes," by L. J. Flynn, S.J., unpublished Ph.D. Dissertation, University of Florida, 1955. University of Microfilms order no. HUJ 100–16926. See also A. P. Farrell, S.J., *The Jesuit Code of Liberal Education: Develop-

ment and Scope of the Ratio Studiorum (Milwaukee, 1938); G. Codina Mir, *Aux sources de la pédagogie des Jésuites: le "modus parisiensis"* (Rome, 1968); J.-M. Valentin, *Le Théâtre des Jesuites dans les pays de langue allemande (1554–1680)*, 3 vols. (Bern, Frankfurt, Las Vegas, 1978), especially vol. I., pp. 205–57, and Marc Fumaroli, *L'Age de l'Eloquence. Rhétorique et 'res literaria' de la Renaissance au seuil de l'époque classique* (Geneva, 1980).

16. G. C. Fiske and M. A. Grant, "Cicero's 'Orator' and Horace's 'Ars Poetica'," *Harvard Studies in Classical Philology*, 35 (1924) and "Cicero's *De Oratore* and Horace's *Ars Poetica*," *University of Wisconsin Studies in Language and Literature* 27 (1929). Oddly enough, W. S. Howell has taken it upon himself to assert that Horace's literary treatise is not rhetorical: see his collection of essays, *Poetics, Rhetoric, and Logic* (Ithaca, N.Y., 1975), pp. 45–49, 62–71.

17. O. B. Hardison, Jr., *The Enduring Monument. A Study of the Idea of Praise in Renaissance Literary Theory and Practice* (Chapel Hill, N.C., 1962). See also T. C. Burgess, *Epideictic Literature* (Chicago, 1902), and Vinzenz Buchheit, *Untersuchungen des Genos epideictikon von Gorgias bis Aristoteles* (Munich, 1960).

18. J. Spingarn, *A History of Literary Criticism in the Renaissance* (New York, 1899, 1908); Marvin Herrick, *The Fusion of Horatian and Aristotelian Literary Criticism, 1531–1555* (Urbana, Ill., 1946); A. H. Gilbert, ed., *Literary Criticism, Plato to Dryden* (1940; repr. Detroit, 1962); Baxter Hathaway, *The Age of Criticism: The Late Renaissance in Italy* (Ithaca, N.Y., 1963); Bernard Weinberg, *A History of Literary Criticism in the Italian Renaissance*, 2 vols, (Chicago, 1961); ed., *Trattati di Poetica e Retorica del '500* (Bari, 1970–74).

19. *The Language of History in the Renaissance. Rhetoric and Historical Consciousness in Florentine Humanism* (Princeton, 1970), p. 65.

20. On the links between rhetoric and painting see J. J. Pollitt, *The Ancient View of Greek Art. Criticism, History, and Terminology* (New Haven, 1974); W. G. Howard, "Ut Pictura Poesis," *PMLA* 24 (1909), pp. 40–123; Rensselaer Lee, *Ut Pictura Poesis. The Humanistic Theory of Painting* (New York, 1967, with preface adding further bibliography; originally published in *The Art Bulletin*, 1940); J. R. Spencer, "Ut Rhetorica Pictura," *Journal of the Warburg and Courtauld Institutes*, 20 (1957), pp. 26–44, and the important essay by Wesley Trimpi, "The Meaning of Horace's *Ut Pictura Poesis*," *Journal of the Warburg and Courtauld Institutes* 36 (1973), 1–34. For the humanist theorists (Dolce, Lomazzo, Alberti, Bellori) see Paola Barocchi ed., *Trattati d'arte del cinquecento fra manierismo e controriforma*, 3 vols., (Bari, 1960–). See also E. H. Gombrich, *Art and Illusion* (London, 1960); "The Debate on Primitivism in Ancient Rhetoric," *Journal of the Warburg and Courtauld Institutes* 29 (1966), 24–38; and *Norm and Form* (London, 1966); Jean Hagstrum, *The Sister Arts* (Chicago, 1958); and Mark W. Roskill, *Dolce's "Aretino" and Venetian Art Theory of the Cinquecento* (New York, 1968), who shows that, as a substitute for Alberti's three divisions of the art of painting, "drawing, composition, and the manipulation of light" (*Della Pittura*, 1436), Dolce applied to painting the three first parts of rhetoric, *inventio, dispositio*, and *elocutio*. Dolce also translated the *Ars Poetica* (Venice, 1535).

21. Bacon, *Works*, ed. J. Spedding et. al., 14 vols., (London, 1857–74), 3:348–49.

22. Schering, "Die Lehre von den musikalischen Figuren," *Kirchen-musikalisches Jahrbuch* 21 (1908), 106–14; Heinz Brandes, *Studien zur musikalischen Figurenlehre im 16. Jahrhundert* (Berlin, 1935); Hans-Heinrich Unger, *Die Beziehungen zwischen Musik und Rhetorik im 16.–18. Jahrhundert* (Würzburg, 1941; repr. Hildesheim, 1969). A

brief but important article by Wilibald Gurlitt, "Musik und Rhetorik. Hinweise auf ihre geschichtliche Grundlageneinheit" appeared in *Helicon* 5 (1944), and is reprinted in Gurlitt's *Musikgeschichte und Gegenwart*, ed. H. H. Eggbrecht, 2 vols. (Wiesbaden, 1966), 1:62–81. See also Martin Ruhnke, *Joachim Burmeister. Ein Beitrag zur Musiklehre um 1600* (Kassel und Basel, 1955), and his facsimile re-edition of Burmeister's *Musica poetica* (Kassel und Basel, 1955); Claude V. Palisca, "A Clarification of 'Musica Reservata' in Jean Taisnier's 'Astrologiae,' 1559," *Acta Musicologica* 31 (1959), 133–61, and "Ut Oratoria Musica: the Rhetorical Basis of Musical Mannerism," in *The Meaning of Mannerism*, ed. F. W. Robinson and S. G. Nichols, Jr. (Hanover, New Hampshire, 1972), 37–65; Gregory G. Butler, "Fugue and Rhetoric," *Journal of Music Theory* 21 (1977), 49–109, and "Music and Rhetoric in Early Seventeenth-Century English Sources," *The Musical Quarerly* 66 (1980), 53–64; Gerrard Le Coat, *The Rhetoric of The Arts, 1550–1650* (Bern and Frankfurt, 1975); Frederick Wessel, *The Affektenlehre in the 18th Century* (Indiana University dissertation, 1955; University Microfilm Dissertation Pub. no. 14,674); "Affektenlehre" and "Figurenlehre" in *Die Musik in Geschichte und Gegenwart*, ed. Friedrich Blume (Kassel and Basel, 1955); Maria R. Maniates, *Mannerism in Italian Music and Culture, 1530–1630* (Chapel Hill, N.C., 1978); H. J. Jensen, *The Muses' Concord: Literature, Music, and the Visual Arts in the Baroque Age* (Bloomington, Ind., 1976); Ursula and Warren Kirkendale, *Studien zur musikalischen Rhetorik* (Vienna, forthcoming).

23. Ripa: cf. Le Coat, op. cit., p. 59.

24. See James J. Murphy, "The Scholastic Condemnation of Rhetoric in the Commentary of Giles of Rome on the *Rhetoric* of Aristotle," *Arts Libéraux et philosophie au Moyen Age* (Montreal and Paris, 1969), pp. 833–41, and "Aristotle's *Rhetoric* in the Middle Ages," *Quarterly Journal of Speech* 52 (1966), pp. 109–15.

25. *Republic*, X, 607; *Laws*, II, 659–61; VII, 801 ff.; *Protagoras*, 325–26. See O. B. Hardison, op. cit., p. 26 f., and G. A. Kennedy, *The Art of Persuasion in Greece* (London, 1963), pp. 152–203.

26. Hardison, p. 30.

27. *Rhetoric*, I. 9 (1366a–1368a 38).

28. See Hardison, op. cit., Baxter Hathaway, *The Age of Criticism: The Late Renaissance in Italy* (Ithaca, N.Y., 1963); and my paper "Epideictic and Epic in the Renaissance," forthcoming in *New Literary History*.

29. Hardison, pp. 34 ff.; Weinberg, *History of Literary Criticism in the Renaissance*, II, 751, 764 f., I, 209, and index s.v. "Averroes."

30. For a convenient list of these *loci* see Wesley Trimpi, "The Quality of Fiction: The Rhetorical Transmission of Literary Theory," *Traditio* 30 (1974), pp. 1–118, at p. 100 note 117.

31. Weinberg, op. cit., I, 3, 17, 22.

32. See M. A. Finocchiaro, *Galileo and the Art of Reasoning: Rhetorical Foundations of Logic and Scientific Method* (Dordrecht, Reidel, 1980).

33. I regret that I have mislaid the source for this quotation. Neither Michael Winterbottom nor Bryan Reardon, both experts in many fields, have been able to trace it, although they both assure me that such events were not unusual, even after Pompey had cleared the sea of pirates.

34. See McKeon's celebrated essay, "Rhetoric in the Middle Ages," *Speculum* 17 (1942), pp. 1–32.

35. John O. Ward, *Artificiosa Eloquentia in the Middle Ages* (Ph.D. Dissertation, Toronto University, 1972), and an important series of articles: "The Constitutio Negotialis in Antique Latin Rhetorical Theory," *Prudentia* 1 (1969), pp. 29–48; "The date of the commentary on Cicero's *De Inventione* by Thierry of Chartres (c. 1095–1160?) and the Cornifician attack on the Liberal Arts," *Viator* 3 (1972), pp. 219–273; "From Antiquity to the Renaissance: Glosses and Commentaries on Cicero's *Rhetorica*," in *Medieval Eloquence* (cited in note 36), pp. 25–67.

36. J. J. Murphy, *Medieval Rhetoric. A Select Bibliography* (Toronto, 1971); *Rhetoric in the Middle Ages. A History of Rhetorical Theory from Saint Augustine to the Renaissance* (Berkeley and Los Angeles, 1974); ed. *Three Medieval Rhetorical Arts* (Berkeley and Los Angeles, 1971); ed. *Medieval Eloquence. Studies in the Theory and Practice of Medieval Rhetoric* (Berkeley and Los Angeles, 1978).

37. See Edmond Faral, Les Arts Poétiques du XIIe et du XIIIe siècle (Paris, 1924), pp. 61–74.

38. Murphy, *Rhetoric in the Middle Ages*, p. 257.

39. ". . . Cicero holds that, while invention and arrangement are within the reach of any man of good sense, eloquence belongs to the orator alone, and consequently it was on the rules for the cultivation of eloquence that he expended the greatest care. That he was justified in so doing is shown clearly by the actual name of the art of which I am speaking. For the verb *eloqui* means the production and communication to the audience of all that the speaker has conceived in his mind, and without this power all the preliminary accomplishments of oratory are as useless as a sword that is kept permanently concealed within its sheath. Therefore it is on this that teachers of rhetoric concentrate their attention, since it cannot possibly be acquired without the assistance of the rules of art: it is this which is the chief object of our study, the goal of all our exercises and all our efforts at imitation, and it is to this that we devote the energies of a life-time; it is this that makes one orator surpass his rivals, this that makes one style of speaking preferable to another." Book VIII, par. 14–17; tr. H. E. Butler (Loeb Library, London, 1933) vol. 3, pp. 185 f.

40. See my comments on Croce below.

41. *De oratore* 2. 102 f; tr. E. W. Sutton and H. Rackham (Loeb Library; London, 1959), vol. 1, pp. 272 ff.

42. See Rosemund Tuve, *Allegorical Imagery. Some Medieval Books and Their Posterity* (Princeton, 1966); D. C. Allen, *Mysteriously Meant. The Rediscovery of Pagan Symbolism and Allegorical Interpretation in the Renaissance* (Baltimore, 1970).

43. *Rhetorica ad Herennium*, tr. H. Caplan (Loeb Library; London, 1954), pp. 386 f.

44. *Agamemnon*, 896 ff., tr. R. Lattimore; for further comment on this scene see Brian Vickers, *Towards Greek Tragedy* (London and New York, 1973, 1979), p. 365 f.

45. *Handbuch der literarischen Rhetorik*, 2 vols. (München, 1960).

46. *Elizabethan and Metaphysical Imagery* (Chicago, 1947), part II: "The Logical Functions of Imagery," pp. 251–410.

47. In his *Renaissance Thought and its Sources* (New York, 1979), pp. 252 f., he has repeated this judgment.

48. Isaiah Berlin, *Concepts and Categories* (Oxford, 1980), p. 11.

49. *Rhetoric*, 1408a 20 ff., 1413b 3 ff., 1414a 8 ff.

Part I

The Rhetorical Tradition

The Variety of Classical Rhetoric

A. D. LEEMAN
University of Amsterdam

RHETORIC IS a chameleonic notion. Few words have covered more different and diverse concepts—and provoked more different emotional reactions. It has something to do with everything, however narrowly we define its *materia artis*. In the beginning was the Logos. According to a wide-spread myth in Antiquity, found in Isocrates as well as in Cicero, the Orator, master of the Logos, *(o)ratio*, had been the founder of truly human, orderly culture, and by means of the gift of language, which distinguishes men from beasts, had persuaded his fellow-men to give up their primitive, 'beastly' way of life for a human, orderly and humane society.[1] The Sophist Gorgias, however, praised the Logos as the power that had persuaded Helen to follow her adulterer,[2] and as the power that enables the individual to win over the members of a jury or a political assembly;[3] moreover, as the power that enabled him, Gorgias, and his pupils that would pay him for it, to speak eloquently about anything his audience wished, *pour épater le bourgeois*: the so-called Gorgian epangelma.[4] Plato protested: logos is universal, concerns every kind of human utterance and communication, public or private, and should be honest and 'philosophical', based on knowledge and truth.[5] Young Isocrates, the philosophical orator, was his man, not the arch-persuader Lysias or the arch-nihilist Gorgias.[6] Unfortunately, however, it proved later that Isocrates' words were of a higher quality than his thinking; his Orator is a pleasant talker about high-pitched but banal generalities. Aristotle did not like him, and he again reduced rhetoric to what he thought it should scientifically be: the study of the means of persuasion—no questions asked.[7] On the other hand, he enormously widened the scope of rhetoric by considering self-presentation (*ethos*) and the handling of the emotions of the audience (*pathos*).[8] But he restricted the field of activity of the orator to public meetings—the law-court, the political assembly, the ceremonial gathering.[9]

Thus, at the death of Aristotle already, rhetoric was a manifold notion, holding very divergent germs for further development. However, the decline of political life in the Greek world during the following centuries hampered the sprouting of the most fertile ones. In the Hellenistic age, rhetoric was in the hands of rhetoricians — schoolmasters who pretended that their more and more elaborate scholastic *techne* was the best training for a young man. They accepted Aristotle's threefold field of activity, thus restricting rhetoric to public speaking only, but not his penetrating views on *ethos* and *pathos*; they took over the division of the tasks of the orator (*inventio, ordo, elocutio, memoria, actio*) from Aristotle's pupil Theophrastus;[10] they elaborated the system of *inventio* (Hermagoras) and took over all kinds of technicalities from the Isocrateans. They introduced the discussion of general topics (*theseis*), and they conducted a feud against the various philosophical schools of their time on the issue of what was the best type of higher education, rhetoric or philosophy.[11] They neglected philosophy (dialectics and psychology) and other forms of human utterance besides public speaking, like literature or the art of conversation (Cicero complains that there were no *praecepta rhetorum* in these fields).[12] They just concentrated on their divisions and subdivisions. As a result, philosophers, especially in the Academy, endeavoured to adopt the undernourished child, and Philo and Antiochus gave courses on rhetoric *i.a.* as an art to test the tenability of certain positions.[13] In their opinion the mythical founder of human culture was the Wise Man, not the orator.[14]

This was, in the broadest outlines, the heritage which Cicero, orator, and at the same time in love with philosophy, had to cope with.[15] In a way, his problems are still ours, if we seriously want to determine what is, and what is not rhetoric. Cicero was learned and well-read in Greek and Latin literature, but he was not a speculative philosopher or a shrewd scholar. A Roman of the first century B.C., he lived in a society characterized by political liberty and political license. His own influence resided in his rich and versatile oratorical power rather than in his political ideas or charismatic leadership. He valued Roman moral traditions at least as high as the Greek cultural heritage. Such factors determined his attitude to the Greek rhetorical traditions. In his student-days, he had written — mostly copied — a rhetorical handbook in the tradition of Hellenistic school-rhetoric, esp. Hermagoras; but later on he was ashamed of this *De inventione*, which he then thought a puerile achievement.[16] In the *De oratore*, written when he had had a long experience of oratorical practice, he repeatedly warns against an over-estimation of pedantic school-rhetoric and its pretentious cut-and-dried system.[17] Yet he does not abandon it altogether. The *De oratore* itself, especially Book II and III, is based on the traditional *partitiones oratoriae*, which he considers as a useful general reference-system for the orator — as a help rather than as a method.[18] Indeed, none of his own orations can be fully and satisfactorily analysed with the categories of the rhetorical system in the sense that an individual oration can be explained as the *ad hoc* embodiment of what the rhetorical precepts taught.[19] The art of oratory, Cicero realized, was infinitely more than the art of rhetoric plus talent plus exercise plus practice. Therefore, he 'humanized' rhetoric by making rhetorical *techne* one of the many attributes of the person of the orator. Moreover, by '*De oratore*' he means *de oratore perfecto*, thus establishing an ideal, though not a mere abstraction.[20] At the same time he does not describe this ideal systematically, but makes it the subject of a learned discussion by a group of outstanding Roman orators of the past, firmly rooted in the Roman traditions, but by no means unacquainted with Greek culture, philosophy and rhetoric.[21] In the first place, the orator is given the political and forensic context in which he must be able to function: he must have a first-hand knowledge of public and civil law, and of history.[22] But Cicero goes a step further. The orator is the master of Logos, and Logos is the human gift of speech. Speech is a means not only of persuasion, but also of communication. In Book III we read what amounts to the following: "eloquence is one, whatever the subject it deals with may be, whatever the circumstances in which it operates may be, whatever the intention of the speaker may be, whatever the audience he addresses may be: few people or many, strange people or friends . . . or oneself."[23] In this remarkable statement Cicero opens the way for a conception of rhetoric including every kind of human utterance, even soliloquy, and ultimately for a general theory of human communication. This happens at the expense of rhetoric as a more or less closed system, such as Aristotle had defined it and such as it had been adopted in an even narrower form in the Hellenistic schools. In fact Cicero returns to the position of Isocrates and the ancient Sophists.

Oratory was one of the three major prose genres which Antiquity recognized, the other two being historiography and philosophical writing. Next to these prose forms, Quintilian in Book X discusses poetry, because he believes that extensive reading in all kinds of good literature is indispensable for the development of the orator's style. In fact the relations between rhetoric and literature had always been very close, from the times that Gorgias demonstrated the magic power of Logos with the help of poetry.[24] Throughout the history of ancient rhetoric the examples for the right use of rhetorical devices were often taken from the poets, especially Homer and Virgil. On the other hand, literary analysis of poetry was often based on the elements of the rhetorical system, which in fact was the only system of literary creation and devices available, and whose traces are palpable throughout Aristotle's *Poetics* and especially Horace's *Ars poetica*, neither of which had a strong impact itself on the analysis of poetry in Antiquity. Thus, literary prose and poetry were considered by the rhetoricians to be domains contiguous to rhetoric, especially close to the ill-defined epideictic genre, though in general they did not venture to extend their territory to include other fields of literature. Cicero, however, in Book II of his *De oratore* makes the main speaker of that book, Antonius, present an outline of a theory for the writing of history, which he states expressedly never to have found its place in the handbooks of the rhetoricians, though, he says, historiography is a great task for the orator.[25] Then he passes on to other literary and philosophical topics, but he checks himself and announces that he will limit himself to forensic oratory only: "if a sculptor has mastered the art of making a statue of Hercules, there is no need to instruct him also in the art of sculpting his lions-skin and the Hydra." At which one of the others rightly remarks: "Who knows if the other departments of eloquence are not Hercules, and the traditional rhetorical genres the skin and the Hydra—not to mention the other Labours of Hercules?"[26] Cicero does see the opening to a kind of general prescriptive theory of literature, but he considers forensic oratory so difficult an art that it can serve as a basis for the writing of every other kind of literature. He considers himself, the orator Cicero, as the very man who can *qualitate qua* endow Rome both with a historical work, *opus oratorium maxime*, that really would be up to the standard—a plan which he often mentions but never was able to execute[27]—and with a philosophical literature: for who can better deal with philosophical questions than the orator who has learned to speak *copiose ornateque* about everything?[28] He even writes epic and didactic poems that are at least better than one would have expected.

As we have seen, the Hellenistic schools of rhetoric and the schools of philosophy conducted a violent feud about who could best educate the young. Cicero's *perfectus orator* is a man who possesses universal knowledge; by this he understands legal, historical, political, literary, but above all philosophical knowledge. He enthusiastically adopts Aristotle's views on the importance of *ethos* and *pathos*, which had found no place in Hellenistic rhetoric.[29] He also adopts the Aristotelian and later Academic method of the *disputare in utramque partem* on general topics.[30] He 'philosophizes' rhetoric to such an extent, that in the third book of his *De oratore* he can state that it does not matter much, whether his perfect orator is called *orator sapiens* or *philosophus eloquens*; for originally, in pre-socratic times philosophy and eloquence were one, or two halves of one whole: the Logos.[31] The old Catonian, Roman definition of the orator as *vir bonus dicendi peritus* is thus expanded and glorified by the incorporation of the whole of Greek cultural tradition.

We need not stress the enormous impact of this Ciceronian conception on Western education and civilization after the Middle Ages.[32] The *orator perfectus* has become the humanistic ideal of the *uomo universale*, based on the unity of all human knowledge and all human values. But this process, interesting as it is, has not contributed to clarify the notion of rhetoric—on the contrary it has totally blurred its outlines. On the other hand we should realize that rhetoric is not a static notion. Its *materia artis* has constantly changed from Gorgias to Perelman. One of the problems that faces our society is to define its own *materia studiorum*. Does Cicero's *De inventione* wholly belong to it, whereas most of the *De oratore* is at best marginal? Should we leave rhetoric alone where it is most interesting, though ill-defined? As far as Antiquity is concerned, 'the art of persuasive public speaking' should perhaps be considered the most usable definition; but it would certainly be useless when we turn to later ages. 'Rhetoric' means 'the art of the orator'; but Cicero already tends to distinguish between a scholastic, Greek *ars rhetorica* and a practical, Roman *ars oratoria*. In the course of the centuries the name rhetoric, just because it could easily be detached from its obsolete connection with *rhetor* = orator, could cover meanings which have little or nothing to do with an orator—a process that has continued until the present day.

Notes

1. Isocrates, *Ad Nicoclem*, 5; Cicero, *De Oratore*, 1, 33–34. The fullest survey of the history of the topos is H. K. Schulte, *Orator* (Frankfurt am Main, 1935), pp. 9–24.

2. Gorgias, *Encomium Helenae*, 8.

3. See Plato, *Gorgias*, 452d.

4. Cicero, *De Oratore*, 1. 103.

5. *Gorgias*, 452d ff.

6. Plato, *Phaedrus*, 279.

7. Aristotle, *Rhetorica*, 1, 2.

8. loc. cit. 2, 1.

9. loc. cit. 1, 3.

10. W. Kroll, "Rhetorik" in Pauly-Wissowa, *Real-Encyclopädie, supplement* 7 (1940), c. 1075 ff.

11. H. von Arnim, *Dion von Prusa* (Berlin, 1898), ch. 1: "Sophistik, Rhetorik, Philosophie in ihrem Kampf um die Jugendbildung."

12. Cicero, *De Oratore*, 2, 62; *De Officiis*, 1, 132.

13. Cicero, *Tusculanae Disputationes*, 2, 9; *De Oratore*, 3, 110; see W. Kroll, c. 1086 f.

14. Cicero, *Tusculanae Disputationes*, 5, 5; *Pro Sestio*, 91.

15. See e.g. K. Barwick, *Das rednerische Bildungsideal Ciceros* (Berlin, 1963).

16. Cicero, *De Oratore* 1, 5. Later ages, however, preferred the *De Inventione* (with the *Rhetorica ad Herennium*) to the *De Oratore*.

17. Cicero, *De Oratore*, 2, 75; 139; 3, 54; 70; 75; 92; 121; 125. Compare L. Laurand, *De M. Tulli Ciceronis studiis rhetoricis* (Paris, 1907), pp. 1–19; and R. Weidner, *Ciceros Verhältnis zur griechisch-römischen Schulrhetorik seiner Zeit* (Erlangen, 1925), pp. 28–64.

18. Cicero, *De Oratore*, 1, 145 *artificium doctrina . . . , quam ego si nihil dicam adiuvare, mentiar: habet enim quaedam quasi ad commonendum oratorem, quo quidque referat et quo intuens ab eo, quodcumque sibi proposuerit, minus aberrat.*

19. See W. Stroh, *Taxis und Taktik* (Stuttgart, 1975), pp. 7–30 for a recent discussion of the problem.

20. This appears from passages like Cicero, *De Oratore*, 1, 118; 3, 84.

21. Cicero, *De Oratore*, 1, 23.

22. E.g. *De Oratore* 1, 18, and *passim*.

23. *De Oratore* 3, 22–24.

24. Gorgias, *Encomium Helenae*, 9.

25. Cicero, *De Oratore*, 2, 62.

26. *De Oratore* 2, 71.

27. On these projects and the reason why they were never executed compare A. D. Leeman, *Orationis ratio* (Amsterdam, 1963), pp. 168 ff.; the quotation is from Cicero, *De legibus*, 1, 5.

28. Cicero, *Tusculanae Disputationes*, 1, 7.

29. Cicero, *De Oratore*, 2, 114–216; compare F. Solmsen, "Aristotle and Cicero on the orators playing upon the feelings," *Classical Philology* 33 (1938), pp. 390–402; *id*. "The Aristotelian tradition in ancient rhetoric," *American Journal of Philology*, 62 (1941), pp. 35–50; 169–90.

30. E.g. *De Oratore*, 3, 80.

31. *De Oratore*, 3, 142; the relations between rhetoric and philosophy in Cicero's works are discussed at great length in Alain Michel, *Rhétorique et philosophie chez Cicéron* (Paris, 1960).

32. Just one example for curiosity's sake: K. O. Apel, "Die Idee der Sprache in der Tradition des Humanismus von Dante bis Vico," *Archiv für Begriffsgeschichte* 8 (1963), pp. 148, 179, shows the influence of the Ciceronian version of the topos of the orator as the founder of civilization.

Invention, imagination, et théorie des émotions chez Cicéron et Quintilien

P. H. SCHRYVERS
University of Leiden

Au livre II du dialogue *De oratore* de Cicéron, paragraphe 196 où l'auteur traite de la théorie des émotions, Antoine donne aux jeunes orateurs une règle de conduite conçue en ces termes: "Quand vous parlerez, sachez trouver de la colère, de la douleur, des larmes." Ce précepte conclut un développement qui partait du principe que les auditeurs ne sauraient être amenés à la douleur, à la haine, à l'envie, à la crainte, aux larmes, à la pitié, si l'orateur ne paraît pas éprouver lui-même profondément les passions qu'il veut leur communiquer.[1] Le principe et le précepte posent au rhétoricien un problème qu'Antoine discute aux mêmes paragraphes: comment se fait-il que le même homme puisse se livrer aussi souvent aux transports de la colère, de la douleur et des autres passions, surtout pour des intérêts qui ne sont pas les siens? Antoine nous donne en passant la réponse: l'orateur sait toujours éveiller en lui-même les émotions voulues grâce à la force des pensées et des *loci* qu'il emploie et développe,[2] c'est-à-dire grâce à l'*inventio*. L'art de persuader autrui est ainsi considéré en premier lieu comme l'art de se persuader soi-même.

A l'appui de sa thèse, Antoine évoque les émotions qu'éprouve véritablement le comédien en jouant son rôle chaque jour dans les pièces dramatiques, et le poète tragique Pacuvius ne pouvait—selon Antoine—être calme et de sang-froid en écrivant ses tragédies.[3] Remarquons que les deux citations tirées de Pacuvius ont été très bien choisies par Antoine; dans la première, il s'agit d'un vers où Télamon reproche à Teucer d'être revenu sans son frère Ajax. Bien qu'Antoine méprise la théorie rhétorique et se fasse fort de n'appliquer jamais les pensées et les *loci* de l'*inventio*, ceux qui assistaient au dialogue, ou les lecteurs de Cicéron, auront reconnu sans aucun doute les *loci* de l'*indignatio*, et rattaché, comme Antoine le demandera plus tard, la citation de Pacuvius à la théorie rhétorique en question.[4] Dans la deuxième citation, où les larmes et les sanglots se mêlent aux paroles et aux plaintes de Télamon, les *loci* de la *miseratio* sautent aux yeux. Sous l'influence de l'*inventio*, des émotions véritables sont éveillées chez le comédien et chez le poète dramatique, joueur et écrivain des fictions, à plus forte raison—selon Antoine—chez l'orateur, qui est en même temps l'acteur et l'auteur de la réalité.

En évoquant les émotions que le poète Pacuvius doit avoir ressenties pendant la création de sa tragédie, Antoine se réfère aux opinions de Démocrite et de Platon, selon lesquelles il n'y a point de véritable poète sans accompagnement d'enthousiasme et sans une inspiration qui tient du délire. Dans certaines études allemandes et françaises, on a indûment déduit de cette référence qu'Antoine (ou bien Cicéron) aurait ici adopté la théorie platonicienne de l'enthousiasme surnaturel (la θεῖα μανία).[5] Ce qui frappe, c'est la réserve avec laquelle Antoine utilise cette référence: il l'introduit par les mots "j'ai souvent ouï-dire," "cette opinion passe pour avoir été transmise." Pour ajouter à la force persuasive de son argumentation, il emprunte l'autorité de Démocrite et de Platon, dont il veut en même temps neutraliser les implications non voulues. En outre, contrairement à d'autres passages où Cicéron se réfère aux mêmes opinions de Démocrite et de Platon,[6] Antoine ne recourt pas à des qualificatifs tels que *divinus* et *caelestis*. L'introduction d'une théorie sur l'inspiration surnaturelle serait d'ailleurs déplacée dans un raisonnement où il s'agit justement de prouver combien il est naturel que l'orateur se livre chaque jour aux transports des émotions. De plus, l'explication rationaliste et naturelle vient d'être trouvée dans la force de l'*inventio* rhétorique. Finalement, au cours du livre II, Antoine se moque de la vénération religieuse que les jeunes Sulpicius et Catulus ont pour Crassus et pour lui-même, et s'efforce de démystifier la conception de l'orateur "divin." Ainsi, à la fin du livre, un des jeunes orateurs témoigne de son soulagement d'avoir été délivré de son étonnement et de pouvoir considérer le talent "divin" comme résultat du zèle, du travail et du savoir.[7] A juste titre, Fiske et Grant ont comparé sur ce point l'attitude rationaliste et réaliste d'Antoine à la conception du *perfectus poeta* dans l'*Art Poétique* d'Horace.[8] Le poète romain renvoie également à l'opinion de Démocrite sur le *poeta insanus*, qu'il va développer dans un sens tout-à-fait réaliste et même médical. Aux temps de Cicéron et d'Horace, les Muses de l'Hélicon appartiennent aux fables d'antan.[9]

Au coeur de la discussion d'Antoine, le célèbre paradoxe du comédien (ou ici de l'orateur) fait son apparition.[10] D'une part, Antoine exige que dans l'orateur les sentiments ne soient pas faux, imités ou contrefaits, d'autre part ceux-ci ne sont pas non plus spontanés mais cherchés au moyen des *loci* de l'*inventio*. Si l'on considère l'oeuvre entière de Cicéron, ce paradoxe apparaît avec encore plus d'évidence. Au chapitre 25(§55) du quatrième livre des *Tusculanes* on lit: "Quant à l'orateur, il est fort mauvais qu'il se fâche, s'il n'est pas mauvais qu'il s'en donne l'air. Franchement, crois-tu que nous nous mettions en colère quand en plaidant nous nous animons et haussons le ton? Penses-tu que le comédien Esope ait jamais été en colère en jouant ce passage, et l'écrivain Accius lorsqu'il l'écrivait?" A la fin de cette tirade, Cicéron nous dit: "je veux bien que leur fameuse colère soit bonne à quelque chose chez un centurion, un porte-étendard, d'autres encore, dont il vaut mieux ne rien dire pour ne pas dévoiler les secrets de la rhétorique."

C'est à ces mots de Cicéron dans les *Tusculanes* que Quintilien paraît faire allusion lorsqu'il introduit son examen de la théorie des émotions par les mots suivants: "Mon dessein est de produire au jour les principes secrets de cet art et d'ouvrir profondément les sanctuaires de ce sujet."[11] Pour Quintilien, comme pour Cicéron et Horace dans l'*Art Poétique*, l'essentiel quand on désire émouvoir les sentiments, est d'être ému soi-même. D'où le problème qui se pose, comme il dit: Comment faire pour l'être? l'émotion n'est pas en effet à notre disposition. Ici, Quintilien développe une théorie – empruntée aux Grecs mais unique dans la rhétorique latine – selon laquelle les émotions sont liées aux *phantasiai* (en latin *visiones*), par lesquelles l'homme est capable de se représenter les images des choses absentes au point qu'il ait l'impression de les voir de ses propres yeux et de les tenir présentes devant lui. Comme nous le dit Quintilien, quiconque aura pu bien les concevoir aura le pouvoir de faire naître les émotions (ajoutons: en lui-même et en conséquence chez son public). A propos de cette faculté humaine, Quintilien dit que c'est un pouvoir qu'il nous sera au reste facile d'acquérir, si nous le voulons. Puis, il compare les *phantasiai* aux espoirs chimériques et à ces sortes de rêves, que l'on fait tout éveillés, pour conclure: ne pourrons-nous pas mettre à profit ce désordre de l'esprit (*hoc animi vitium*)?[12]

Bien que Quintilien déclare que sur ce point il ne se fonde pas sur l'enseignement reçu d'un maître[13] – ce qui veut dire ici tout au plus qu'il n'a rien trouvé chez Cicéron – essayons de retrouver quelque peu les sources ou, du moins, les influences qui auraient pu contribuer à la formulation de cette théorie. Ce sont d'abord trois éléments qui nous intéressent: le terme grec φαντασία, la comparaison ou plutôt l'identification établie entre les rêves et l'imagination, et le fait que cette dernière faculté est qualifiée de désordre de l'esprit (*vitium animi*).

On a toujours rapproché, avec raison, la théorie de Quintilien et le chapitre 15 du traité *Du Sublime*, où il est question des images (φαντασίαι) poétiques et rhétoriques. Depuis l'étude de Striller sur les études rhétoriques des stoïciens, on a reconnu l'influence de la Stoa chez l'auteur *Du Sublime*, aussi bien dans sa définition générale de la *phantasia* que dans l'exemple des images d'Oreste μαίνομενος (en délire), exemple destiné à illustrer l'imagination du poète et de l'orateur.[14] Si l'on émet l'hypothèse de l'influence stoïcienne chez l'auteur *Du Sublime* et, en conséquence, chez Quintilien, on doit, à mon avis, considérer en même temps que l'épistémologie et la psychologie descriptive de la Stoa, qui ont leur origine chez Aristote, se sont raffinées et développées au cours des controverses avec les Sceptiques.[15] Ceux-ci se sont toujours acharnés contre l'adoption par la Stoa d'une représentation évidente imprimée dans l'esprit par un objet extérieur, comme d'ailleurs contre l'axiome de l'évidence sensorielle, en vigueur chez les Epicuriens. La mise en rapport de l'imagination et des rêves apparaît plusieurs fois chez Sextus Empiricus, mais surtout dans les discussions épistémologiques entre la Stoa d'Antiochus d'Ascalon et le scepticisme de la nouvelle académie, présentées par Cicéron au livre II de ses *Académiques*. Dans ce dialogue (15,48), pour soutenir que rien ne peut être perçu d'une façon évidente ni tenu pour vrai, l'interlocuteur sceptique nous dit: "l'esprit est capable de se mouvoir tout seul, comme il apparaît de la faculté de l'imagination, des rêves et des hallucinations chez les gens en délire. Or, il est probable que l'esprit est mis au mouvement à un tel point qu'il n'existe plus de différence entre les présentations vraies et les représentations illusoires. De même, on ne peut pas distinguer l'effroi et la pâleur suscités par l'esprit tout seul en soi-même (*per se*) de la crainte causée par un objet extérieur.[16] C'est dans ces perspectives épistémologiques et psycho-pathologiques que s'explique l'expression *vitium animi*, utilisée par Quintilien pour qualifier la faculté de l'imagination.

Ainsi l'épistémologie et la psychologie descriptive de l'époque hellénistique, tout comme la critique littéraire plus tardive (Quintilien, l'auteur de *Du Sublime* et aussi la critique ancienne d'Homère) associent l'imagination, les rêves, le délire et – ajoutons – la folie amoureuse (chez Lucrèce et Plutarque par ex.)[17]. A propos d'un orateur qui s'enflammant obtient le plus grand succès grâce à son improvisation inspirée, Quintilien déclare au livre X (7.2): les orateurs anciens disaient dans ce cas: un dieu l'a inspiré (*deum tunc adfuisse*); mais non, dit Quintilien, la raison est claire: le succès était dû aux émotions bien conçues et à une vive imagination. La théorie des *phantasiai* est utilisée encore dans la discussion de l'*actio* pour résoudre dans la mesure du possible le paradoxe de l'orateur. L'importance que Quintilien accorde à l'imagination, apparaît avec force au début de son *Institution Oratoire* (I 2, 30), où il déclare: "l'éloquence dépend principalement de l'état de l'âme: l'âme doit être émue, concevoir les images des choses et se modeler en une certaine mesure sur la nature du sujet traité."

Dans la théorie des *phantasiai*, exposée au livre VI de Quintilien, on rencontre deux éléments fondamentaux, discutés et même appliqués dans la philosophie hellénistique (Stoa et Epicurisme), à savoir que les émotions sont liées aux représentations mentales, et, deuxièmement, que l'imagination dépend de nous, de notre vouloir.[18] Je voudrais illustrer l'application de ces deux principes en partant de l'exemple qu'Antoine donne au livre II du *De oratore* (47, 194–95). Voici ce qu'il dit: "de jour où il me fallut empêcher M'. Aquilius, un général renommé, de perdre son droit de cité, si-je me comportai comme je le fis dans ma péroraison, c'est que j'étais sous le coup d'une sincère douleur. Je me rappelais que cet homme avait été consul, imperator, et honoré par le sénat de l'ovation, qu'il était monté au Capitole, cet homme que je voyais maintenant abattu, brisé, dans l'affliction, aux prises avec une situation des plus critiques. A cette pensée, je fus saisi le tout premier d'une pitié que je voulais communiquer aux autres etc. etc. . . . ." Quoiqu'Antoine déclare dans ce même contexte qu'il ne saurait rien dire de l'art rhétorique, ses auditeurs auront tôt fait d'assimiler l'exemple au lieu commun le plus pathétique de la *miseratio*, celui qui consiste à opposer le passé, heureux et honorable, d'une personne à la situation actuelle, malheureuse, imméritée et inattendue.

Mesdames, messieurs, représentez-vous maintenant, si vous voulez bien, les réactions du Stoïcien et de l'Epicurien vis-à-vis des expériences racontées par Antoine: le stoïcien nous aurait dit que si le général ou son avocat avait anticipé par l'imagination sur ce malheur éventuel, ils ne se seraient pas laissé surprendre et émouvoir; l'épicurien nous aurait expliqué que le général ne devrait jamais se représenter d'avance ce malheur, car dans ce cas-là il se trouverait toujours dans le chagrin; plutôt, au moment de la catastrophe, il devrait détourner son esprit de cette situation pénible pour le concentrer sur son passé si heureux.[19] Ce que je voudrais démontrer par cet exemple, c'est que les deux principes de base, à savoir que les représentations mentales se trouvent à notre disposition et que les émotions sont provoquées par elles, inspirent deux développements opposés: *a.* la méditation philosophique qui vise à combattre les émotions, et *b.* l'*inventio* rhétorique qui, au contraire, veut les susciter aussi bien chez l'orateur que chez le public.[20]

Différents éléments de la discussion de Quintilien sur l'imagination humaine se trouvent reúnis dans le discours *pro Milone* de Cicéron. Là, Cicéron fait un tableau admirable de ce qu'aurait fait Clodius s'il s'était emparé de la préture (89 ff.). En s'adressant aux juges Cicéron commence par dire (79): "eh bien, représentez-vous — car notre imagination est libre et se figure ce qu'elle veut aussi clairement que nous distinguons ce qui est sous nos yeux." On constate dans cette phrase l'identification de la pensée à l'imagination dans l'emploi du substantif *cogitatio* et le parallélisme établi entre l'esprit et les yeux. "Représentez-vous," Cicéron continue, "en imagination la convention que voici: si je pouvais obtenir de vous l'acquittement de Milon mais à la condition expresse que Clodius revînt à la vie." Le fait que l'émotion est liée à l'image est exploité par Cicéron d'une façon suggestive, puisqu'il ajoute: "eh quoi? vos visages expriment la terreur. Quelle serait votre émotion, s'il était vivant, puisque, tout mort qu'il est, il vous a ainsi bouleversés par une vaine imagination (*vos quos mortuus inani cogitatione percussit*)." C'est Quintilien lui-même qui, au livre IX (2.41) a renvoyé au passage cité du *pro Milone*. A ce propos il fait observer que la transposition des temps, effectuée ainsi par Cicéron — c'est-à-dire l'évocation d'un événement tout à fait imaginaire — était plus modestement employée par les anciens orateurs. C'est pourquoi ils recouraient à des formules préparatoires telles que "imaginez que vous voyez" ou — formule d'un caractère déjà topique — "ce que vous n'avez pas vu avec les yeux, vous pouvez vous le représenter en imagination." Dans le fond, la formulation de Cicéron — *inani cogitatione* — est ambigüe: n'étant pas suscitée par un objet extérieur, la représentation mentale pourrait être déclarée vaine (*inanis*) par l'épistémologie stoicienne et sceptique. De plus, il s'agit ici d'actions imaginaires, puisque Clodius est déjà mort. Ici apparaît un certain glissement du sens, une certaine ambiguité dans le concept de la *phantasia* et les termes équivalents latins *imago, visio*. Pour Quintilien, la *phantasia* désigne encore la faculté de se représenter des choses absentes, de même que l'*imago* désigne l'apparence des personnes et des choses, mais comme les philosophes, il rapproche, lui-aussi, l'imagination et les espoirs illusoires des rêves éveillés et parle à ce propos d'un désordre de l'esprit. En outre, Quintilien et l'auteur *Du Sublime* se réfèrent à la hardiesse des déclamateurs postclassiques qui dépassent par leurs images les limites du probable. C'est pourquoi l'auteur *Du Sublime* les compare à Oreste (15,8).[21] Ces deux facteurs, épistémologique et littéraire ont sans doute contribué à la confusion qui règne chez les *Rhetores Latini Minores* et Macrobe à propos du mot *imago*. Ainsi le rhéteur tardif Julius Victor définit *imago* comme une image ressemblante que l'on forme bienque l'objet représenté n'existe pas (*quamvis non sit in rerum natura*); exemple *Scylla* (339, 33 H). Dans son commentaire sur Virgile, Macrobe nous offre deux définitions de l'*imago* (IV 9–10): il y a image quand on décrit l'aspect extérieur d'un objet absent ou quand on imagine de toutes pièces un être qui n'existe pas (l'exemple de cette pure création est chez lui aussi *Scylla*).

Après avoir énoncé sa théorie sur le rôle de l'imagination dans la provocation des sentiments, Quintilien va démontrer par quelle méthode il sera facile d'acquérir le pouvoir de se représenter de la façon la plus vraie les choses, les paroles, les actions. La démonstration se déroule comme suit; elle part de la donnée de base suivante: "un homme a été tué." Alors, ne pourrais-je me représenter tout ce qui a dû vraisemblablement se produire dans la réalité, voir l'assassin bondir, la victime pâlir, crier . . . , l'assaillant frapper, la victime tomber? N'aurais-je pas présents à l'esprit le sang, la pâleur, les gémissements et enfin la bouche ouverte, pour la dernière fois, de l'agonisant? De là procédera l'ἐνάργεια (la clarté), qui nous semble non pas tant raconter que montrer, et nos sentiments suivront comme si nous assistions aux événements eux-mêmes.[22]

La technique employée pour développer ce tableau est une répétition de la méthode appliquée par Quintilien au premier chapitre du livre VI (1, 15 sqq.) de l'*Institution Oratoire* pour montrer de quelle manière on peut représenter un acte comme le plus horrible ou comme le plus digne de pitié qui soit. La donnée de base est la suivante: nous nous plaignons d'avoir reçu des coups. Or, comme l'explique Quintilien, l'horreur s'accroît par les considérations suivantes: qu'est-ce qui a été fait? par qui? contre qui? dans quel esprit? en quel moment? en quel lieu? de quelle façon? C'est donc l'application du système des *circumstantiae* ou – en grec – περίστασεις, que l'on se rappelle le plus facilement à l'aide de l'hexamètre bien connu: *quis, quid, ubi, quibus auxiliis, cur, quomodo, quando.*

Depuis qu'en 150 av. J. Chr. Hermagore de Temnos avait défini les περίστασεις,[23] cette liste des circonstances a connu une application très répandue aussi bien dans la philosophie que dans la rhétorique. On a l'impression que la classification d'Hermagore a presque évincé dans l'antiquité plus tardive le système des catégories aristotéliciennes. Bienque Cicéron et Quintilien n'utilisent guère le terme de *circumstantiae* et jamais dans le sens donné par Hermagore, on reconnaît ce système dans la théorie sur les *elementa* ou *partes narrationis*, destinée à composer un récit probable ou à démolir un récit improbable.[24] C'est ainsi que la plus grande partie du discours *Pro Milone* a été construite selon ce schéma. La critique ancienne des mythes s'en est servie également.[25] On retrouve le schéma dans l'éthique de la Stoa Moyenne, appliqué pour distinguer les devoirs absolus et les devoirs qui s'imposent "selon les circonstances."[26] Dans les discussions philosophiques, chez Cicéron et Lucrèce par ex., le système des *circumstantiae* constitue l'inventaire des *loci* utilisés pour combattre la thèse de l'adversaire.[27] Dans la psychagogie ancienne, les circonstances constituent un topique de la méditation, comme l'a formulé Paul Rabbow dans son livre sur les exercices spirituels.[28] Quintilien l'applique avec l'intention de développer un tableau plein d'ἐνάργεια ; ainsi l'orateur peut susciter la pitié et l'indignation.

Ce qui frappe dans la discussion de Quintilien, c'est qu'une fois qu'il a mis en rapport les *phantasiai* et l'ἐνάργεια, il cite 3 exemples poétiques, tirés de l'*Enéide* de Virgile. Tandis que j'ai essayé de chercher la base philosophique de la théorie des *phantasiai* dans les débats épistémologiques et psychologiques entre la Stoa et l'école sceptique, les liens entre *phantasiai*, ἐνάργεια et poésie apparaissent pour la première fois, à ma connaissance, dans la critique hellénistique d'Homère, conservée dans les scholies.[29] C'est dans ces scholies que la critique poétique s'imprègne de la rhétorique et, en outre, d'une philosophie de marque plus ou moins stoicienne.[30] D'ailleurs, le rapprochement des rêves et des *phantasiai*, que l'on retrouve dans les scholies sur Homère, s'explique mieux chez Quintilien si l'on admet que, chronologiquement, ce rapprochement se rapportait en premier lieu aux représentations fabuleuses du poète, non pas à celles du rhéteur, qui tiennent du vraisemblable. C'est dans cette direction que nous devons, à mon avis, chercher l'origine de la théorie de Quintilien.

Au livre VIII (3, 67–70), dans sa discussion de l'ἐνάργεια, Quintilien utilise le même procédé pour démontrer de quelle manière s'accroît la pitié sur le sort des villes prises. Il faut, dit-il, développer ce qui est contenu dans le seul mot *expugnatio*. Ensuite, grâce à l'élaboration des circonstances du sac d'une ville, apparaîtront les flammes, les toits qui s'écroulent, les cris, la fuite, les lamentations etc. etc., et Quintilien présente un tableau imagé du sac d'une ville, qui ressemble en tous points à maintes descriptions dans Tite-Live ou même au chant II de l'*Enéide*. Quintilien ajoute que l'on atteint à la même clarté en décrivant les particularités accidentelles (en latin: *accidentia*), qui sont propres aux personnes. Les circonstances appartiennent aux choses (*res*), selon la division qu'il fait entre *res* et *persona* dans l'*inventio*.

Aussi bien la pensée que la terminologie de Quintilien à propos de l'ἐνάργεια se rencontrent dans le chapitre X du traité *Du Sublime*. L'auteur déclare: "puisque à toute chose s'attachent de par la nature certaines particularités coexistantes avec sa substance, ne pourrions-nous pas nécessairement trouver la cause du sublime dans le fait de toujours choisir dans ses parties consécutives les qualités les plus appropriées et de savoir, par une accumulation successive, en former comme un seul corps?" C'est ce que fait Sappho, dit-il; elle décrit les souffrances inhérentes au délire amoureux, et le choix des traits dominants et leur réunion dans un tableau d'ensemble ont crée le chef-d'oeuvre (à savoir le célèbre poème φαίνεταί μοι . . .). D'autres exemples, dans le traité *Du Sublime*, de ce genre de descriptions nous ramènent de nouveau à la critique ancienne d'Homère. D'ailleurs, les remarques de Quintilien sur l'ἐνάργεια, qui, selon lui, est le résultat d'une accumulation de détails, rappellent les observations relatives à l'ἐνάργεια d'Homère, qui apparaissent fréquemment dans les scholies.[31]

Pour terminer, esquissons brièvement une dernière application de cette théorie de l'*inventio* dans un domaine tout différent. Au dixième chapitre du livre XII, Quintilien donne un aperçu du développement stylistique de la peinture et de la sculpture grecques. A l'instar de la critique d'art de l'époque hellénistique, il mentionne aussi le peintre Théon le Samien, dont l'excellence résidait dans la faculté de concevoir les images que les grecs appellent *phantasiai* (XII 10, 6) Grâce à un renseignement de Pline l'Ancien (35, 144) Théon le Samien nous est connu comme le peintre du délire d'Oreste. C'est pourquoi le commentateur anglais Austin s'est demandé s'il fallait rapprocher ce renseignement et le fait que l'auteur *Du Sublime* cite l'*Oreste* d'Euripide pour illustrer les *phantasiai* poétiques. Je ne crois pas que dans le jugement de Quintilien sur Théon le terme de *phantasiai* se rapporterait au premier chef à la peinture des hallucinations du délire.[32] Plus importante me paraît être l'anecdote qu'Elien raconte dans ses *Histoires Variées* (II 44) à propos d'un célèbre tableau de Théon, figurant un hoplite et intitulé ὁ ἐκβοηθῶν (celui qui part pour porter secours). Partant des détails de cette peinture, Elien va reconstruire la conception de l'artiste, c'est-a-dire l'ensemble des circonstances et des particularités que le peintre s'est représenté dans l' imagination et qu'il a essayé d'exprimer par tous les détails de sa peinture, de même que Quintilien a développé ce qui était contenu dans le mot "sac d'une ville," et Sappho a décrit les particularités inhérentes au délire amoureux. De ce fait, le tableau de Théon mérite la qualification qu'en donne Elien: ἐναργῶς. A la fin du passage, Elien raconte l'anecdote selon laquelle le peintre avait loué pour le vernissage un trompettiste qui devait jouer la chanson de guerre au moment où le tableau serait montré. Comme le dit Elien, le son de la trompette rendait encore plus évidente dans l'esprit des spectateurs l'image de l'ἐκβοηθῶν (ἐναργεστέραν τὴν φαντασίαν). Je crois qu'il faut rapprocher cette anecdote, qui s'inspire sans doute de la critique d'art hellénistique, des réflexions esthétiques du sophiste tardif Philostrate. Ce dernier mentionne aussi dans sa *Vie d'Apollonius de Tyane* (II 22, VI 19) et dans ses *Eikones* W (II 340, 35) le rôle de la φαντασία – cette faculté de représenter ce qu'on n'a pas vu – dans la création de l'artiste et dans la re-création par le spectateur. Pour résumer les opinions de Philostrate, c'est le rôle de la φαντασία de sélectionner et de réunir les moments caractéristiques du thème de base (les *accidentia* / συμβαίνοντα propres aux personnages, comme il dit) dans une seule statue ou – ajoutons – tableau, poème, description.[33]

Ces réflexions anciennes sur l'imagination, l'invention et l'émotion nous rappellent peut-être qu'un homme, un événement, une action ne sont jamais des faits isolés mais plutôt des structures de circonstances et de particularités et qu'il faut reconstruire ces structures dans l'imagination pour comprendre, juger et ressentir les *personae* et les *res*. Les oeuvres d'art présentent les exemples, l'*inventio* nous offre les préceptes.

Notes

1. Dans son article "Rhetorik" (*Pauly-Wissowa, Suppl.* 7, 1940, 1059), W. Kroll fait remarquer: "Der Gedanke, dass der Redende selbst diese Affekte fühlen müsse, um sie auf die Hörer zu übertragen, ist im Keim (Aristoteles) *Poet.* 17 enthalten, später dann deutlich entwickelt worden"; voir pour la tradition scolaire aussi *Auctor ad Herennium*, IV 43, 55: *item mutatur res tractando si traducitur ad exsuscitationem, cum et nos commoti dicere videamur et auditoris animum commovemus.*

2. *De Oratore*, II 46, 191 . . . *magna vis est earum sententiarum atque eorum locorum quos agas tractesque dicendo.*

3. Cf. G. C. Fiske and M. A. Grant, *Cicero's De oratore and Horace's Ars Poetica* (Madison 1929), 41: "An examination of the index of Wilkins' edition of Cicero's *De oratore* under the headings *histrio, scaena, tragicus, tragoedus, tragoedia, comoedia, Roscius, tibicen, tibia,* shows how frequently Cicero draws upon analogies from the stage for his delineation of the orator's art."

4. *De Oratore*, II 48, 199: *si placuerit, vos meam defensionem in aliquo artis loco reponetis,* cf. la réaction de Sulpicius ibid. 203–204.

5. Contra: L. Voit, Δεινότης, *Ein antiker Stilbegriff* (Leipzig, 1934), 140–42, A. Michel, *Rhétorique et Philosophie chez Cicéron* (Paris 1960), 105; sur l'application de la théorie poétique de l'ἐνθουσιασμός à la rhétorique, l'historiographie et la philosophie, voir aussi K. Adam, *Docere – Delectare – Movere, Zur poetischen und rhetorischen Theorie über Aufgaben und Wirkung der Literatur* (diss. Kiel 1971), 123; pour la tradition plus tardive, cf. K. Dockhorn, *Die Rhetorik als Quelle des vorromantischen Irrationalismus*

in der Literatur–und Geistesgeschichte (Nachrichten Akademia der Wissenschaften, Göttingen, 1948–49), 147 sqq.

6. Cicero, *Tusculanae Disputationes*, I 26, 64, *De Divinatione*. I 36, 80, *De Natura Deorum* II 66, 167, cf. pro *Archia* 8, 18.

7. Cf. *De Oratore*, II 42, 179; 45, 188; 74, 298; 89, 363; La divinité de l'orateur constitue ainsi une sorte de Leitmotiv au cours du livre II.

8. Fiske and Grant, *o.c.* 128–30.

9. Sur les rapports entre le génie et la mélancolie (Aristote *Problem.* 30), voir aussi J. Pigeaud, "Une physiologie de l'inspiration poétique, De l'humeur au Trope," *Les Etudes Classiques* 46 (1978), 24; les observations d'Antoine dans le *De oratore* peuvent contribuer à l'étude déjà suggérée par E. R. Dodds concernant les différentes formes du délire: "how far did they modify them under the influence of advancing rationalism" (*The Greeks and The Irrational*, Berkeley 1951, 65).

10. Voir sur ce point aussi N. Rudd, *Lines of Enquiry, Studies in Latin Poetry* (Cambridge, 1976), 170–73.

11. Cf. Cicero, *Tusculanae Disputationes*, IV 25, 55: *ne rhetorum aperiamus mysteria* et Quint. VI 2, 55 *sed promere in animo est quae latent et penitus ipsa huius loci aperire penetralia.*

12. Quintilianus, VI 2, 28–31.

13. VI 2, 25: *non aliquo tradente.*

14. F. Striller, *De stoicorum studiis rhetoricis* (Breslau, 1886), 56 sqq.; voir aussi le comm. de D. A. Russell sur *De Sublimitate*, 15 (Oxford, 1964).

15. Cf. A. O'Brien-Moore, *Madness in Ancient Literature* (diss. Princeton, Weimar 1924), 157 et note 2 à propos de Cicero, *Academica Priora* II 17, 52 et 27, 88.

16. Cf. Sextus Empiricus, *Adversus Mathematicos*, VII 241, ἡ φαντασία γίνεται ἤτοι τῶν ἐκτὸς ἢ τῶν ἐν ἡμῖν παθῶν.

17. *De Sublimitate* 9, 15, *Scholia Vetera in Iliadem* XXII 199 (cf. M. L. von Franz, *Die aesthetischen Anschauungen der Iliasscholien*, diss. Zürich 1943, 19), Sextus Empiricus, *Adversus Mathematicos*, VII 227 (cf. Cicero, *De Divinatione*, II 61, 126, et Diogenes Laertius VII 50), la suite des sujets traités par Lucrèce à la fin du chant IV, Plutarque, *Amatorius* 759 c.

18. Lucrèce souligne les rapports entre l'imagination et la volonté (*De Rerum Natura* IV 777). Dans son étude "The Theory of Imagination in Classical and Mediaeval Thought," *University of Illinois Studies in Language and Literature* 12 (1927), 88 sqq., M. W. Bundy remarque à juste titre: "The significant fact for the Stoic is that these phantasies, these mental impressions which impel our acts are within our power."

19. Sur la *praemeditatio* des stoiciens et l'*avocatio* des épicuriens, voir P. Rabbow, *Seelenführung, Methodik der Exerzitien in der Antike* (München 1954), 160 sqq.

20. C'est Antiochus d'Ascalon qui le premier pourrait avoir établi les rapports esquissés ici entre l'éthique et la rhétorique; sur son influence dans le *De oratore*, voir W. Kroll, "Studien über Ciceros Schrift De oratore," *RhM* 58 (1903), 566, 583, "Cicero und die Rhetorik," *Neue jahrbücher für das klassische Altertum* 6 (1903), 687 sqq., et Fiske-Grant *o.c.* 16.

21. Pour l'exemple d'Oreste dans l'épistémologie stoicienne, voir Bundy *o.c.* 88 sqq., pour la tradition médicale Celse III 19: *nam quidam imaginibus, non mente falluntur, quales insanientem Aiacem vel Orestem percepisse poetae ferunt.*

22. Quintilianus, VI 2, 31–32.

23. Sur son rôle, cf. Striller *o.c.* 27.

24. Cf. H. Lausberg, *Handbuch der literarischen Rhetorik* (München, 1960), §328.

25. Voir R. M. Grant, *Miracle and Natural Law in Graeco-Roman and Early Christian Thought* (Amsterdam, 1952), pp. 48, 58–59.

26. Diogenes Laertius, VII, 109, 121.

27. Voir P. H. Schrÿvers, "Le regard sur l'invisible, Étude sur l'emploi de l'analogie dans l'oeuvre de *Lucrèce*" (Genève, 1978), pp. 83, 98.

28. Rabbow *o.c.* 55: "Circumstanzen sind die einzelnen Momente eines Gegenstandes der Betrachtung; sie stellen eine Topik der Meditation dar."

29. Voir von Franz *o.c.* 22 sqq.

30. Voir après les études de Striller, von Franz et G. Lehnert (*De scholiis ad Homerum rhetoricis*, diss. Leipzig 1896, 97, cf. la critique de Kroll dans *Rhetorik* 1082) les remarques judicieuses de M. Schmidt dans *Die Erklärungen zum Weltbild Homers und zur Kultur der Heroenzeit in den BT-Scholien zur Ilias* (München 1976), 60–63.

31. Cf. von Franz *o.c.* 25.

32. R. G. Austin (Oxford 1954); Quintilien nous dit *concipiendis visionibus, quas* φαντασίας *vocant, Theon Samius*, texte mal traduit dans Pauly-Wissowa II 5, 1934, 2083 par "die Darstellung von *visiones*," cf. Quintilianus, VIII, 3, 81: φαντασία *in concipiendis visionibus.*

33. Cf. Philostratos, *Die Bilder, Griech.-deutsch herausg., übersetzt, erläutert von* O. Schönberger (München 1968), 55, B. Schweitzer, *Mimesis und Phantasia*, Philologus 89 (1934), 297; dans son étude *Die kunsttheoretischen Gedanken in Philostrats Apollonios* (Philologus 88, 1933, 392 sqq.), E. Birmelin souligne trop à notre avis l'influence aristotélicienne chez ce sophiste et néglige les rapports entre Philostrate et la rhétorique.

Schoolroom and Courtroom

MICHAEL WINTERBOTTOM
Worcester College, Oxford

Aт the very end of what we have of Suetonius' *de grammaticis et rhetoribus*[1] we are told of the death of Gaius Albucius Silus of Novara. He was suffering from a tumour, and, returning to his home town, he ceased taking food. But before dying he called the people together and gave the reasons for his decision to take his own life. Suetonius tells us that he did this *more contionantis*; but it would be more correct to say that it was *more declamantis*. There seems no reason to suppose that giving reasons for one's suicide was a custom commonly indulged in ancient Italy: though Valerius Maximus[2] witnesses to something like it among the Greeks of Massilia. Albucius' death was surely consciously modelled, with an élan worthy of Petronius himself, on the law that he will so often have treated in his declamation-hall: QUI CAUSAS VOLUNTARIAE MORTIS IN SENATU NON REDDIDERIT, IN-SEPULTUS ABICIATUR.[3]

This same Albucius reminds us in a less bizarre way of the intimate connections between declamation and real-life oratory. He was mainly a declaimer; but, at least before an unfortunate incident in the centumviral court, he also pleaded cases.[4] It was not only that the schools influenced the courts by training future lawyers; Albucius, like other declaimers,[5] led a double life between lecture hall and courtroom. I want in this paper, in what must be a random fashion, to discuss some of the ways in which this interaction affected both declamation and legal oratory.

Chronology might seem to make it difficult for us to see declamatory elements in the preserved speeches of Cicero. They stretch from the 80s to the 40s B.C. Declamation, on the other hand, was said by the elder Seneca to have been a thing born later than himself; and he was born not earlier than 55.[6] But this information can hardly be taken literally. Declamation was something with its roots in the Greece of the era between Demetrius of Phaleron and Hermagoras of Temnos. It was a Hellenistic creation, that brought its apparatus of tyrants and piracy and New Comedy sexuality over the Adriatic to Italy. Such influence will have been reaching a peak in the philhellene years of the late second century B.C., and there is nothing to prove that the lectures Cicero took down as the basis for the *de inventione* were given anywhere else but in Rome. The declamation themes that occur in that treatise may not be as extravagant as those that we find later in the elder Seneca. But it may well be that the schools were already in the early first century moving towards the sort of melodramatic and even epigrammatic style that was later characteristic of them.

In the *orator*[7] Cicero claims to have found the ears of Rome "hungry for this varied style that spreads equally into every type;" "I was the first to turn them to an astonishing enthusiasm for this manner." Now observe the illustrations Cicero gives us. First—received by what clamours!—the famous extravaganza beginning "Quid enim tam commune quam spiritus vivis, terra mortuis, mare fluctuantibus, litus eiectis."[8] It may not be a coincidence that this passage found so ready acceptance into the declamatory style of the Quintilianic *declamationes minores* 299; I have found it echoed in the elder Seneca and Apuleius too, not to speak of Martianus Capella and a Donatist council. It is perfectly on the cards that what went to feed declamation came originally from declamation; the youth who had to defend Roscius of Ameria on a charge of parricide mentions in the *de inventione*[9] the case of a father-murderer who suffered the horrors of the *culleus*. And if we had a fourth book of the *de inventione* it would show us, as does the fourth book of the *ad Herennium*, a schoolroom milieu perfectly well aware of all the stylistic tricks of the declaimers' trade. Indeed, that emerges from Cicero's second example from his early, though maturer style: "uxor generi, noverca filii, filiae paelex." What are these words of the *pro Cluentio*[10] if not declamatory? Was not the champagne bubble of the unregenerate Cicero the product of the declamation school? It is the argument of the *Brutus*[11] that his visit to Asia enabled him to calm down his hectic oratory: a paradox meant to explain away what critics of his Asianism must have used as a trump card. But he had seen Asian orators before he left Rome: they were the *rhetores* who ran the schools, the forerunners of persons we meet in Seneca: "Grandaus, Asianus aeque declamator," "Adaeus, rhetor ex Asianis,"[12] Glaucippus of Cappadocia, Hybreas of Mylasa. . . .

Cicero, however, matured, and grew away from the schools, even grew to look down on *rhetores* who had done so much for him. He became an *exemplum* in his turn. It is easy for the historian to think that Cicero's speeches were published as part of a series of propaganda campaigns intended to recommend Ciceronian policies or gloss over Ciceronian errors. And indeed something approaching that reason is given when Cicero sends to Atticus the corpus of consular orations: "Since you like my writings as well as my doings the same compositions will show you both what I did and what I said." But we should notice a little earlier the stress placed on another motive for publication: "it appears," says Cicero to Atticus, "that you too find pleasure in these performances which the enthusiasm of my young admirers prompts me to put on paper."[13] *Adulescentulorum studiis excitati.* And it is not unreasonable to expect that, in writing up speeches for the public, Cicero kept in mind the interests of the *adulescentuli*, still in their schools or already launched on the courts with Cicero, perhaps, as their mentor.

He was particularly free to do this in the *pro Milone*. The spoken speech, if not a disastrous failure, was shorter and less grand than Cicero wished it to become for posterity. I shall say something later about a particular addition he made to the spoken version. But in general I think we should see in the peculiar faithfulness of our speech to the precepts of rhetoric a reflection of Cicero's care to educate the youth. This is a speech, as he almost says of his consular orations, that he hopes to see read in the schoolroom with the attention accorded to the *Philippics* of Demosthenes. But as a bonus it was to exemplify in action the rhetorical rules that seem so lifeless when they are merely placed end to end in an *ars rhetorica*. That, too, is a theme to which I shall return.

The *pro Milone* is exceptional, and there are good reasons for the exception. But I shall discuss briefly two other examples of my point. The *pro Caelio* was, I take it, in another sense *for* Caelius; it would be sent to Cicero's old protégé in the hope that this brilliant example of a defence speech might turn to better ways one who was showing such disconcerting signs of a *rabies accusatoria*.[14] But it also recalled to Cicero's old pupil the days when he had been his model in oratory; it is almost as a private joke that he says: "I can also make other enquiries of the accuser, after my own custom and that of advocates generally: where did Caelius meet Lucceius' slaves, how did he gain access? . . . I can take my speech through all the thickets where suspicions may lurk: there will be found no motive, no place, no means, no accomplice, no hope of achieving or concealing the crime, no reason, no trace of so terrible a deed."[15] This all has word for word correspondence with the *ad Herennium*; and I think that Cicero included it, together with the following[16] technical distinction between the πίστεις ἔντεχνοι and ἄτεχνοι, not because his original speech indulged in such coy allusion to the schoolroom, but because the *adulescentuli* could profitably be reminded that their masters' precepts were not irrelevant to a real case. He is employing a trick we shall see used later in declamation: pedagogy intrudes into the fair-copy oration.

I add a further example of a rather more far-reaching kind. At the start of the fourth speech against Catiline, Cicero says: "I see, conscript fathers, that the faces and eyes of you all are turned towards me. I see that you are anxious not only about the danger to yourselves and to the republic, but also, if *that* is repelled, about the danger that threatens *me*." As Professor Nisbet once wrote of another aspect of these speeches: "When faced with a concrete and urgent problem did the Roman senate really waste time on this stuff?"[17] The answer, as Nisbet implied, is surely 'No'. But it is more interesting to speculate why the fourth *Catilinarian* has come to us in the form it has. It is partly a matter of changed circumstances. The words *si id depulsum sit* show right from the start that Cicero wrote up his speech with more than half an eye on what was to follow the events of 63, on the wave of feeling which, fostered by Clodius, was to remove him into exile. Hence—and this is an obvious point, often made before—the unnatural emphasis on the peril to Cicero, on the 'perpetual war' that he has undertaken with 'desperate citizens'.[18] Less obvious, perhaps, is the effect this new viewpoint has had on the very *genus* of the speech. It is true that the speech remains in its general direction deliberative. Its penultimate sentence is a plea to the senators to make their decision carefully and bravely. But it is significant that the last sentence of all redirects their attention to the consul, a consul prepared to stand up for their decision *quoad vivet*:[19] again the note of personal concern. And it seems to me that the speech has been recast in ways that bring it close to a *legal* speech, and one written in self-defence: not *in Catilinam* so much as *pro Cicerone*.

In this recast speech the deliberative kernel—which, I take it, represents things spoken on the actual occasion[20]—takes on a new aspect. The arguments for execution become, as well, arguments for Cicero's correctness in desiring and carrying out that execution. Around this kernel, Cicero has placed proem and epilogue hardly conceivable in the original senatorial speech. In the proem, he evokes the tears of his brother, *carissimi atque amantissimi*, and present to hear him, but says he will die with mind untroubled and prepared.[21] In the epilogue he commends to his hearers his small son.[22] These are topics, surely, more proper to judicial oratory, and through them Cicero appeals not so much to the senatorial audience of 63 as to a wider body of Romans in the years that immediately followed. But this was one of the corpus of consular speeches that, as we have seen, was published by Cicero partly in answer to the enthusiasms of young admirers. And I should not be surprised if Cicero wrote up his senatorial speech to some extent in judicial form because judicial speeches were what the schoolroom wanted. The *suasoria* was not taken too seriously at school: it was reserved for the young.[23] It was the *controversia* that engaged the attention of the older pupils.

I have come to the schools, and shall now turn to the second half of my topic. It has been a cliché not only of modern but of ancient critics that the declamation schools were disastrously adrift from reality. I need only mention the splendid assault on the *rhetores* at the start of Petronius' *satyricon*—"pirates with chains in their hands standing on the beach, tyrants writing edicts instructing sons to cut off their fathers' heads"—along with the devastating parody of the declamatory style: "These wounds I received for the freedom of all, this eye I forfeited for you. Give me a guide to lead me to my children: my knees are hamstrung and cannot support my body."[24] And clearly there was something excessive about some first-century practices. We know this because Quintilian, himself a *rhetor*, goes on the defensive when he discusses the topic. His premiss is that "things that are naturally good can be put to good use," and declamation is for him a naturally good thing. It is only thanks to its teachers that (he says) "it has now so degenerated that the licentious ignorance of declaimers has become one of the principal causes of the corruption of eloquence."[25]

Now Quintilian's point in this chapter is that declamation was started as a preparation for the forum. It should therefore "follow the pattern of the speeches it was invented to train for." Quintilian sees that the whole business, especially the feeling of unreal emotions, trembles on the brink of absurdity: the only defence can be that we are "as it were, on manoeuvres to prepare us for the real battle and the serious fighting." At the same time, declamation *does* have an element of display about it, and that justifies it being given a certain brilliance (*nitor*) that might be improper in the lawcourts. Quintilian tries to have it both ways: declamation as pure training combined with the declamation of ἐπίδειξις.

Now, whatever the excesses of some of the *rhetores*, it is exceedingly difficult to believe that declamation was not on the whole regarded as a practical as well as an attractive way of training the public speaker. Consider it. From 100 B.C. or even earlier till the times of Ennodius, the *rhetores* held sway over the secondary education of a people we are accustomed to laud for their practical genius. Did these same Romans who built aqueducts and amphitheatres and established a masterful legal code really consign their children to an education system that patently had no advantages in the formation of a lawyer or politician or, later, civil servant? We should at least give them the benefit of the doubt, and try to see what declamation could offer besides its superficial absurdities.[26]

It is difficult to use the evidence of the elder Seneca in this enquiry. He reports with some favour the forceful views of Cassius Severus on the gulf between schoolroom and courtroom.[27] But Seneca's own book is constructed in such a way that we find it hard to be sure what a complete declamation was like. And that is the crucial thing. Quintilian, or the pseudo-Quintilian, draws a distinction between the bones of a speech and its flesh:[28] a distinction not so much between the argumentation and the less essential elements as between the skeleton of the speech, its formal division, and the language which clothed the skeleton. In this terminology Seneca is particularly interested in the flesh: the bulk of his work consists of striking phrases culled from many speeches, grouped together by theme. But it would be quite wrong to imagine that a speech by, say, Albucius Silus consisted entirely of epigrams. On the contrary, it is clear from the sections that Seneca devotes under each topic to *divisio* that the declaimers were very much concerned with the structure of their argumentation. The tiresome thing is that nowhere[29] are we given a complete declamation from which we could see how much this division dictated the overall pattern—how far, for instance, it was obscured or swamped by more meretricious elements.

Where, then, can we look? Primarily, I suggest, to the Minor Declamations that are transmitted under the name of Quintilian. Here are 145 extant declamations, some long, some short, some supported by *sermones* where the *rhetor* advises how the subject should be treated, others left on their own. They are the fragments, posthumously published as I should judge, from a practising teacher's workshop. I stress 'practising.' In the elder Seneca we can never be quite sure in what circumstances the various declaimers uttered their more or less scintillating *sententiae*. I should guess that there was a considerable range of possible situations, stretching from the purely teaching declamation, given as a 'fair copy' behind closed doors, to the purely epideictic declamation, given to impress friends and attract publicity for the school: the context we should, I think, imagine for the *Major* Declamations. But the Minor Declamations do not make sense except as the notes of a *rhetor* involved in the day-to-day business of teaching the young.[30] And from them we can see how it is possible to regard declamation as a training for real life.

I should perhaps enter a caveat here. The collection shows the most unmistakeable signs of knowledge of the *institutio oratoria*; and I do not feel able to confute, on linguistic or other grounds, anyone who thinks them the work of Quintilian himself. In that case, and perhaps in any case, we may have to regard these declamations as exceptions: I mean as composed with exceptional attention to reality by someone who felt strongly that declamation must not lose contact with the courts.

A prima facie objection at once emerges: are not these declamations, like all others which we know from the ancient world, based on themes that cannot, *ut parcissime dicam* (to use the *rhetor*'s own cliché), often have found counterparts in real life? The tyrants writing edicts, the pirates carrying chains are still familiar figures. Worse still, the laws that govern the declamations are usually unreal. Now there is an answer to this objection, and I am surprised that Quintilian himself did not formulate it. If you make an unreal speech to train your powers of argument and expression, it is positively preferable that it should be on an unreal topic and subject to unreal laws. This is clearest from a 'historical' declamation like 323. "Alexander," it is stated in the theme, "was besieging Athens, and he burned a temple outside the walls. He began to suffer from a plague. An oracle stated that the plague would only finish if he restored the temple. . .:" and so on. Now Alexander did not lay siege to Athens at all; *a fortiori* this particular incident can only be fictional.[31] It was therefore possible for a schoolboy to treat the theme without any distraction: all he needed to know was that Alexander was a young and bold general, and that Athens was famous for religious observance. The rest was up to his ingenuity. If he had been faced with a real historical incident, he would, or should, have felt the need to read his history books, name names, allude to further events. Faced with a fiction, he can fall back on pure argument. Those who regard the learning of facts as more important than learning how to argue will find this deplorable; but *rhetores* taught rhetoric, not history.[32] The same is true of non-historical cases. And here we know that my point was seen in antiquity. In court, says Cicero in the *de oratore*, we must get to know the case at issue very thoroughly. "But," he goes on, "this precept is not applicable to the schoolroom. For the cases that boys treat are simple. 'The law forbids a stranger to ascend the wall. A stranger has ascended it and repulsed the enemy. He is accused.' It takes no trouble to learn up a case like this."[33] Exactly so: the boys could get to know how cases are argued without the distraction of unnecessary detail. Quintilian once suggested that declamations might be improved by the use of proper names, longer and more complex themes, an infusion of ordinary words, and—optimist that he was—jokes.[34] But he did not suggest that real-life cases, past or present, would provide better material. They would have too many ramifications; and anyway, in the nature of things, neither master nor pupil would have access to the detils.

So too with declamatory laws. Even in the early days of Greek declamation they can hardly have been more than a very simplified reflection of Attic practice. By the time of the early Roman empire they are a hopelessly confused mixture of Greek and Roman, fact and fiction. To try to disentangle the ravelled skein is not a waste of time;[35] but to commit oneself to the general proposition that declamatory law is somehow a 'source' for Roman law is amongst other things to ignore the point that these laws were so regularly chosen just because they were largely fictional. You learned your law at a law school or in the practice of the courts. You learned to argue at the declamation school. And the two were kept apart for a very good reason. The use of fictional laws encouraged flexibility and ingenuity of argument. If the laws had been real one would have had to step more carefully. And one might have got used to asserting things about the law that turned out to be false when one appeared in the courts. "Cum ad veros iudices ventum. . . ." When the great lacuna of the *dialogus*[36] cuts him short, Messala is about to use the contrast between school and courtroom as a stick with which to beat the declaimers. But it was not quite so simple. When one first arrived in the courtroom one *knew* that one did not know the law; that was better than thinking one knew it when one in fact did not.

To come more specifically to the Minor Declamations: I want to suggest two ways in which they achieve their pedagogic purpose. First, they show in action what in an *ars rhetorica* would normally be stated as a precept. Thus in the *de inventione* Cicero gives detailed heads of arguments to be used in cases with different στάσεις. Each of the Minor Declamations clearly has its own στάσις, and the arguments appropriate to it are deployed not abstractly, but with reference to the particular theme.[37] Now this, of course, does not count as a link between schoolroom and reality if, as may have been the case, the niceties of the στάσις-system were scorned or neglected in the law courts. Aper—no sympathetic witness, it is true—speaks in the *Dialogus* of 'the items prescribed in the dry-as-dust handbooks of Hermagoras and Apollodorus'[38] as being a feature of the old unenlightened courts of the Republican past. But the fact is that, even if the Hermagorean system took its classification of arguments too far, the arguments themselves remained indispensable; and someone trained in the system would know where to look for his proofs, have, as it were, a checklist to ensure he had made no important omission.[39]

Secondly, the fair-copy declamations in this collection are designed quite consciously to show the *ossa controversiae*, the bones. Thus, to take an example at random, a speech purporting to be made by Demosthenes supporting a bill to prevent those captured by Philip at Chaeronea from taking part in Athenian assemblies (339). The speaker starts: "Priusquam causas rogationis meae persequar," making it clear that what immediately follows is a proem *extra causam*. After this proem, he says that the other side contends that bills cannot be accepted if they are against the law or if they are directed at individuals. Each of these points is discussed, carefully marked off at the start of each: "neque adversus leges esse existimo" and "illud minus existimari possum, adversus singulos scripsisse legem." A further *divisio*, between consideration of the interests of the former captives and the interests of the state, is made explicitly, and it dictates, again with the appropriate signposts, the structure of the rest of the piece. It is just the same impulse, to make the shape of the speech intelligible *in advance*, that causes the frequent use of such phrases as 'postea videbo', answered by 'interim. . . .'[40] These techniques could, of course, be used to mark off the parts of a speech laid out on Hermagorean principles; but they could still teach something to a speaker who when he arrived in court might wish to forget everything he had ever learned about Hermagoras. The *rhetor* by these methods was inculcating something that would always have its uses, the practice of lucid and organised thought. The point was to train the pupil to speak a declamation that had a shape, that advanced from argument to argument in a logical sequence, and to have the shape of the whole in his head at the same time as he spoke a part. As I read my students' essays, I sometimes wish that the art of *divisio* were imparted along similar lines in the schools of today.

Now one constant method of dividing a *controversia* was to move from treatment of the law to treatment of equity. This fitted in well with the movement through argumentation to the emotional epilogue, but it was a different level of division. Was it a division with no relevance to the courtroom?

It is worth stressing here that the point at issue is not that still argued about in the wake of Stroux's classic *Summmum ius summa iniuria*.[41] Stroux was concerned to argue that rhetoric — and of course in particular the contrast of *ius* and *aequitas* — affected the interpretation of the law far earlier than the Byzantine period to which others so confidently relegate any part of the *Digest* that smacks of rhetoric. Without being in the least qualified to decide this grave point, I should not be in the least surprised if Stroux were right. Orators and lawyers must have gone to the same secondary schools, and spoken much the same language. Indeed it would be very desirable that the Minor Declamations should be studied by someone with a mastery of legal texts and legal terminology.[42] Furthermore, I have been struck, in such parts of the *Digest* as I have read consecutively, by the resemblance between the tricks of the two trades of rhetorician and lawyer. Both had pupils to teach, and both stimulated them in a similar way; as Cicero puts it in the *topica*: "fictitious examples ... have their value, but they belong to oratory rather than to jurisprudence, although even you" (he is addressing the lawyer Trebatius) "even you are wont to use them."[43]

Now Gaius constantly mentions the differing views of the legal schools. And Cicero's *de oratore* tells the same tale of dissension among the learned. "It is not difficult," says Antonius, "for an orator to find a lawyer to back the side he is supporting, whichever it happens to be."[44] If all law were straightforward, the lawyer would be out of business: but so too would the orator. And when the law was doubtful it would often happen that *aequitas* was brought in to make one view rather than another more plausible: "ius dubium aequitatis regula examinandum est" is what Quintilian expressly says.[45] I should be astonished if, even before the decadent days of Byzantine sentimentalism, lawyers themselves did not sometimes find themselves arguing in these terms.

But my more confident, and different, point is that whatever the lawyers did, practical oratory, at least in the early empire, was as open to considerations of equity as the declamation school. It is true that the *rhetor* of the Minor Declamations at one point follows up his detailing of the legal topics by remarking: "after *that* we may say the things that people tend nowadays to restrict themselves to"[46] — by which he must mean that modern declaimers were too keen on *aequitas*. It is also true that it was only when Cicero came to write up his *pro Milone* for publication that he ended it with the argument that if Milo *had* killed Clodius he would have been abundantly justified in doing so.[47] But we can use the *institutio* itself to show that practical oratory too laid stress on equity. Stroux demonstrated in his famous *libellus* how such arguments were the stock-in-trade of the late Republic.[48] One need only read the *pro Caecina*, or Cicero's various accounts of the famous *causa Curiana*,[49] to see that those hours in the classroom were not wasted when it came to the forum. But Stroux's argument can be carried forward to the next century. Quintilian was no stranger to the lawcourts: he several times lays stress on his forensic experience.[50] He can speak with equal authority of declamation and of actual practice. Thus, as to the schoolroom, he tells us, in connection with a declamation on Alexander and the Thebans, that, "as the Amphictyones are the judges, the most effective part of the case will be the *tractatio aequi*;"[51] or again in a declamatory context he remarks that "generally we will find a treatment of *aequitas* at the end of cases, because judges" (note the slide over into reality) "listen to nothing with greater pleasure."[52] But elsewhere Quintilian says much the same when he is undoubtedly speaking of the courts. Thus he says: "we must get to know the nature of the judge: is he more inclined to *ius* or to *aequum*?"[53] Or, speaking of *ipsae actiones*, he stresses the importance of the decision whether to use first arguments from *ius* or from *aequum*.[54] Or again, in that most real of chapters where he discusses the need for morality in the practising orator, he says: "Who does not see that a great part of oratory consists in the treatment of *aequum* and *bonum*?"[55] So too had Cicero said, specifically of *iudicia privata*, that the contest is often not about the act, but about *aequitas* and *ius*.[56] In the empire, as under the Republic, equity was an important part of a case; and declamation, at least in the hands of a Quintilian, was here as elsewhere a more realistic form of training than it is fashionable to think it.

Notes

1. 30.7 Brugnoli. The passage was juxtaposed with the declamation law by J. Sprenger, *Quaestiones in rhetorum Romanorum declamationes iuridicae* (Halle, 1911), 238; but Sprenger did not draw my conclusion.

2. 2.6.7–8. See Sprenger, 237.

3. E.g. *declamationes maiores*, 4.

4. Suetonius, *de grammaticis*, 30. 4–5.

5. Quintilian is the most distinguished example. It was true even of *grammatici* (Suetonius, *de gramm.* 22.1). So too in Greece: see Philostratus, *vit. soph.* 511,516 etc.

6. *Controversiae* 1 pr. 12. For Seneca's date of birth, see Griffin, *Journal of Roman Studies*, 62 (1972), 5. The difficulties of this passage, and the development of declamation generally, are discussed e.g. by S. F. Bonner, *Roman Declamation* (Liverpool, 1949), ch. 1.

7. 106–7.

8. *Pro Roscio Amerino* 72, echoed in *declamationes minores*, p. 181 Ritter; Seneca, *controversiae*, 7.2.3.; Apuleius, *met.* 4.11; Martianus Capella 522 (citation for metrical purposes). For the Council see E. Norden, *Antike Kunstprosa*[5] (Stuttgart, 1958), 626.

9. 2.149.

10. 199. Compare Seneca, *controversiae* 6.6 'generi adultera, filiae paelex'; 9.6.1 'nefaria mulier, filiae quoque noverca.'

11. Especially 316.

12. *Contr.* 1.2.23; 9.1.12.

13. *Epistulae ad Atticum*, 2.1.3 (Shackleton Bailey's translation).

14. Note e.g. *Pro Caelio*, 76–77.

15. 53, with Austin ad loc.

16. 54.

17. In *Cicero*, ed. T. A. Dorey (London, 1965), 62.

18. In *Catilinam*, 4.22; cf. 3. 27.

19. 24.

20. It would not surprise me if Cicero spoke only at the end of the debate, and summing it up as a chairman does. For the kernel note e.g. 6 ("illa praedicam quae sunt consulis") and the tell-tale "nunc antequam ad sententiam redeo, de me pauca dicam"(20).

21. 3.

22. 23.

23. So at least later: Tacitus, *dialogus*, 35.4.

24. *Satyricon*, 1.3 and 1.1. "Haec vulnera pro libertate publica excepi, hunc oculum pro vobis impendi" is very like the repetitiousness so prevalent in the *declamationes minores* (e.g., at random p. 28, 26 Ritter "quidquid asperrimum leges, quidquid crudelissimum habent iura, occupas"). *Succisi poplites* seems to me to strike a note of absurdity, despite (or because of) its echo of Virgil, *Aeneid* 9.762 and 10.699–700.

25. 2.10.3. In what follows I allude especially to 2.10.4, 8 and 12.

26. See now for a sympathetic assessment of declamation S. F. Bonner, *Education in Ancient Rome* (London, 1977), esp. ch. 21.

27. *Contr.* 3 pr. 8–18. Cf. 9 pr. (also 2.3.13).

28. *Decl. min.* p. 102 Ritter.

29. In *contr.* 2.7 Seneca gives a good deal of a declamation of Latro's, but this is cut short by a lacuna in the manuscripts. It is noticeable, however, as Dr. J. A. Fairweather stresses to me, that much of what remains is (fairly) sober argument.

30. A new idea (I think), which I shall develop in the introduction to a forthcoming edition of the work.

31. Cf. Sen. *contr.* 7.2.8 on fictions over Popillius (also *suas.* 6.14–15). This is what Cicero means when he makes Atticus say "concessum est rhetoribus ementiri in historiis, ut aliquid dicere possint argutius" (*Brut.*42). It was of course *possible* for declaimers to be historically accurate: so Aristides (see B. P. Reardon, *Courants littéraires grecs des IIe et IIIe siècles après J.-C.* [Paris, 1971], 105.

32. Quintilian encouraged his pupils to read historical works (e.g. 2.5.19); but that is a different matter.

33. 2.100.

34. 2.10.9.

35. See especially Bonner, *Roman Declamation*, ch. 5–6.

36. 35.5. Cf. e.g. Petr. *sat.*1.2.

37. For example, the topics of the conjectural στάσις are run through in *decl. min.*321. See also Bonner, *Roman Declamation*, 15. The system and declamation fed each other; I doubt if the system had much to do with real life.

38. 19.3.

39. Cf. e.g. *Brut.*263 (where it is noticeable that Cicero regards an orator trained in the details of the Hermagorean system as exceptional).

40. *decl. min.* p. 125, 7 Ritter.

41. Republished in *Römische Rechtswissenschaft und Rhetorik* (Potsdam, 1949).

42. I cannot judge the knowledge of law displayed by F. Lanfranchi, *Il diritto nei retori Romani* (Milan, 1938), but his knowledge of rhetoric left something to be desired.

43. 45.

44. 1.242. For Gaius, see e.g. *inst.* 1.7.

45. 12.3.6.

46. p. 103, 11 Ritter. Cf. Quint.5.8.1.

47. See Asconius p. 41 Clark.

48. *op. cit.*, 42 seq.

49. E.g. *Brut.* 143 seq. (with Douglas ad loc., valuable on what exactly the opposition of *ius* and *aequum* means: a topic also covered by D. Nörr, *Rechtskritik in der römischen Antike* [Munich, 1974], 36 seq.).

50. Contrast Cicero on the ivory-tower academic: "quod ipsi experti non sunt, id docent ceteros" (*de orat.* 2.76). Correspondingly Quintilian was not content to use examples from declamation alone, but continually cited real orators, unlike the minor rhetoricians such as Fortunatianus and Sulpicius Victor. In Greek, compare the constant examples from Demosthenes as well as from declamation in e.g. Hermogenes' *de inventione*.

51. 5.10.118.

52. 7.1.63.

53. 4.3.11.

54. 6.5.5.

55. 12.1.8.

56. *de orat.* 1.173.

The Material of the Art
in the Latin Handbooks
of the Fourth Century A.D.

MICHAEL C. LEFF
University of Wisconsin-Madison

> Seeing then, that not only rhetoric works by persuasion, but other arts
> do the same, . . . a question has arisen which is a very fair one: Of what
> persuasion is rhetoric the artificer, and about what?—is not that a fair
> way of putting the question?[1]

In THESE WORDS, Socrates asks Gorgias to define the subject matter of his
art. The question is certainly fair, but it is also very difficult. Not only Gorgias
but many of his successors have confounded themselves in the attempt to answer
it. Since Aristotle, we have found a convenient refuge in the reply that rhetoric
studies a process, and hence it has no definite subject. But this tactic can afford
only a temporary shelter, since, as McKeon observes, rhetoric is "an art which,
although it has no special subject matter according to most rhetoricians,
nonetheless must be discussed in application to some subject matter."[2] That
is, sooner or later the theorist must connect the process he describes to some
set of objects. Every rhetorical theorist must make a conscious or unconscious
choice about the subjects that are relevant to his inquiry.

One of the virtues of "Rhetoric in the Middle Ages" is that it clearly recognizes
and confronts this central problem. McKeon urges historians of rhetoric to
focus their attention on the shifting conceptions of the matter and function
of the art as it evolves through time.[3] And he proceeds to outline a history
of medieval rhetoric based on this approach. The result is an essay of startling
scope and brilliance. Nevertheless, our knowledge of medieval rhetoric has increased dramatically during the past thirty-five years, and it now seems appropriate to retrace McKeon's steps, to invoke his original statement of purpose and to augment and emend his findings in light of recent research.

In this paper, the re-interpretation is limited to a single issue—the transition
between classical and medieval rhetoric as it is evidenced by the Latin technical

handbooks of the fourth century. This narrowing of the topic is somewhat arbitrary, but it is mandated by the lack of space and justified by the studies of Ward, Fontaine, and others that invite a new examination of these works.[4] Specifically, I intend to argue that the fourth-century handbooks subtly alter the classical conception of the subject matter of rhetoric and thereby anticipate some of the characteristic developments of later medieval theory.

As a starting point, it is necessary to attempt a definition of the classical view of the matter. Fortunately, this task is simplified because of the general clarity and consistency of the classical texts. Rhetoric originated as an art in response to the exigencies of Greek political and legal institutions in the fifth century B.C. and thus drew its material and defined its function within the context of civic activity. Despite changing conditions, most of the later classical authorities remained loyal to this original conception of the art. As Kennedy has noted, classical rhetoric was "defined by its function within Greek and Roman political and legal systems."[5]

From Aristotle to the end of the fourth century A.D., the mainstream of the tradition limited the *materia* of rhetoric to issues that arose in "civic" or "public" debate. Aristotle and his followers made this limitation implicitly when they restricted rhetorical discourse to the forensic, deliberative, and epideictic genres of oratory.[6] The Hermagoreans made it explicitly when they defined the art in terms of the civil question.[7] In all cases, however, the concept of civil discourse provided an answer to the "fair question" posed in the *Gorgias*: Persuasion remained the subject of rhetoric, but only that kind of persuasion which touched on the problems of citizenship. Negatively, this view excluded the issues considered in medicine, philosophy, or any other specialized or contemplative art. On the positive side, it embraced all the issues of normal civic deliberation. In the words of Fortunatianus, the civil issue involved whatever fell "into common mental conception – that is, what everyone can understand, as for example the question of justice and goodness."[8] Hence, the classical tradition conceived of the function and subject matter of the art in terms of something we might call "public knowledge."

Within this broad consensus, however, certain important differences arose about how the rhetorician ought to approach his subject matter. McKeon has argued persuasively that by late antiquity these differences revolved around two major traditions.[9] The first stemmed from the Hellenistic rhetorician Hermagoras of Temnos, and it stressed the systematic analysis of public issues according to a field invariant set of topics. Relying on categories derived from Hellenistic logic, the Hermagorean system sought to locate and classify issues prior to the construction of the message and without reference to the specific audience. Its major doctrines, such as the figure and mode of the case, *peristasis*, and *stasis*, might be regarded as preliminaries to invention. Thus, some later Greek and Roman treatises incorporated these matters under a separate canon called *intellectio* or νόησις (understanding).[10]

The second tradition devolved from Cicero's *De inventione* and other Latin treatises of the late Republic and early Empire. In *De inventione*, Cicero defined rhetoric as a part of political science and equated the subject matter of the art with the Aristotelian *tria genera causarum*. Analysis of the art, consequently, was field dependent (i.e. dependent on the type of civil issue involved). Neither the *Auctor ad Herennium* nor Quintilian directly connected rhetoric with political science, but both retained Cicero's empirical interest in civil issues. Both used the Ciceronian quinquepartite system to organize the art, and used the *genera causarum*, not the divisions of *stasis*, to organize the doctrine of invention.

Thus, it seems fair to make a tentative division between a Hellenistic and early Latin tradition in respect to the treatment of rhetorical subjects. The difference between the two is not absolute, but it is significant: The Latin approach maintains contact with the vagaries of political circumstance, while the Hellenistic approach verges toward a fixed logic of public argument.

This distinction becomes crucially important when we turn to Latin handbooks of the fourth century.[11] Since all of the handbooks identify civic or political affairs as the substance of rhetoric, it follows that differences in the conception of the art in this period should manifest themselves in terms of the division between the Hermagorean and Ciceronian views of the civil question. In part this is a matter of definition, and all of the relevant treatises make some reference to the issue in their introductory sections. Seizing on this point, McKeon makes a careful study of the preliminary definitions in the handbooks and concludes that both traditions are well represented.[12] His findings, then, tend to emphasize the continuity of the classical tradition in the fourth century.

Yet, exclusive concentration on the preliminary definitions obscures some of the most important features of these handbooks. When one considers their contents as a whole, certain characteristic differences between the structure of the handbooks and the older Latin tradition begin to emerge. These changes, I believe, have an important bearing on the conception of the scope and subject matter of the art, and in order to understand them, we must review briefly each of the relevant fourth-century treatises.

Of the four extant technical rhetorics, Julius Victor's *Ars rhetorica* conforms most closely to the Ciceronian pattern. After a brief introduction, Julius proceeds to analyze the art in terms of the conventional five divisions. Nevertheless, the doctrine of invention dominates the work, taking up eighteen of the twenty-seven chapters and eighty percent of the text. *Stasis* is placed under the heading of invention, as in the earlier Latin rhetorics, but, in proportion to the rest of the treatise, it is given more detailed treatment.[13] Disposition, memory, and delivery each account for a single chapter, while style is the subject of three rather long chapters. The work ends in an unusual manner with discussion of rhetorical exercises, conversation, and letter-writing.[14] Aside from these concluding sections, however, there is no evidence of interest in any type of rhetoric other than the forensic.

Fortunatianus' *Ars rhetorica* consists of three short books written in catechical form. The treatise opens with a hexameter poem inviting those interested in legal cases to study its contents. There follows a series of definitions in which the civil question is not only explained, but also broken down into the three sub-classes of epideictic, deliberative, and forensic. The rest of the treatise adheres to the pattern manifested in Julius Victor's *Ars rhetorica*. The first book is devoted to *stasis*, the second to the remaining components of inventional theory. (The relative emphasis on *stasis* is even greater than in Julius' treatise, both because Fortunatianus gives less attention to the other devices of invention, and because a considerable portion of the second book explains how to correlate the circumstances of the case with the various divisions of *stasis*.)[15] The third book deals with disposition, style, memory, and delivery, with style again receiving the most detailed treatment. After the preliminary definitions, there is no further reference to deliberative or epideictic oratory. The work is devoted entirely to the forensic branch of rhetoric.

The third treatise, a work sometimes attributed to Saint Augustine, comes to us in the form of a short, fragmentary text bearing the title *De rhetorica*.[16] The initial paragraph lists seven *officia* for the orator, adding "understanding" and "judgment" to the standard five elements. The surviving fragment of the rest of this text presents a detailed definition of the civil question and a discussion of such aspects of issue analysis as the circumstances and forms of the case and the divisions of *stasis*. In general, the *De rhetorica* relies more heavily on Greek sources than the treatises by Julius Victor and Fortunatianus, but it exhibits a similar preoccupation with the technical analysis of *stasis* and its application to legal cases (or at least to forensic exercises).

Finally, the *Institutiones oratoriae* of Sulpitius Victor dramatically restructures the elements of rhetorical theory. Following certain Greek sources, Sulpitius holds that the *officia* of the orator are three: understanding, invention, and disposition. The "canon" of understanding consists of *stasis* and the attendant doctrines that relate to issue analysis. Disposition, in this scheme, includes both style and delivery as well as organization. But neither the elements of disposition nor invention receive more than passing attention, since ninety percent of the text deals with understanding.[17]

Having examined the structure of these handbooks, we are now in a position to recognize a number of ways in which they depart from the conceptual framework of earlier Latin theory. In the first place, there is a tendency to distort and contract the general design of the art. *De inventione*, of course, restricts itself to a single aspect of the rhetorical process. But in the *Ad Herennium*, in Cicero's mature works, and in Quintilian the quinquepartite design of the art emerges with great clarity and force. In the fourth century, however, the *De rhetorica* tampers with this scheme, and Sulpitius Victor abandons it. Even

Fortunatianus and Julius Victor, who retain the conventional pattern, distort it considerably because of their overwhelming concern for invention. Style still maintains a position of relative importance in the handbooks, but memory and delivery receive only perfunctory notice. When one remembers how important they are to the practicing orator, the atrophy of these two canons suggests a declining interest in oral performance.[18]

Secondly, the doctrine of *stasis* becomes an increasingly formative part of rhetorical theory. The *Ad Herennium* and *De inventione* give considerable attention to *stasis*. Neither work, however, develops the system in its full detail, and both refuse to organize invention under the analytic categories of the *stasis* system. By the fourth century, Hermagorean influences have increased notably. Fortunatianus and Julius Victor devote the first third of their works to an analysis of *stasis; stasis* totally dominates the *Institutiones oratoriae* of Sulpitius Victor, and the *De rhetorica* consists of a minute analysis of Hermagorean doctrine. Consequently, one must conclude with Solmsen that "Hermagoras with his reorganization of the material under the *constitutiones* carries "the day over alternative theories and tendencies."[19]

Third, while the Latin rhetoricians had always placed primary emphasis on forensic speaking, the fourth-century authors exaggerate this emphasis to the point of excluding all other oratorical genres. In fact, only Fortunatianus makes any reference to deliberative or epideictic oratory, and they receive no more than token recognition. His preliminary definition and division of the civil question is a purely mechanical gesture; it has no bearing on the doctrine contained within the work.

All told, then, the handbooks alter the earlier Latin tradition by distorting and contracting its design, by exhibiting a preoccupation with the details of the *stasis* system, and by concentrating exclusively on judicial rhetoric. It is tempting to dismiss these changes in the configuration of the art as the product of confusion and degeneration. But recently John Ward has advanced the more interesting theory that these alterations may reflect the court procedures of the late Empire. The late imperial law courts offered little opportunity for the type of forensic oratory that Cicero had practiced. Advocates became increasingly concerned with minor, technical cases; the jury system declined; trials were often "broken up into a number of separate investigations;" written materials rose in prominence; oral arguments became less important, and advocates no longer had an opportunity to present closing arguments.[20]

It certainly seems plausible to connect these circumstances with contemporary developments in rhetorical theory. The atrophy of delivery and memory may well be a response the the diminished use of oral argument in court. This same factor, coupled with the increased technicality of court procedure, may account for the preoccupation with the minutiae of the *stasis* system. Whatever the relationship between the moot cases in the system and the actual law, training in the use of *stasis* must have offered good mental exercise for the would-be advocate of the fourth century. As Ward puts the point, we can speculate that the late Latin manuals "were written less for training in the actual presentation of court briefs and more for practice in identifying the correct issue category of a situation at law."[21]

If there is any merit in these conjectures, then we have reason to believe that some of the characteristics of medieval rhetorical theory already begin to surface as early as the fourth century, e.g.: the shift in focus from oral to written discourse, the decline of a holistic conception of the art in favor of a loose borrowing of particular elements of the classical system, and an implicit assumption that rhetoric is something to be used for specialized purposes, that it is not the main organizing force in the liberal education of a citizen.

By the fifth and sixth centuries, we can recognize conscious attempts to redefine the subject of rhetoric. Augustine, for example, rejects the civil issue entirely, since he believes that the only authentic function of the orator relates "not to the temporal welfare of man, but to his eternal welfare. . . ."[22] And Boethius, extending the tendencies of Hermagorean theory to their limit, makes the civil issue a subordinate part of dialectical logic.[23] These explicit changes in the conception of rhetoric, however, are anticipated by the implicit changes apparent in the handbooks of the fourth century. Despite preliminary references to the earlier and more liberal Latin tradition, these treatises functionally dismantle the civil question, remove it from the realm of genuine public discourse, and restrict it to the analysis of technical legal issues.

In closing, I would like to suggest that the study of these technical Latin manuals may help clarify our understanding of both earlier and later conceptions of rhetoric. As we witness the disintegration of the classical form of the art, we are better able to recognize the assumptions that framed and preserved its unity. Demetrius, Dionysius, and Longinus notwithstanding, the integrity of classical rhetoric depends on the concept of civil discourse, on the central interest in oral argument before an audience about subjects of public knowledge and concern. Nowhere in the later history of rhetoric do we find consensus on such a specific and limited conception of the art. The Middle Ages dispersed the elements of rhetoric into a vast number of learned and practical disciplines, and subsequent attempts to re-establish its integrity have stressed the unity of the art as process, not as substance. Moreover, one glance at Perelman's *New Rhetoric*, or Burke's *Rhetoric of Motives*, or the proceedings of this society should convince us that we still lack agreement about the subject matter of the art. This situation has its advantages, since we have a broad field in which to pursue our interests in the name of rhetoric. Yet, it leaves us without a satisfactory answer to Socrates' fair question, and thus complicates the attempt to locate the center from which these interest radiate.

Notes

1. Plato, *Gorgias*, trans. Benjamin Jowett (New York, 1937), p. 454.
2. Richard McKeon, "Rhetoric in the Middle Ages," *Speculum*, 17 (1942), 3.
3. Ibid.
4. John O. Ward, *Artificiosa Eloquentia in the Middle Ages* (Diss.: Toronto, 1972), I, 72–119, "The Constitutio Negotialis in Antique Latin Rhetorical Theory," *Prudentia* 1 (1969), 29–48. Jacques Fontaine, *Isidore de Séville et la Culture Classiques dans L'Espagne Wisigothique* (Paris, 1959), I, 211–340. See also James J. Murphy, *Rhetoric in the Middle Ages: A History of Rhetorical Theory from Augustine to the Renaissance* (Berkeley and Los Angeles, 1974), pp. 43–46.
5. George Kennedy, "The Present State of Ancient Rhetoric," *Classical Philology* 70 (1975), 280.
6. *Rhetoric*, 1356a, and see also *De inventione*, I.7 for an important interpretation of the function of the genres in defining the scope of rhetoric.
7. For a good short account of Hermagoras on the civil question see George Kennedy, *The Art of Persuasion in Greece* (Princeton, N.J., 1963), pp. 304–306. In the recent scholarship, the best analyses of Hermagoras' rhetorical theory are Dieter Matthes, "Hermagoras von Temnos 1904–1955," *Lustrum* 3 (1958), 58–214, 262–78, and Karl Barwick, "Zur Rekonstrucktion der Rhetorik des Hermagoras von Temnos," *Philologus* 109 (1965), 186–218. The ancient testimony on Hermagoras is collected by Dieter Matthes, *Hermagorae Temnitae testimonia et fragmenta* (Leipzig, 1962).
8. *Ars rhetorica*, I.1, in C. Halm, ed. *Rhetores Latini minores* (Leipzig, 1863; rpt. Frankfurt, 1964), p. 81.
9. McKeon, 14.
10. The term *intellectio* is used in this technical rhetorical sense in only two extant classical Latin works, the *De rhetorica* attributed to Augustine (Halm, p. 314), and the *Institutiones oratoriae* of Sulpitius Victor (Halm, p. 315). *Intellectio* apparently is the Latin translation for the Greek νόησις , which appears in a number of late classical manuals. See, for example, the anonymous treatise in *Rhetores Graeci* VI (Stuttgart, 1832), 34. The origins of this concept are unclear. Barwick, 192–200, attempts to trace it back to Hermagoras.
11. Four handbooks (or "technical rhetorics") survive from the fourth century: Sulpitius Victor's *Institutiones oratoriae*, Julius Victor's *Ars rhetorica*, Fortunatianus' *Ars rhetorica*, and the *De rhetorica* attributed to Augustine. All these works are edited in Halm's *Rhetores Latini minores*. We cannot be very secure about the date of these handbooks, but the consensus of modern opinion is that they belong to the fourth century. See W. S. Teuffel, *A History of Roman Literature*, revised by Ludwig Schwabe, trans. George C. W. Ward (London, 1892), II, 427.
12. McKeon, 14–15.
13. Julius devotes chapters II–IV to *stasis* (Halm, pp. 374–95). These chapters are quite long, and taken together, they occupy about one-third of the text.
14. The section on letter-writing is especially interesting as a precursor of the medieval *ars dictaminis*. See Murphy, pp. 195–97.
15. II. 5–1/1, Halm, pp. 105–108.

16. The attribution of this work to Augustine remains a matter of considerable controversy. Recent scholars who argue that Augustine authored the treatise include: B. Riposoti, "Agostino o pseudo-Agostino," *Studi in onore di Gino Funaioli* (Rome, 1955), pp. 378–93, Barwick "Augustins Schrift De rhetorica und Hermagoras von Temnos" *Philologus*, 105 (1961), 97–99, and Otto Dieter and William Kurth, "The *De rhetorica* of Aurelius Augustine," *Speech Monographs*, 35 (1968), 91–92. On the other hand, Joseph Miller, *Readings in Medieval Rhetoric* (Bloomington, Indiana, 1973), pp. 6–7, argues that Augustine did not write this work, and B. Darrel Jackson, *Augustine: De Dialectica* (Dordrecht and Boston, 1975), p. 31, n. 17, finds the arguments in favor of Augustine's authorship unconvincing. All scholars agree, however, that this fragmentary work follows Hermagoras very closely and provides one of the best available sources for the reconstruction of Hermagorean rhetoric.

17. For a fuller account of the structure of the *Institutiones*, see my note in *Quarterly Journal of Speech* 63 (1977), 441–43.

18. See Fontaine, I, 223–25, Ward, *Artificiosa Eloquentia*, I, 76–78, and Ward, *Prudentia* I, 43.

19. Friedrich Solmsen, "The Aristotelian Tradition in Ancient Rhetoric," *American Journal of Philology* 62 (1941), 177.

20. H. F. Jolowicz, *Historical Introduction to Roman Law* (Cambridge, 1954), p. 470. See also Ward, *Artificiosa Eloquentia* I, 76–78, and Ward *Prudentia* I, 43–45.

21. Ward, *Artificiosa Eloquentia*, I, 77.

22. *On Christian Doctrine*, trans. D. W. Robertson, Jr. (Indianapolis, 1958), IV. 35.

23. Concerning Boethius' interpretation of the subject matter of rhetoric, see my essay "The Logician's Rhetoric: An Analysis of Boethius' *De differentiis topiciis*, Book IV," in James J. Murphy, ed. *Medieval Eloquence: Studies in the Theory and Practice of Medieval Rhetoric* (Berkeley and Los Angeles, 1978), pp. 3–24.

The Teaching of Rhetoric in the Middle Ages

R. R. BOLGAR
King's College, Cambridge

THE STUDY OF RHETORIC had been the backbone of the educational system of Imperial Rome, and we know that it left a surprisingly deep imprint on many areas of Graeco-Roman culture. In the period we are considering, its role was less momentous, but it was not by any means negligible.

In the Dark Ages, which were not as dark as scholars used to think before the appearance of Pierre Riché's monumental survey[1], rhetorical knowledge came from two sources. Two systems of education existed side by side: the one dying, the other struggling to be born.

The Romanised upper classes that survived in the new barbarian kingdoms continued to cling, though with an ever diminishing zeal, to their old way of life. The public schools of the Empire had with a few exceptions closed their doors by the end of the fifth century, but many parents did their best to give their children a literary education within the home. They produced an élite that had some notion of the standards of literacy which had existed in the past.

Alongside this privately organised education, there was another offered to rather larger numbers by the Church. This too looked to the past: inevitably perhaps since the ecclesiastical authorities continued to use the Latin of Jerome's Bible and the Early Fathers for their official purposes. Jerome's language gave some trouble even to the Romanised whose slipshod spoken idiom differed from it in many respects, and learning it presented clerics of barbarian origin with a formidable task. The basic course that monastic and episcopal schools offered their students consisted merely of learning the Psalter by heart, so that some clerics never learnt Latin, and there were many more who could not write a grammatical letter. Only a few progressed further. But these few, taking the Bible and the Fathers for their models, did gain some knowledge of rhetoric through imitation. They certainly learnt to use figures of speech, and indeed used them to excess.

By the end of the seventh century however, the number of those whom instruction at home made acquainted with good Latin and classical literature had shrunk to a mere handful, and this created an urgent problem, since the Church had to a great extent relied on the dwindling Romanised upper class to provide it with administrators. If the Church was to retain its use of Latin, its intellectual traditions and complex organisation, the time had plainly come when Latin would have to be systematically taught as a foreign language.

It was at this point that Ireland and the Anglo-Saxon world made their unexpected contribution to Europe's development. Latin had come to Ireland under the auspices of the Church, and the Irish were inclined to regard everything written in the Church's language as deserving of respect. Unlike their continental contemporaries, they welcomed antiquity with open arms; and they communicated this tolerant attitude to the disciples their missionary zeal collected both on the continent, and most especially in the Anglo-Saxon kingdoms.

Ireland and England had from the beginning been in the position that was now coming to obtain in Europe as a whole. They possessed no educated Romanised upper class and had to provide the whole of their clergy's education. This the Irish had done; and it was evident that the new-fledged Anglo-Saxon Church would somehow have to follow suit. Since paganism still had strong roots in England, and since its Christian population was divided between those who observed the Roman and those who observed the Celtic rite, there was a measure of confusion that underlined the need for competent administrators.

In 664 Pope Vitalian sent Theodore of Tarsus and Abbot Hadrian to take the Anglo-Saxon Church in hand. His choice of two learned men with unorthodox backgrounds—the one a Greek, the other a Greek-speaking African—indicates perhaps that he realised that more was required than the education the Church had been accustomed to provide since the days of Gregory the Great.

One can learn rhetoric from the Bible as Augustine noted, but it does not provide many examples of the sort of language that is commonly required in the conduct of business, nor does it tell us much about human behaviour or the handling of public affairs. The dependence of the Church on its privately educated Romanised subjects during the previous two hundred years demonstrates that the pagan classics had something to offer the seventh century and could perhaps contribute to solving the educational problem the Church was facing.

We have no evidence that could help us decide whether or not Theodore and Hadrian used pagan authors in their teaching. Their acquaintance with Greek culture may have inclined them to a certain catholicity of approach. But Bede who was a product of the educational tradition they inaugurated was still suspicious of paganism although he certainly knew Virgil and the elder Pliny[2] first hand. On the whole, it seems likely that the Irish and their disciples may have done more than Vitalian's special envoys to promote a revival of

classical studies. But however it was, by the end of the eighth century the ancient authors were certainly being read in England.

The English experience is regarded as important because Alcuin was the man
who eventually organised the new education. But it ought to be noted that,
like Theodore and Hadrian, coming into a country where the Irish had been
at work, he had some foundations to build upon. The eighth century had seen
the reappearance of urban schools in northern Italy. It had seen churchmen
taking over notarial tasks in France, and bishops making some attempts to
organise legal education. The formulary of Marculf with its examples of legal
phraseology was composed *ad exercenda initia puerorum*,[3] and there were saints'
lives written in Aquitaine that show some knowledge of Caesar and Virgil.[4]
Thanks to the pressure of events and thanks too to the activity of Irish mis-
sionaries, the old narrow education of the clerical schools was already widen-
ing before Alcuin came on the scene. It would be wrong however to
underestimate his achievement. He found tentative innovations and left a system.

Behind the Carolingian restructuring of education there lay first of all that
need for administrators which has already been mentioned. Both the Church
and the Carolingian State were short of men who could understand organisa-
tional problems and could express their ideas in a clear and persuasive manner. Secondly, there was a genuine interest in ancient writings, mediated by
the Irish, but not unconnected with the desire for a better understanding of
civil life, and finally there was the revival of the belief, formulated originally
by Augustine, that a knowledge of pagan literature could contribute to a better understanding of the Bible.

It is in the Carolingian age that rhetoric reappears as a school subject. The
Irish had limited their studies to grammar, though it is true that they had added to this some systematic work on tropes which might be held to belong
more properly to rhetoric. *Elocutio* interested them; but the problems of *inventio* and *dispositio* escaped their attention. As for Bede, he had classed rhetoric
and dialectic with heresy,[5] and had dismissed them as branches of learning
that served only worldly interests.

Alcuin therefore was a genuine innovator when he wrote *De rhetorica et virtutibus*. The very title is revealing. Classical writers on rhetoric had hovered
between three conceptions of their subject. It was seen as an art of persuasion,
which brought it close to dialectic; or as an art of writing, which threatened
to identify it with some varieties of literary criticism;[6] and finally as the art
of speaking about public affairs which was the view taken by Cicero. Alcuin
significantly adopted the Ciceronian theory; and Luitpold Wallach has described
his little work as an 'art of kingship'.[7]

What made it possible for Alcuin to treat his subject at this impressively
general level was the circumstance that apart from occasionally listing figures
of thought and speech, the writers of this period did not pay much attention

to the theoretical study of their craft. They learnt to write by imitation, or so one might guess from the popularity of formularies. The early ones like Marculf's, which were for the use of notaries, were later supplemented by collections intended to illustrate private as well as business correspondence. A selection of Alcuin's own letters was assembled in the eleventh century for educational use.

It is true that we do not know what models Alcuin himself set in front of his pupils. His own manner of writing was simple and very different from the highly ornamented mandarin style favoured by Aldhelm. A close study may one day trace its line of descent from Bede and Gregory I, and these may have been the exemplars he selected. In any case, the use of figures of speech and thought appears to have been taught in part through poetry. We know that verse composition was practised in the Carolingian schools, and it is plain that a student who has learnt to imitate Virgil or Ovid or some of the Christian poets will at the end of the day have come to master most of the common rhetorical devices and will have done so more quickly and more thoroughly than if he had been writing prose. In fact, some Carolingians also learnt to handle classical techniques of description as T. R. Anderssen has pointed out in a recent book.[8]

The three hundred years that followed Alcuin's death were the most important period in the history of medieval rhetoric. This was the time during which men became familiar with the subject, and when its different uses were carefully explored. Alcuin's attempt to link the study of rhetoric with political science did not bear much fruit.[9] The conditions of the age did not favour such a coupling. On the other hand, rhetoric enjoyed great popularity as an art that would teach men how to argue. The distinction between rhetorical proofs (enthymeme, example etc) and the more rigorous forms of proof demanded by Aristotelian logic was not properly understood, and as late as the eleventh century we find a controversialist like Anselm of Bisate describing himself as a rhetorician. However, in this area rhetoric was bound in the end to give place to its more exact rival. Dialectic was introduced into the curriculum in the ninth century by Heiric of Auxerre as a humble auxiliary to rhetoric. A hundred years later its popularity was greatly stimulated by Gerbert's teaching at Rheims, and by the end of the eleventh century it was dominant in a great many schools to the virtual exclusion of rhetoric.

Much the same happened over the same period in the case of law. Some schools, which seem for the most part to have been located in northern Italy, were accustomed to give their rhetorical instruction a legal slant. "Eruditus est," says Lanfranc's biographer, "in scholis liberalium artium et legum secularium ad suae morem patriae."[10] But then in the next generation Irnerius systematised the teaching of law, and here again rhetoric took a back seat.

In an epoch which offered few opportunities for persuasive oratory that would make an immediate impact on public assemblies, the weaknesses of rhetorical argument were bound to come to light, and specialists were bound to look for something better. But as had already been noted, the usefulness of rhetoric was not limited to the art of controversy. Intending orators had always been encouraged to study literature, and reading the major classical authors came to play an important part in the work of some medieval schools. Alcuin had still regarded pagan writings with some suspicion. But in the next generation we find two scholars, Servatus Lupus and Paschasius Radbertus, whose enthusiasm for antiquity had no bounds. The Roman satirists were studied at the end of the ninth century in the schools of Auxerre, while in the tenth we have the plays of Hroswitha inspired, if distantly, by Terence, and the epic *Waltharius*, which contains some notable reminiscences of Virgil.[11] In spite of the growing interest in dialectic, it is evident that by the end of the tenth century classical learning had a well-defined place in education. The foundations were laid for that so-called renaissance of the twelfth century which was to bring into being a literature of undoubted merit deeply indebted to its Roman models. The best account we have of the teaching in these literature-directed schools is John of Salisbury's famous description of the methods employed by Bernard of Chartres. He would lecture on a classical text explaining grammatical problems and pointing out the figures of rhetoric, putting special emphasis of metaphors and unusual epithets, and he would then set a theme for composition so that his pupils might apply what they had just learnt.[12]

In the twelfth century the work of the previous three hundred years came to a head. Dialectic, law and literature, the three offshoots of rhetorical study, all flowered. But the flowering of rhetoric was short, and during the remaining portion of the Middle Ages its historian is reduced to depicting survivals rather than new developments. It was the founding of the great universities that occasioned this change. With their emergence, educational interest came to focus on the professional disciplines of law, medicine and theology, adding only the study of dialectic that was regarded as the best introduction to all three. In Alcuin's day, the utilitarian requirements of society could still be satisfied by a general education. Now they had become more specialised, and specialist forms of training had evolved to satisfy them. Rhetoric was demoted to the initial stage of the school course, and in most places it was taught alongside grammar only to young boys. Such literary schools as survived—the one at Orleans was quite well-known—dragged out a shadowy half-life, producing little of note.

It was this neglect of rhetoric and literature in the thirteenth and fourteenth centuries that was to enable the humanists to describe the Middle Ages as an epoch of barbarism.

However, we should be wrong to assume that the rhetoric course designed for schoolboys represented the totality of thirteenth century interest in the subject.

The drafting of letters that involved questions of law had from the Dark Ages onwards been entrusted to trained notaries, and we know that they possessed collections of set formulas to guide them. But with the thirteenth century, the volume of this kind of correspondence increased enormously. Private people as well as public officials needed on occasion to have letters carefully drafted, and there emerged a special class of professional letter-writers, the *dictatores*, who were trained in what came to be known as the *ars dictaminis*. The first systematiser of this legal variety of rhetoric was Buoncompagno. His *Rhetorica novissima* (1235) claimed to be a rejection of Cicero's teachings, but has been proved to owe a good deal to the *De inventione* and the *Ad Herennium*,[13] a debt which later practitioners like Brunetto Latini freely acknowledged.

Mention must also be made of the work of the chancelleries that were responsible for official correspondence. Under the influence of Frederick II's chancellor, Pietro della Vigna, they developed a highly mannered style, peppered with rare words and figures of speech, which was to have a marked influence on Latin prose writing until the coming of the Renaissance. The popularity of this style did not, one feels, represent an advance in men's understanding of the possibilities of rhetoric, but was simply the use (or misuse) of techniques that had been acquired much earlier.

Rhetorical techniques were also employed by writers on sacred subjects and more particularly by preachers. When Gerald Owst turned his attention to medieval pulpit literature half a century ago,[14] he was not concerned with the rhetorical element in sermons and was anyway more interested in English than in Latin sources, but even so it is impossible to read the passages he cites without noticing how frequently their authors employed figures of speech and thought. *Exempla* in particular took on a life of their own as realistic anecdotes about everyday behaviour. Since the great majority of people listened regularly to sermons, and many were concerned in their composition, preaching was probably the principal source through which rhetoric reached the medieval public, and through which its devices could pass into common usage.

Rhetoric had been studied with the help of Cicero's writings from the Carolingian age onwards, and by the thirteenth century most of what Cicero could teach had passed into the general stock of knowledge familiar to educated men. The *dictatores*, the clerks in the chancelleries, the authors of sermon books could draw on this common stock without needing to look further. They added little to the understanding of rhetoric, but they certainly disseminated to a wider public what had been even in the twelfth century the special possession of an élite.

Finally it is worth noting that an analogous dissemination occurred about the same time through the medium of vernacular writings. Latin literature, which had flourished so brilliantly in the twelfth century, declined rapidly after the rise of the universities as the interests and energies of the public that wrote

and read Latin were diverted from literary study. But thanks to the growth
of prosperity and the spread of literacy that accompanied it, there was now
a public for writings in the vernacular of a more popular sort; and enough
was known about literary techniques, enough in particular had passed into
the easily accessible Latin literature of the time, to provide clerks who had
a taste for producing popular works with the materials they needed. Consequently, the decline of Latin literature of the poetic and fictional sort was
matched by a corresponding proliferation of vernacular writings, which as far
as technique was concerned were substantially indebted to the Latin tradition.

We have therefore in the Middle Ages four successive, though somewhat
overlapping periods. The years 450–700 see the final collapse of the old Roman
civilisation. From 650–850 we have the gradual development of a new attitude to the pagan past and the emergence of an educational system that will
enable medieval man to make good use of the classical heritage. From 800–1200
we have four centuries during which the rhetorical tradition of antiquity is
explored from several points of view and its possibilities are developed. From
1200 to the point when humanism becomes dominant in the fifteenth century, we have an epoch when the study of rhetoric is relatively speaking
neglected, but knowledge of it reaches a wider public through a number of
channels.

Rhetoric was the gateway through which medieval scholars came to dialectic, law and literary achievement. It left its mark on vernacular literature, on
popular preaching, even on the writing of hymns. Without it, the culture of
the Middle Ages would have been very different.

Notes

1. Pierre Riché, *Education et culture dans l'Occident barbare 6e–8e siècles* (Paris, 1962).
English tr. by John J. Contreni (Columbia, SC. 1976).
2. M. L. W. Laistner, *The Intellectual Heritage of the Early Middle Ages* (Ithaca, New
York, 1957) pp. 97–98.
3. Riché, op. cit., p. 286, n. 464.
4. Id. p. 413.
5. Id. p. 439.
6. The most striking example of this approach was the pseudo-Longinus's *On the
Sublime*.
7. Luitpold Wallach, *Alcuin and Charlemagne* (Ithaca, New York, 1954) chapter 4.
8. Theodore R. Andersson, *Early Epic Scenery* (Ithaca, New York, 1976) pp. 104–44.
9. Alcuin's *De dialectica*, like his *De rhetorica*, seems designed for adult rather than
school reading. The master's interlocutor is not a schoolboy but Charlemagne himself.

10. Milo Crispinus, *Vita Lanfranci*, Patrologia Latina CL 39.

11. E. P. M. Dronke, "Functions of classical learning in medieval Latin verse" in *Classical Influences on European Culture A.D. 500–1500*, ed. R. R. Bolgar (Cambridge, 1971).

12. John of Salisbury, *Metalogicon* I, ch. 24 (in C. C. Webb's edn., pp. 55–56.)

13. H. Wieruzewski, "*Ars Dictaminis* in the time of Dante," *Medievalia et Humanistica* I, (1943).

14. Gerald R. Owst, *Literature and Pulpit in Medieval England* (Cambridge, 1943; revised edn. 1961).

Twelfth-Century Ciceronian Rhetoric: Its Doctrinal Development and Influences

KARIN MARGARETA FREDBORG
University of Copenhagen

COMMENTARIES on Cicero's *De Inventione* and the *Rhetorica ad Herennium* were but one branch of medieval instruction in rhetoric, and had to compete for the students' favour with the *Artes praedicandi*, the *Artes dictaminis* and the teaching of the elements of Style in the courses on Grammar.

This, however, is not the only reason why these Ciceronian commentaries are only little known, since the study of the approximately 40 or more extant major Ciceronian commentaries from the Middle Ages has only recently begun and is still beset with numerous problems of listing the Mss, of identification of different versions, authenticity and search for identification of authorship. Hence, the sources are not yet readily available, and so far only a fragment of one commentary has been edited (from a single Ms) and shorter excerpts from others must be gleaned from the pioneering studies of R. McKeon, H. Caplan, M. Dickey and J. O. Ward.[1]

I shall here confine myself to only a few of the major commentaries of the twelfth century, for which the following chronological table might be useful:

Rhetoric masters in the late eleventh and twelfth centuries:

	Laon	mainly Paris	Northern Italy
c. 1080	Manegold		
c. 1095	William of Champeaux		
c. 1110?	Anon. *Materia Tullii*		
		(Abelard)	
c. 1130		Thierry of Chartres	Anon. *Rhetorica est*
c. 1140		Petrus Helias	
c. 1170?		Alanus (de Insulis?) with anon. cognate versions	William of Lucca

This list is based partly on historical information from the period, from which we know that Abelard studied rhetoric under William of Champeaux,[2] and the Thierry taught Petrus Helias and both taught John of Salisbury, the secretary of Thomas Beckett,[3] and partly on quotations in the commentaries themselves. The quotations indicate that the anonymous commentator excerpting the gloss *Materia Tullii* was well acquainted with William of Champeaux[4] and that Alanus had read Thierry's and Petrus Helias' commentaries.[5] Further study of the commentaries themselves confirms this grouping of commentaries, even in the case of Abelard, whose *Rhetorica* (as well as his *Grammatica*) is now lost, but who has left us a short summary of his views on the rhetorical topics and the issues in one of his dialectical works.[6]

However, the doctrinal development in the twelfth century moved by small steps, and the readers should be warned that the understanding of this abundant, but not easily accessible material, presupposes a ready knowledge of the classical rhetorical authorities, with whose diverse and at times conflicting positions concerning details of doctrine and terminology the medieval masters were intimately acquainted, and set out to organize into some coherent body of doctrine, according to their individual preferences.

In this process Boethius' *De Differentiis Topicis* Bk. 4 and Victorinus' commentary on the *De Inventione* played the most important part. The *De Oratore* was either considered lost: "quo nos caremus" according to Alanus,[7] or known from garbled quotations, as in Thierry's work.[8] The latter may be said for Quintilian as well, although he is occasionally appealed to.[9] Further, Aristotle's *Rhetoric* was (apart from an implicit quotation in the obscure sixth-century commentator, Grillius) not known to the Latin West before Hermannus Alemannus translated it into Latin (from Arabic) in 1256 and William of Moerbeke again translated it (from Greek) in about 1270.[10]

A study of this particular sequence of twelfth-century commentaries as well as the students' digestions thereof, suggests that the major efforts were given to the study of Invention and Style. The other parts of rhetoric were more reluctantly developed, e.g. the system of mnemonics in *Rhetorica ad Herennium*, which found little favour. This is clear from Geoffrey of Vinsauf, who in his *Poetria Nova* preferred his own system of mnemonics to that of the *Rhetorica ad Herennium*.[11] Also John of Salisbury complains in his *Metalogicon* (1159) that he never grasped the mnemonics of *Rhetorica ad Herennium*,[12] a statement which is fully understandable when compared with the bald treatment of mnemonics in his teacher's, Thierry of Chartres', commentary on *Rhetorica ad Herennium*. Interestingly, it was rather the ubiquitous eleventh- and twelfth-century drill in analyzing a text into arguments and topics for arguments which served as a system of mnemonics. Thus the rhetorically interested abbot Wibald of Corvai writes in a letter from 1149: "and I have the habit, having read a book which holds any kind of difficult subject matter, to lay aside the book and by memory unfold the topics and arguments, the premises in the discussion and the traps of the conclusions."[13]

In the medieval doctrine of Style it is well known that the list of figures of Style in the *Rhetorica ad Herennium* played a major role not only in the school rhetoric, but also in the twelfth-century Latin Poetics. In fact, the very first commentaries on the *Rhetorica ad Herennium* dealt only with that part, where e.g. the poet and scholar Marbod of Rennes, who taught in Angers in the 1060s, quoted the definition of each figure of Style from the *Rhetorica ad Herennium* and then illustrated it with verses of his own:[14]

> Complexio est quae utramque complectitur exornationem, et hanc quam modo exposuimus, ut et repetamus idem verbum saepius et crebro et ad idem postremum revertamur, hoc modo   (*Ad Her*. IV. 14. 20):

> Qui sunt qui pugnant audaciter? Andegavenses.
> Qui sunt qui superant inimicos? Andegavenses.
> Qui sunt qui parcunt superatis? Andegavenses.
> Egregios igitur livor neget Andegavenses.

(The example given by the author of *Rhetorica ad Herennium* is very similar in structure, but turns on a harangue against the Carthaginians!) And, even as late as the fourteenth century, John of Jandun considered these definitions of the figures of Style as a necessary part of a course in rhetoric and added them to his commentary on Aristotle's *Rhetoric* "because of their usefulness."[15]

It is however in the field of Invention that the greatest doctrinal development in twelfth-century rhetoric appears to take place, since the masters had to account for conflicting positions in the classical authorities, as well as take a stand in the inherent conflict between dialectic and rhetoric with regard to the topics and definitions of types of arguments.

As a result of this juxtaposition of authorities Cicero's complicated list of issues, the four 'constitutiones in ratione' and the five 'status in scripto' became eventually subsumed under and replaced by the more simple threefold system of the *Rhetorica ad Herennium* (an sit, quid sit, iurene sit).[16] Still, the status and divisions of the issues might be hotly disputed in the schools, but they were not to play any important practical role in contemporary legal practice. So Petrus Helias complains (c. 1140): "Now, when the issue should be decided on and worked out, people of our time are corrupt. For, when the defendant is called to court by the bailiff or prince, he usually upon hearing the charges defers his defence by saying that he had not come to plead his case, but to hear his opponents' charges, and he promises to answer them at a time appointed by the judge. . . . In this delay of the defence there is a peculiar kind of corruption, since the defendant ought immediately, when he has heard the charges, to defend himself, in order that the issue should be worked out."[17] Here Petrus Helias' claim agrees with our earliest extant gloss on *De Inventione* (in MS Oxford Laud. Lat. 49) from c. 1020, which criticizes contemporary legal practice for showing negligence of the issues, and deplores the annulment of the ancient threat of losing the case if the issue is not handled correctly.[18]

Conversely, in the doctrine of the topics both theoretical and practical interest prevailed and it is in this field that we find the most explicit doctrinal development of medieval rhetoric. The topics listed from the *De Inventione* with a number of subdivisions and modes of interaction and combination were filed into one sequence, providing the storehouse of arguments from character, another sequence being concerned with details of the case itself.

The topics served a double purpose: as means of invention as well as a tool for literary analysis. Accordingly, all details in a text (whether literature, theology, or a textbook) being subject to interpretation and commentary were analyzed into topics for argument, a habit that accounts for the topics being used as a system of mnemonics, as mentioned above. More importantly, these lists of rhetorical topics also served the twelfth-century Latin Poetics as the established categories for description of character and action, in a way clearly showing the dependence of these Poetics on contemporary rhetorical instruction.[19] That the authors of these Poetics not only used the same (classical) authorities, but had recourse also to contemporary commentaries is obvious from Matthieu of Vendôme, who in his *Ars Versificatoria*, directly or indirectly, borrowed half a page from Thierry of Chartres' commentary on the *De Inventione*.[20]

This overall emphasis on the topics is not only widespread in related subjects of literary analysis and Poetics, but becomes more evident when we look to those authors who deal with Ciceronian rhetoric outside the proper commentary tradition. John of Salisbury, in his defence of the Trivium in the *Metalogicon*, deals only sporadically with rhetoric, but when he does so it is in his discussion of topics, more precisely of Aristotle's *Topics*,[21] and in the thirteenth century the university masters simply turned to commentating Boethius' *De Differentiis Topicis* IV rather than the *De Inventione* and the *Rhetorica ad Herennium*.[22]

Within the discussion of those rhetorical topics that have a strong affinity to dialectical topics, such as "locus a genere," "locus a contrario," etc., the old conflict between the proper subject matter for dialectic and rhetoric springs forth. Three main positions can be traced for the twelfth and thirteenth centuries. In one, with Thierry[23] and Petrus Helias,[24] the Boethian view is maintained that rhetoric is strictly tied to a particular subject matter, and when using such topics we argue e.g. from a particular contrary, not from contrariety. Others, such as William of Champeaux and Abelard,[25] admit that by using such general topics rhetoric simply borrows from dialectic. A slight variation of this view is found in Manegold's work,[26] who would "only borrow such topics when the proper particularly rhetorical topics did not suffice to convince the audience." A third, conciliatory position is found in Alanus[27] and the thirteenth-century Boethian commentators, who hold that the rhetorical argument is drawn from a rhetorical, particular topic, e.g. from a particular contrary, but that the strength or validity of such arguments is warranted by the corresponding dialectical (general) topic, to use the phrase of Nicolaus of Paris (c. 1250).[28]

In the theory of rhetorical types of arguments Cicero's and Victorinus' terminology proved too loose. Accordingly, Thierry of Chartres strongly denied Cicero's claim that the five-part argument (= Victorinus' five-part syllogism) was accepted by Aristotle as a rhetorical syllogism.[29] For a proper *syllogismus* has only three parts. Likewise Cicero's rejection of the enthymeme or two-part argument made the commentators uneasy, since it conflicted with Boethius' explicit recommendation of the enthymeme as an argument suitable for rhetoric.[30] William of Champeaux[31] took Cicero's side by pointing to the baldness of the enthymeme, for according to him rhetorical arguments should primarily be ornate. To this view Thierry added a historical (guess or) interpretation, believing that Cicero was led to reject the enthymeme due to the first century B.C. discussions over the value of this type of argument.[32]

In a similar manner, formal dialectical training and stricter terminology made the twelfth-century masters reject Cicero's three kinds of necessary arguments as *argumenta* proper. Instead they discussed them in terms of either *consequentiae*, or modes of arguments springing from the *locus a divisione*, or subclasses of this topic.[33] Likewise, the kinds of probable arguments from *De Inventione* were subsumed under the classification of rhetorical topics, as initiated by Victorinus.[34]

Just as the medieval masters had been careful to be explicit on the relation of rhetoric to legal practice when discussing the issues, and the relation to dialectic with regard to subject matter (topics) and common terminology (*syllogismus*, *argumentum*) they occasionally ventured into more explicit discussions of the specific aims and function of rhetoric as distinct from other literary genres. Of the commentators dealt with here William of Champeaux is the most informative: The aim of rhetoric is to persuade, which marks it off from other literary genres, poetry, historiography, composition of didactic prose; all these genres might well produce edifying literature, but not primarily persuade. However, these related genres might proceed rhetorically, without being proper rhetorical speeches, as does Horace in his praise of Augustus, or Sallustius in the inserted speeches in his history, and Boethius in his prologues[35] — here William presumably directed the students' attention to the Boethian Trinitarian treatises, which, in fact, were usually analyzed rhetorically in twelfth-century theological exegesis.[36] Likewise students of the Quadrivium paid great attention to rhetorical figures in Boethius' *De Arithmetica*.

Finally, it might be permitted to mention here a more formal contribution of rhetoric to all the Artes within the medieval curriculum, namely a new Accessus-scheme, which was very popular in the twelfth century. By that the introductions to the commentaries on all kinds of textbooks discussed the following topics: what is this particular art, of what branch of knowledge is it a subclass, what subject matter, which species and parts does it have, which aim, which duty, which instrument or means, which 'artifex,' what is the etymology of its name. Readers of *De Inventione* and more specifically, *De Differentiis Topicis*, will identify most of these items from there, but contemporary twelfth-century sources[37] pointed to its rhetorical origin, and in all probability it first originated in this authoritative form with Thierry of Chartres, and gained enormous popularity by being adopted by the Spanish scholar Dominicus Gundissalinus for all the Artes in his encyclopedic *De Divisione Philosophiae*, which was much quoted by later masters.[38]

We may end this brief summary of the doctrinal development in a few major twelfth-century Ciceronian commentaries by the following conclusions, however tentative they must remain because of the difficult access to the material. Masters like William of Champeaux, Abelard, Thierry of Chartres, Petrus Helias and Alanus show a profound interest in delineating the borderlines between rhetoric and the other arts of discourse according to its specific means of persuasion – in the topics, the status of rhetorical kinds of arguments (against dialectic); its specific aim (against other kinds of prose and poetry); and its subject matter – the issues as determined by their particularly required topics and elegant argumentation (against Law). In this process of development more and more emphasis was given to the topics, which thoroughly permeated the Ciceronian discussion of rhetorical kinds of necessary and probable arguments, and which were to prove very influential in related subjects. This peculiar line of development is partly due to Boethius' influence as well as to the exigencies of stricter terminology learnt from dialectic, but also due to a faulty knowledge of Quintilian and Aristotle.

These conclusions are as yet only tentative since editorial work as well as exploration of details of interrelationship must first be carried out. However, the sheer bulk of the material confirms that rhetoric was indeed the concern of these masters, though they are today better remembered for their contributions to grammar, logic and theology. And we can but admire their concern to sharpen their doctrine by basing it upon a subtle, well-discussed and firmly established terminology, in which this kind of rhetoric might compare favourably with some later attempts.

Notes

Abbreviations: *CIMAGL* = *Cahiers de l'Institut du Moyen-Age grec et latin* (Copenhagen); *Pl* = Migne, *Patrologia Latina*.

1. W. H. D. Suringar edited a fragment of Thierry's commentary in *Historia Scholiastorum Latinorum* (Leyden, 1834) pp. 213–53, covering *De Inventione* I.1.1-I.5.7. R. McKeon, "Rhetoric in the Middle Ages," *Speculum* 17 (1942) p. 1–32, esp. p. 16 sqq. M. Dickey, "The teaching of rhetoric in the eleventh and twelfth centuries, with particular reference to the schools of Northern France," B.litt. thesis, now Oxford, Bod. L. MS B.litt. d. 150; id., "Some commentaries on the *De Inventione* and *Ad Herennium* of the eleventh and early twelfth centuries," *Medieval & Renaissance Studies* 6 (London, 1968) p. 1–41; H. Caplan, "A mediaeval commentary on the *Rhetorica ad Herennium*," in "*Of Eloquence*," (ed.) A. King & H. North (London, 1970); J. O. Ward, "Artificiosa Eloquentia in the Middle Ages," Ph.D. thesis (Toronto, 1972); id., "The date of the commentary on Cicero's *De Inventione* by Thierry of Chartres (c. 1095-1160?) and the Cornifician attack on the Liberal Arts," *Viator* 3 (Berkeley, 1972) pp. 219–73.

2. Abelard, *Historia Calamitatum* ed. Monfrin (Paris, 1967), p. 65.

3. Cf. R. B. C. Huygens, "Guillaume de Tyr étudiant, une chapitre xix. 12, de son Histoire rétrouvé," *Latomus* 21 (Bruxelles, 1962) pp. 811–29; John of Salisbury, *Metalogicon* II.10, ed. Webb (Oxford, 1929) p. 80; cf. K. M. Fredborg, "The commentary of Thierry of Chartres on Cicero's De Inventione," *CIMAGL* 7 (1971) pp. 1–36; id., "Petrus Helias on rhetoric," *CIMAGL* 13 (1974) p. 31–41.

4. Cf. K. M. Fredborg, "The commentaries on Cicero's *De Inventione* and *Rhetorica ad Herennium* by William of Champeaux," *CIMAGL* 17 (1976), pp. 1–39.

5. Cf. "Petrus Helias on rhetoric," *CIMAGL* 13, p. 31 n. 2.

6. Abelard, *Scritti di Logica* ed. Dal Pra (Firenze, 1969), commentary on Boethius' *De Differentiis Topicis* p. 256–67; for the relation to William's rhetorical views see "The commentaries . . . by William of Champeaux," *CIMAGL* 17 p. 16–20.

7. Alanus, *Commentary on Rhetorica ad Herennium*, MS London, Brit. L. Harley 6324 f. 2vb. However, the well-read John of Salisbury had a copy of *De Oratore*, which he left at his death to the cathedral of Chartres, *Cartulaire de Notre-Dame de Chartres* III, p. 202, ed. E. de Lépinois & L. Merlet (Chartres, 1864).

8. Thierry, *Com. ad De Inv.* I.5. 7: "NAM GORGIAS etc. Ostendit qui ultra modum materiam assignant, illi scilicet qui in verbis Gorgiae erraverunt, putantes quod ille philosophus omnem rem artis rhetoricae materiam assignasset dicens ORATOREM POSSE OPTIME DICERE etc. Sed ille veram sententiam protulit, quam Tullius quoque in libro De Oratore confirmat" (*viz.* Cic.'s own view in *De Oratore* I.15. 64–65). "Non enim dixit quod de omnibus rebus loqueretur, quod illi putaverunt, sed optime de omnibus rebus, id est de quacumque re loquitur de ea optime loquitur" (*contra* Gorgias' views mentioned in *De Oratore*. I.22. 103; III.32. 129). I here quote from my edition of Thierry's commentaries on *De Inventione* and *Ad Herennium* as prepared for publication.

9. John of Salisbury quotes Quintilian readily enough, but his teachers knew less. For Thierry cf. "The commentaries of Thierry . . ." *CIMAGL* 7, p. 32 (but he implicitly paraphrases Quint. at times, cf. ibid., p. 19); P. Helias wrongly attributes to Quint. a subsummation of the four issues under the ten Categories, which he inherited from Thierry, though without the attribution, cf. "Petrus Helias on rhetoric," *CIMAGL* 13, pp. 40 sq.

10. Cf. W. F. Bogess, "Hermannus Alemannus's rhetorical translations," *Viator* 2 (Berkeley, 1971), pp. 227–50; K. M. Fredborg, "Buridan's *Quaestiones super Rhetoricam Aristotelis*," in *The Logic of John Buridan, Acts of the 3rd European Symposium on Medieval Logic and Semantics, Copenhagen 16–21 Nov. 1975*, Opuscula Graecolatina 9, Museum Tusculanum (Copenhagen, 1976), pp. 47–59.

11. Geoffrey of Vinsauf, *Poetria Nova* vv. 2017–2030, ed. Faral, *Les Arts Poétiques du xiie et du xiiie siècle*, Bibliotheque de l'Ecole des Hautes Etudes 238 (Paris, 1923), p. 259.

12. John of Salisbury, *Metalogicon* I.20, *PL* 199, 851A: "Seneca se artem comparandae memoriae traditurum facillime pollicetur. Et utinam innotuisset mihi, sed quod eam tradiderit omnino non recolo. Tullius in Rhetoricis operam dedisse visus est, sed similibus mei multum non prodest."

13. Wibald of Corvai, *Ep.* 147, *PL* 189, 1251D: "et in hoc me exercere soleo, ut post lectum aliquod cuiuspiam nodosae quaestionis volumen, locos et argumenta et disputandi vias et conclusionum laqueos, amoto libro, memoriter replicem". The letter as a whole is well worth reading, not in the least the section on rhetoric which is full of implicit quotations from Grillius (col. 1255A), *De Inventione* and *Ad Herennium* as well as showing mannerisms of contemporary school-rhetoric. (Go, read Quintilian col. 1254C, cf. Thierry's commentary, where this section is available in W. H. D. Suringar's edition, *Historia critica scholiastorum Latinorum* [Leyden, 1834], p. 219 and also *Med. Stud.* 26 [Toronto, 1964], p. 282.)

14. Marbod of Rennes, *PL* 171, 1687–1692.

15. John of Jandun, *Quaestiones s. Rhetoricam Aristotelis*, MS Padova U.B.1472 ff. 285rb–286rb. For other MSS cf. Schmugge, *Johannes von Jandun* in *Pariser Histor. Studien* 5 (Paris, 1966), pp. 135–39.

16. Cf. "Petrus Helias on rhetoric," *CIMAGL* 13 p. 37, with longer excerpts and parallels.

17. Cf. Petrus Helias, MS Cambridge, Pembroke Coll. 85, sect. iii, f. 85ra: "In formanda vero constitutione dolo fere omnes apud nos hodie tenentur. Cum enim reus a pretore vel a principe devocatur in ius, audito quid intendatur in eum, differt depulsionem plerumque dicens se non ideo venisse ut causaretur, sed ut audiret quid ei adversarius imponere vellet et die prestituta a iudice responsurum super hoc promittens. . . . Nescio quid doli subest in huiuscemodi depulsionis dilatione cum intentione audita, ut cause constitutio formaretur, deberet statim depellere."

18. MS Oxford, Bodl. L. Laud. Lat. 49 f. 131vb: "Erat praeterea institutum ut [e] causa caderet is qui non quemadmodum [oportebat] egisset. Quod tamen nostro tempore minime fit, cum utique ad causam agendam quivis accurrat et quod dicat non respiciat, et sic causam male definiat vel male transferat," quoted from M. Dickey's B. Litt. thesis (o.c. in note 1), p. 200.

19. Cf. Faral, *Les Arts Poétiques* . . . p. 135 sqq.

20. Matthieu of Vendôme, *Ars Versificatoria* ed. Faral, '*Les Arts Poétiques* . . ." p.

136-37, to which compare Thierry, *Com. ad De Inv.* I. 24. 35: "Sumuntur autem argumenta a naturalibus, a SEXU ut Vergilius: Rumpe moras. Varium et mutabile semper femina. A NATIONE ut si quis probet aliquem cautum esse quia Graecus sit, ut Ovidius: Vix bene barbarica Graeca notata manu. A COGNATIONE ut Statius: Cadmus, origo patrum. A PATRIA: Tellus mavortia Thebae. Ab AETATE ut Ovidius: A iuvene et cupido credatur reddita virgo. Ab attributis CORPORI ut Statius de Polynice: Celsior ille gradu procera in membra. Ab ANIMO ut idem Statius de Tydeo: Sed non et viribus infra Tydea fert animus totosque infusa per artus. Maior in exiguo regnabat corpore virtus."

21. *Metalogicon* III. 10, *PL* 199, 910c–D, as pointed out by McKeon, o.c. *Speculum* 17 p. 18 n. 4.

22. Only four of the six extant Boethian commentaries go as far as to *De Diff. Top.* IV, two are anonymous and one by Nicolaus of Paris (mid 13th c.) and one by Radulphus Brito, now edited by N. J. Green-Pedersen, *CIMAGL* 26 (1978) pp. 1–92. For the general tenor of these commentaries see "Buridan's *Quaestiones* . . . *super Rhetoricam Aristotelis*," pp. 48–51.

23. Thierry, *Com. ad De Inv.* I. 24. 34: "In ratione igitur disserendi sedes argumentorum sunt haec maxima propositio 'unde abest definitio et quod definitur' et haec alia 'cui adest species, et genus' et consimiles . . . et sic aliae generaliter ad multa pertinent. In rhetorica vero sedes argumenti est vel hoc genus vel haec species . . . quae particularia esse quantum ad praedictas maximas patet cuilibet," but this view had difficulties too, cf. "The commentary of Thierry. . . ." *CIMAGL* 7 p. 21 sqq.

24. Petrus Helias, MS Cambridge Pembroke Col. 85 sect. iii f. 92va: ". . . Sed hec est dialecticorum locorum et rethoricorum differentia, quod loci dialectici universales sunt, loci vero rethorici particulares. Dialecticus sumit argumentum a genere universaliter, id est a communi natura generis . . . rethor vero sumit argumentum ab hoc genere, non a genere universaliter."

25. William, *Com. ad De Inv.* II. 5. 19: "Assumunt enim rhetorici dialecticos aliquando locos . . .", for the full texts see "The commentaries . . . by William of Champeaux," *CIMAGL* 17 pp. 23 sqq., Abelard, *Scritti di Logica* p. 262: "In adiunctis vero Tullius negotio locos dialecticos includit, quibus quandoque orator utitur. Cum enim orator proprios locos suos, per supra positas videlicet circumstantias ex quibus coniecturae capiuntur, senserit ad probationem non sufficere, confugit ad dialecticos, ut rethorica, quae est copia dicendi, copiam argumentationum habeat. Hos itaque ex dialecticis locis quibus orator maxime utitur Tullius adiuncta vocat. . . ."

26. Manegold, MS Köln, Dombibl. 197 f. 24r (below = K) and MS Berlin, Deutsche Staatsbibl. lat. oct. 161 f. 36ra (below = B): "Et postquam negotium de qua agitur (quareritur K) probabitur per supradicta (*viz.* the 7 circumstantiae), si fides adhuc in aliquo claudicarit (-caret B claudutur K) inducemus haec (vel *add.* K) adiuncta negotio."

27. Alanus, MS London B. L. Harley 6324 f. 27rb: "Sunt autem adiuncta circumstantiae extrinseci negotii et extrinsecae personae, relatae ad praesentem personam et ad praesens negotium et ex relatione vim probandi recipientes."

28. Nicolaus of Paris, *Com. S. Boethium, Top.* MS München clm 14460, f. 166va: "Loci dialectici sumuntur ab ipsa natura generis, scil. a genere secundum intentionem. Loci vero rhetorici non sumuntur a natura generis . . . sed a re ipsa quae genus est . . . et ideo sumunt confirmationem loci rhetorici a dialecticis." For parallels and a broader discussion, see "Buridan's *Quaestiones* . . ." p. 48–51.

29. Thierry, *Com. ad De Inv.* I. 35. 61: "NOBIS AUTEM etc. Priori parti consentit Tullius inducens testes et argumenta. QUARE AUTEM etc. Post testes ponit argumenta non quae suam sententiam probent, sed quae sententiam aliorum falsificent, quasi Tullio constaret quod, illa falsificata, staret illa cui favebat. Mihi autem videtur quod utraque sententia falsa sit. Nam neque probatio pars est syllogismi nec semper propositio syllogismi probatione indiget."

30. Boethius, *PL* 64, 1206C.

31. William: ". . . enthymemate, ubi non est ingens ratio, quia non habet expolitum argumentum et satis firmum, sed solis nudis verbis expositum. . . . Quaeritur . . . quare enthymema non sit secundum istum expolitio, sicut et exemplum? Quia non est perfecta expolitio nisi ad minus ibi sint tres partes (cf. *De Inv.* I. 32. 54). For the full text see "The commentaries . . . by William of Champeaux," *CIMAGL* 17 p. 26.

32. Thierry, *Com. ad De Inv.* I. 40. 72: "BIPERTITA. Quidam putabant ratiocinationem bipertitam esse . . . , quod denegat Tullius, ideo dixit illud esse in controversia."

33. There is an excellent summary of these views in P. Helias' *Com. ad De Inv.* I. 29. 44: "Et videntur quibusdam hec esse genera sillogismorum quibus argumenta necessaria tractantur. Est autem complexio quidem secundum eos sillogismus qui ab antiquis 'cornutus' dicitur propter duplicem quam habet conclusionem (= the view of Abelard's scholar, William of Lucca, *Summa Dial. artis*, ed. Pozzi (Padova, 1975), p. 144) . . . Dicitur autem a dialecticis indirecta ratiocinatio (cf. Abelard, *Dialectica* ed. De Rijk, p. 447. 9, Boethius, *PL* 64, 1192 Dsq.). Sunt etiam qui dicant quod complexio est species divisionis, disiuncta scilicet cuius utraque pars reprehenditur . . . (= Thierry, text in *CIMAGL* 7 p. 26–29, cf. the anon. *MATERIA TULLII* MS Durham C. iv. 29 f. 208vb: "Complexio similis est loco a divisione") Quidam enim ausi sunt etiam complexionem, enumerationem et simplicem conclusionem locos argumentorum, secundum quod sunt necessaria, dicere, ut sub his attributa omnia personae et negotio vellent includere" (= the view in a commentary cognate with the Alanus-com. This commentary is found in two versions: complete and abbreviated in MS Venezia B. Marc. XI. 23 (4686), longer and fragmentary in MS Uppsala 928 ff. 140r–146, ad *De Inv.* I. 21. 29–41. 77) For the full text see "Petrus Helias on rhetoric," *CIMAGL* 13 pp. 39–40.

34. Victorinus, *Com. s. De Inv.* ed. Halm in *Rhetores Latini Minores* (Leipzig, 1863), p. 239.

35. William, basing himself on Victorinus o.c. p. 171: "Civilis scientia alia in dictis, alia in factis . . . scientia in dictis alia cum lite, alia sine lite. Sine lite ut scientia historiographorum et poetarum. Utilia enim sunt dicta poetarum rei publicae. Magis enim Romanum nomen scripta quam facta extulerunt, magis incitaverunt ad virtutem homines facta antiquorum audita quam modernorum . . . Cum lite, ut scientia causidicorum. Scientia cum lite subdividitur ita: alia artificiosa, alia inartificiosa. Artificiosa cum lite ut oratorum, qui utuntur argumentis in disputationibus suis, inartificiosa cum lite ut in iurisperitis, id est iudicibus, quae inartificiosa vocatur quia cum inter se de sententia litigant non utuntur argumentis, ut oratores, sed solum auctoritatibus legum . . . Est autem eius officium solis auctoritatibus uti. Potest tamen usurpare alienum officium quod est oratorum, utendo argumentis in disceptationibus suis. . . . Nota, si poetae aliquando loquuntur apposite ad persuasionem, tamen non est officium eorum, sed alienum usurpant . . . Si autem poetae faciunt demonstrationem agendo de laude alicuius non tamen ad persuasionem faciunt, sicut Horatius laudando

Augustum non laborat ut homines credant eum esse deum, sed tantum quaerit ut faciat hymnum laudis qui placeat Augusto . . . Sciendum est quod quamvis officio oratoris in hoc prologo utatur . . . tamen non est oratio rhetorica, quia non sunt ibi sex partes, sed tantum exordium. Non enim qui rhetorice agit, id est rhetoricas curialitates in verbis suis observat, semper rhetoricam orationem facit illam quam in hoc libro facere docet, sicut Sallustius in orationibus, Boethius in prologis." (fuller excerpts in *CIMAGL* 17 p. 27 sqq.).

36. E.g. Thierry of Chartres, *Commentaries on Boethius*, ed. N. M. Häring, P.I.M.S. Studies & Texts 20 (Toronto, 1971), pp. 119, 126, 316, 483.

37. *Summa Sophist. Elench.*, ed. De Rijk, *Logica Modernorum* I (Assen, 1962), p. 265.

38. Cf. R. W. Hunt, "The introduction to the Artes in the twelfth century," in *Studia Mediaevalia in honorem R. J. Martin* (Brügge, 1948), pp. 85–112; Fredborg, "The commentary by Thierry of Chartres . . ." *CIMAGL* 7, p. 6–11; *pace* N. M. Häring, "Thierry of Chartres and Dom. Gundissalinus," *Med. Stud.* 26 (Toronto, 1964), pp. 271–86.

Since completion of this paper I have learned that William of Lucca was the donor, not the author of MS. Lucca 614; cf. F. Gastaldelli, "Note sul codice 614 della Biblioteca Capitolare di Lucca e sulle edizione del *De Arithmetica compendiose tractata* e della *Summa dialetice artis*," *Salesianum* 39 (1977), pp. 693–702.

L'inventio Nell'Ars Poetica Latino-Medievale

PAOLO BAGNI
University of Bologna

L'IMMAGINE CHE la retorica nel suo sviluppo storico abbia conosciuto una progressiva riduzione del proprio campo, è diventata chiave di lettura abituale della sua storia, quasi luogo comune. Senza dubbio questa immagine ha, a proprio vantaggio, una buona evidenza empirica: se mettiamo su un piatto Aristotele con la sua retorica "antistrofe" della dialettica, e sull'altro un John Smith, ad esempio, con il suo *The Mysterie of Rhetorique unvail'd* (1657) "eminently delightful and profitable for young Scholars," quale bilancia non segnerà la differenza di peso e di ambizioni?

Tuttavia, ogni evidenza è tale in rapporto a qualche criterio, che, nel nostro caso, è rappresentato dal riferimento all'edificio retorico consolidatosi nell'antichità, strutturato sulle cinque fasi di elaborazione del discorso (*inventio dispositio elocutio memoria actio*) e sui tre campi di applicazione (giudiziale deliberativo dimostrativo). Cosi, è quanto fa Florescu, si può leggere la storia della retorica come progressiva riduzione del suo campo di applicazione, perdita dell'ambito deliberativo e giudiziale, restrizione al dimostrativo e conseguente *letteraturizzazione* della retorica.[1] Oppure, come Genette, si può privilegiare l'attenzione alle parti della retorica, vedere come essa si restringa all'*elocutio* al punto che "da Corace ad oggi, la storia della retorica coincide con una *restrizione generalizzata*."[2]

Il rischio metodologico di simili operazioni, pur legittime e utili, è di promuovere la nozione di retorica a *categoria tipologica*, forse capace di efficacia polemica, ma di scarsa fruibilità storiografica; lungo questa via non è difficile scivolare in presunzioni strutturaliste-semiologiche di operare sulla retorica un'inconfessata *Aufhebung* hegeliana, una soppressione-conservazione della retorica, empirica e ideologica, linguaggio imperfetto, da parte della semiologia, scientifica, linguaggio rigoroso.[3]

Per sfuggire a questa sorta di nuovo senso comune sulla retorica, credo sia per prima cosa necessario, nel lavoro storiografico, avvalersi in modo diverso del riferimento all'edificio retorico antico. Il problema vero, infatti, non è tanto constatare quanto e cosa venga sottratto all'edificio antico per essere dislocato altrove (esempio ricorrente è il trasferimento ramista di *inventio* e *dispositio* alla logica) e vedere solo in quanto resta alla retorica il filo conduttore della sua storia; il vero problema è costituito dalle trasformazioni di configurazione e significato che, in questo gioco di spostamenti, investono la retorica *nel suo assetto complessivo di disciplina* e le sue singole categorie costitutive (*inventio dispositio* etc.) nei loro percorsi "dentro e fuori" la disciplina retorica.[4]

L'ipotesi di lavoro dentro cui si muovono queste pagine è dunque un'indagine sull'*inventio*: più precisamente, secondo una linea d'indagine che ricerca il rapporto, se vi sia e quale, fra *inventio* retorica antica e *invenzione* estetica moderna. Rapporto da studiare percorrendo molti campi (non ultimo, per importanza, l'ambito delle teorie della pittura fra '400 e '600), al di fuori della disciplina retorica in senso stretto; qui, intanto, ci occuperemo del caso dell' *ars poetica* medievale.

E' noto che il *trivium* non contempla l'esistenza di una autonoma *ars poetica* tra grammatica e retorica; dalla tradizione antica vengono assegnati materiali poetici alla grammatica, per la duplice competenza dell'*ars* a trattare *vitia et virtutes orationis* e dedicarsi alla *enarratio poetarum*.[5] Accade perciò che nel concreto dei processi di trasmissione culturale, nelle scuole, sia l'*ars grammatica* la disciplina che controlla i fatti, per dirla con termine moderno, "letterari". In questo, opera dall'origine un'interferenza della retorica sulla grammatica, poiché concetti e criteri retorici intervengono nei meccanismi di spiegazione dei poeti e l'intero sistema di tropi e figure si trasferisce al capitolo "dei vizi e delle virtù" del discorso.

Quando, attorno al XII secolo, sorge sul terreno dell'*ars grammatica* una poetica, di cui è netto l'orientamento didattico,[6] è in gioco anche un'aumentata intensità dell'interferenza retorica: l'attenzione viva a testi quali la *rhetorica ad Herennium* e il *de inventione* prolunga e rafforza una mai spenta tradizione di trattatistica *de figuris*.[7] Non è riducibile però a ciò l'apparizione della poetica, che anzi la si può intendere come effetto e momento di una più generale e profonda crisi del sistema delle arti liberali: c'è una generale tensione a riarticolare il quadro del sapere, l'ordine e la gerarchia delle *artes*, nel complessivo maturare di nuove esigenze civili e culturali della "rinascenza del XII secolo." Si vedano, ad esempio, le preoccupazioni di un Ugo di S. Vittore nel tracciare e motivare un ordine delle discipline nel *Didascalicon*; e, per la poetica, la decisa presa di posizione di Giovanni di Salisbury a favore della stabilità del *trivium, aut poeticam grammatica obtinebit, aut poetica a numero liberalium disciplinarum eliminabitur*,[8] mentre nel *de divisione philosophiae* di Gondissalvi, con suggestioni aristoteliche, emerge una poetica come specifica disciplina, ancora legata a un'accezione grammaticale della poetica come metrica ma pur pensata in un coerente sviluppo del *loqui*.[9]

Un nuovo assetto della vita culturale e nuove rappresentazioni teoriche dell'ambito del sapere delineano l'orizzonte della situazione in cui appare l'*ars poetica*, germoglio della grammatica proiettata verso la retorica, e disposta nella costellazione delle nuove "arti verbali," *ars poetica, dictatoria, praedicatoria*.

Come si propone in questa poetica la categoria dell'*inventio*? Trattandosi di testi in cui il decorso delle parti è accuratamente delineato (il loro stesso carattere didattico ne impone l'esemplarità), cominciamo con l'osservare lo schema dell'*ars*;[10] si ricava il seguente materiale:

Matteo di Vendôme (Faral, pp. 151, 153–54, 179–80)

triplex versificandi elegantia:

1) interior favus (modus describendi) — venustas interioris sententiae — iudicium sententiarum in attributis negotio et personae — ornatus interioris sententiae — imaginatio sensus: sententiae conceptio
2) verba polita — superficialis ornatus verborum — sermo interpres intellectus: verborum excogitatio
3) dicendi color — modus dicendi — qualitas dicendi in scematibus et tropis — qualitas dicendi — ordinatio in qualitate tractatus: qualitas materiae sive tractatus dispositio inoltre,
4) exsecutio materiae

Gervaso di Melkley (Gräbener, pp. 6, 89, 155)

schema tripartito più supplementi:

1) idemptitas (locus ab eodem): oratio sine omni transumptione vel contrarietate absolute prolata
2) similitudo (locus a simili): prolatio vocis aliqua similitudinariam equipollentiam assignantis sive expresse sive inexpresse
3) contrarietas (locus a contrario): a rebus vel dictionibus contrariis ornata sententia
4) paroemia
5) munditia
6) argumenta

Goffredo di Vinsauf (Faral, pp. 198–99, 260)

schema a cinque punti:

1) inventio commoda 2) sermo continuus 3) series urbana 4) retentio firma 5) recitatio facta venuste

1) mentis in arcano cum rem digesserit ordo, materiam verbis veniat vestire poesis . . . circinus interior mentis

praecircinet omne materiae spatium . . . mens discreta
praeambula facti tractet diu de themate secum   *inventio*

2) quo limite debeat ordo currere, qua compensare statera
pondera (ordo naturalis et artificialis, amplificatio et
abreviatio)   *dispositio*

3) corpus verborum (ornatus facilis et difficilis)   *elocutio*

4) assente nella prefazione ma presente nella trattazione   *memoria*

5) vox castigata modeste   *actio*

Giovanni di Garlandia (Lawler, pp. 2, 4)

schema in accessus:
      ars inveniendi – eligendi – memorandi – ordinandi – ornandi

schema in prefazione:

1) doctrina inveniendi	2) de modo eligendi materiam (contiene dottrina della memoria)
3) de dispositione et de modo ordinandi materiam	4) de partibus dictaminis
5) de viciis vitandis	6) de rhetorico ornatu
7) exempla litterarum, etc.	

Come si vede, né Matteo né Gervaso fanno cenno dell'*inventio*;[11] lo schema di Gervaso si costruisce su categorie completamente estranee alla partizione a cinque di *inventio dispositio etc.*; in Matteo se ne può forse leggere una traccia indiretta, quando egli giustifica la partizione del trattato nella *triplex versificandi elegantia* appellandosi alla successione effettiva *in poeticae facultatis exercitio*, dove si verifica un'analoga sequenza tripartita.[12] Sembra tuttavia insufficiente l'opposizione tra *sententiae conceptio* e *verborum excogitatio* per potersi riferire, qui, alla categoria dell'*inventio*. In Goffredo, se la menzione esplicita dell'*inventio* si limita a quella formula riassuntiva nella parte finale del trattato che parafrasa le categorie classiche,[13] è anche presente nella parte introduttiva una serie di esortazioni e consigli che configurano una sorta di *inventio*: dico una sorta di *inventio* perché non è tanto per il loro contenuto che sono assegnabili a questa categoria, quanto piuttosto per la loro collocazione nell'ordine del trattato. Per il loro contenuto, infatti, esse raccomandano in sostanza la priorità della *manus cordis* sulla *manus corporis*, la necessità di una preliminare meditazione e misura interiore della *materia* nella sua interezza:[14] tanto da profilare un'opposizione netta, come tra *interior* e *exterior*, con tutta la restante precettistica. Possiamo considerare ciò come *inventio* soprattutto considerando i compiti che vengono di seguito enunciati: 1) *quo limite . . .* e 2) *qua compensare . . .* (dottrina dell'*ordo* e dell'*amplificatio*), assimilabili alla *dispositio*; 3) *corpus verborum . . .* (teoria dell'ornato), assimilabile all'*elocutio*; 4) *vox castigata. . .*, assimilabile all'*actio*. Se poi osserviamo che l'effettivo sviluppo del trattato comporta una sezione sulla *memoria* ma non contiene nessuna trattatistica specifica per l'*inventio*, si può affermare che siamo di fronte a uno schema che ricalca le cinque categorie antiche, risolvendosi però l'*inventio* in un momento esortativo-preliminare.

Una vera e propria trattazione dell'*inventio* l'abbiamo solo in Giovanni, nell'ambito di uno schema che riprende quello classico, escludendo l'*actio* e aggiungendo altri punti più marcatamente didattici (e, tranne l'*ars eligendi*, eterogenei rispetto allo schema antico).

Quanto sinora emerso ci autorizzerebbe a concludere per una sostanziale assenza dell'*inventio* nell'insieme dell'*ars poetica* latino-medievale, se già la presenza dello schema retorico a cinque punti è incerta e l'*inventio*, all'interno di questo schema, non è certo la parte forte. Il contenuto dell'*inventio* di Giovanni ci presenta tuttavia un materiale largamente presente nelle altre *artes*: è possibile unificarlo sotto criteri e categorie comuni? eccone intanto gli elementi essenziali:

definizioni: invenire est in ignote rei noticiam ductu proprie rationis
                venire

                invencio est rerum verarum et veri similium excogitatio
                que causam probabilem reddant

sub invencione species sunt quinque:

1) Ubi: tria   — persona: tria genera hominum (curiales, civiles, rurales)
                — exempla
                — ethimologia

2) Quid: — in personis: laus vel vituperium
                — in exemplis: facta, auctoritates et proverbia
                            (ars inveniendi proverbia)
                — in ethimologis: ethimologica expositio manifestat

3) Quale: materia honesta / turpis (insinuacio)

4) Ad Quid: finis inventoris (utilitas et honestas)

5) Qualiter: — VII colores quibus adornatur et ampliatur materia
                (annominatio, traductio, repetitio, gradatio, interpretatio,
                diffinitio, sermocinatio)
                — de arte inveniendi nomina substantiva: habita et
                excogitata materia, excogitanda sunt omnia nomina illa
                que pertinent ad talem materiam ... cognata verba et
                propria materie
                — de arte inveniendi adiectiva: ab effectu, eventu, habitu,
                loco, genere, quantitate, qualitate

—de arte inveniendi verba: raro licet nova verba invenire
(fingere de dictione nota)
—de arte transumendi verba
—de circumlocutione: rei verbi et nominis
—conversio verbi in nomen
—quot modis dicatur materia: secundum sex casus
nominis
—de arte inveniendi materiam: volentes ampliare et
variare materiam, non pretermittentes causas principales
IV (efficiens, materialis, formalis, finalis)

(Lawler, pp. 8-30)

Si inizia con due definizioni, una delle quali di stile nettamente etimologico,
l'altra citata dalla *Rhetorica ad Herennium*, 1, 2, 3. La suddivisione in *species*
riecheggia—*ubi, quid, quale, qualiter, ad quid*—la dottrina antica degli *attributa
negotio*. Vengono trattati rapidamente *quale* e *ad quid*: per l'uno si richiama
la doppia possibilità di una *materia honesta* o *turpis* (suggerendo la figura
dell'*insinuacio*); per l'altro si richiama il *finis inventoris* che è l'*utilitas et honestas*.
Ubi viene tripartito in *persona, exempla, ethimologia* (con una ulteriore ripartizione
delle *persone* in *tria genera hominum, curiales, civiles, rurales*) su cui si articola
a sua volta *quid* ottenendo: *laus vel vituperium (in personis); facta, auctoritates
et proverbia (in exemplis); ethimologica expositio manifestat (in ethim.).* Il punto
che ha maggior sviluppo è *qualiter*. Elencati 7 colori con i quali *adornatur et
ampliatur materia*, si propongono altri 8 procedimenti il cui criterio di
articolazione è in parte decisamente grammaticale. Lawler osserva che di questo
materiale ben poco pertiene al campo dell'*inventio* classica[15] (*persona, exempla,
ethimologia* e, aggiungiamo noi, la serie di *attributa* menzionati per l'*ars inveniendi
adiectiva*) e suggerisce la possibilità di interpretare lo schema della trattazione
in rapporto alle cause della filosofia scolastica: *ubi* e *quid* = *causa materialis,
quale* e *qualiter* = *c. formalis, ad quid* = *c. finalis*. Non mi pare, però, che si
possa cogliere il senso dell'articolazione che Giovanni dà all'*inventio* senza operare
confronti analitici con le altre *artes*. Per quanto riguarda la tripartizione interna
a *ubi* e *quid*, troviamo che:

1. *persona*: incontriamo le *proprietates personarum* in Matteo a
   proposito della *descriptio*, con un'ampia e analitica trattazione,[16]
   coincidente nella finalità con il *quid invenitur* di Giovanni, *laus vel
   vituperium*; analogamente in Goffredo è a proposito della *descriptio*
   che si raccomanda di osservare le *proprietates personarum et
   rerum*,[17] mentre Gervaso riserva una specifica appendice del suo
   trattato per gli *argumenta*.[18] C'è poi da notare che Giovanni tratta
   gli *attributa persone* non al capitolo dell'*inventio* ma in

chiusura del capitolo *de ornatu metri*, dopo la lista dei *colores verborum et sententiarum*, ricordandone la necessità sia *in amplianda* che *in abbrevianda materia*. I *tria genera hominum* con cui si specifica la *persona* dell'*inventio* hanno il loro riscontro, in Giovanni, nella teoria dello *stilus materie*, che pone *tres stili secundum tres status hominis* a motivare il precetto contro la *incongrua stilorum variatio*[19] (medesima definizione in Goffredo dello stile, e in un analogo contesto, sui vizi da evitare).[20] In Giovanni ricompare la tripartizione degli stili come tecnica dell'*ars memorandi* inserita nell'*ars eligendi*, con la conclusione che *eligenda sunt verba inventa ad quemlibet stilum in suo stilo;*[21]

2. *exempla*: in Matteo si consiglia l'uso di un *generale proverbium* o *communis sententia* come tecnica dell'esordio;[22] in Goffredo, *exemplum* e *proverbium* tra i colori dell'*ornatus facilis* e a proposito dell'*ordo artificialis*;[23] in Gervaso, un'altra appendice è dedicata a *paroemia*;[24]

3. *ethimologia*: Matteo indica l'*argumentum a nomine* nella *descriptio personae*;[25] Gervaso, a proposito dell'*annominatio* (come figura della *polita idemptitas per conservantiam*), nomina un caso in cui essa è *adeo ampla quod fere repetitionem parit*:[26] l'esempio dato, *fortuna fortis una*, è sovrapponibile ad una *expositio* etimologica.[27]

Trascuriamo le species *quale* e *ad quid* per la loro brevità e generalità, e soffermiamoci su *qualiter*:

1. *VII colores*: sono colori riferibili, per Goffredo e Gervaso, rispettivamente all'ornata *facilitas* e all'*idemptitas*; si osservi come Giovanni assegni loro il compito di *adornare et variare materiam*;

2. *de arte inveniendi nomina substantiva*: è questo un passaggio estremamente significativo, poiché vi si esprime un nesso tra *materia* e *verba* analogo a quello rilevato per la teoria dello stile: *cognata verba et propria materie*, questo nesso mostra l'esigenza di una omogeneità della *materia*, omogeneità che possiamo comprendere solo se intendiamo con *materia* non tanto un'astratta *res* pre-linguistica, ma una *res* cui compete una "propria," "naturale" estrinsecazione linguistica: il *verbum proprium et cognatum materiae* è la "faccia linguistica" della *materia*. L'omogeneità, la congruità a sè della *materia* comporta dunque un aspetto tematico e linguistico, che non sono disgiungibili[28]. Analoga dottrina in Goffredo, sempre a proposito di *vitia* da evitare, o a ribadire il precetto di osservare le *proprietates* affinchè vi sia congruità fra *verba* e *res*, o anche in quella tecnica di

abreviatio che si appunta sui *nomina rerum in quibus consistit vis materiae.*[29]

Osserviamo poi come Giovanni riconosca due motivi per "uscire" dalla stretta e assoluta chiusura e coerenza a sè della *materia: causa materiam ampliandi (digressio)* e *causa ydemptitatis vitande (materie variatio);*[30]

3. *de arte inveniendi adiectiva*: come già visto, si concreta in una lista di *attributa*;

4. *de arte inveniendi verba*: sul fatto che *raro licet fingere nova verba* Giovanni concorda con Goffredo; trascurando il dettaglio dell'argomentazione limitativa di Goffredo, è più interessante notare che egli ne parla (dopo aver raccomandato l'osservanza degli *attributa personae*) solo come di un supplemento rispetto al compito di porre *verbum notum in nova significatione*, compito che è più pienamente assolto dai tropi della *difficultas ornata* che opera sull'improprietà, sullo spostamento semantico della parola.[31] Gervaso tratta dei *nova verba* in un contesto più sistematicamente analitico. Siamo nell'ambito della *similitudo*, al cui interno si distingue tra *assumptio* e *transumptio*;[32] distinguendo poi tra *ass. vocis non significative / vocis sign.*, si hanno come casi di *ass. vocis non sign.*:

a) *nomen barbarum*

b) *penuria dictionum compositarum*

c) *nova verba*: il *novum verbum* deve essere *signatum presente nota, idest expressa ratione inventionis presente;*[33] la *nota* può essere *intrinsecus et extrinsecus* oppure solo *intrinsecus*; negli esempi e nella argomentazione emerge una parentela con i procedimenti di *expositio* etimologica: l'espressione della *ratio inventionis* del *novum verbum*, ossia la *nota*, è una sorta di etimologia: *preliliat lilia* esprime correttamente *intrinsecus et extrinsecus* la propria *nota*, mentre sarebbe scorretto *preliliat nivem;*[34]

d) ulteriori classificazioni secondo categorie grammaticali più l'*inventio* per *onomatopeia*.

Medesimo decorso secondo categorie grammaticali ha la classificazione dell'*ass. vocis sign.*, con l'aggiunta finale della *catachresis*. C'è in Gervaso un altro cenno all'*invenire nomina*, a proposito della *transumptio orationis per apparentiam, alia sensualitatis, alia rationis*: "per sensualitatem etiam adinventa sunt multa nomina deorum et dearum et etiam multe fabule gentilium. sed de demonibus nihil ad presens . . . rationis apparentia deorum numerum et nomina sua constituit fantasia".[35] Non è certo una tematica dei *nova verba* nel senso sopra visto, tuttavia il problema esegetico dei *nomina* delle *fabule* non è senza relazioni con la tematica, propria dell'*ars poetica*, dei *verba* della *materia*;

5. *de arte transumendi verba*: una *congrua transumptio* si effettua dal "corpo" all' "anima" e viceversa; da rilevare che è l'unica menzione esplicita di un procedimento nettamente assegnabile all'*ornatus difficilis*;

6. *de circumlocutione*: consueta tecnica di *amplificatio* e *descriptio*; ·

7. e 8. *conversio, quot modis dicatur materia*: tecniche simili di trasformazioni grammaticali sono elencate da Gervaso sotto la categoria generale di *idemptitas* e quella più particolare di *diversio*;[36] Goffredo, tratta delle conversioni grammaticali come di operazione preliminare alla *transsumptio*, che si effettua al livello di parole *proprie sumpta*;[37]

9. *de arte inveniendi materiam*: più che le 4 *causae principales*, abbastanza ovvie, mi pare vada sottolineata la motivazione, in certo modo riassuntiva di tutta la dottrina dell'*inventio*: *volentes ampliare et variare materiam*.

Per tentare adesso qualche considerazione sintetica, vorrei partire proprio da queste parole di Giovanni, *ampliare et variare materiam*, emblematicamente rappresentative della problematica essenziale dell'*ars poetica*, che consiste nell'articolare e combinare *identià* e *variazione*.

Dalla lista di Giovanni e dai successivi riscontri sulle altre *artes* ricaviamo infatti un blocco di procedimenti riferibile a:

ampliare materiam: *ordo, amplificatio, descriptio, proprietates personarum et rerum*: siamo a quel livello che Matteo denomina *venustas interioris sententiae* e *modus describendi*;

variare materiam: colori e tecniche della *facilitas ornata*: è il livello di *variatio* che non fa intervenire i tropi, livello al quale non si altera la congruenza-proprietà dei *verba* alle *res*, l'identità a sè della *materia-sententia* nel suo sviluppo di *res et personae*.

Si tratta complessivamente di procedimenti che operano secondo criteri di addizione, diversione e accumulo su un piano omogeneo, mediante paradigmi retorici (*attributa personae et negotio*) e grammaticali (*sex casus nominis, conversio* etc.) che non fanno intervenire lo scarto semantico, l'improprietà dei tropi.

Il tono e il linguaggio, schiettamente grammaticali, di molta parte di questa precettistica non devono essere letti in maniera riduttiva, come mera adeguazione

PAOLO BAGNI

a una prassi didattica: allo stesso modo che in ambito esegetico la grammatica
è il criterio di quel livello di senso che è la *littera-historia*,[38] cosi qui non va
dimenticato che la grammatica è necessariamente pertinente ad una *materia*
da intendersi come ambito di *res et personae* nella loro rappresentazione
linguistica.[39]

In questa parziale grammaticalizzazione, in questo disporsi per *loci* grammaticali
oltrechè retorici, l'*inventio* diviene dunque dottrina dell'*ampliare et variare
materiam*, criterio di elaborazione di una *materia proposita*, in contiguità e
continuità con la grammatica che governa la necessità-proprietà verbale della
materia. In ciò, evidentemente, via via si affievolisce ogni opposizione tra *inventio*
e *dispositio*: lo schema di Giovanni che distingue *ars inveniendi* e *ordinandi* non
rende pienamente giustizia al contenuto effettivo delle *artes*, che tendono appunto
ad accorpare blocchi di procedimenti che valgano come criterio di sviluppo
della proprietà-identità della *materia*, su cui semmai interviene un'opposizione
tra *res* e *verba* tale da prospettare una *venustas interioris sententiae* contro un
superficialis ornatus verborum (Matteo) o una dottrina di *ordo, amplificatio, abreviatio*
contro una *facilitas ornata* (Goffredo). Da un lato, dunque, integrazione di *inventio*
e *dispositio* in una dottrina dell'*ampliare et variare materiam*; d'altro lato, però,
emerge anche una nuova connotazione dell'*inventio* proprio dove questa
integrazione è di fatto completa. In Goffredo, infatti, mentre la precettistica
si ordina sotto le categorie di *ordo* e *amplificatio*, affiora un'idea di *inventio* o
piuttosto di *invenire* che, con caratteristiche di interiorità-anteriorità, *prius in
pectore quam in ore*, si oppone a tutte le restanti operazioni: un *invenire* che
non si coordina tanto nella sequenza funzionale classica (*inv., disp.*, etc.), quanto
piuttosto si propone come "pensamento"[40] che abbraccia la totalità della opera,
suo "disegno interiore" più che fase della sua elaborazione.[41]

In questa direzione di significato dell'*invenire* va collocata anche la prima
definizione di Giovanni, nella forma di *expositio* etimologica;[42] di contro alla
definizione classica che blocca le *res* oggetto dell'*inventio* in una ferma struttura
categoriale (*res verae aut veri similes*), secondo un punto di vista funzionale (*quae
causam probabilem reddant*), la definizione etimologica sottolinea piuttosto il
processo intellettuale soggettivo di investigazione e ricerca, senze dir nulla
dell'oggetto *inventum* (in —*ignote rei noticiam* — *ductu proprie rationis* —venire).
Forse, le qualità del prodotto, dell'*inventum*, si possono correlare a certe tracce
lessicali che affiorano in Gervaso,[43] e che sembrano quasi suggerire il gesto
di una motivata, consapevole scoperta: si veda quell'aggettivo *inventicium* che,
in coppia endiadica con *ficticium*, rimanda a un'area di esercizio dell'*invenire*
in cui affiora il tema dell'inedito, del "nuovo," come sviluppo *fictivus* di una
materia data, riferito qui alla sola dimensione verbale della *materia*, ma non
senza un presagio della prossimità, che tempi successivi produrranno, fra i termini
"invenzioni" e "finzioni."[44]

Sono tracce minime, ma siamo probabilmente su quella via lungo cui si produrrà un'accezione di *inventio* oggettuale e plurale, a significare non più l'operazione prima dell'atto di costruzione retorica, bensì *inventiones*, effetti tematici, inediti sviluppi della *materia*; si vedano le *peregrinas et inauditas inventiones*, gli *inventa perlucida atque peregrina* del Boccaccio, all'interno di una definizione della poesia giocata su due termini, *invenire* e *dicere*.[45] E si potrà, poi, correlare a queste *inventiones* come effetti tematici l'accezione che acquista il termine *poetrie* in ambiente francese tra XIV e XV secolo: quando, incentrandosi la sua definizione sul *fingere*, "la fin et l'entencion de poetrie si est de faindre hystoires ou aultres choses selon le propos duquel on veult parler, et de fait son nom se demonstre, car poetrie n'est aultre chose a dire ne mais science qui aprent a faindre," accade che il suo contenuto si riparta fra una lista delle "figures contenans en brief ficcions et histoires" e una delle "hystoires plus essenciels de la Bible, prouffitables pour ditter les propos qui amennent."[46] Qui, sul livello narrativo della *materia*, la *poetrie* si flette in repertorio di temi, di *fabulae*, catalogo di *inventiones*. Ma torniamo ai nostri testi. Ora, stimolati da quell'*inventicium et ficticium* di Gervaso, vorrei un momento riprendere la tematica dei *nova verba*, che mi sembra il punto cruciale dell'*inventio*. Cruciale perché lì s'insinuano le categorie dello spostamento tropico, estraneo, come s'è visto, all'*inventio* in quanto *ampliare et variare materiam*. Il tema dei *nova verba* va connesso con l'etimologia, perché si annodano insieme nella problematica della congruità tra *nomina* e *res*. Ricordiamo che l'etimologia appare appena nelle nostre *artes*, come *argumentum a nomine* in Matteo oltre alla menzione di Giovanni; ma il suo meccanismo concettuale (riducibilità di un *nomen* alla sua *vis*) viene usato da Goffredo in un movimento simmetrico e contrario all'espansione dell'*expositio* etimologica: la restrizione all'essenziale dell'*abbreviatio*, l'operazione che riduce la *materia* alla sua *vis*, ai *nomina in quibus consistit vis materiae*. *Nomina*, dunque, come contenuto essenziale, "verità" della *materia*; ma accanto a questo *nomen* in perfetta adeguazione alla sua *materia* si profila la possibilità di un *nomen inventicium et ficticium*, non pensabile come "proprietà" della *materia* e che ci rinvia a quella *sensualitatis apparentia* mediante la quale *adinventa sunt multa nomina deorum et dearum et multe fabule gentilium*, e a quella *rationis apparentia che deorum numerum et nomina sua constituit fantasia*.[47] Certo Gervaso accenna e chiude immediatamente con questo tema dei *nomina deorum* e delle *fabule gentilium, sed de demonibus nihil ad presens*: è infatti tema più esegetico che di *ars poetica*, ma riguarda pure in profondità la poesia. Vorrei anch'io limitarmi a un accenno e lo farò disponendo l'uno accanto all'altro tre testi:

Goffredo, Faral, p. 253: si . . . rebus verba coaptes
  (introduce la parte conclusiva della teoria dell'*ornatus*, contenente precetti generali; segue immediatamente il richiamo alle *proprietates personae et negotio*)

Corrado di Hirsau, *Dialogus*, ed. Huygens 1970, p. 113:
> necesse est ut in stilo tuo iuxta materiae initium semper sit consequentia rerum
>
> (a commento dell'*ars poet*. di Orazio, della sua *utilitas*)

Dante, *Vita Nuova*, XIII:
> lo nome d'Amore è sì dolce a udire, che impossibile mi pare che la sua propria operazione sia ne le più cose altro che dolce, con ciò sia cosa che li nomi seguitino le nominate cose, sì come è scritto: "Nomina sunt consequentia rerum."

Corrado, p. 99:

> (D) . . . videri possunt loca vel personae vel quarumcumque corporalium vel contrectabilium rerum substantiae, qualitates earum . . . videri non possunt – (M) Recte sentis . . . cuiuscumque coloris videri quidem possunt substantiae, albedo, rubedo, nigredo nec videri nec tangi possunt, quia subiectorum suorum qualitates vel accidentia sunt; sic de fide quamvis substantia sed invisibili . . . – (D) Qualiter igitur me vis intelligere duellum singulare viciorum vel virtutum sine personali materia? – (M) Tropice, id est per figuram metonomiam haec accipienda sunt.
>
> (a proposito della *materia* della Psicomachia di Prudenzio)

Dante, *Vita Nuova*, XXV:
> Potrebbe qui dubitare persona degna da dichiararle onne dubitazione, e dubitare potrebbe di ciò, che io dico d'Amore come se fosse una cosa per sè, e non solamente sustanzia intelligente, ma sì come fosse sustanzia corporale: la quale cosa, secondo la veritate, è falsa; ché Amore non è per sè sì come sustanzia, ma è uno accidente in sustanzia.

C'è una *consequentia* tra *verba* e *res* che si articola, senza soluzioni di continuità, in tre momenti:

a) elaborazione con le tecniche adeguate, in ogni punto dell'*opus*, dei *verba* congrui alle *res: res condita tota est condita*;[48]

b) omogeneità dello *stilus* nello sviluppo sequenziale dell'*opus*: *iuxta materiae initium semper sit consequentia rerum*;

c) congruità del *nomen* alla *res* come sua verità "etimologica".

Rispetto a ciò il problema dei *nomina ficticia* si pone come problema di un *nomen* senza *materia*, di un *nomen* cui non corrisponde una *persona*, in assenza di *personalis materia*. Se l' "accidente in sustanzia" dantesco pare rimandarci al linguaggio filosofico, i medesimi termini in Corrado rimandano chiaramente all'ambito retorico delle *proprietates personarum et rerum*: interessante perciò la spiegazione *tropice*, che evoca uno spostamento tropico, *per figuram metonomiam*, ma a livello della *materia* non dell'*elocutio*. Per questa via, evidentemente, verremmo a trovarci sul terreno di questioni quali *fabula, allegoria, integumentum*: ci basti intanto osservare come tale tropicità a livello della *materia* può gettare qualche luce sulla dottrina dell'*invenire* che abbiam tentato di ricostruire, sul modello di poesia che essa implica.

Per concludere riassumendo, si è visto che l'*inventio*, quanto alla sua collocazione nell'*ars*, o si contrae in una virtuale opposizione *inventio/elocutio* (*prius in pectore quam in ore*) che apre ampio spazio alle tecniche dell'*ordo* e dell'*amplificatio* per articolare la dottrina della *materia*; o assume su di sè parte di questa dottrina disponendola per *loci* grammaticali e retorici. Se l'assenza dell'*inventio* è leggibile come funzionale al livello didattico dell'*ars grammatica*, c'è anche una parziale dislocazione dell'*inventio* sulla grammatica, un suo disporsi per categorie grammaticali. Inoltre, affiora una connotazione di interiorità-anteriorità (*mentis in arcano, circinus interior mentis*) non riducibile a fonti antiche, accanto a cui certe tracce lessicali in Gervaso e la dottrina dei *nova verba*, con il tema della *nota*, della *ratio inventionis*, ci richiamano alla definizione che Giovanni dà di *invenire*, incentrata sul *ductu proprie rationis*.

L'idea di *inventio* che così si disegna, insieme alla verifica che i procedimenti assegnati da Giovanni all'*ars inveniendi* insistono sulla, e sviluppano la, *proprietas* della *materia*, porta in primo piano, quale correlato di questo *invenire*, la nozione appunto di *materia* (ambito di *res et personae* nella sua "propria" rappresentazione linguistica).

Avanzando poi qualche proiezione su testi ulteriori alle *artes* di cui ci siamo occupati (e con la cautela che compete ad ipotesi di lavoro più che ad asserzioni verificate), una dottrina della *materia* che si presenti come elaborazione di un tema dato (*propositum*) nella sua necessità-proprietà e narrativa e verbale, fa emergere il tema dell'etimologia. Più esattamente, lo statuto ambiguo dell'etimologia, che si colloca tra *proprietas* dei *nomina rerum* (con la connotazione di "verità", di *vis materiae*) e *improprietas* dei *nomina per apparentiam* (con un rimando ai criteri della *similitudo*), propone l'interessante questione, da Corrado a Dante, di una tropicità della *materia* come tipo di rapporto, di *ratio*, fra "nome" e "personaggio."

Quando infine, in Boccaccio, troviamo una *inventio* obiettivata in *inventiones* cui son pertinenti qualità (*dilucida et peregrina*) che l'*ars poetica* riservava semmai all'*elocutio*; mentre la nozione di *materia* si divarica, da un lato, nel repertorio di temi o *fabulae* (la *poetrie* francese, le stesse Genealogie del Boccaccio), e dall'altro nella codificazione della verità poetica in una strategia di lettura (tecniche dell'*explanatio* allegorica); ebbene, in tutto questo possiamo vedere alcuni segni, alcune delle condizioni che consentiranno all'*inventio* ricchi sviluppi nella direzione di senso delle "peregrine invenzioni," quando importano più gli effetti tematici del *costrutto* retorico che non l'efficacia persuasiva del *costruire* retorico.

Note

1. V. Florescu, *La retorica nel suo sviluppo storico* (Bologna 1971) (Bucureşti 1960).
2. *Figure III*, Torino 1976 p. 18 (Paris 1972, già in *Communications*, 16, 1970).
3. Si veda il pur notevole Paul Zumthor, *Essai de poétique médiévale*, Paris 1972, e "Erich Auerbach ou l'éloge de la philologie," *Littérature* 5 (1972), pp. 107–16.
4. Metodologicamente utili le nozioni di "démantèlement," "écartelèment," "retour de l'écarté" in P. Kuentz, Le "rhétorique" ou la mise à l'écart, *Communications*, 16, 1970, pp. 143–57.
5. Cfr. K. Barwick, *Probleme der stoischen Sprachlehre und Rhetorik*, (Berlin 1957) e *Remmius Palaemon und die Römische Ars Grammatica*, (Leipzig 1922); D. van Berchem, "Poètes et grammairiens. Recherche sur la tradition scolaire d'explication des auteurs," *Museum Helveticum*, 9, 1952, pp. 79–87.
6. Cfr. J. J. Murphy, *Rhetoric in the Middle Ages*, (Berkeley-Los Angeles-London 1974).
7. La *Poetria Nova* di Goffredo di Vinsauf, ad esempio, è nota anche con la denominazione *Galfredi rethorica*; cfr. D. Kelly, "The Scope of the Treatment of Composition in the Twelfth – and Thirteenth-Century Arts of Poetry," *Speculum*, XLI, 1966, p. 271.
8. *Metalogicon*, I, xvii.
9. "Poetica est sciencia componendi carmina metrice," "cum grammatica sit prima et post grammaticam poetica profecto post poeticam discenda est consequenter rethorica; racio enim exigit, ut qui primum per grammaticam docetur recte loqui, consequenter discat per poeticam qualiter delectet auditorem vel prosit; deinde qui per poeticam delectare vel prodesse iam novit, continuo discat per rethoricam, qualiter persuadere et movere auditorem possit," L. Baur (ed.), *Dominicus Gundissalinus, de divisione philosophiae*, (Münster 1903), pp. 54, 68–69.
10. In riferimento ai seguenti testi: Matteo di Vendôme, *Ars versificatoria* e Goffredo di Vinsauf, *Poetria Nova*, editi in E. Faral, *Les Arts Poétiques du XIIe et du XIIIe siècle*, (Paris 1924), Gervaso di Melkley, *Ars poetica*, ed. H.-J. Gräbener, (Münster 1965),Giovanni di Garlandia, *Parisiana Poetria*, ed. T. Lawler, (New Haven-London 1974.)
11. D. Kelly, op. cit., correla l'assenza e la presenza dell'*inventio* ad un livello didattico più elementare, grammatica, o più complesso, retorica.
12. "Prior est sententiae conceptio, sequitur verborum excogitatio, subjungitur qualitas scilicet materiae, sive tractatus dispositio," Faral, p. 180.
13. "Inventio commoda, sermo continuus, series urbana, retentio firma, recitatio facta venuste," Faral, p. 260.
14. "Circinus interior mentis praecircinet omne materiae spatium," Faral, p. 199.
15. Cfr. pp. 229–30.
16. Cfr. Faral, pp. 119, 135 sgg.

17. Faral, p. 310.
18. Gräbener, pp. 202–3.
19. Lawler, p. 86.
20. "Ratione personarum vel rerum de quibus fit tractatus," Faral, p. 312.
21. Lawler, p. 38.
22. Faral, p. 113.
23. Faral, pp. 201, 236.
24. Gräbener, p. 182.
25. Faral, p. 136.
26. E aggiunge: "cognata est ubi una inflectitur ex reliqua . . . fit quasi per quandam derivationem", Gräbener, pp. 14–15.
27. Cfr. in Faral, p. 65, come esempio di *interpretatio per dictiones* "fortuna, quae forte una".
28. "Incongrua materie varitio: . . . incidit poeta in vicium narrando gravem materiam per iocosa et comica, iocosam materiam per gravia," Lawler, p. 88; "potest et humilis materia exaltari, ut in gravi materia coli muliebres vocantur 'inbelles haste' ", Lawler, p. 86.
29. Faral, pp. 253–54, 256, 279, 317.
30. Lawler, p. 8; crf. in Matteo la perifrasi come *permutatio materiae*, Faral, p. 185.
31. Faral, p. 311.
32. "Similitudo est prolatio vocis aliqua similitudinariam equipollentiam assignantis", Gräbener, p. 89; "assumptio est accomodatio vocis ad significationem vel consignificationem quam ex institutione non habet per similitudinem extra sumptam", ibid.; "transumptio est translatio vocis a propria signifi ad alienam per similitudinem intransumptam," ibid., p. 108.
33. Gräbener, pp. 91–92.
34. Ibid.
35. Gräbener, p. 143.
36. "Causa ornatus ab ordinis planicie digredimur", Gräbener, p. 59; Goffredo usa *planities* per caratterizzare l'*ornatus facilis*, Faral, p. 231.
37. Faral, pp. 246–47.
38. "Ad litteram constructio et continuatio pertinet", Ugo di S. Vittore, *Didascalicon*, ed. C. H. Buttimer, Washington 1939, p. 126.
39. Cfr. F. Quadlbauer, *Die antike Theorie der genera dicendi im lateiniscen Mittelalter*, (Wien 1962).
40. Termine di Brunetto Latini, *La Rettorica*, ed. F. Maggini, (Firenze, 1915; 1968), pp. 73–.
41. In Goffredo e Brunetto ricorre l'immagine della costruzione, della *inventio* come "pensamento" o "disegno interiore" anteriore alla esecuzione, e che abbraccia la totalità dell'opera. E. Gallo riconduce ciò a Quintiliano, "This image occurs in Quintilian (VIII. pref., 1) in the same context as in the *Poetria Nova*—that is, in reference to the arrangement of the parts of a work." *The Poetria Nova and its Sources in Early Rhetorical Doctrine* (The Hague-Paris, 1971) p. 137. Ma l'uso dell'immagine non è omogeneo perfettamente, per chè riferito qua alla *dispositi* e là all'*inventio*; oltre a questo, se vale un'opposizione *res/verba* in Quintiliano, *res* designa una fase di elaborazione del discorso (punto di vista funzionale), mentre *materia-res* in Goffredo designa e una fase di elaborazione e uno strato del discorso (punto di vista sequenziale).

42. Cfr. R. Klinck, *Die lateinische Etymologie des Mittelalters*, (München 1970), pp. 30 sgg.

43. *Inventio modernorum, invenimus quaesita, ratio inventionis, inventicium et ficticium*, Gräbener, pp. 3, 22, 90–91, 101, 104.

44. Solo per gettare un'altra traccia, osserviamo poi che sarebbe interessante indagare distanza e parentela tra il *nomen ficticium* di Gervaso e quel *nomen facticium* che Papia dà come caso di *derivatio* "per immutationem a proprietate sonorum, quod facticium dicitur, ut tyntinabulum turtur," in Klinck, op. cit., p. 26.

45. "Poesis est fervor quidam exquisite inveniendi atque dicendi, seu scribendi, quod inveneris," *Gen. deor. gent.*, XIV, 6–7.

46. E. Langlois, *Recueil d'Arts de Seconde Rhétorique*, Genève 1974 (Paris 1902), p. IX .

47. Gräbener, p. 143.

48. Faral, p. 254.

Zur Theorie der Komposition in der mittelalterlichen Rhetorik und Poetik

FRANZ QUADLBAUER
University of Kiel

I

WAS DIE MITTELLATEINISCHEN Poetiken und *Artes dictaminis*, die ja im Mittelalter die wesentlichen Träger literarischer Theorie sind, zur Komposition literarischer Werke, zur *dispositio*, wie der rhetorische Terminus für den Werkaufbau lautet (*compositio* wird seit der Antike normalerweise für den Satzbau, die Wortfügung im Satz verwendet[1]), zu sagen haben, ist im Vergleich zu ihren umfangreichen und differenzierten Praecepta für Ausdruck und Stil recht knapp.[2] Diese relativ karge mittellateinische Theorie der *dispositio* hat — typisch für den Hang des Mittelalters zum Formalistischen — als prominenten Bestandteil ein Schema von zwei Aufbautypen, das Schema des *ordo naturalis* und *artificialis*, der natürlichen und der 'künstlichen,' der kunstgemäßen, kunstvollen Anordnung.

Das Schema bezieht sich im Normalfall auf die Darbietung von Erzählstoffen, von Geschehensfolgen. Geschehenes, *res gestae*, kann man nun, und das ist auch die in dem Schema zugrundegelegte Scheidung, entweder in der tatsächlichen zeitlichen Folge erzählen (das gibt dann den *ordo naturalis*), oder man kann in der Erzählung von der Chronologie der Ereignisse abweichen, die Aufbauform der Inversion wählen: das gibt den *ordo artificialis*, wie ihn — das bekannteste Beispiel — Vergil in der *Aeneis* anwendet. Denn Vergil berichtet am Beginn der *Aeneis* zunächst vom Seesturm und von der Landung des Aeneas in Karthago, und erst während des Gastmahls bei Dido läßt er — das Kunstmittel des 'Nachberichts', der Rückblendung anwendend — Aeneas das zeitlich Frühere, die Zerstörung Troias und die Irrfahrten erzählen und nachholen. Die tatsächliche Ereignisfolge ist also hier in der Erzählfolge verschoben, invertiert, aber in einer Weise natürlich, die den Leser über den 'wirklichen' Geschehnisablauf nicht im Unklaren läßt.

Die Knappheit der für das Referat zur Verfügung stehenden Zeit drängt dazu,

das angegebene Thema "Zur Theorie der Komposition" einzuengen auf die
mittelalterliche Lehre vom *ordo naturalis* und *artificialis*, die die Forschung bis
jetzt noch nicht in einer einläßlichen speziellen Studie, sondern in verschiedenen
Arbeiten jeweils nur als Teil– oder Nebenthema behandelt hat.[3] Über Herkunft
und Wandlung dieser Ordineslehre möchte ich ein paar Gedanken vortragen.

II

WIR TREFFEN DAS SCHEMA der *ordines* im Mittelalter zunächst, wie schon Faral
a.O. (Anm. 3) 56 hervorgehoben hat, in den Scholia Vindobonensia ad Horatii
artem poeticam, die im "Codex Vindobonensis nr. 223 (phil. 244)" in einer
Niederschrift des 10./11. Jahrhunderts überliefert sind, aber möglicherweise
schon in karolingischer Zeit verfaßt wurden.[4] Sehen wir nun zunächst kurz
die Horazpassage an, zu der der Scholiast seine Ordinestheorie vorträgt. Horaz
empfiehlt da einen *lucidus ordo* und sagt dann (*Ars poetica* 42–44):

> *Ordinis haec virtus erit et venus, aut ego fallor,*
> *ut iam nunc dicat iam nunc debentia dici,*
> *pleraque differatet praesens in tempus omittat.*

> Das ist die Tugend (Vorzüglichkeit) und die Anmut (Eleganz) des
> Aufbaus, oder ich täusche mich, daß er (der Dichter) schon jetzt sagt,
> was schon jetzt zu sagen ist, daß er sehr vieles aber verschiebt und für
> den Augenblick wegläßt.

Schon jetzt, also gleich, zu Beginn, zu sagen, was schon jetzt zu sagen ist
(natürlich auf Grund künstlerisch-aesthetischer Erwägungen), vieles aber für
den Augenblick wegzulassen und zu verschieben, das ist die Inversionstechnik
der Erzählung, wie sie z.B. Vergil anwendete.[5] Horaz bezeichnet solche Inversion
als *virtus et venus ordinis*.

Obgleich nun unser Scholiast manches hier recht eigenartig deutet, bemerkt
er zu V. 45 (mit Bezug auf den Inhalt der zitierten Verse 42–44) doch richtig,
daß Horaz hier den *ordo artificialis*, wie der Scholiast sagt, also die Inversion
der Erzählung, empfehle. Dann fügt der Scholiast hinzu:

> *Omnis ordo aut naturalis aut artificialis est. naturalis ordo est, si quis narret*
> *rem ordine, quo gesta est; artificialis ordo est, si quis non incipit a principio*
> *rei gestae, sed a medio, ut Virgilius in Aeneide quaedam in futuro dicenda*
> *anticipat et quaedam in praesenti dicenda in posterum differt.*

> Jede Anordnung (Aufbau) ist entweder natürlich oder 'künstlich'.
> Natürlich ist die Anordnung, wenn man die Handlung in der Ordnung

(Folge) erzählt, wie sie abgelaufen ist. 'Künstlich' ist die Anordnung, wenn man nicht mit dem Beginn der Handlung anfängt, sondern mit der Mitte, wie Vergil in der Aeneis manches, das erst später zu sagen wäre, vorausnimmt und manches, das 'im Augenblick' (sogleich) zu sagen wäre, auf später verschiebt.

Fragen wir uns nun, woher diese Theorie der *ordines* kommt: Das Terminipaar *naturalis* und *artificialis (ordo)* stammt offenbar aus der Ordineslehre der spätantiken Rhetorik; da bedeutet *ordo naturalis* allerdings (zum Unterschied von unserem Scholiasten) normalerweise das Beibehalten der üblichen Abfolge der bekannten Teile einer Rede: *prooemium, narratio, argumentatio, epilogus; ordo artificialis (artificiosus)* ist da das Abweichen von dieser Folge durch Invertieren oder Auslassen von Rede-Teilen,[6] etwa das Beginnen einer Rede mit der Narratio, also unter Weglassen des Prooemiums. Es ist zwar im Rahmen dieser rhetorischen Ordinestheorie auch die Rede etwa von einem Einhalten des *naturalis temporum ordo* im Anordnen der Argumente,[7] aber eine Beschreibung eines *naturalis* oder *artificialis ordo* in der Art unseres Scholiasten findet sich in diesem Zusammenhang nicht.[8] Die inhaltliche Bestimmung, die Definition der *ordines* beim Scholiasten ist also trotz der Gleichheit der Termini *naturalis/artificialis ordo* nicht aus der spätantiken rhetorischen Ordineslehre abzuleiten.

Aber die begriffliche Festlegung des *naturalis* beim Scholiasten (*si quis narret rem ordine, quo gesta est*) kommt doch aus der Rhetorik, nur aus einem anderen Teil des rhetorischen Lehrgebäudes, aus der Narratiolehre. Die um 80 vor Christ entstandene *Rhetorica ad Herennium*, die im Mittelalter als Werk Ciceros galt und wohlbekannt war, sagt über die *narratio dilucida* 1, 9, 15:

> *Rem dilucide narrabimus, si . . . rerum ac temporum ordinem conservabimus, ut gestae res erunt etc.*: Wir werden das Geschehen (die Handlung) klar darstellen, wenn wir die Reihenfolge der Fakten und Zeiten bewahren, wie die Dinge eben geschehen sind, *etc.*

Das ist offenkundig die Vorlage für die Definition des *naturalis* bei unserem Scholiasten.

Doch der *artificialis ordo*, den der Scholiast gegeben sieht, *si quis non incipit a principio rei gestae, sed a medio*, und für den er Vergil als Beispiel anführt, steht inhaltlich und formulierungsmäßig augenscheinlich in der Tradition der antiken Poetik, die (wie z.B. Servius) die Inversionstechnik Vergils als *a medio (a mediis) incipere* bezeichnet hat.[9] Die antike Poetik hält diese Inversionstechnik nun für die poetische Kunst, die *ars poetica* schlechtin (Servius), für die 'poetische Tugend,' die *virtus poetica* (Donat),[10] bzw. für die *virtus et venus ordinis* (so Horaz, wie wir oben gesehen haben).[11] Diese Hochbewertung des *a medio*–Verfahrens, die natürlich eine Abwertung des chronologischen Verfahrens einschließt, übernimmt der Scholiast für seinen *ordo artificialis* nicht, ebensowenig die Abwertung des chronologischen Verfahrens für seinen *ordo naturalis*. Denn der Scholiast betrachtet offenbar den *naturalis* im Sinne des rhetorischen Praeceptums für die *narratio dilucida*, das augenscheinlich auch seinem eigenen Empfinden entspricht, betrachtet den *naturalis* als das eben natürlich gegebene und anzuwendende Verfahren; und er konnte in dieser Wertung auch durch die antike rhetorische Ordineslehre bestärkt werden, die ihren *ordo naturalis* auch als das natürliche Normalverfahren ansieht, von dem man nur aus Gründen der Zweckmäßigkeit (*utilitas*) oder der Notwendigkeit (*necessitas*) abweichen solle.[12]

Aus dieser positiven Einstellung zum *naturalis*, der für den Scholiasten als das grundsätzlich Gegebene auch Maß und Richtpunkt ist, erklären sich auch seine oben zitierten, zunächst etwas eigenartig klingenden Worte über Vergils Vorgehen: a) Vergil nehme in der *Aeneis in futuro dicenda*, Dinge, die erst später zu sagen wären, voraus: das heißt hier, diese Dinge wären später zu sagen *secundum naturalem ordinem*, nach dem natürlichen *ordo*, der nach dem Scholiasten eben normalerweise angewendet werden müßte; b) ebenso sind die *quaedam in praesenti dicenda*, die Vergil, wie der Scholiast sagt, auf später verschiebt (*in posterum differt*), Dinge, die nach dem *naturalis ordo* 'sogleich zu sagen' wären. Anschließend an den oben S.116 zitierten Text bemerkt der Scholiast dann auch, erläuternd, ausdrücklich, Vergil hätte den Untergang Troias vorher (also am Beginn der *Aeneis*) schildern müssen (*prius debuisset dixisse*); dies hätte er tun müssen *secundum ordinem naturalem*; aber Vergil habe den *ordo* geändert und die Schilderung von Troias Untergang für eine bessere Zeit reserviert (*reservavit in melius tempus*), nämlich für den Zeitpunkt, da Aeneas dann beim Gelage an Didos Hof zum besonderen Vergnügen (*oblectamen*) der Gäste darüber habe berichten können. *Oblectamen*, ein gewählterer Ausdruck für *delectatio*, ist offenbar im Anschluß an die horazische These gesagt, die das *delectare* zu den Aufgaben der Poesie zählt (*Ars poetica* 333). Der Scholiast anerkennt also verbal, daß Vergil hier einen guten, aesthetisch fundierten Grund hatte für seine Änderung des *ordo*; aber man hat das Gefühl, daß das Anerkennen dieses Grundes vielleicht mehr nur der Autorität Vergils (der eben grundsätzlich der große Dichter ist und schon richtig verfahren sein wird) zuliebe geschieht: der Ausgangs– und Richtpunkt des Denkens und Urteilens des Scholiasten bleibt doch der *ordo naturalis*. Den Gedanken eines Invertierens des natürlichen *ordo* aus aesthetischen Gründen kann er, scheint es, nicht so richtig, nicht innerlich mitgehend nachvollziehen, mochte dieser Gedanke auch durch die – ihm wohl bekannte – Vergilerklärung (besonders Servius auctus) suggeriert werden[13] und mochte er auch in den Versen 42–44 der *Ars poetica*, die der Scholiast hier kommentiert, impliziert sein (vgl. oben am Anfang unseres Abschnittes II).

Es kommen also in der Ordineslehre des Scholiasten die Termini *naturalis/artificialis* aus der spätantiken rhetorischen Ordinestheorie, die inhaltliche Bestimmung stammt beim *naturalis* aus der rhetorischen Narratiolehre, beim *artificialis* aus der antiken Poetik. In der Wertung, vor allem in der sehr positiven Einschätzung des *naturalis* setzte sich die Einstellung der Rhetorik durch, die offenbar hier auch der vorgegebenen Ansicht des Scholiasten vom rechten Aufbau der Erzählung entsprach.

Die positive Einschätzung des *ordo naturalis* findet sich, wenn auch zum Teil etwas anders nuanciert, auch bei weiteren Autoren, so im 11. und 12. Jahrhundert bei Bernhard von Utrecht, Bernhard Silvester, Anselm von Laon und im *Accessus Lucani* (die übrigens alle Lukan, der chronologisch erzähle, als Muster für den *naturalis* anführen),[14] ferner bei Konrad von Hirsau[15] und Hugo von St. Victor.[16] (Abgesehen von Hugo und dem *Accessus Lucani* figuriert bei den hier aufgezählten Autoren stets Vergil als Repraesentant des *artificialis*).[17]

III

EINEN WANDEL in der aesthetischen Wertung der *ordines*, die bisher beide als positiv (zum Teil sogar bei stärkerem Hinneigen von Autoren zum *naturalis*) galten, bringt zu Beginn des 13. Jahrhunderts Galfrid von Vinsauf mit seiner *Poetria nova* (um 1210), die er bewußt als 'modernes' Gegenstück zur 'Poetria vetus' des Horaz verfaßte; Galfrid führt da zunächst das übliche Ordinespaar vor: er umschreibt den *artificialis ordo* versgerecht mit *limes artis*, Pfad der Kunst, den *naturalis* mit *strata naturae*, Straße der Natur (V.87f.); dann stellt er den *artificialis* V.91 als *aptior ordo* und V.100 gar als *longe prior ordo*, als weit überlegenen *ordo*, hoch über den *naturalis*. Damit hat Galfrid, aesthetisch wertend, dem *artificialis* jene hohe Wertschätzung gegeben, die in der antiken Poetik die Inversionstechnik, das *a medio*–Verfahren, genossen hatte, während sonst, nachweisbar seit dem Wiener Scholiasten, der *artificialis*, dank dem Einfluß der die *dispositio* nach Zweckmäßigkeit wertenden und den *naturalis* schätzenden Rhetorik, eine geringere Bewertung erfahren hatte. In der Beschreibung des *artificialis ordo* unterscheidet Galfrid in der *Poetria* acht Unterarten, die aber weitgehend nicht mehr richtig als Ordotypen, sondern mehr nur als Beginntypen gesehen sind, als Möglichkeiten, den Eingang eines Gedichtes zu gestalten.[18]

Konsequenterweise spricht dann Galfrid in seinem bald nach der *Poetria nova* verfaßten Prosatraktat, im *Documentum de modo et arte dictandi et versificandi*,[19] auch direkt von Principiatypen, von einem *principium naturale* und *artificiale*. Das *naturale* ist gegeben, "wenn die Darstellung dort beginnt, wo auch das Geschehen abzulaufen beginnt" (*quando sermo inde incipit, unde res geri incipit*), wenn also das Werk direkt mit der Schilderung des Handlungsbeginns einsetzt, ohne daß dem irgendetwas, etwa eine allgemeine Bemerkung (z.B. ein *proverbium*: vgl. unten), vorausginge. Dieses *principium naturale* bezeichnet

Galfrid, weil so etwas jeder könne, abwertend als bäurisch und gemein, *agreste vel vulgare*, was die höhere Einschätzung des *principium artificiale* impliziert, welche in der (oben erwähnten) Hochbewertung des *artificialis ordo* in der *Poetria nova* ihre *expressis verbis* geäußerte Parallele hat.

Das *artificiale principium* nun kann auf acht Arten (*octo modis*) gebildet werden:[20] Man setzt ein entweder direkt (also ohne der Narratio etwas vorauszuschicken) mit der Mitte des (Erzähl-) Stoffes (*a medio*, Typ 1), oder direkt mit dem Ende des Stoffes (*a fine*, Typ 2).[21] Man kann weiters einsetzen mit einem *proverbium*, *a proverbio*, (wobei es drei Möglichkeiten gibt), oder *ab exemplo*[22] (wofür wieder drei Variationen existieren). Die drei Möglichkeiten mit einem Proverb (die Typen 3–5) sind die, daß das Proverb (das übrigens inhaltlich auf den jeweiligen Narratiobeginn abgestimmt wird) neben dem Anfang (*principium*), der Mitte (*medium*) oder dem Ende des Erzählstoffes (*finis materiae*) stehen, das heißt, daß nach einem Proverb der Erzähleinsatz mit dem *principium*, *medium* oder dem *finis* der Handlung erfolgen kann. Dieselben 3 Möglichkeiten (das sind die Typen 6–8) hat man auch bei einem *exemplum* am Werksbeginn.

Wenn man sich die acht Arten des *principium artificiale*, die Galfrid nach einer Äußerung im *Documentum* offenbar, wenn auch nicht in sehr klarer Weise, als zum *ordo artificialis* in Beziehung stehend betrachtet,[23] näher ansieht, so zeigt es sich, daß zwei Arten nicht zu vereinbaren sind mit dem Begriff des traditionellen *ordo artificialis*: das sind die Typen 3 und 6, bei denen jeweils auf ein Proverb oder Exempel eine chronologisch verlaufende Narratio (die also mit dem Handlungsbeginn, dem *principium materiae*, einsetzt) folgt: eine chronologische Narratio gibt aber nach der traditionellen Ordineslehre einen *ordo naturalis*. Die Typen des artifizialen Beginns sind also von Galfrid, wenn auch mit dem *artificialis ordo* der Intention nach in Beziehung gesetzt, doch in der praktischen Ausführung nicht konsequent auf das Wesen dieses *ordo*, wie er üblicherweise gesehen wurde, ausgerichtet worden.

Die Schwierigkeit, die Ordines– und Principialehre aufeinander abzustimmen, ergibt sich daraus, daß die Ordineslehre andere Bestimmungskriterien hat als die Principiatheorie. Die Ordineslehre faßt nur den Erzählstoff (*materia*) und dessen Darstellung ins Auge; ist der Aufbau der Narratio chronologisch, so ist das *ordo naturalis*, wird die *a medio*- bzw. *a fine*-Technik in der Erzählung angewendet, gibt das den *ordo artificialis*. Was der eigentlichen Narratio eventuell vorausgeht, z.B. ein Prooemium wie in der *Aeneis*, ist für die Entscheidung, ob der *naturalis ordo* oder der *artificialis* vorliege, irrelevant.

Die Principialehre hingegen nimmt das gesamte Werk, also die Narratio samt dem, was ihr etwa vorausgeht, in den Blick. Für sie ist daher das, was der Narratio eventuell vorangestellt ist, qualifikationsrelevant, wesentlich für die Entscheidung, welcher Typ von *principium* vorliege. Und die Principialehre qualifiziert mit den Praedikaten 'natürlich' bzw. 'künstlich' den Werksbeginn,

der mit dem Narratio-Einsatz identisch sein kann, aber nicht muß. Ist der
Werksbeginn identisch mit einem Narratio-Einsatz *a principio materiae*, so gibt
das ein *naturale principium (operis)*; ist der Werksbeginn identisch mit einem
Narratio-Einsatz *a medio* bzw. *a fine materiae*, ergibt das ein *artificiale principium
(operis)*. Ist der Werksbeginn ein Proverb oder Exempel, so konstituiert allein
schon das Proverb/Exempel in dieser Position ein *artificiale principium (operis)*;
und es ist in diesem Fall irrelevant, ob die folgende Narratio mit *principium*,
medium oder *finis materiae* einsetzt, irrelevant also, ob die Narratio chronologisch
oder invertiert gebaut ist. Wie also die (eigentliche) Erzählung auch aufgebaut
sein mag: wenn ihr noch etwas vorangestellt wird (wenn der Narratiobeginn
also nicht zugleich der Werksbeginn ist), so ist damit nach der Principialehre
ein artifizialer Beginn (des Werkes) gegeben.

Man hatte übrigens schon vor Galfrid Beginntypen, façons de commencer,
wie Faral sagt,[24] unterschieden, nicht nur den Beginn mit Proverb oder Exempel,
sondern auch z.B. mit Stilfiguren wie Zeugma und Hypozeuxis (so Matthaeus
von Vendôme am Anfang seiner *Ars versificatoria* um 1175); aber man hatte
nicht einen natürlichen und 'künstlichen' Beginn geschieden. Galfrids Lehre
vom *principium artificiale* und *naturale* ist offenbar aus Elementen dieser Theorie
der façons de commencer und der traditionellen Ordineslehre, allerdings, wie
wir oben gesehen haben, nicht ganz harmonisch und ausgeglichen,
zusammengebaut. Da nun die Principialehre Galfrids nur einen Werksbeginn
direkt mit der Narratio oder mit Proverb bzw. Exempel kennt, ist ein Werk
mit Prooemium wie Vergils *Aeneis* mit dieser Lehre gar nicht zu erfassen. Bei
Galfrid wird dieses Problem allerdings sozusagen nicht akut, da er für seine
Principiatypen nur lauter 'moderne' (eben kein Prooemium antik-epischer Art
enthaltende), ganz knappe, von ihm selbst formulierte Muster anführt, immer
je eines in Vers und eines in Prosa.[25] Er, der Verfasser der *Poetria nova*, verzichtet
als selbstbewußter Vertreter der 'neuen' Zeit, so scheint es, bewußt auf ein
Illustrieren seiner Theorie durch Werke der 'Alten'.[26] Die *brevitas* der von Galfrid
vorgeführten *principia*-Muster illustriert die im Mittelalter vielfach zu
beobachtende Tendenz, bei der Erörterung von Aufbaufragen mit kleinen
kompositionellen Einheiten zu arbeiten, wenn man die Illustrationsbeispiele
selber entwirft.[27]

Johannes von Garlandia, der Galfrids Principialehre übernahm (und sie
allerdings ausdrücklich nur auf *materiae poeticae* bezog),[28] merkte offenkundig,
daß ein antikes Epos mit Prooemium in Galfrids Principiatheorie nicht
unterzubringen war; er sah in diesem Nicht-Berücksichtigen der 'alten' *carmina*
wohl eine Unzulänglichkeit und beseitigte dieses Manko, indem er zu Galfrids
acht *modi* des *principium artificiale* einen *nonus modus* hinzufügte.[29] Johannes
sagt da zunächst, im Rahmen der acht Beginntypen bewegten sich die *carmina*
der *moderni*, und fährt dann, den *nonus modus* nun beschreibend, fort:

> *Quidam tamen antiquorum, sicut Virgilius et Lucanus, artificiale principium observaverunt narrationi preponentes propositionem, invocationem et causam hystorie:*

> Manche der Alten aber, wie z.B. Vergil und Lukan, befolgten den kunstgemäßen Beginn, indem sie der Erzählung eine Themenangabe, Anrufung und Darstellung der Ursachen für das (in ihrer Dichtung geschilderte) Geschehen voranstellten.

Vergil und Lukan haben also nach Johannes ein *artificiale principium*, weil sie der Narratio ein (wie wir sagen würden) Prooemium (bestehend aus *propositio, invocatio, causa hystorie*) vorausschicken. Hier in der Principialehre konstituiert, im Geiste Galfrids, das der Narratio vorangestellte Prooemium, ebenso wie ein Proverb und Exempel in dieser Position, allein schon den 'künstlichen' Beginntyp. So können der sonst als Vertreter des *ordo naturalis* genannte, chronologisch erzählende Lukan und der sonst als typischer Vertreter des *artificialis* angeführte, invertiert erzählende Vergil beide hier friedlich als Repraesentanten des (*nonus modus* des) *principium artificiale* nebeneinanderstehen. Eine Spannung zwischen Principialehre und Ordinestheorie entsteht dabei für Johannes selbst nicht, da er nur die Principialehre vorträgt, einen *ordo naturalis* oder *artificialis* aber nirgends nennt.

IV

EINE BESONDERE ENTWICKLUNG der Ordineslehre finden wir im Bereich des *dictamen*. Hier wird die Ordinestheorie auf die 'Ordnung der Worte,' auf Wortstellung und Satzbau, also—soweit es dabei um das *recte dicere*, die Sprachrichtigkeit, geht—in den grammatischen Bereich übertragen. Die volle Übertragung des fixen Terminipaares *naturalis / artificialis* auf Typen der Satzkonstruktion (Wortfügung) liegt vor, um zunächst ein Werk, dessen Autor bekannt ist, zu nennen, in Guido Fabas *Summa dictaminis* (wahrscheinlich um 1230).[30] *Naturalis ordo* heißt da eine Wortfügung, in der das Subjekt (*nominativus*) mit seiner 'Bestimmung' (*cum determinatione sua*) vorangeht und das Prädikat (*verbum) cum determinatione sua* folgt (Beispiel: *Ego amo te*). Der *artificialis ordo* ist nach Guido ein schöneres Anordnen, ein *pulcrius disponere* der Worte (*partes, scil. orationis*), und wird von ihm mit der bei 'Tullius' definierten (eleganten rhetorischen) *compositio (verborum)* identifiziert;[31] damit repraesentiert der *artificialis* außer der entsprechenden Wortstellung auch eine (gehobene) aesthetische Qualität. Mit dem *pulcrius* der Wortfügung sind wir eben nicht mehr im grammatischen Bereich der Sprachrichtigkeit, sondern im rhetorischen der *compositio*, der eleganten rhythmischen Wortfügung, im Bereich der Sprachschönheit, des *bene dicere*. Der *artificialis* wird daher nach Guido in anspruchsvollen (literarischen) Texten (*dictatio*) verwendet, der *naturalis* aber in der *expositio*.[32]

Das *pulcrius ordinare* der Worte, wie es eine anonyme (in einer Handschrift des frühen 13. Jh. überlieferte, also möglicherweise zeitlich vor Guidos Werk liegende) *Summa dictaminis* nennt, die wie Guido einen *naturalis* und *artificialis ordo* des Satzbaus scheidet und zum Teil auch wörtlich gleich definiert, das *pulcrius ordinare* äußert sich nun (wie die anonyme *Summa* zusätzlich ausführt)[33] in einem angemessenen Umstellen der Worte (*transponere partes, scil. orationis*) und besonders in einem rhythmischen Fluß der Rede mit entsprechenden Klauseln, mit entsprechendem *cursus*, wie das Mittelalter sagt: Das angeführte Beispiel (*Petrum sincera dilectione prosequor et amplector*) hat, abgesehen von der Voranstellung der *determinatio* vor das Verbum, in den Schlußworten *prósequor et ampléctor* den *cursus velox*.

Die volle Übernahme des festen Terminipaares der traditionellen Ordinestheorie in die *artes dictandi* zur Bezeichnung von Wortfügungsarten – wobei *ordo* (vor allem der *ordo artificialis*) nicht bloß die reine Wortstellung, sondern auch damit verbundene stilistische Qualitäten charakterisiert – ist also noch vor der Mitte des 13. Jahrhunderts (z.B. Guido Faba) nachweisbar; als *naturalis ordo* wird dabei der von der grammatischen Theorie der Zeit als Norm des *recte dicere* festgelegte, wortstellungsmäßig rigoros und starr reglementierte Satzbau bezeichnet, als *artificialis ordo* gilt die rhetorische, freie, auf Eleganz ausgerichtete Satzkonstruktion, die man mit Hilfe eines – nach eigenen Vorstellungen zurecht gemachten – 'Zitats' aus 'Tullius' definiert.[34] Aus der traditionellen Ordineslehre übernommen und auf die Satzbauarten übertragen werden hier, wie die angeführten Stellen zeigen, nur die zwei wichtigen Termini *naturalis / artificialis*, jedoch keine inhaltlichen Elemente.

Konrad von Mure (um 1210–1281) bietet in seiner *Summa de arte prosandi*[35] eine weitere Entwicklungsstufe der Theorie der Wortfügungsarten, die hier zum Abschluß noch kurz vorgeführt werden soll:

> *Naturalis hic est ordo, quando nominativus precedit et verbum cum suis determinationibus . . . subsequitur. Et iste ordo rem, prout gesta est, ordine recto, plano modo . . . exponit. Artificialis ordo est, partibus materie artificialiter transpositis, rei gestae . . . narratio per verba polita . . . , quasi diceretur: Artificialis ordo est, qui rem gestam . . . a medio incipit narrare. . . . Et hoc ordine Virgilius utitur in Eneide.*

Natürlich ist die Anordnung, wenn der Nominativ (Subjekt) vorausgeht und das Verb (Praedikat) mit seinen Bestimmungen . . . nachfolgt. Und diese Anordnung legt das Geschehen, wie es vor sich gegangen ist, in rechter Folge, in schlichter (einfacher, klarer) Weise dar. Die kunstgemäße Anordnung ist eine Erzählung des Geschehens in gefeilten Worten bei kunstgerechter Umstellung der Teile des Stoffes . . . , als ob es hieße:

Kunstgemäß ist die Anordnung, die die Erzählung mit der Mitte des
Geschehens einsetzen läßt. . . . Und dieser Anordnung bedient sich Vergil
in der *Aeneis*.

Konrad verwendet also zwar zur Charakteristik der Wortfügungsart einerseits
noch die grammatische Nomenklatur (so beim *naturalis* die Folge *nominativus –
verbum cum suis determinationibus*); andererseits zieht er aber – das ist neu
gegenüber den oben genannten *artes* – zur Charakterisierung von Wortstellung
und Satzbau auch Formulierungen aus der traditionellen Ordineslehre heran,
die ursprünglich zur Beschreibung des Aufbaus der Erzählung dienen, so in
der Definition des satzbaumäßig, stilistisch schlichten *(planus) ordo naturalis* die
Formel, daß dieser *ordo rem, prout gesta est, . . . exponit*. In der Definition des
artificialis bei Konrad ist die (bei Guido Faba und anderen hervorgehobene)
Eleganz der Wortfügung durch die Erwähnung der *verba polita* praesent. Aber
daß Konrad dabei von einem Umstellen *(transponere)* der *partes materiae* spricht,
zeigt, daß er nicht rein die Wortfolge als solche, sondern auch das Wortgefüge
als Sinn- und Stoffträger vor Augen hat,[36] was durch die anschließenden Worte
'*rei gestae . . . narratio*' noch verdeutlicht wird. In Form eines Vergleichs (*quasi
diceretur*) schließt dann Konrad zur Verdeutlichung der 'künstlichen' Wortfügung
noch eine zweite Definition des *artificialis* an, die besonders typische Elemente
aus der traditionellen Beschreibung des artifizialen Erzählungsaufbaus enthält,
nämlich die Formulierung, daß der *artificialis a medio incipit narrare*, und den
Hinweis, daß Vergil diesen *ordo* verwende. Besonders auffällig mutet hier im
ersten Augenblick die Tatsache an, daß auch Vergils Aufbautechnik in der *Aeneis*
als Muster für den artifizialen Satzbau bemüht wird. Denn Vergils
Aufbauverfahren wird, wo es inhaltlich erläutert wird, immer als großräumig
gesehen und durch die umfangreiche Einblendung der Zerstörung Troias und
der *errores* (in Aeneas' Erzählung beim Gelage) illustriert. Aber wie weit ist
diese Großräumigkeit hier in Konrads Formulierung (*hoc ordine Vergilius utitur*),
in der also der *ordo* Vergils zwar genannt, aber nicht beschrieben wird, noch
aktiv gegenwärtig? Die Anwendung von Formeln, die an sich ursprünglich
größere Erzählabläufe bezeichnen, auf den Satzbau wird gerade für den Verfasser
einer *Ars dictaminis* der Umstand erleichtert haben, daß die Narratio eines Briefes,
wie Beispiele bei Konrad von Mure zeigen, in der Tat nicht selten in einem
Satzgefüge gegeben wurde, so daß da Narratioaufbau und Satzbau tatsächlich
miteinander identisch werden konnten. Übrigens arbeiten aber auch etwa die
Poetiken (Galfrid von Vinsauf, Johannes von Garlandia) vielfach schon mit
sehr kleinen *materiae*, z.B. in den oben S.121 bereits erwähnten (für den
Schulbetrieb berechneten) Beispielen zur Illustration der Ordines- und
Principialehre: ein Zeichen, daß diese Tendenz zur kleinen Einheit in der
Erörterung von Kompositionsfragen schon traditionell gegeben ist.
Diese Tendenz, Aufbauprobleme durch kleine kompositionelle Einheiten,

durch Stoffquanten im Ausmaß eines Satzes zu illustrieren, macht auch die Ungeniertheit verständlich, mit der Konrad die neuen (bestimmte Typen der Wortfügung, des Satzbaus darstellenden) *ordines* durch (auch das Stoffliche betreffende) Elemente aus der traditionellen (von den Aufbautypen der Narratio handelnden) Ordineslehre näher erläutert und bestimmt, die Selbstverständlichkeit, mit der er die neue Ordinestheorie durch die alte, abgesehen von der Gleichheit der Termini *naturalis/artificialis*, auch dem aufbautheoretischen Gehalt nach überlagert und so die neuen *ordines* (der Wortfügung) und die alten (der Stoffgliederung) nicht nur terminologisch, sondern auch substanzmäßig miteinander verbindet und verquickt.[37]

V

ZUSAMMENFASSEND können wir festhalten, daß die recht formal ausgerichtete mittelalterliche, Aufbauarten der Erzählung scheidende Ordineslehre, die uns (zuerst in den Wiener Horazscholien faßbar) als eine Verschmelzung von Dispositionspraecepta aus der antiken Rhetorik und Poetik entgegentritt, erstens doch ins Gewicht fallende inhaltliche Wandlungen durchmachte (Entwicklung der Principialehre; Anwendung der Ordinestheorie auf den Satzbau und zwar zunächst nur hinsichtlich der Termini *naturalis/artificialis*, dann auch hinsichtlich des dispositionstheoretischen Gehalts), festhalten auch, daß, zweitens, in der Wertung der *ordines* ein deutlicher Umschwung stattfand. Denn anfangs gilt der *naturalis ordo* als gleichwertig, ja zum Teil wird er als der von Natur gegebene *ordo* sogar eher vorgezogen: dies wohl unter dem Einfluß der antiken rhetorischen Ordinestheorie und Narratiolehre, der aber hier eine offenbar schon vorgegebene Einstellung stützt, die das chronologietreue Erzählen als das 'natürliche' und daher eigentlich gebotene betrachtet, die jedoch (wie der Wiener Horazscholiast) dem artifizialen Aufbau, dem Invertieren gegenüber, selbst wenn der große Vergil es übt, eine gewisse Hemmung nicht ganz überwinden kann.[38] Aber bei Galfrid, für den nur der Gehalt an *ars* zählt, die den Gebildeten über den *agrestis vel vulgaris* hinaushebt, wird dann der *artificialis ordo* (den der Ungebildete nicht beherrscht) als künstlerisch-aesthetisch höher eingestuft; eine ähnliche Höherbewertung gilt auch für das *principium artificiale* und – im Bereich des *dictamen* – für den *artificialis ordo* des Satzbaus mit seiner eleganten, rhythmischen *compositio verborum*.

Die festgestellten Wandlungen treten zum Großteil in der ersten Hälfte des 13. Jahrhunderts ein, eine nicht uninteressante Parallele zu der wesentlichen Wandlung und Entwicklung der *ars praedicandi* in dieser Zeit.[39]

Die traditionelle Lehre vom *ordo naturalis* und *artificialis* (der Narratio) ist und bleibt im Mittelalter eine formalistische Theorie einer recht schematisch nach dem chronologischen oder nach dem Inversions-Prinzip reihenden Anordnung (*dispositio*) der Teile eines gegebenen Stoffes, ob die Theoretiker nun die *ordines* als gleichwertig betrachten, den 'natürlichen' *ordo* glauben vorziehen zu sollen oder schließlich den 'künstlichen' eben auf Grund seines gesteigerten Gehaltes an *ars* als künstlerisch-aesthetisch überlegen einstufen.[40] Die Vorstellung einer Komposition im Sinne eines Gestaltens der Erzählung—eines Zusammenfügens der Handlungsteile—zu einem organischen, mit innerer Konsequenz ablaufenden Handlungsgefüge, zu einer künstlerischen Einheit im vollen antik-aristotelischen Sinne wird im Rahmen dieser Ordineslehre nicht konzipiert. Aber immerhin erhebt Galfrid von Vinsauf, jedoch an einer Stelle, wo er die beiden *ordines* nur nebenbei erwähnt, die Forderung nach einem— allerdings anscheinend recht formalistisch verstandenen—wechselseitigen Zusammenhängen, einem *sibi cohaerere* der *partes materiae*.[41] Und auch Konrad von Hirsau, um das noch anzuführen, erklärt in einer Passage, wo er nicht vom *ordo naturalis* und *artificialis* spricht, Horaz verlange in der *Ars poetica* zur Vermeidung der *confusio* im Aufbau das Einhalten des—von Konrad wieder mehr formalistisch gefaßten—*ordo legitimus (principium-medietas-finis)* für das *totum corpus operis*.[42]

Anmerkungen

1. Vgl. H. Lausberg, *Handbuch der literarischen Rhetorik* (München, 1960) S. 455 (Paragr. 911); A. Scaglione, *The Classical Theory of Composition* (Chapel Hill, 1972) S. 24 ff.

2. Das gilt auch schon für die antike Rhetorik: E. R. Curtius, *Europäische Literatur und lateinisches Mittelalter* (Bern, 1967[6]), S. 491.

3. Vgl. etwa E. Faral, *Les arts poétiques du XIIe et du XIIIe siècle* (Paris, 1924; Nachdruck 1962) S. 55–60; J. J. Murphy, *Rhetoric in the Middle Ages* (Berkeley-Los Angeles-London 1974) S. 170 f.; E. Gallo, *The Poetria Nova and its Sources in Early Rhetorical Doctrine* (The Hague-Paris 1971), S. 137–150 (besonders 137–140); P. v. Moos, "Poeta und historicus im Mittelalter," *Beiträge zur Geschichte der deutschen Sprache und Literatur* 98 (1976), 94–96; F. Quadlbauer, "Lukan im Schema des ordo naturalis/artificialis," *Grazer Beiträge* 6 (1977), 67–71; 73–83; 87–101. Speziell zur Anwendung der Ordinestheorie auf die Wortstellung im Satz: Scaglione a.0. (Anm. 1) 105–22.—Vgl. Anm. 29, Zusatz.

4. Vgl. die Ausgabe von J. Zechmeister (Wien 1877) praef. p.I; II ff.

5. So wurde die Horazstelle jedenfalls schon von Servius (4.Jh.) in seinem Aeneiskommentar (praef. p. 4/5 der editio Harvardiana, vol. II, Lancastriae Pennsylvanianorum 1946) verstanden und, offenbar in seiner Nachfolge, von Bernhard von Utrecht (11.Jh.); vgl. F. Quadlbauer a.0. (Anm. 3) 70.

6. Vgl. Sulpicius Victor (4.Jh.) *rhet.* 14 p. 320 Halm und Martianus Capella (um 400), *De nuptiis Philologiae et Mercurii* 5 (de rhetorica) 506 p. 249 Dick, ferner *Rhetorica ad Herennium* 3, 9, 16f. (wo allerdings der spätere *ordo artificialis* als *dispositio, quae*

... *oratoris iudicio ad tempus adcommodatur*, bezeichnet wird).

7. Martianus Capella a.0. (Anm. 6) 5, 507 p. 249 Dick; auch Fortunatian (4.Jh.) kennt in seiner *Rhetorica* 3, 1 p. 141 Calboli für den *naturalis ordo* u.a. einen *modus per tempora* (ohne nähere Bestimmung).

8. Nicht bei Martian und nicht bei Fortunatian (vgl. Anm. 7).

9. Servius a.0. (vgl. Anm. 5) p. 5. Quintilian (*Institutio oratoria* 7, 10, 11) spricht von einem *more Homerico a mediis vel ultimis (incipere)*, Donat in seinem *Commentum Terenti* (*Andria*, praefatio 2, 2 p. 38 Wessner) von einem *a novissimis argumenti rebus (incipere)*, Macrobius (*Saturnalia* 5, 2, 9) sagt: *a rerum medio coepit (Homerus)*.

10. Vgl. Servius a.0. (Anm. 9) und Donat a.0 (Anm. 9).

11. Daß *virtus poetica* und *virtus ordinis* Übertragungen aus dem Griechischen sind, legen Ausdrücke wie 'poetische Tugend' (*aretè poietikè*) bzw. 'Tugend der Poesie' (*aretè poiéseos*) nahe, die in den Scholien zu Homer, *Ilias* 1, 1 als Bezeichnungen für das Inversionsverfahren im poetischen Erzählungsaufbau fungieren: nachzulesen bei H. Erbse, *Scholia Graeca in Homeri Iliadem (Scholia vetera)*, vol. I (Berolini, 1969) 4, 24–26 bzw. bei I. Bekker, *Scholia in Homeri Iliadem*, tom. I (Berolini, 1825) 1, 33–34 (links).

12. Fortunatian a.0. (Anm. 7) z.B. bezeichnet den *artificialis* grundsätzlich als *modus utilitatis* und betont, man wähle den *artificialis ordo* (statt des 'normalen' *naturalis*) nur, *si aliquid occurrerit necessitate utilitatis*. Zur Einstellung von Martianus Capella vgl. Quadlbauer a.0. (Anm. 3) 73.

13. Die Formulierung des Scholiasten, daß Vergil Troias Untergang *reservavit in melius tempus*, wird in eine Kommentartradition zu stellen sein, die faßbar wird: a) in der Äußerung des Vergilkommentators Claudius Donatus (5.Jh.) p. 6 f. Georgii, daß Vergil Troias Zerstörung auf eine andere Zeit verschob (*in aliud tempus . . . distulit*), damit sie beim Dido-Gelage erzählt werde, auf daß es, für den Fall, daß die Zerstörung gleich zu Beginn des Epos geschildert würde, dann nicht etwa lästig (*odiosum*) wäre, dasselbe auf Bitten der Dido beim Gelage noch einmal erzählen zu lassen; b) in der Ansicht des Servius auctus zu *Aeneis* 9, 83, daß Vergil den Bericht über den Bau der Schiffe des Aeneas, der (chronologisch) ins dritte Buch gehört, verschob (*narratio . . . dilata est*), damit er im neunten Buch 'günstiger' (*opportunius*) – also offenbar künstlerisch wirkungsvoller – gegeben werde (ähnlich über dieses Verschieben, aber ohne aesthetische Wertung, Pseudo-Acro zu Horaz, *Ars poetica* 43/4). Nur hat unser Scholiast, der dieser Verschiebetechnik Vergils seiner Formulierung nach aesthetischen Wirkungswert zuerkennt (vgl. Servius auctus), doch seiner eigentlichen Einstellung nach – durch die Brille seiner gegebenen Vorliebe für den *naturalis* die Dinge betrachtend – eben diese Technik nicht vollen Herzens positiv zu werten und zu würdigen vermocht.

14. Vgl. Quadlbauer a.O. (Anm. 3) 67–69; 87–90; 92; Bernhard Silvester nennt neben Lukan noch Statius als Vertreter des *naturalis* (vgl. ibid. 88).

15. *Dialogus super auctores* p. 77, 194 ff. Huygens (R. B. C. Huygens, *Accessus ad auctores, Bernard d'Utrecht, Conrad d'Hirsau* (Leiden, 1970); p. 104, 1002 ff. wird hier nicht Lukan als Vertreter des *naturalis* genannt, sondern eine Prosaschrift, Sallusts Catilina-Monographie. Zu Konrads Stellung zum 'legitimen' Ordo vgl. unten mit Anmerkung 42.

16. *Didascalicon* 3, 9 (Migne PL 176, 771 D: die Ausgabe von Ch. H. Buttimer, Washington, DC, 1939, war mir nicht rechtzeitig erreichbar); ibid. 6, 7 (806 C) erklärt Hugo, daß *scriptura divina* teils den *naturalis ordo* verwendet, teils "Späteres dem Früheren voranstellt" (*posteriora prioribus anteponit*). Das entspricht dem *artificialis*, der

hier also nur *per circumscriptionem* erwähnt wird. Das (im Mittelalter üblicherweise *artificialis ordo* genannte) Inversionsverfahren als Vertauschung von Früherem und Späterem, also mit einer Hysteroproteron-Formel, zu bezeichnen, hat erwartungsgemäß seine antiken Vorstufen: so schreibt z.B. der Vergilkommentator Claudius Donatus Vergil das *posteriora primitus et prima posterius (ponere)* zu (p. 6 Georgii), und Cicero (ad Atticum 1, 16, 1) spricht von einem *hýsteron próteron homerikōs* (einem "*hýsteron próteron*–Verfahren auf homerische Art"), elegant eine damals offenbar übliche – im legeren Briefstil auch dem Römer gestattete – griechische Formel einfließen lassend. – Varianten der Hysteroproteron-Formel finden sich etwa auch in der (oben auszugsweise zitierten) Passage des Wiener Scholiasten zu Horaz, *Ars poetica* 45 (Vergil habe *primum* gesagt, was *posterius* hätte gesagt werden sollen, nämlich nach dem *ordo naturalis*) und bei Bernhard von Utrecht: vgl. Quadlbauer a.0. (Anm. 3) 67.

17. Vgl. Konrad von Hirsau a.0. (Anm. 15) p. 77, 195 ff.; zu Bernhard von Utrecht, Bernhard Silvester (der außer Vergil auch Terenz als Musterautor des *artificialis* anführt) und Anselm von Laon vgl. Quadlbauer a.0. (Anm. 3) 67; 87 f.

18. Vgl. *Poetria nova* 101 ff., besonders 151–202 (mit Vers-Beispielen für die acht Typen).

19. 1, 1–2 p. 265 Faral a.0. (Anm. 3).

20. Beschrieben im *Documentum*: 1, 7–17 p. 266–68 Faral.

21. Gallo a.0 (Anm. 3) 139 bemerkt, den Typ des Beginnens *a fine* (neben *a medio*) könne Galfrid aus Quintilians Formel (vgl. Anm. 9) *more Homerico a mediis vel ultimis (sc. incipere)* haben. Man darf vielleicht auch Donats *a novissimis argumenti rebus* (vgl. Anm. 9) hier mit im (möglicherweise wirksamen) Hintergrund sehen.

22. Unter *proverbium* scheint Galfrid einen allgemeinen, sentenzartigen Ausspruch zu verstehen, der (vorwiegend) abstrakte Vorstellungen ausdrückt (z.B. *citius fata serena ruunt*: allzu rasch gehen freundliche Geschicke vorbei), unter *exemplum* dagegen einen Ausspruch über einen üblichen Vorgang in der konkreten, dinglichen Welt (z.B. *saepe venenator, alii quod porrigit, haurit*: oft bekommt der Giftmischer selbst zu trinken, was er einem anderen zudenkt; die Beispiele aus Documentum 1, 1, 11 und 17 p. 267–68 Faral).

23. Documentum 2, 1, 1 p. 268 Faral.

24. A. O. (Anm. 3) 55; 106.

25. Die Beginnmuster sind alle, didaktisch sehr instruktiv, für eine und dieselbe *materia*, die Geschichte von Minos, Androgeos und Scylla, entworfen, die Galfrid a.0. (Anm. 19) zunächst, zugleich das *principium naturale* anwendend und illustrierend, ganz knapp und gedrängt, aber kunstreich formuliert, erzählt.

26. Ob er dabei realisierte, daß die *Aeneis*, die er sicher kannte, zu keinem seiner artifizialen Beginntypen stimmte, und sie deswegen nicht erwähnte, oder ob er von vornherein gar nicht an ein eventuelles Illustrieren seiner 'modernen' Typen durch 'alte' *opera* dachte, bleibe dahingestellt. – Ein sprechendes Zeichen seines Selbstbewußtseins ist übrigens etwa das Faktum, daß er bei der Besprechung der *vitia stylorum* bemerkt, Horaz zeige keinen Weg, wie man diese *vitia* vermeiden könne; er, Galfrid, werde aber dieses Versagen, dieses 'Auslassen' (*defectus*) der horazischen 'Poetria' ausgleichen: *Documentum* 2, 3, 153–54 p. 313–14 Faral.

27. *Docum.* 2, 2, 46–60 p. 280–82 Faral wählt Galfrid ein einziges Wort, *lego*, als *materia* (Stoff zur Darstellung) und zeigt 'kunstvoll', wie man aus dieser kürzesten *materia* die drei obligaten Teile eines (Erzähl-)Stoffes, *principium, medium* und *finis materiae* (die alten aristotelischen, aber nicht mehr im Sinne der aristotelischen Einheits-

idee verstandenen Teile des künstlerischen 'Ganzen') herausholt und dann bei dieser *materia* die acht 'künstlichen' Beginntypen für die Darstellung, für das zu schaffende literarische *opus* (die *octo modi* des *artificiale principium, scil. operis*) bilden kann.

28. *Parisiana Poetria* 3 p. 52–56 Lawler (New Haven and London 1974) = p. 905–7 Mari (*Rom. Forsch.* 13, 1902) beschreibt Johannes die acht Typen; er bringt nur Versbeispiele zu ihrer Illustration, er läßt die Principiatypen ja auch, wie erwähnt, nur für poetische Stoffe gelten. Seine Illustrationsbeispiele für die acht galfrid'schen Typen sind (wie bei Galfrid) knapp und (für eine bestimmte *materia*) von ihm selbst gebildet.

29. Ibid. p. 56 Lawler = p. 907 Mari.–Ohne Bezug zur Principialehre erwähnt Johannes auch das (bei ihm sechsteilige) Schema der Teile einer (auf *persuadere* angelegten) Rede: *exordium, narratio, partitio, confirmatio, confutatio, conclusio*: p. 66 Lawler = p. 911 Mari.-Zusatz: Dieses antike Schema der Teile der (Gerichts-)Rede wird auch mit der mittelalterlichen Theorie der Ordines (des Erzählungsaufbaus) nicht verknüpft; es bleibt daher in diesem Referat die Erörterung seiner Funktion in der mittellateinischen Aufbaulehre ausgespart (zur Rolle dieses Schems in der antiken rhetorischen Ordineslehre vgl. oben mit Anm. 6).

30. P. 338 A. Gaudenzi (*Il propugnatore*, nova series III, 1, 1890).

31. Gemeint ist die Definition in der *Rhetorica ad Herennium* 4, 12, 18 p. 166 Calboli: *compositio est verborum constructio, [quae facit omnes partes oratio]nis aequabiliter perpolitas.* Guido 'zitiert' die–verderbte–Stelle mehr paraphrasierend und auf seine These hinbiegend: *compositio artificialis est constructio dictionum equabiliter perpolita.*

32. Zu der Frage, ob dieser *naturalis ordo* (mehr) nur für didaktische Exposition im Unterricht gedacht war, vgl. Anm. 34 Abs. 2.

33. MS Paris Bibl. Nat. Lat. 16253, fol. 1; der Traktat enthält noch eine Reihe von Detailvorschriften für den Satzbau, die Guido nicht hat: vgl. Scaglione a.0. (Anm. 1) 117 mit Anm. 24. Dieselbe Theorie, mit gewissen Varianten, zum Teil näher an Guido, bietet eine Handschrift des 14.Jh. (Paris Bibl. Nat. Lat. 11386, fol. 30: vgl. Scaglione 118 mit Anm. 26).

34. Etwas anders ist die Theorie des Bene von Florenz, der in seinem *Candelabrum* (bald nach 1220) eine *compositio naturalis, fortuita* und *decora* bzw. *artificialis* unterscheidet und beschreibt (1, 1–9 p. 134 f. Vecchi: *Atti e memorie*, N.S. 10, 1958–9, Bologna 1963) und *ordo naturalis / artificialis* rein nur auf die Wortfolge (ohne Berücksichtigung der aesthetischen Aspekte, die die *compositio* umfaßt) bezieht, also als untergeordnete Kategorien behandelt (vgl. ibid. und 6, 1–5, p. 150 f. Vecchi; vgl. dazu Quintilian, der *Institutio oratoria* 9, 4, 22 *ordo, iunctura* und *numerus* der *compositio* als Glieder unterordnet). Inhaltliche Vorstufen des späteren *ordo naturalis / artificialis* der Wortfügung stellen die in den (früher Alberich von Montecassino zugeschriebenen) *Rationes dictandi* (12.Jh.) geschiedenen Wortfügungstypen, *recta et simplex constructio* einerseits und *appositio* andererseits, dar: vgl. Scaglione a.0 (Anm. 1) 114.
Zur Entwicklung der oben aus Guido Faba angeführten 'logischen' Wortfolge (Nominativ = Subjekt = Prädikat = Determinationen) und ihren zusätzlichen Details und Variationen bei den mittelalterlichen Grammatikern, die diese Folge gelegentlich auch *ordo naturalis* nennen, vgl. Scaglione a.0. 105–114; zum Zusammenhängen dieser Wortfolgethese mit Wortstellungstendenzen in den romanischen Sprachen und zu dem Problem, wie weit dieser *ordo* nur als Verständnishilfe im Lateinunterricht (logisches Ordnen der Satzteile, 'Konstruieren'), wie weit auch als Norm für außerschulische (schriftliche) Äußerung gedacht war, einiges ibid. 110–13.–Es ist interessant, daß

auch zu Quintilians Zeiten (1.Jh.) die Forderung nach einer starren Wortfolge (Substantiv [allgemein, nicht wie im Mittelalter *nominativus*]–Verb-Adverb *etc.*) ventiliert wurde, die Quintilian aber (für Latein) energisch ablehnt (*Institutio oratoria* 9, 4, 24), ebenso wie vor ihm für das Griechische Dionys von Halikarnaß (1.Jh. vor Chr.), *De compositione verborum* 5, 33 ff.: vgl. H. Jellinek, *Geschichte der neuhochdeutschen Grammatik*, II 4, 429 f. (Heidelberg 1914).–Als *naturalis ordo* bezeichnet Quintilian übrigens, ganz speziell, Wortverbindungen wie *viros ac feminas, dies noctesque* (*Institutio oratoria* 9, 4, 23).

35. P. 67 Kronbichler.

36. In dem schon erwähnten handschriftlichen Traktat aus dem frühen 13.Jh. (vgl. oben mit Anm. 33) ist von einem *transponere* der *partes (orationis)*, also der Worte (*pars, scil. orationis*, für Wort geht auf die antike Grammatik zurück), im *artificialis ordo* die Rede.

37. Diese Verschmelzung der beiden Ordinestheorien läßt Scaglione a.0. (Anm. 1), der den Passus Konrads nur nebenbei (114 Anm. 19) zitiert mit dem kurzen Hinweis, bei Konrad zeige sich die "analogy between word order and topical disposition," unerörtert.

38. Zu dieser *pro-naturalis*-Haltung vgl. auch noch Albert von Stade (13.Jh.), der *Troilus* 3, 235 Homer (der auch 'lüge') tadelt, weil er den Trojakrieg nicht *recto . . . ordine* erzählt habe, und den Vorspruch der *Anonymi Historia Troyana Daretis Frigii* (um 1150), deren Verfasser sich rühmt, die *ordinata Troyani belli historia* nach (dem geschichtstreuen) Dares zu erzählen (p. 266 J. Stohlmann, Ratingen, 1968): hier steht nun als Gegensatz zum *rectus ordo*, scheint es, nicht so sehr das Invertieren vor Augen, als vielmehr ein Pervertieren, ein Verfälschen des (wahren)'historischen' Ablaufs. (Das komplexe Problem des Wahrheitsanspruchs der Autoren, auf das der *ordo* damit führt, kann hier nicht erörtert werden.)

Es ist reizvoll, neben die *pro-naturalis*-Haltung auch die These des Byzantiners Eustathios (12.Jh., im Vorwort zu seinem Iliaskommentar 7, 8 ff., p. 11 van der Valk) zu stellen, daß der 'natürliche' Erzählbeginn mit dem Anfang (des Stoffes) nichts 'Neues' an sich habe und daß der Hörer normalerweise dieses Erzählverfahren erwarte; bei Eustathios ist aber impliziert, daß der Hörer das 'natürliche' Erzählverfahren erwartet, weil (fast) alle Dichter es pflegen, nicht weil er es für das gebotene hielte – im Gegenteil, das 'neuartige' Invertieren Homers würde dem Hörer nach Eustathios offenbar zur Abwechslung, als etwas Neues, besser behagen.

39. Vgl. den Artikel 'Artes praedicandi' im *Artemis Lexikon des Mittelalters* (München und Zürich, 1978 ff.).–Die Frage der Auswirkung der Ordinestheorie (vor allem der traditionellen, die Narratiotypen scheidet) auf die literarische Praxis wurde hier mit Rücksicht auf die gebotene *brevitas* ausgeklammert. Vgl. im übrigen dazu D. Kelly, "Theory of Composition in Medieval Narrative Poetry and Geoffrey of Vinsaufs *Poetria Nova*," *Medieval Studies* 31, 1969, 132: artificial order in der poetischen Praxis des Mittelalters sei 'rar'; W. Ziltener, *Chrétien und die Aeneis* (Graz-Köln, 1957) 16: ob die Beispiele von *ordo artificialis* bei Chrétien aus der mittelalterlichen Theorie oder aus der Aeneisimitatio zu erklären seien, könne 'letzthin' nicht entschieden werden. Als ein Beispiel für die Anwendung des *artificialis* kann das (lateinische) Bibelgedicht des Eupolemius (um 1200) genommen werden (ed. K. Manitius, Weimar 1973, MGH, *Quellen zur Geistesgeschichte des Mittelalters IX*).–Zu polemisch bewußtem Eintreten für einen *rectus ordo* vgl. Anm. 38 Abs. 1.

40. Die künstlerische Höherwertigkeit wird beim *ordo artificialis* des Satzbaus konsequenter und durchgehender betont (vgl. Abschnitt IV). Hier entspricht der *ordo* ja der *compositio verborum*, für die auch die antike Rhetorik die aesthetische Qualität, das künstlerische 'Zusammenfügen', viel intensiver fordert als für die *dispositio* (Stoffanordnung, Redeaufbau), die in erster Linie dem Gesetz der Zweckmäßigkeit (*utilitas*) der Anordnung (im Hinblick auf das Durchsetzen des eigenen Standpunkts) unterliegt: vgl. Anm. 12 und Lausberg a.0 (Anm. 1) 241 (Paragr. 443); 247 (Paragr. 452).

41. *Documentum* 2, 3, 154–55 p. 314 Faral: Er handelt da von der Vermeidung des Vitiums des unpassenden Setzens der Materiateile, der *incongrua partium positio* (von der Horaz zu Beginn der *Ars poetica* spreche), und verlangt, man müsse beim ausführlichen Behandeln (*diffuse tractare*) einer *materia* alle ihre *lineamenta* (Einzelzüge) darstellen, nach dem *naturalis* oder nach dem *artificialis ordo* vorgehend, damit eben dann die *partes materiae* (*principium, medium, finis*) untereinander zusammenhängen (*sibi cohaereant*: vgl. Horazens Lob *Ars poetica* 151–52, daß bei Homer *primum, medium* und *imum* zusammenstimmen). Mit diesen Worten meint Galfrid, nach seiner Lehre vom *continuare*, von der Verbindung der Werkteile (ibid. 2, 1, 1–12 p. 268–71 Faral) zu schließen, daß die einzelnen *partes materiae* durch geeignete Übergangsformeln verknüpft werden sollen. Das hier vorliegende Konzept einer formal verbundenen Reihe der Stoffteile (Anfang-Mitte-Ende, bzw. in invertierter Folge) möchte man zunächst als Ansatz zur Vorstellung einer inneren aufbaumäßigen Handlungseinheit, eines *unum* nach antiker, aristotelisch-horazischer Auffassung nehmen. Doch weiteres Umsehen mahnt zur Vorsicht, denn in seiner Interpretation der horazischen Forderung des *simplex et unum* (*Ars poetica* 23) deutet Galfrid ibid. 2, 3, 158 p. 315 Faral dann das *unum* zwar im Sinne einer Einheit, aber nur einer Einheit und Gleichartigkeit des *stylus* (*unus et uniformis sit stylus*). Die Poetik des Aristoteles, die den Begriff eines kompositionellen *unum*, eines in sich kausal verknüpften Handlungsgefüges hätte klar vermitteln können, war eben dem Mittelalter infolge der mangelnden Griechischkenntnisse zunächst unbekannt, blieb aber auch nach ihrer Übersetzung ins Lateinische (13.Jh.) weitgehend ohne Einfluß und Wirkung, jedenfalls ohne direkte Wirkung—und die indirekte Wirkung durch Horaz erwies sich, wie Galfrid zeigt, als unzureichend für die konsequente Konzeption einer organischen Handlungseinheit. Zu *principium, medium* und *finis materiae* bei Galfrid vgl. auch Anm. 27.

42. A.O. (Anm. 15) p. 112, 1268 ff. Konrad meint mit dem 'legitimen' Ordo das Beibehalten der in einem (gegebenen) Stoff vorliegenden Handlungsfolge in der Darstellung, also wohl das, was man sonst—auch er selbst an anderer Stelle (vgl. oben mit Anm. 15)—als *ordo naturalis* bezeichnet (ein Terminus, den er aber hier, wie gesagt, nicht nennt); die Vorstellung eines in seinen Teilen kausal verbundenen, also im antikaristotelischen Sinne einheitlichen, organischen Handlungsgefüges liegt aber auch hier eben nicht, zumindest nicht klar vor.

Literaturnachtrag zu Anm. 3: P. Klopsch, *Einführung in die Dichtungslehren des lateinischen Mittelalters* (Darmstadt, 1980), S. 129 f.

On the Practicalities
of Renaissance Rhetoric

BRIAN VICKERS
Eidgenössische Technische Hochschule Zürich

During the European Renaissance—a period which, for convenience, I take as stretching from 1400 to 1700—rhetoric attained its greatest preeminence, both in terms of range of influence and in value. The quantity of rhetoric texts known to have been published is immense. J. J. Murphy, who is engaged in compiling a primary bibliography, estimates that it will include 1,000 authors and 2,500 books. If each text was issued in an average of 1,000 copies, and if each copy was read by anything from one reader to the dozens using a school text, then we have a total of several million Europeans who had a working knowledge of rhetoric. These included many of the kings, princes, and their counsellors; Popes, bishops, ordinary clergymen (whether Catholic, Jesuit, Protestant, Calvinist, Baptist, Methodist); all the professors, schoolteachers, lawyers, historians; all the poets and dramatists, including the women, who were otherwise not granted much education.

Throughout this period rhetoric was a major concern of most writers at the formative period of their lives, when habits of reading and writing are picked up, seldom to be shaken off. We need to re-live this culture in order to appreciate the importance of rhetoric, not only to major writers like Shakespeare but in hundreds of contexts in life then, and to habits of mind which have since disappeared. To do so, we need far better working-tools: there is no adequate bibliography of rhetoric in any language for this period.[1] There is no fully satisfactory history of rhetoric in any language;[2] there are only two modern studies of Renaissance rhetoricians which I would regard as satisfactory by scholarly standards, uniting biographical and bibliographical accuracy with a knowledge of the rhetorical tradition, namely Father Ong on Ramus and John Monfasani on George of Trebizond.[3] What of Melanchthon and Sturm, Vives, Vossius and Caussinus, Scaliger, Minturno, Soarez, Nizolius, etc.? As for texts, there are not more than six editions of Renaissance rhetoric-texts which satisfy modern standards of editing while also offering adequate historical and critical notes. We urgently need a whole series of studies of the rhetorical tradition, of the ways in which rhetoric was handed down, re-shaped according to the needs of place, language, social context; of how syntheses were made, of Hermogenes with Cicero, Aristotle with Quintilian; of how work in the schoolroom was actually related to educational theory. The re-discovery of Renaissance rhetoric has barely begun.

II

THE STUDIES that have been made over the last thirty years or so tend to fall into two main groups. First, rhetoric has been studied in its general form, in relation to politics, history, philosophy, above all for Quattrocento Italy, by such scholars as Eugenio Garin, Paul Kristeller, Peter Herde, J. E. Seigel, Nancy Struever and others[4] – all historians. Second, rhetoric as a particular discipline of language has been studied by what used to be known as philologians – literary critics, editors, who have gone into the details of structure, form, and style. Writers in the first group have not concerned themselves with literary matters, reasonably enough, while the literary students have not always considered the broader cultural questions. That is, historical and philological studies of rhetoric have been carried out by two different groups, with substantially different trainings, interests and expectations, which has resulted in a split not only in the manner and method of studying rhetoric but also in its evaluation. Scholars in the first group, for instance, tend to take at face value what the Humanists claim about rhetoric, fail to see the rhetorical forms and procedures which govern most Humanist utterances in praise of their own discipline. They also tend to undervalue the detailed rhetorical teaching on language and technique, dismissing it as arid, or dry, or mechanical. Literary scholars who understand the detail tend sometimes to forget what it is all for. They can tell an *epizeuxis* from an *anadiplosis* but they do not always see the purpose or cultural significance of the whole.

I wish to urge that since, as Cicero said, "eloquence is one," rhetoric was a unified, coherent discipline, then our study of it should be unified: historians must learn the values of *elocutio*, philologians must be aware of rhetoric as a social, political, and psychological tool. The great justification for the study of rhetoric in the Renaissance was that it was not "theoretical" (a term of abuse to most Humanists), but useful, of practical value: it taught you how to win over friends, and either persuade enemies or make them look ridiculous. The well-known classical texts had taught that rhetoric was useful, or indeed essential, in civic life, and the great humanists of the Quattrocento arguing *de laudibus eloquentiae* demonstrated both by the eloquence with which they re-stated the

Isocratean-Ciceronian concepts and by their own practical success in politics that, as Francis Bacon was to put it, "it is eloquence that prevaileth in an active life."[5] What is striking as one follows the rise of rhetoric between 1500 and 1700 in England, France and Germany is to see how writers connected with civic life re-discover the same classical texts and make the same propaganda with them. Rhetoric is essential to governors and counsellors because it can persuade men to do what you want them to do. All the doctors agree on that point. But it leads humanists, whatever their language and status, on to a further and more dangerous position: rhetoric is useful, the rival disciplines are useless. In the Renaissance the Disputes of the Liberal Arts were often reduced to the level of an intellectual Punch and Judy show, in which philosophy, or dialectic, or medicine retired with a bleeding head, while rhetoric held the stage alone. All of the humanists' utterances on this topic are governed by the practices of epideictic oratory, which has its own methods but knows of no rules of fair play. In constructing a *laus* or *vituperatio* you strive for the maximum effect. Success is measured by striking-power, not by reason or judgment. The literary critic's advice to the historian, then, is: never trust a rhetorician when he is praising his own subject.[6]

The Renaissance valued rhetoric because it could move people to thought or action, whether they wanted to or not, by mobilizing the will. Renaissance rhetoricians differ from their medieval counterparts in an increased stress on persuasion and the greater prominence given to the will, a development much helped by voluntarist theories in psychology. The route to the will lay partly through the reason, since the role of argument was to convince by rational means, and it is a false emphasis to describe rhetoric as irrational. Yet the more effective route lay through the passions, the feelings and emotions which the orator or poet either re-created in himself or represented in language with the aim of awakening the same feelings in the audience. We must beware of using the modern clear-cut distinction "between feelings and thoughts": as the great pioneer of this area of rhetorical criticism, Rosemond Tuve, wrote thirty years ago, "several of the faculties are concerned, in both parties to the communication." Rhetorical devices "move a reader's affections," but also "affect his judgments; they move him to feel intensely, to will, to act, to understand, to believe, to change his mind"[7]. I would add that the student of rhetoric must also study ethics, as in the concept of appetite, which plays a significant role in the theory of epideictic oratory.

The unity of rhetoric as a system is seen in the connections it makes between language and the feelings: it moves from psychology to style (or *elocutio*) and back again, offering a coherent model of how language can influence behaviour. The links between rhetoric and psychology are important, and inadequately studied. Aristotle had made his only large-scale discussion of the emotions in Book II of the *Rhetoric*, which was to become a scholastic textbook in ethics and psychology.[8] Cicero in Book II of *de oratore*, (II. xliv, 125–216) had given an extremely influential account of how the orator ought himself to be moved by the passions he is describing or arousing, and of the successes he can have, in setting audiences aflame; while Quintilian devoted a chapter to the passions (6.2), stating that the orator's main goal is to win power over his audience's feelings: without this his activity is pointless. The 16th century Italian critics show an increasing concern with the passions both in the traditional idea that the poet's goal is to arouse them, and in the newer concern with such concepts as the marvellous, and purgation, both of which are referred to theories of the passions.[9] When Daniel d'Auge published his *Deux dialogues de l'invention poétique*. . . . in 1560 he gave 5 pages to the analysis of the passions;[10] when the Jesuit Caussinus published his *de Eloquentia Sacra et Humana* in 1619 he could give nearly a hundred pages to the topic.[11] The increasingly systematic treatment of the emotions in the 17th century has been well studied recently by German scholars, such as Joachim Dyck, Heinrich Plett, Erwin Rotermund, F. G. Sieveke, and Birgit Stolt.[12] It resulted in a new sub-discipline of rhetorical psychology, *pathologia*, which has certain eccentricities, such as what Peter France has described as "the weird imaginings" of Cureau de la Chambre in *Les Caractères des passions* (1640) and *Le Système de l'âme* (1664).[13] All the same, this was clearly a significant development in rhetorical-psychological theory and practice. We need to know much more about the psycho-physiology of this period, whether Aristotelian, Stoic, or Cartesian, and the ways in which it may have affected theories of language.

The increasing stress on persuasion via the passions led to an important re-adjustment of emphasis within rhetoric between 1540 and 1640. Of the three goals of rhetoric, *movere, docere*, and *delectare, movere* became the most sought-after; of the five parts of the compositional process, *elocutio* received the greatest attention. The two changes were connected, of course, since the resources of language were developed by *elocutio* in the service of persuasive ends. The dominance of *movere* (shown by Dockhorn, Muntéano, Plett, and Weinberg)[14] applied to sacred as well as secular speakers, and St. Augustine's insistence that the preacher will accomplish nothing if he does not move the hearts of his congregation was taken up by many Renaissance writers on religion and rhetoric.

For *elocutio* the evidence is equally strong. Quintilian had said that *elocutio* was the hardest part of rhetoric to master; he is echoed by Melanchthon, Richard Sherry, Webbe, Du Bellay, Peletier, Speroni, Vida, Tasso, Puttenham and many more—some actually say that *elocutio* is more important than *inventio*.[15] W. S. Howell[16] distinguished 4 types of rhetoric-book in the 16th century: 1) Ciceronian, teaching all five processes; 2) Ramist, teaching the last three; 3) elocutionary, teaching *elocutio* alone; and 4) formulary, teaching the *progymnasmata* methods. I note that *elocutio* figures in three out of the four types, and plays a dominant role in those. The text-books give more space to *elocutio* than to the other processes, and while, as A. Kibédi-Varga had reminded us[17], this may partly be because it needs more room to set out all the definitions and examples, it is clear that the Renaissance pursued *elocutio* with enormous zest. Susenbrotus listed 140 figures; Shakespeare has been shown to know nearly 200; while the *Thesaurus* of Giovanni Baptista Bernardo (1599) lists approximately 5,000 rhetorical devices.[18] Modern disapproval of stylistic rhetoric, then, is wholly unhistorical. If you cannot pick up a list of the figures and read it through avidly, thinking of all the instances of their application and re-creation in Petrarch or Racine or Shakespeare or Milton, then you ought not to be studying rhetoric.

III

THE INTEREST in *elocutio* applies not only to composition but to criticism. Bernard Weinberg's massive history has shown how Italian criticism became more rhetorically influenced in the course of the 16th century: poetics was reduced to the doctrine of the three styles, with the result that poetry was virtually equated with *elocutio*, and questions of style and diction were given by far the greatest attention.[19]

If we regard *elocutio* as mere ornament then its rise to dominance in the 16th century would be inexplicable and unforgivable. But the link between rhetoric's role in the civic life and the details of style, this inner coherence of rhetoric, lies precisely in the power of the figures of rhetoric to move the feelings. The figures were divided into three groups, traditionally, which were then classified according to their emotive power, as were the individual figures. Similarly the three styles were ranked in terms of emotional intensity. The Grand Style was allowed to use all the figures, to achieve maximum effect: it was 100 Octane, or 5 star petrol; the middle style was 3 star, the *genus humile* 1 star, a good all-purpose means of motion, but unable to produce the strongest effects by use of the most intense figures. This most effective category consisted of the *figurae sententiae*, "les grandes figures" as the French called them, which comprised such figures as *exclamatio, apostrophe, imprecatio, aposiopesis, prosopopoeia* (and all types of visual representation). In a few weeks' reading I counted, for the period between 1545 and 1657, no less than 23 rhetoricians who describe the *figurae sententiae* as being an automatic way of arousing the feelings. They include Ramists, such as Talaeus, Fenner, Fraunce and Butler; non-Ramists, such as Susenbrotus, Sherry, Puttenham; Italian poetic theorists, Lionardi and Minturno; French theorists, such as d'Auge, d'Aubignac, La Mesnardière; the Jesuit Caussinus, the encyclopedist Alsted. The types of rhetoric book which make this identification include the standard Ciceronian and Ramist texts, works of epistolary rhetoric, preaching, poetics, and dramatic criticism.[20] We are dealing with a central rhetorical tradition, found throughout Europe, in all types of school, that appeal to the feelings is most effective through the most emotive figures.

One of the tasks of modern studies of rhetoric will be to understand the attention paid to *elocutio*, and to validate an interest in the figures and tropes. We have begun to see that they have a function,[21] but we need to see how many different functions they can have. In analysing the figures I suggest that we have to consider a triple relationship:

Form   :   Meaning   :   Feeling.

The form is fixed, in the rhetoricians' classification of verbal devices; but both *meaning* and *feeling* are infinitely flexible, as varied in expressive potential as language itself. This was recognized by the classical rhetoricians: Cicero said that the figures could be used either as "weapons for menace and attack" or for display. "For example, sometimes the repetition of words will produce an impression of force, at other times of grace" (*de Oratore*, 3.206; cit. Quint. 9. 1. 33). Demetrius gives three different effects possible from *anaphora*; Quintilian gives three uses for *aposiopesis* (9. 2. 54 ff), Susenbrotus four, Puttenham five[22]. Renaissance rhetoricians are just as sensitive to the polysemous quality of the figures: Hoskins[23] says that figures are to be used "as the passion of the matter shall serve," and that *polyptoton*, for instance, "may be used with or without passion" (17, 21); Peacham[24] says that the *figurae sententiae* "attend upon affections, as ready handmaids at commaundement to expresse most aptly whatsoever the heart doth affect or suffer" (120), and in discussing individual figures he asserts that this or that "may serve to any affection" (eg. pp. 44, 47, 105, etc.). I should like to know how effective these figures are; what kinds of effects they represent, or reproduce; and whether the same psychological-emotional effects can be produced by other means. It would be interesting to compare the various treatments of specific figures, to trace the *stemma* of influence, and to gauge their functions in literature. Not all of the connections are equally convincing, of course: the reader still has to test the effects ascribed according to his experience of reading the text. But until we take this doctrine seriously we will not be able to appreciate the coherence of rhetoric, the chain of cause and effect – rather like the chain of the "Hercules Gallicus"[25] leading all his hearers captive – which links rhetoric's public and civic function, its power to control will and feelings, with the minute practicalities of language.

Notes

1. The only bibliography of English rhetoric for the period is that contained for the works dicussed in W. S. Howell, *Logic and Rhetoric in England, 1500–1700* (Princeton, 1956), which, however, pays too little attention to neo-Latin works and to a large number of minor texts. A useful survey is W. J. Ong, "Tudor Writings on Rhetoric, Poetic, and Literary Theory," *Studies in the Renaissance* 15 (1968), 36–69, expanded in Ong, *Rhetoric, Romance, and Technology* (Ithaca, N.Y., 1971), 48–103. For the French 16th century see A. L. Gordon, *Ronsard et la Rhétorique* (Geneva, 1970), who notes "Il n'existe aucune bibliographie exhaustive de la rhétorique en France au XVIe siècle" (p. 11n). For the French 17th century see P. Kuentz in *Dix-Septième Siècle*, 80–81, (1968) 133–40, and Peter France, *Rhetoric and Truth in France, Descartes to Diderot* (Oxford, 1972), "Bibliographical Essay," 265–77. For Italy, Bernard Weinberg, *A History of Literary Criticism in the Italian Renaissance* (2 vols., Chicago, 1961) and his invaluable collection, *Trattati di Poetica e Retorica del '500* (4 vols., Bari, 1970–74). There is no reliable bibliography of the secondary literature, but for poetics and criticism, with some reference to rhetoric, see A. Buck, K. Heitmann, and W. Mettman (edd.), *Dichtungslehre der Romania aus der Zeit der Renaissance und des Barock* (Frankfurt, 1972), texts with short bibliographies. Some guidance can be obtained from the books by John Monfasani (note 3 below), J. E. Seigel and Nancy S. Struever (note 4). For recent work on German rhetoric see Birgit Stolt, "Tradition und Ursprünglichkeit. Ein Ueberblick über das Schrifttum zur Rhetorik in den sechziger Jahren im Bereich der Germanistik," *Studia Neophilologica* 41 (1969), 325–388; Joachim Dyck, "Rhetorical Studies in West Germany 1974–76. A Bibliography," in *Rhetoric Society Quarterly* 7 (1977), 1–19; and the books by German critics listed in note 12 below.

2. Apart from Howell (whose work is in many ways unsatisfactory: see my article "Rhetorical and antirhetorical tropes: On writing the history of *elocutio*," *Comparative Criticism* 3 (1981), pp. 105–32), there is no over-all view of English rhetoric, although useful studies include E. Sweeting, *Early Tudor Criticism, Linguistic & Literary* (Oxford, 1940; New York, 1964); V. L. Rubel, *Poetic Diction in the English Renaissance* (New York, 1941); F. R. Johnson, introduction to R. Rainolde, *The Foundacion of Rhetorike* (Gainesville, Fla. 1945; Delmar, N.Y. 1977) and further works cited in Brian Vickers, *Classical Rhetoric in English Poetry* (London, 1970), 170–74. For France and Germany see the works cited in notes 1 and 12; for Italy the works cited in notes 3 and 4, also Alfredo Galletti, *L'Eloquenza / Dalle Origini al XVI Secolo* (Milano, 1938), limited to ecclesiastical and political rhetoric, sketchy and outdated in many ways; Francesco Tateo, *Retorica e Poetica fra Medioevo e Rinascimento* (Bari, 1960). The important collection of studies by Cesare Vasoli, *La dialettica e la retorica dell'Umanesimo. "Invenzione" e "Metodo" nella cultura del XV e XVI secolo* (Milano, 1968) is concerned largely with the new Humanist logic. The study of literary rhetoric in the Italian Renaissance is amazingly incomplete.

3. Walter J. Ong, S.J., *Ramus, Method and the Decay of Dialogue* (Cambridge, Mass., 1958) and *Ramus and Talon Inventory* (Cambridge, Mass., 1958). John Monfasani, *George of Trebizond. A Biography and a Study of his Rhetoric and Logic* (Leiden, 1976): see my review in *Quarterly Journal of Speech* 63 (1977) pp. 443–48.

4. E. Garin, *Italian Humanism. Philosophy and Civil Life in the Renaissance* (Oxford, 1965; tr. P. Munz from the second (1958) edition of *L'Umanesimo italiano*); "Discussione sulla Retorica," *Medievo e Rinascimento* (Bari, 1954), 117–39; and numerous other works. P. O. Kristeller, *Renaissance Thought. The Classic, Scholastic, and Humanist Strains* (New York, 1961), including "Humanism and Scholasticism in the Italian Renaissance," from *Byzantion* (1944) and *Renaissance Thought and Its Sources* (New York, 1979), pp. 213–59. Peter Herde, "Politik und Rhetorik in Florenz am Vorabend der Renaissance," *Archiv für Kulturgeschichte* 18 (1965), 141–220; J. E. Seigel, " 'Civic Humanism' or Ciceronian Rhetoric? The Culture of Petrarch and Bruni," *Past & Present* no. 34 (July 1966), 3–48, and *Rhetoric and Philosophy in Renaissance Humanism. The Union of Eloquence and Wisdom, Petrarch to Valla* (Princeton, 1968). Nancy S. Struever, *The Language of History in the Renaissance. Rhetoric and Historical Consciousness in Florentine Humanism* (Princeton, 1970) with exceptionally detailed bibliographical notes.

5. Bacon, *Advancement of Learning* (1605), in *The Works of Francis Bacon* ed. J. Spedding *et. al.* (14 vols.; London, 1857–74), 3. 409.

6. This caveat applies in particular to the polemics of Valla, as treated by J. E. Seigel (note 4 above); but it applies also to most historical and philosophical treatments of this dispute.

7. *Elizabethan and Metaphysical Imagery* (Chicago, 1947), ch. VIII: "The Criterion of Rhetorical Efficacy," at p. 183.

8. James J. Murphy, "The Scholastic Condemnation of Rhetoric in the Commentary of Giles of Rome on the *Rhetoric* of Aristotle," *Arts Libéraux et philosophie au Moyen Age* (Montreal and Paris, 1969), pp. 833–41, and "Aristotle's *Rhetoric* in the Middle Ages," *Quarterly Journal of Speech* 52 (1966), pp. 109–15.

9. Weinberg, *History* (note 1 above) 137, 172, 283, 545, etc. (see Index, s.v. "Passions" and "Moving of passions (*movere*)").

10. Gordon (note 1 above), 37.

11. F. G. Sieveke, op. cit. in next note, 55.

12. Joachim Dyck, *Ticht-Kunst. Deutsche Barockpoetik und rhetorische Tradition* (Bad Homburg v.d. Höhe, Berlin, Zürich, 1966, 1969); Heinrich F. Plett, *Rhetorik der Affekte. Englische Wirkungsästhetik im Zeitalter der Renaissance* (Tübingen, 1975); Erwin Rotermund, "Der Affekt als literarischer Gegenstand: Zu Theorie und Darstellung der Passiones im 17. Jahrhundert," in H. R. Jauss (ed.) *Die nicht mehr schönen Künste* (München, 1969) 239–69, and *Affekt und Artistik. Studien zur Leidenschaftsdarstellung und zum Argumentationsverfahren bei Hoffman von Hoffmanswaldau* (München, 1972). F. G. Sieveke, "Eloquentia sacra. Zur Predigttheorie des Nicolaus Caussinus S.J." in *Rhetorik* ed. H. Schanze (Frankfurt, 1974), 43–68. B. Stolt, *Wortkampf. Frühneuhochdeutsche Beispiele zur rhetorischen Praxis* (Frankfurt, 1974), especially 1–77.

13. France (note 1 above), 164.

14. See Klaus Dockhorn, *Macht und Wirkung der Rhetorik. Vier Aufsätze zur Ideengeschichte der Vormoderne* (Bad Homburg v.d. Höhe, Berlin and Zürich, 1968: essays dating from 1944–66): Dockhorn may be described as the inspiration for the younger school of German rhetoricians; B. Muntéano, *Constantes Dialectiques en Littérature et en Histoire* (Paris, 1967), which contains several very stimulating essays on the rhetorical tradition in France, and a long study of the Abbé Du Bos. For Plett see the work cited in note 12; Weinberg, *History*, Index s.v. "Moving of passions (*movere*)."

15. On the dominance of *elocutio* see, e.g., (only a small sample is given here) Gordon, op. cit., 42 ff.; Monfasani, 282, 332n; Dyck, 66, 162 etc.; France, op. cit. 10, also *Racine's Rhetoric* (Oxford, 1965, 1970), 32 ff.; Weinberg, *History*, Index s.v. "Elocution" and "Invention-disposition-elocution"; Plett, 18, 28, 77 f., 79, 105, etc.

16. Howell, op. cit. in note 1, ch. 3.

17. A. Kibédi–Varga, *Rhétorique et Littérature. Etudes de structures classiques* (Paris, 1970), 17. Cf. the whole discussion, 16–36, especially the conclusion that in French rhetoric of the 17th and 18th centuries "les *passions* sont considérées comme un chapitre très important, sinon le chapitre principal, de la rhétorique" (35).

18. Susenbrotus, *Epitome troporum ac schematum*, 1540; Sister Miriam Joseph, *Shakespeare's Use of the Arts of Language* (New York, 1947). I owe my knowledge of Bernardo's *Thesaurus Rhetoricae* to an as yet unpublished paper by J. J. Murphy.

19. Weinberg, *History*, 108–10, 151–52, 196–99, 804, etc.

20. It would take too much space to cite all the evidence here: see the works listed in notes 12, 14, 15, 17 for a beginning. A full study of the *figurae sententiae* and the various schemes of classification and explication is a desideratum.

21. I have argued this case at more length in *Classical Rhetoric in English Poetry* ch. 3, 83–121: 'The Functions of Rhetorical Figures.'

22. Demetrius: cit. Vickers, 96 f.,from G. M. Grube, *A Greek Critic: Demetrius on Style* (Toronto, 1961). Susenbrotus: cit. Plett, 74 note; Puttenham: cit. Vickers, 113, from *The Arte of English Poesie*, ed. G. Willcock and A. Walker (Cambridge, 1936, 1970), 166–67.

23. John Hoskins, *Directions for Speech and Style* (c. 1599), ed. H. H. Hudson (Princeton, 1935).

24. Henry Peacham, *The Garden of Eloquence* (1593), ed. W. G. Crane (Gainesville, Fla., 1954; Delmar, New York, 1977). This text, together with that by Rainolde cited in note 2 above, is published in the extremely useful 'Scholars' Facsimiles & Reprints' series, which has also issued Thomas Wilson, *The Arte of Rhetorique* (1553); and Richard Sherry, *A Treatise of Schemes and Tropes* (1550) ed. H. W. Hildebrandt (1961, 1977).

25. On the Hercules Gallicus see M. R. Jung, *Hercule dans la littérature française du XVIe siècle* (Geneva, 1966).

Rhetoric and the Passions, 1760–1800

IAN THOMSON
Eltham College, London

IT WILL BE HELPFUL from the outset to be wary of certain models of literary history: models which tacitly assume developments from one period in which a set of homogeneous rhetorical principles appears to hold, to a later period in which a new set is received. The danger lies in the attendant notion of a "period of transition," while the word "new" itself needs to be more closely defined. The period from 1760–1800 seems more than any other to have lent itself to such labels. In fact, critical emphasis on terms such as "passion," "emotion" and "feeling" during these forty years has inspired an even more lethal label: "pre-romantic"—as if it were not enough to tag the point of departure and the destination with the epithets "neo-classical" and "romantic" without labelling the journey too! Rather than consider the period as one of transition, of development, advancement, progress (with the insidious suggestion of improvement which those words begin to supply)—I prefer to consider it as a period in which deadlock is often a keynote. It is almost a truism to say that what the period brings to rhetorical theory which is *essentially* new is psychology, and in particular, the principle of the association of ideas. But it is not often pointed out that the philosopher-rhetoricians[1] often thought of their enquiries as an attempt to weed out from established rhetorical theory those precepts not founded on nature, and to retain and enforce those that were. It is not often pointed out that what was new was often a question of different emphases on established terms, or more interestingly, on the *relations* between those terms, rather than the evolution of an altogether new terminology. Indeed, in cases where these emphases *did* tend to the radically new, real development was often inhibited by a refusal to rescind superannuated precepts belonging to the rhetorical tradition. I think I can best exemplify what I have called "deadlock" by adducing contradictions that seem to me to arise from it.

Johnson's censure of Lycidas is familiar: "It is not to be considered as the effusion of real passion; for passion runs not after remote allusions and obscure opinions. Passion plucks no berries from the myrtle and ivy, nor calls upon Arethuse and Mincius, nor tells of rough satyres and fawns with cloven heel. Where there is leisure for fiction there is little grief."[2] The same point was made by Kames in *The Elements of Criticism*. He quotes Satan in *Paradise Lost*:

> Then when I am thy captive talk of chains,
> Proud limitary cherub; but ere then
> Far heavier load thyself expect to feel
> From my prevailing arm, though Heaven's King
> Ride on thy wings, and thou with thy compeers,
> Us'd to the yoke, drawst his imperial wheels
> In progress through the road of Heav'n *star-pav'd*.

Kames writes that: "the concluding epithet forms a grand and delightful image, which cannot be the genuine offspring of rage."[3] There is no need to reduplicate examples: the attitude is pervasive and can be found in Blair, Campbell, Priestley and others.

However, another widely received notion implies a contradiction here: it is that theory of the origin of language which urges that in the infancy of a nation men were more passionate, being closer to nature, and that their passion naturally led to bold and figurative language. Thomas Barnes in a usefully eclectic piece written in 1785, with the telling title: *On the Nature and Essential Characters of Poetry as Distinguished from Prose*, remarks on "the *native impulse* of a soul, inspired with sentiments, which it could not express in any language but what was florid and poetical. By this theory, it may be said, we account for the common remark, that the *original* language of mankind was poetical: because, in the infancy of the world, everything would naturally excite admiration, and vehement passion."[4] To summarize, the contradiction is this: that rhetoric is, according to one major definition, the art of persuasion, and one of its resources is to move its audience, and figurative speech assists this end: on the other hand, genuine passion is supposed *not* to resort to figures, which are now seen as an artifice.

The confusion leads to evasions and equivocations. Kames, for example, occupies a very dubious platform when he argues that: "figures are not equally the language of every passion; pleasant emotions, which elevate or swell the mind, vent themselves in strong epithets and figurative expression; but humbling and dispiriting expressions effect to speak plain."[5] It is significant that Horace is cited as an authority for this excuse[6] — and an excuse is surely all that it is. One could easily reverse his position with a greater appearance of veracity: for instance, it is not beside the point to say that I write more florid letters when I am miserable, and that when I am happy, I often don't write letters at all.

It would be unfair to Kames to leave the issue here since at a later point in *The Elements of Criticism* he advances a similar point with greater complexity.

I shall cite the passage in full: "It is evident that a comparison is not proper on every occasion: a man when cool and sedate, is not disposed to poetical flights, nor to sacrifice truth and reality to imaginary beauties; far less is he so disposed when oppressed with care, or interested in some important transction that engrosses him totally. On the other hand, a man when elevated or animated by passion, is disposed to elevate or animate all his objects . . . In general, when by any animating passion, whether pleasant or painful, an impulse is given to the imagination; we are in that condition disposed to every sort of figurative expression, and in particular to comparisons. Rooted grief, deep anguish, terror, remorse, despair, and all the severe dispiriting passions are declared enemies, perhaps not to figurative language in general, but undoubtedly to the pomp and solemnity of comparison."[7] There is a significant shift in emphasis here from one on the differing expressions of pleasant and painful emotions, to a stress on the differing expression of *animating* and *dispiriting* passions. The word *animating* is interesting for it means here, as it does in Priestley (who acknowledges affinities with Kames) expressions which promote action or "those forms of address which are adapted to engage assent."[8] So that while the argument begins as a description of figures as *expressions* of sentiments, it ends with an *affective* direction. "Those forms of address which are adapted to engage assent" is of course a perfectly traditional definition of rhetoric.

I should like to leave some of the implications of this last point in abeyance while I develop my argument a little further. I believe that the concealed confusion which I have tried to illustrate by these evasions is not at all a product of the period 1760–1800. Rather, enquiry within the period developed in such a way that a lack of coherence *inherent* in rhetorical theory *since antiquity* could no longer be glossed over with any appearance of conviction. That this rift between incompatible rhetorics did not entangle earlier rhetoricians is only mildly surprising. Perhaps a favourite occupation of the Italian Renaissance — that of using Horace as a gloss on Aristotle, or more usually *vice versa*,[9] — is indicative of a disease endemic in many rhetorics: the disturbing will to believe that the tradition is homogeneous.

My contention is that the philosopher-rhetoricians of the latter half of the Eighteenth Century were so eager to assimilate primary standards of the rhetorical tradition into their work that they assimilated the lack of coherence already immanent in the tradition, and that this effectively limited the potential of what *was* new in their research. The reasons I want to offer for this are two: both involve disparities between the inescapable implications of what they assert and the conclusions they draw from what they say. The first is a question of aesthetic orientation; the second a confusion of rhetoric and poetic.

In many ways, writers of the period made significant advances in the theory of aesthetic orientation, in assessing the relationships which subsist between a work, its audience, its writer and the phenomenal world. They made a valuable contribution to our understanding of the correlation between actual emotions, both as transmitted and received, and the formal linguistic properties of the utterance. Priestley, for instance, puts the point succinctly: "If," he wrote, "we would wish to communicate to our readers those strong sensations that we feel in the ardour of composition, we must endeavour to express the whole of our sentiments and sensations, in the very *order* and *connection* in which they actually presented themselves to us at that time. For such is the similarity of human minds, that when the same appearances are presented to another person, his mind will, in general, be equally struck and affected with them, and the composition will appear to be natural and animated. Whereas if in consequence of an ill-judged scrupulosity or delay, we once lose sight of any part of that train of ideas, though, separately taken, they may appear better adapted to the subject, [we lose] the power to excite those sensations with which we would wish the composition might be read."[10] This strikes a blow at one kind of understanding of *mimesis*, the relationship between reality and language, for figures are seen, not as the signs of separate ideas (still less of things) but of the relationships between them. Indeed, as Priestley says, even though the ideas "*separately* taken may appear better adapted to the subject," it is "those strong sensations which we feel in the ardour of composition" which are to be communicated. This is perhaps a step towards Eliot's "objective correlative"[11] but it is surely not consonant with the traditional understanding of figures as part of an ornamentation of language "adapted to engage assent." The seeds of the impending dissolution of traditional rhetoric sown by Horace in the maxim *si vis me flere dolendum est primum ipsi tibi*[12] are now germinating. As an interest grew in the personal disposition of the writer the affective orientation came to seem less crucial.

Six years later, in 1783, Blair, in his *Lectures on Rhetoric and Belles Lettres* made a significant move in repudiating the theory of the classical levels of style. Instead, he considered that style might more profitably be examined under a more individual aspect, that of the author's habitual modes of thinking. The psychological constitution of the author, rather than the *a priori* decorums of rhetoric, no matter how skillfully and flexibly attuned to their ultimate purpose, determine the characteristics of his style. In this view, figurative language as part of the affective apparatus is put firmly in its place: "If it shall now be enquired," Blair wrote, "what are the proper sources of the sublime? My answer is, that they are to be looked for everywhere in nature. It is not by hunting after tropes and figures, and rhetorical assistances, that we can expect to produce it. No: it stands clear, for the most part, of these laboured refinements of art. *It must come unsought, if it comes at all* [my italics]; and be the natural offspring of a strong imagination."[13] Strange words to find in a rhetorical treatise, a fit of rhetoric against rhetoric almost, and while Blair is still a very long way away from Keats, one is forcibly reminded of the latter's outburst: "Poetry should come as naturally as the leaves to a tree: otherwise it had better not come at all."[14]

But Keats is talking about poetry: Blair is talking about producing the sublime in discourse, and it seems to me that here and elsewhere there is a lack of distinction about ends. It is consistently disappointing to find that these writers often lose sight of the *kind* of discourse they are talking about, and it is interesting to note that often the more revealing developments in their work are exemplified by quotations from poetry rather than oratory. It is disappointing too to find that despite their acuity, Kames, Blair and Priestley will not let go of certain precepts of the rhetorical stock-in-trade[15] which are not consistent with the implications of their more progressive research. I am thinking particularly of the tiresome recurrence in their work of the dictum "Language is the dress of thought" with the inevitable suggestion that figures serve to adorn the dress. The notion of figures as ornament, whether the object is pleasure or persuasion, is not compatible with a notion of figures as a natural and sympathetic correlative between transmitted and received trains of ideas.

Possibly the beginning of this paper was unnecessarily polemical, an overstatement of emphases. Without doubt, the application of psychological models to literary ideas promoted a good deal of worthwhile research and valuable critical comment, and Blair and Priestley were among the most perspicacious theorists of their time. What such an approach conspicuously failed to do, however, was to show how the resources of language could still serve rhetorical ends; indeed, even to show that the ends which rhetoric had proposed for itself were still realistic in a state where public speaking was expected to be more coolly functional than it had been at Rome, and in a literary ethos where persuasion, moving an audience, and eventually even addressing an audience at all, had less and less to do with the aesthetics of writing. The major accusation to be levelled against late eighteenth-century rhetoric is that it is written in a void. It had come too late; perhaps it was no longer needed. The enormous ambitions of the belle-lettrist rhetoricians, coupled with the limitations they had inherited from a declining tradition, left them open to the snares of dilettantism. They had set themselves the task of revitalising rhetoric without due consideration of the purpose a rhetorical education might be expected to serve in their own era. There can be no doubt that Priestley, lecturing in Warrington, and Blair in Aberdeen, sincerely believed that their contributions to the history of rhetoric had some practical value. They knew from classical theory that the purposes of rhetoric were deliberative, forensic or epideictic and doubtless they envisaged their pupils as potential members of either house, as lawyers, or as literary men. But they took their obligations to utility no further, and it is frequently disturbing to find that they so often promulgated an ideal of style without any regard for the *telos* of a particular kind of composition.

Notes

1. The epithet is P. W. K. Stone's. See his *The Art of Poetry 1750–1820: Theories of Poetic Composition and Style in the late Neo-Classic and early Romantic Periods* (London, 1967).

2. Samuel Johnson, "Life of Milton," *Lives of the English Poets*, ed. G. Birbeck-Hill (Oxford, 1945), vol. I, p. 163.

3. Henry Home, Lord Kames, *Elements of Criticism*, 8th ed. (Edinburgh 1807), vol. I, p. 474.

4. Thomas Barnes, "On the Nature and Essential Characters of Poetry as distinguished from Prose," in *Memoirs of the Manchester Literary and Philosophical Society*, I, 1785, p. 57.

5. Kames, vol. I, p. 497.

6. See Horace, *Ars Poetica*, lines 95–99.

7. Kames, vol. II, p. 204.

8. Joseph Priestley, *A Course of Lectures on Oratory and Criticism* (London, 1777), p. 79.

9. See Bernard Weinberg, *A History of Literary Criticism in the Italian Renaissance* (Chicago, 1961), vol. I.

10. Priestley, p. 77.

11. See T. S. Eliot, *Selected Essays*, (Faber, 1932). In his essay on *Hamlet* (1919) Eliot wrote: "The only way of expressing emotion in the form of art is by finding an 'objective correlative'; in other words, a set of objects, a situation, a chain of events which shall be the formula for that *particular* emotion; such that when the external facts, which must terminate in sensory experience are given, the emotion is immediately evoked."

12. *Ars Poetica*, lines 99–103.

13. Hugh Blair, *Lectures on Rhetoric and Belles Lettres* (London, 1783), vol. I, p. 85.

14. John Keats, Letter to John Taylor, 27 February, 1818.

15. One reason for the persistence of such rags from the stock-in-trade may be the way in which rhetoric was taught in schoolbooks. Many of these manuals were compilations of axioms culled from rhetoricians of all periods without any attempt to form them into a coherent system. One can imagine that later study, no matter how diligent, would scarcely eradicate the effects, or weaken the tenacity, of these dicta.

Antonio de Capmany's Theory of Human Nature

DON ABBOTT
University of California, Davis

Aₙₜₒₙᵢₒ ᵈᵉ Cₐₚₘₐₙy's *Filosofía de la eloquencia* (1777) represents a singular achievement among the rhetorical treatises written by Spaniards in the eighteenth century. Capmany (1742–1813), virtually alone among his countrymen, proposed a philosophic rhetoric, a book which would combine "the origin of ideas with the affections" and exercise "both the minds and the hearts of the readers." Accordingly, the purpose of this paper is to investigate the nature and origins of Capmany's "philosophic" rhetoric.[1] Such an investigation reveals that Capmany constructed a modern theory of rhetoric predicated upon an explicit theory of human nature. In sum, it will be argued that Capmany's study of the psychological foundations of rhetoric yields, in the *Filosofía de la eloquencia*, the Spanish treatise most representative of the spirit of the Enlightenment.

It is apparent from the outset of the *Filosofía* that Capmany intends to challenge the prevailing superiority of neo-classicism in Spanish letters. The preference for the past over the present is the result of an historical myopia. Says Capmany: "The ancients are looked upon in perspective: they are not of flesh and blood to the eyes of the imagination. With the course of centuries they have laid aside all grossness, and only the spiritual remains: the individual in the abstract" (p. iii). This process of abstraction resulted in ancestor-worship which so perverted rhetorical education that "all believe that they possess eloquence, because it is poorly taught. In effect, a few men endowed with a great facility of speech, and a natural abundance of words, dominate over the many in whom the cold lessons of the classroom have extinguished all talent, and believe that to be loquacious is to be eloquent. Sometimes this vulgar opinion derives from the caprice and puerility of many classical rules and exercises which have caused certain writers to disregard all pure sentiment, all simple and natural taste, suffocating it with an infinity of fantastic tastes" (pp. x–xi).

It is particularly noxious to Capmany that these classically inspired perversions are peculiar to Spain. The language of "the parliament of Great Britain and the churches of France moves, softens, and influences the spirits. Only among us are there men who panegyrise the dead in order to depreciate the living; whose rancid taste finds in old books energetic that which was only clear, correct that which was only pure, simple what was base, harmonious what was diffuse, fluent what was languid, natural what was slovenly, sublime what was emphatic, proper what is today antiquated" (pp. xvii–xviii). This veneration of "worthless trash" had been in part perpetuated by the teaching of rhetoric in Latin rather than the vernacular. "The most useful and prudent method for young rhetoricians," says Capmany, "is to cultivate and ennoble, by eloquent compositions, their native language" (p. xvi). The Spaniards should imitate the Romans, who "devoted themselves to writing exclusively in their own language" (p. xvi). Following his own advice Capmany's "little work goes forth in Castilian" (p. xvii).

It is, of course, more than simply composition in Castilian which marks the *Filosofía* as the antithesis of antiquarianism. It is rather Capmany's self-conscious identification with the methods and methodologists of the modern age which results in a rhetoric consistent with Enlightenment epistemology. Capmany is quite clearly enamored of the eloquence of those thinkers who had broken with the past: "To be eloquent, grand objects are enough for a great genius; thus even Descartes and Newton, although they were not orators, were eloquent, when they spoke of God, of time, of space, and of the universe" (pp. 7–8). Not only does Capmany admire Newton and Descartes, but he also seeks to emulate their empirical approach. According to Capmany observation and expression are inextricably linked, for "the method of viewing objects depends much on the force or weakness of perception; if the perception is weak, so too is the expression. Ideas acquired by cold and leisurely reflection in the retirement of the study are less vivid and strong than those which come from observation of the earth's spectacle. It would therefore be a prodigy to find eloquence in a man born blind" (p. 7).

Capmany himself intends to observe "those magnificent expressions and sublime sayings, which in all times and countries have won for their authors the renown of eloquence" (p. vii). The result of this analysis is a book which "does not teach oratory completely" nor one which instructs "how to compose a perfect and uncorrupted discourse" but rather a work which "accustoms its readers, by the light of many observations and natural principles of taste and sentiment, to discern the effects of true eloquence" (pp. xix–xx). It is this dependence upon "observations and natural principles" which justifies the work as a philosophy of eloquence and ensures, in turn, a new treatment of an old subject. "Hitherto," claims Capmany, "eloquence has been treated among us by precepts more than by principles, by definition more than by example, and more by speculation than with sentiment" (p. ix). Consequently, Capmany proffers his philosophic rhetoric, "a rhetoric which gives reasons for its propositions, which analyzes examples, which combines the origin of ideas with the affections, in a word, which exercises both the minds and the hearts of the readers" (p. ix).

This "philosophical rhetoric" is predicated upon an exposition of certain elements of human nature: the "Qualities of Oratorical Talent." These "qualities" are the natural powers or faculties of the mind necessary to produce eloquence. So concerned with mental powers is Capmany that Marcelino Menéndez y Pelayo charged that the *Filosofia* is not a rhetoric at all, but rather a work of psychology.[2] For Capmany, however, there is no distinction between a philosophical and psychological rhetoric—the study of eloquence must begin with the human mind. And the study of the human mind begins with the qualities of oratorical talent.

The first of these qualities is wisdom. Wisdom, or the "philosophic impulse," "is formed by a profundity of ideas, elevation of sentiment, and independence from prejudice. But philosophy of this kind has two foundations: a force of reason, to fathom the principles of things, and to rise to the most perfect knowledge of which man is capable; and a well-informed reason, which, contained within the limits prescribed for the human understanding, delivers it from the errors of pride and a fatal love of singularity" (p. 10).

Taste, the second quality, is the expression of "a feeling of beauty or defect in all the arts. It is a profound discernment, which anticipates reflection" (p. 10). Taste is a habit which must be exercised "by seeing as well as feeling, and judging the beautiful by inspection, and the good by sentiment. It requires exercise and objects of comparison; for how can he who has seen only the pagodas of Hindustan, but never St. Peter's at the Vatican be able to distinguish the miserable from the sumptuous, the deformed from the beautiful, the monstrous from the symmetrical" (p. 10)?

The third oratorical talent is genius. This term, says Capmany, "is derived from the Latin word *gignere*, to engender, to produce; and therefore invention, which pertains to every species of genius. The new and the singular in thought is not enough to merit the name of genius; it is also necessary that ideas should be great, or exceedingly interesting to men." Genius, however, is not "simply invention in the plan of a work, but also the invention of expression. The principles of the art of speaking well are so obscure and imperfect, there are so few fixed rules, that he who is not really an inventor cannot acquire the renown of great genius" (p. 14).

Fourth is imagination, a quality which "consists in a new combination or union of images, as well as in a correspondence or exact comparison of these images with the sentiment that is to be excited. If it is to be one of terror, then the imagination creates sphinxes; animates furies; makes the earth roar, burst asunder, and disgorge fire to the sky. If admiration or enchantment, then it creates the garden of the Hesperides, the enchanted island of Armida, and the palace of Atlantas. Thus we shall say that the imagination is invention in the matter of images, just as genius is in the matter of ideas" (p. 17).

The fifth and final quality of oratorical talent is sentiment. However, "sentiment is to be distinguished from sensation. The latter is a material impression, dependent upon necessities. The former is a delicate affection of the soul, relating to the moral man, and according to some, an internal transitory emotion that precedes passion, when passion begins to rise in our soul with greater vehemence and more forceful activity" (p. 23). Sentiment, says Capmany, is the source of "eloquence which exhalts and moves the soul. Because of this it has been observed that neither sentiments are excited, nor passions painted, if the orator is insusceptible of them, since, to draw a faithful picture, to cause a certain emotion, he who speaks ought to be moved by the same affections as he seeks to inspire" (p. 24).

These then are the five qualities of oratorical talent: wisdom, taste, genius, imagination, and sentiment. These powers are the prerequisites of eloquence without which "the orator is no more than a declaimer" (p. 29). Although all five of these qualities are necessary for the achievement of eloquence, Capmany clearly regards two of them, imagination and sentiment, as most important for the orator. The soul, says Capmany, "has two levers by which it is put in motion, and these are the sentiment and the imagination: The first is undoubtedly of great force, but the second can often supply for it" (p. 25). He continues: "If imagination supplies for sentiment, it is not by the impression that it has upon the orator, but by the impulse that it gives to the affections of the hearers. The effect of sentiment is more concentrated in him who speaks, and that of imagination is more appropriate for communication to others" (pp. 32–33). For Capmany, then, imagination and sentiment are the mental capacities most essential for effective expression.

Only if a man is naturally endowed with imagination, sentiment, and the other qualities of oratorical talent will he profit from the study of rhetoric. For without an examination of "the rules of expression" these five qualities cannot be put into action. By expression Capmany means quite simply elocution, that is, style. Elocution is "such an absolute necessity to the orator that without it he is incapable of producing his ideas, and all his other talents, however great they may be, are entirely useless" (p. 30). So indispensable is elocution to Capmany that he titles the major division of the text a "Treatise on Oratorical Elocution." In contrast, the "Qualities of Oratorical Talent" is merely the introductory essay.

The philosophical and psychological premises found in the introduction do dictate, however, that the dominant theme of work must be elocution. The traditional investigative functions of rhetoric are consigned to natural proclivities, thus leaving style as the only aspect of rhetoric to warrant attention. Inventive ability is co-determined by the qualities of genius and imagination and as such is independent of rules and exercises. Invention, says Capmany, "pertains to every species of genius" (p. 10). Later he adds that "the imagination is invention in the matter of images, just as genius is the matter of ideas" (p. 17). Thus, because the inventiveness of the orator is predetermined by nature, invention is not strictly a part of rhetorical studies, as is style. Capmany, then, sees two dimensions of rhetoric: invention, which is wholly a product of nature; and expression, which is largely the result of the application of rules. The other parts of rhetoric, says Capmany, are "not pertinent" (p. viii).

Capmany must, of necessity, therefore, treat style in a comprehensive manner. This he does in the "Treatise on Oratorical Elocution". It is wide-ranging and divided into three sections: 1) "Of Diction"; 2) "Of Style"; and 3) "Of the Adornment of Eloquence." This last section is the longest of the three parts and consists of a veritable catalogue of tropes and figures. Despite the avowed newness of his approach, Capmany is unable to break from the Spanish ornamental tradition in rhetoric.

Despite Capmany's extensive, and for the most part traditional, treatment of the tropes, he nonetheless manages to present a view of style which is consistent with his theory of human nature. This is because, for Capmany, style, above all else, must reflect the mind of the orator. The principal quality which makes this possible is variously labeled vividness, brightness, or liveliness. Hence an eloquent speaker "is known by a lively and persuasive style, formed of expressions, vigorous, energetic, and bright" (p. 5). Later Capmany remarks that "a strong thought will always be that which causes us the most lively impression that can arise either from the idea, or from the manner of expressing it" (p. 91). In order for the speaker to make a "lively impression" on his hearers he must be capable of a depth of feeling: "Neither sentiments are excited, nor passions painted, if the orator is insusceptible of them; since, to draw a faithful picture, and to cause a certain emotion, he who speaks ought to be moved by the same affections as he seeks to inspire" (p. 24). But such an orator is rare, because "there are very few sensitive souls, on whom the objects of their meditations make a lively impression, and who can transmit to the hearts of their hearers the sentiments with which they themselves are penetrated" (p. 7).

Thus stylistic excellence is dependent upon liveliness of expression which is in turn determined by the perceptions of the speaker. Capmany's theory of rhetoric, then, is clearly the product of his theory of human nature. As such it marks a distinct departure in Spanish rhetoric. Before 1777 no one in Spain had attempted anything like Capmany's psychologically oriented study of oratory. The almost unprecedented appearance of the *Filosofía* strongly suggests the influence of foreign thought on its author. The attribution of influence is illusive, however. With the exception of Newton and Descartes Capmany rarely acknowledges his foreign debts. Moreover, the "Qualities of

Oratorical Talent" (wisdom, taste, genius, imagination and sentiment) reads like a conspectus of Enlightenment commonplaces. All of this assures that the tracing of sources must be largely speculative.

Such speculation led Menéndez y Pelayo to assert, with little elaboration, that Capmany was a follower of Francis Hutcheson.[3] It is an assertion that bears scrutiny. Capmany, like Hutcheson, is a sentimentalist. Both men recognize the importance of sensation, but neither believes that the fundamental characteristics of human nature are ultimately reducible to experiential origins. Sentiment, unlike the physically induced sensation, says Capmany, "is a delicate affection of the soul, relating to the moral man, and according to some, an internal transitory emotion that precedes passion" (p. 23). This statement is consistent with Hutcheson's description of the "moral sense" in *An Essay on the Nature and Conduct of the Passions and Affections* (1728): "All Perception is by the Soul, not by the Body, tho' some Impressions on the bodily Organs are the Occasions of some of them; and in others the Soul is determined to other sorts of Feelings or Sensations, where no bodily Impressions is the immediate Occasion. A certain incorporeal Form, if one may use that Name, a Temper observed, a Character, an Affection, a State of a sensitive Being, known or understood, may raise Liking, Approbation, Sympathy, as naturally from the very Constitution of the Soul, as a bodily Impression raises external Sensations."[4]

So similar are Capmany and Hutcheson that the latter's discussion of oratory in *An Inquiry into the Original of our Ideas of Beauty and Virtue* (1726) could practically serve as a summary of the former's position. Writes Hutcheson: "Upon this moral Sense is founded all the Power of the Orator. The various Figures of Speech are the several Manners which a lively Genius, warm'd with Passions suitable to the Occasion, naturally runs into, only a little diversify'd by Custom: and they only move the Hearers, by giving a lively Representation of the Passions of the Speaker; which are communicated to the Hearers."[5] The sentimental origin of the orator's power, genius, lively representation, and the primacy of the passions in persuasion are all consistent with Capmany's philosophy of rhetoric. Such close correspondence suggests that Capmany may have indeed been influenced by Hutcheson.

Although Capmany does not acknowledge it, indebtedness is certainly possible, for Hutcheson's works were known and respected in Spain by the last decades of the eighteenth century. In his *Investigaciones filosóficas sobre la belleza ideal* (1789) Capmany's contemporary, Esteban de Arteaga, recommended Hutcheson's *Essay on the Passions* as a fundamental work on aesthetics and morality.[6] At approximately the same time, Spain's most ardent Anglophile, Gaspar Melchor de Jovellanos, urged the Collegio Imperial de Calatrava at Salamanca to develop a course in ethics consistent with Hutcheson's *System of Moral Philosophy* (1775).[7] By at least 1790, then, Hutcheson was recognized by the

Spanish as a moralist and aesthetician of considerable note. Although evidence of this recognition generally appears after the publication of the *Filosofía*, such testimony does demonstrate receptiveness to Hutchesonian principles on the part of Spanish intellectuals.

Moreover, even if Hutcheson's works were themselves unavailable to Capmany when he composed the *Filosofía*, Hutchesons's ideas were, nonetheless, in circulation in Spain prior to 1777. Nigel Glendinning suggests that Capmany may have been exposed to Hutchesonian theory by the French *Encyclopédie*.[8] The *Encyclopédie* was apparently circulating in Spain by mid-century and with it the ideas of Francis Hutcheson. The article by Marmontel on beauty, in particular, contains a rather thorough resumé of Hutcheson's work, including his treatment of sentiments.[9] In eighteenth-century Spain the French often served as the intermediaries of English ideas and Capmany might well have gained a basic understanding of Hutcheson from the work of Diderot and D'Alembert.

Thus it is both possible and plausible that Capmany was influenced by Francis Hutcheson. Whatever the precise channels of influence, it is clear that Capmany's concept of communication is the result of a climate of opinion more common to England or France than to Spain. As already indicated, the *Filosofía* reflects genuine respect for Descartes, whom Capmany calls "the father of modern philosophy" (p. 207). Like many enlightened Spaniards, Capmany admired the Cartesian method because it had made possible a new intellectual order, but he did not, as a consequence of his admiration, accept the philosopher as ultimate authority. Capmany approvingly quotes an anonymous author who claims that "time has destroyed the opinions of Descartes, but his glory continues" (p. 22). This statement helps explain why, despite several references to Descartes, the *Filosofía* exhibits a greater affinity for the comparatively more current ideas of Hutcheson. It may be that Capmany discovered in the writings of Rene Descartes the inspiration for a new philosophical rhetoric, and that he found in the work of Francis Hutcheson the means of attaining that end. This receptivity to French and English ideas of human nature and the nature of rhetoric enable Capmany to produce the most "enlightened" rhetoric of eighteenth-century Spain.

Capmany recognized the difficulty of providing the philosophic rhetoric which the title of the treatise so confidently promised. "I know," he writes, "that this book cannot fill so great a void, but meanwhile it will supply what is most common, until another, with more extensive knowledge, will perfect the work" (pp. ix-x). But no one else appeared to "perfect the work" of Antonio de Capmany and his *Filosofía de la eloquencia* remains a singular achievement of the Spanish *ilustración*.

Notes

1. This study is based upon the first edition of the *Filosofia de la eloquencia* (Madrid, 1777). References will be cited parenthetically within the text. Translations are mine.

2. Marcelino Menéndez y Pelayo, *Historia de las ideas estéticas en España* (1883–91; rpt. Madrid, 1947), III, 127.

3. Ibid.

4. Francis Hutcheson, *An Essay on the Nature and Conduct of the Passions and Affections* ed., Paul McReynolds (Gainesville, Florida, 1969), p. 241.

5. Francis Hutcheson, *An Inquiry into the Original of Our Ideas of Beauty and Virtue* (New York, 1971), p. 258.

6. Esteban de Arteaga, *La belleza ideal*, ed., Miguel Batllori, Classicos Castellanos, v. 122 (Madrid, 1943), p. 108.

7. J. H. R. Polt, "Jovellanos and His English Sources," *Transactions of the American Philosophical Society*, New Series, v. 54, pt. 7 (Philadelphia, 1964), p. 10.

8. Nigel Glendinning, "Influencia de la Literatura inglesa en España en el siglo XVIII," in *La Literatura española del siglo XVIII y sus fuentes extranjeras*, Cuadernos de la Cátedra Feijóo, No. 20 (Oviedo, 1968), pp. 51–52.

9. "Beau," *Encyclopédie*, Geneva Folio Edition (1771–76), IV, 608–36.

Part II

Rhetoric and Literature

Rhetorical Status in Horace, *Serm.* 2, 1

A. D. LEEMAN
University of Amsterdam

THE MOST PROMISING young lawyer of the Ciceronian age was C. Trebatius Testa.[1] Cicero, quick to pick out excellent young men, recommended him in 54 B.C. to Caesar during his Gallic campaign and kept up a correspondence with him. Cicero's letters survived and show Trebatius to be not only intelligent, but also full of wit, moreover a keen swimmer and a keen drinker of a good glass of wine.[2] In 46 B.C. Cicero dedicated his *Topica* to his young friend—a work dealing with a subject half-way between philosophy and rhetoric, which he provided, rather unexpectedly, with an appendix on rhetorical status.[3] We shall meet all these features of his early life again.

Twelve years after Cicero's death, Trebatius, by then a highly respected iurisconsultus, makes his second entry into the history of Latin literature. In the dramatized first satire of his second book of *Sermones* (published in 30 B.C.) Horace introduces his own person consulting the famous lawyer on the subject of his satire-writing.[4] His first book (published some years earlier)—he tells Trebatius—has encountered severe criticism from the public: some think him too violent a satirist (*ultra legem*), others think him too weak a poet. What is he to do in order to avoid attacks on the second book which he is going to write? (v. 1–5). The fiction here is apparently that of the threat of a trial to be averted, and of the satirist asking legal advice from a lawyer.[5] This "metaphorical" situation is brilliantly exploited by the poet, who in reality is explaining his conception of satire and the ways in which his second book differs from the criticized first one. Listen for yourself. To Horace-the-consultant's question "what am I to do?" Horace the poet makes Trebatius reply: "Just keep quiet," *quiescas*, which is ambiguous: "take a rest and don't mind," or "do nothing at all." Horace understands it in the second meaning, and asks: "you advise me to write no more poetry whatever?." "Yes I do." Trebatius reacts in the lapidary manner typical of lawyers of all ages. "I would if I could," Horace sighs, "*verum nequeo dormire*" (but I cannot sleep, or: do nothing, pursuing the

ambiguity of *quiescas*, Latin *dormire* also meaning "to keep quiet, to do nothing").
In a splendid *ethopoiia* Horace makes the jurisconsult reply: "my remedy against
sleeplessness is to take a good swim in the Tiber and to round the day off
with a strong drink" (v. 8–9), thus showing the three traces characterizing his
person in Cicero's letters: wit, and a predilection for wetting the outer and
the inner man. "But seriously," Trebatius continues, "if you really must write,
then write safer and more profitable poetry, e.g. an epic on Octavian's wars,"
(at the time Octavian had just got rid of Antony and Cleopatra and was busy
pacifying the Roman Empire). "Oh no, that is far above my poetical capacities,"
is Horace's reaction (v. 10–15). "But you can write a laudatory poem on
Octavian's person." "I will in due course, but it is not the right moment yet
for that" (v. 16–20). – "At any rate such poetry is better than writing violent
and offensive satires in which every reader feels a potential victim himself" (v.
21–25). This warning of the lawyer voices the dangers to which the
satirist – whether he is called Lucilius or Horace or Persius or Juvenal – exposes
himself.[6] All four satirists give the same kind of answer: mother Nature made
me a satirist, so I cannot help writing satire. Horace formulates it in the following
way: "Everybody has his whims and follies; mine is writing verse in the manner
of the great Lucilius, thus showing myself a worthy descendent of my bellicose
forefathers in Apulia and Lucania" (v. 24–39). "But," Horace goes on, "I promise
not to attack in the future unless provoked and offended, so help me Jupiter;
however, if touched in my weak spots, I will counterattack with my own
weapon: satire. And write I will as long as I live" (v. 39–60). Dryly, Trebatius
replies with a quotation from Homer[7], Thetis' warning to her son Achilles
that he will not live long, if he follows his bellicose nature: "Horace, my boy,
beware of the chilling reaction of an offended high and mighty person" (v.
60–62). Horace's proud answer amounts to the following: "Just as Lucilius
was safe from such dangers by his close relations with mighty friends, so I
feel protected by my acquired social status as a friend of men like Maecenas"
(closest friend himself of Octavian).

I will save up the finale of the poem for my own finale, and first turn to
some problems concerning the consultation sofar, which is usually misinterpreted
by Latinists. Thus it is stated that the situation of the consultation is
contaminated with a situation of the trial itself: Trebatius attacks and Horace
defends himself – successfully. No less a scholar than Eduard Fraenkel
characterizes the dialogues as *Scheinpolemik*, and Niall Rudd's verdict is that
the satire is a brilliant piece of shadow-boxing, a light-weight poem which should
not be taken too seriously.[8] However, we should first try to give Horace some
more credit and ask ourselves how far he makes Trebatius act as a
pseudo-professional and competent jurisconsult. Unfortunately, we possess no
sources informing us how exactly the consultation of a lawyer took place, but
we do happen to have a passage in Cicero's *De oratore* telling us how a patron

undertaking the defence of a client acted in similar circumstances. In Book 2, 102–4 he tells us how an orator, asked to act as a patron, should take on the role of an advocatus diaboli and bring forward all the arguments against his future client he—and supposedly the adversary—could think of. With the help of the counterarguments of his client he should form a preliminary idea of the nature of his client's case and of its *status — coniecturalis, finitionis* or *qualitatis*, the three statuses in descending order of strength: the client has not done the deed (say murder) he is accused of; or he has done the deed, but it falls under a different definition (murder of a traitor); or he has done the deed, but he had more or less good reasons for it (e.g. murder in self-defence or other extenuating circumstances).

Returning to the consultation of a lawyer, we should first state that the situation here is only partially analogous. In most cases of legal advice the procedure is that of *respondere*, that is interpretation of the law or advice for the formulation of legal documents. But there is another important activity of the jurisconsult, *cavere*, which is giving advice as to how the client should avoid falling into legal pitfalls resulting in legal procedures against him.[9] It is clear that this is the situation in our *Sermo* 2, 1: how is Horace going to avoid nasty consequences in writing his second Book of Satires, given the criticism uttered by the public against Book I. We can say that this is a deliberative aspect of a juridical causa to be avoided: the advice concerns a future course of action, not a deed done. This has its consequences for the question of *status*, which—as you will by now understand—I want to use as a problem-solver in our satire. Now in Cicero's—and Trebatius'—*Topica* due attention is paid to status in a deliberative case. There the statuses are, whether a certain action (e.g. a war) is to be undertaken altogether; if not, whether it can be undertaken under a different heading (e.g. not a war of conquest, but one in accordance with a treaty of mutual assistance); or whether it can be excused and defended as a preventive war for self-protection.

What happens in Horace's satire? First, Trebatius dissuades his consultant from writing poetry altogether: the most radical and safest course (*status coniecturalis*). Failing this, he advises him—if he must write by all means—to write poetry under a different heading: in the epic or in the encomiastic tradition (*status finitionis*). This is safer than writing offensive satire. Horace refuses again: he simply must write satire, but, warned by Trebatius, he will write defensive, not offensive satire, and thus be safeguarded as far as possible against actions which might be undertaken against him (*status qualitatis*).

In this way Trebatius helps Horace the consultant to formulate the real 'status' of his poetry, and Horace the poet to formulate his satirical program.

You will remember that Trebatius then warns Horace that attacks on the mighty, even provoked attacks, will endanger his social position. This passage provided an opportunity to stress his social rise in recent years and his friendship with the great Maecenas – a favorite topic in his satires – and it serves as a transition to the finale, in which quite unexpectedly Trebatius turns the pseudo-juridical situation into a real one: "I warn you (*caveas*) there is an old law against *mala carmina*" – properly, magic formulae, but interpreted here as invective poetry (v. 80–83). Horace appeals to the verdict of Octavian, who judged his satires to be *bona carmina*, meaning this in the literary sense of good poetry; moreover he used them in the service of the good cause of exposing only those who deserve it (v. 83–85). "All right," is Trebatius' last word, "under the general laughter of the jury the accusation will not be admitted, and you will be dismissed from trial" (v. 86). I venture the guess that here we meet with the fourth *status* – often omitted in the system – called *translationis*, which implies that a case should be dismissed because the court is not competent – in this case apparently because of the previous verdict of *iudex* Octavian, the highest authority in the state.[10] In this highly fanciful final passage with its legal jokes and word-play Horace rounds off – as is so often the case in Latin literature – by returning to the beginning, where he had stated that he was criticised as being violent *ultra legem* and a weak poet – i.e. as a writer of *mala carmina* in both meanings.

The relations between rhetoric and Roman Law are highly disputed. In a book on *Rhetorische Statuslehre und Gesetzauslegung der römischen Juristen* (1967) Uwe Wesel rejects the famous theory of Stroux concerning the influence of the *status legales* on Roman legal interpretation and on the *Causa Curiana* in particular. However that may be, it seems to me that the refined *ethopoiia* of the lawyer Trebatius enabled Horace to present him as a jurisconsult well versed in rhetorical *status* and well aware of Cicero's advice on the right procedure during a consultation – thanks to Cicero's guidance in his earlier years. The highly educated Roman public for which Horace wrote, men like Maecenas, who was to employ the services of Trebatius later in a divorce case, and also like Octavian himself, could appreciate the rhetorical games which I think are an essential part of the fun in this satire, in which Horace again managed to follow his own device: *ridentem dicere verum*.[11] His second book contains in fact less violent satire and more refined poetry.

Notes

1. Comp. P. Sonnet, *C. Trebatius Testa* (diss. Giessen 1932); RE s.v. (same author).
2. Cicero's letters concerning Trebatius are *Ad fam.* 7, 5 (recommendation to Caesar); 7, 6–18 (54–53 B.C., to Trebatius in Gaul); 7, 19–21 (44 B.C.), 7, 22 (?). Comp. Ed. Fraenkel, Some notes on Cicero's letters to Trebatius, *JRS* 47 (1957), 66–70 (= *Kleine Beiträge* 2, pp. 75–85). On his swimming *Ad fam.* 7, 10, 2, on his drinking *Ad fam.* 7, 22, 1.
3. *Topica* (44 B.C.), a treatise on argumentation totally different from Aristotle's Topica. The appendix on quaestiones infinitae and finitae begins at 80; the status of definite quaestiones is found 91–96 (in all three genera causarum); comp. B. Riposati, *Studi sui Topica di Cicerone* (Milan 1947), 234–63.
4. Already Book I, published in 35 B.C., contained two programmatic satires, in which he discusses his relationship toward his great predecessor Lucilius, founder of the genre, who in Horace's view was a great wit but a careless poet (*Serm.* 1, 4; 10).
5. For the juridical lore in Horace comp. – apart from the studies mentioned in note 1 – L. Wenger, *Die Quellen des römischen Rechts* (Vienna, 1953), 227–28; F. Stella Maranca, *Orazio e la legislazione romana* (Milano 1936). Much attention is paid to legal problems in *Serm.* 2, 1 by P. Lejay, *Les Satires d'Horace* (commentary) 1911.
6. Comp. L. R. Shiro, The Satirist's Apologia, *Univ. of Wisc. St. in Lang. and Lit.* 15 (1922), 148–67.
7. Homer, *Iliad* 18, 95–96.
8. N. Rudd, *The Satires of Horace* (Cambridge, 1966), 128–31.
9. On the important notion of cavere see F. Cancelli, "Per una revisione del 'cavere' dei giureconsulti reppublicani" *Studi in Onore di Ed. Volterra* (Milan, 1971, 611–45).
10. *Serm.* 2, 1, 84; 10.
11. *Serm.* 1, 1, 24.

Rhetoric and Poetics
in Twelfth-Century France

TONY HUNT
University of St. Andrews

THE PURPOSE of this paper is to emphasize the significance of the association of *rhetoric* with *ethics* in the twelfth century, especially for poetics and the production of literature. In this connexion I distinguish three types of literary rhetoric in twelfth-century France: demonstrative rhetoric, scholastic rhetoric, and philosophical / poetic rhetoric.

§

IT MUST BE ASSUMED that it was Grammar that gave most would-be writers in the twelfth century their insight into the processes of literary creation. Grammar, in the broad sense of Philology, was concerned with the "enarratio poetarum." We know that Bernard of Chartres would expound "figuras gramatice, colores rethoricos, cavillationes sophismatum et qua parte sui proposite lectionis articulus respiciebat ad alias disciplinas."[1] In his grammatical seminars or *declinationes* "proponebatur materia que fidem edificaret et mores, et unde qui convenerant, quasi collatione quadam, animarentur ad bonum."[2] We can thus be sure that the matter treated merited the description we invariably find in the *accessus ad auctores*: 'ethice subponitur'. The author of the *De septem septenis* stresses how the arts of the *trivium* tend to the same goal: "Grammaticus namque viam grammaticae recte ingreditur, et per eam graditur, quando post rectam locutionem vitae et morum sequitur aequitatem . . . ille ergo aequam dialecticae viam sequitur, et tam opere quam sermone veraciter argumentatur, qui verum a falso, rectum a curvo dividendo ratiocinatur . . . hic ergo in via recta rhetoricis vestigiis incedit, qui lingua censoria rotunda auditores persuadendo commonefacit, et de jure stricto in aequum revocando instruit." He concludes, "Sic igitur trivium eloquentem reddit, ad virtutes vias construit."[3]

The association of the arts of the *trivium* with ethics[4] had the notable consequence of emphasizing eloquence as a means rather than as an end. The functional view of eloquence, emphasized by Augustine in the *De doctrina christiana* and later by Abelard, led to a move away from a narrow view of rhetoric as intrinsically valuable local verbal arrangement to a wider view which might be called poetics and which helped to dissolve the traditional dichotomies of pagan v. Christian, rhetorical v. plain style etc. Both Augustine and Abelard attempted to show that Scripture afforded an excellent display of rhetoric rightfully employed. Abelard, indeed, points out that the famous reproof administered to Jerome in his dream was not a criticism of the fact that he read pagan authors at all, but of the fact that he read them *non pro utilitate aliqua sed pro oblectatione eloquentiae.*[5]

In twelfth-century France rhetoric appears in the service of some religious or philosophical truth in three different forms which I have already described as *demonstrative, scholastic* and *poetic*.

DEMONSTRATIVE RHETORIC:

The source of this was clearly Cicero, especially the *De inventione* and *De officiis*. It enters Old French literature with the Saints' Lives, which show a high incidence of the figures of *exclamatio, repetitio* and antithesis. From these works, such as the *Eulalie, Clermont Passion* and the *Vie de Saint Léger*, the procedures of demonstrative rhetoric pass to the *chansons de geste* whose origins are so intimately connected with paraliturgical developments and with hagiography. This demonstrative rhetoric is not so much learned in the schools from the study of the *auctores* as elaborated according to the expressive techniques of oral literature (especially parallelism and formulae).[6] Professor Zumthor has therefore called it *la rhétorique coutumière*.[7] It arises from the practical exigencies of oral address to a largely illiterate audience. With the passage of time, however, the influence of the schools is gradually felt, so that the *Vie de Saint Alexis*, for example, is clearly constructed according to the scheme *exordium-narratio-conclusio* and makes frequent use of figures of words (*repetitio, contentio, exclamatio, sententiae*) and of tropes (*circuitio, superlatio, intellectio, permutatio* etc). This in the middle of the twelfth century. The point to stress is that this tradition of demonstrative rhetoric is primarily designed to serve certain **expressive** aims which are a function of the audience envisaged—the unlettered congregations recognized by the Council of Tours in 813. The function of the rhetoric is **expressive, affirmative, celebratory**.

SCHOLASTIC RHETORIC:

In the twelfth century this rhetoric was transformed by the influence of logic and grammar, to produce a scholastic rhetoric whose function was not simple, positive affirmation, but rather **critical investigation**. The source here, of course, is Aristotle, particularly the *Topica* and *Sophistici Elenchi*. Together with the *Analytica Priora* and *Posteriora* they constituted the Logica Nova and furnished more advanced treatment of sophistical argumentation and the detection of fallacies which became the central territory of dialectic. Whilst their introduction in Latin translation is associated with the pioneering work of James of Venice (c. 1130) and they are utilized by Adam of Petit Pont (c. 1132) and Thierry of Chartres (c. 1140), they were probably not firmly established before Otto of Freising's reference to them in his chronicle and John of Salisbury's famous discussion of them in the *Metalogicon* (c. 1159). The *Topica* provides a full treatment of dialectical reasoning, especially the role of opposition in the development of an argument and its refutation. It is in effect a handbook of debate and its precepts are often contiguous with those of rhetoric. The *Elenchi*, effectively the Ninth Book of the *Topica*, deals with fallacious syllogism and is a method for detecting fallacies. The establishment of the Logica Nova coincides with the appearance of a quite new scholastic rhetoric in courtly literature. This scholastic rhetoric can most clearly be seen in the *Cliges* and *Yvain* of Chrestien de Troyes and the *Tristan* of Thomas.[8]

Its dialectical base leads to three innovations:

(i) on the level of topical reasoning it is applied to the comparison of divergent views—divergent authorities in the case of Abelard's *Sic et Non*. Whereas earlier Old French literature, the Saints' Lives and *chansons de geste*, are unifocal, that is to say they provide only one view of events, beliefs and feelings described, the new courtly romance is multifocal, that is, it offers more than one view or interpretation of the phenomena described:

(ii) the second innovation is that on the grammatical-logical level it is applied to the analysis of meaning. In both Abelard's *Sic et Non*[9] and John of Salisbury's discussion of the *Topica*[10] emphasis is placed on the role of dialectic in establishing semantic nuances and distinctions. The scholastic rhetoric of courtly literature promotes a heightened consciousness of the ambiguity and polyvalence of particular concepts and terms, thus replacing the transparency of earlier literature with a much more complex texture, where, for example, irony becomes possible on a completely different scale;[11]

(iii) the third innovation is that dialectic issues on the practical level in constant questioning—Abelard had already declared "prima sapientiae clavis definitur, assidua scilicet seu frequens interrogatio"—questioning in the sense of both enquiring and doubting: "dubitando enim ad inquisitionem venimus; inquirendo veritatem percipimus." This explains why Chrestien's romances are much more open-ended, ambiguous even, ironical also, than, say the *chansons de geste*, and elicit from the audience an enquiring, critical response rather than affirmative recognition. Further, it highlights an essential compositional feature of these courtly works, namely the way in which school-trained poets like Chrestien developed their themes in dialectical manner, exploiting contrast, opposition, repetition, inversion and the like, all with the effect of unsettling received notions. What we may call the technique of **binary opposition** in these works supports irony and paradox in such a way that the significance of events and motifs is grasped by the audience through the **apprehension of oppositions** which isolate and give prominence to the real issues of the work.

Here rhetoric in the narrower sense has a crucial role to play. Far from being mere surface decoration or redundant virtuoso display, its most important purpose is to achieve a satisfactory formulation of the paradoxes which bear the ideological structure of the work. One might make three subsidiary points in this connexion:

(i) the very concept of courtly love and the experiences it embodies is of a dialectical nature and lends itself to dialectical treatment, for it represents a tension between *mezura* and extravagance, action and inaction, hope and despair, aspiration and achievement, life and death etc.

(ii) Chrestien de Troyes' concept of *bele conjointure* consists fundamentally in the ordering of oppositions, complementary and contradictory, as is already suggested by Wolfgang Brand's recent study of motif duplication in Chrestien.[12] Students of the *trivium* would see how important oppositions, rhetorically formulated as paradoxes, might be resolved *ex negativo*, through the refutation or elimination of one of the elements of the antithesis (as in the Epic), or resolved transcendentally through the semantic manoeuvre of a *coincidentia oppositorum* or else straight supercession (as in the Romance), or else left unresolved as tension (as in the Lyric).

(iii) Dialectic lies behind the prominence given to *ratiocinatio* which leads to that self-questioning which is a characteristic of many romance characters and of the best romances themselves.

PHILOSOPHICAL RHETORIC

The sources here, of course, are Plato, Augustine and the Neoplatonism of Chartres, especially the work of William of Conches.[13] So far as literature is concerned, the assumption behind symbolic and mythopoeic thought in the twelfth century might be expressed in John of Salisbury's famous dictum *mendacia poetarum serviunt veritati* (*Policraticus*, III, 6). The attraction of Plato for Augustine in the *De doctrina christiana* and Abelard in several of his theological works lay in the way he showed how the values of moral thought and action might be expressed. The platonizing and humanistic tradition of the twelfth-century schools eagerly took up the idea of *narratio fabulosa* by using the notion of *integumentum* or *involucrum* with which they had been impressed in Macrobius, who included an important discussion of fables in his commentary on the *Somnium Scipionis*.[14] Abelard saw myth as a necessity for philosophy when it came to the discussion of mysterious realities and Alan of Lille saw it as part of a necessary intellectual modesty when dealing with the great mysteries of Nature. The idea of the *involucrum* became so well established that about 1200 a poet composed a short poem about a poet who instead of using *integumenta* to present his philosophy, profaned Natura by exposing her naked to the common view.[15]

In the *De doctrina christiana* Augustine confines himself to literary figures rather than myth or symbolism. He defends obscurity, by which he largely means "verborum translatorum ambiguitates," on three accounts: (a) what is won by the reader through toil and application is the more highly prized — *teguntur ne vilescant*; (b) intellectual pride is subdued by the effort of interpretation so imposed; (c) there are certain things, difficult of true understanding, which are better hidden from simple people. In the *Liber contra mendacium* he strenuously argues against calling all transferred meanings lies.

Macrobius goes much further in taking up the discussion of fables and myth. He resolutely rejects for philosophical purposes, however, those myths and fables which are intended merely for entertainment and delight, what he calls the "childrens' nurseries," by which he means schooling in the profane poets. Whilst Abelard, too, operates a similar restriction, William of Conches in his commentary on Macrobius, greatly extended the use of the *narratio fabulosa*. He is prepared to envisage the possibility of metaphorical reading in a far wider range of fictional material than Macrobius is.[16] He takes Macrobius's rejected group of fables and shows that even here valid moral and cosmological meanings can be elicited. Even where the words themselves (e.g. adultery) are base they may, in the *contextio narrationis*, represent something *pulcrum et honestum*. There is gradually elucidated, therefore, a new mythopoeic vocabulary: *aenigma, fabula, figura, imago, integumentum, involucrum, similitudo, symbolum, translatio* which alerted poets in the vernacular to the new possibilities of metaphorical expression.[17] Thus in Chrestien de Troyes and Marie de France[18] we have an entirely new incidence of tropes. Poetry is in the service of *sapientia*. A much more ambitious rhetoric is required and metaphorical writing becomes possible on a new scale.

Notes

1. See John of Salisbury, *Metalogicon* ed. C. C. J. Webb (Oxford, 1929), lib. I, c. 24, p. 55 and the transl. by D. D. McGarry (Berkeley / Los Angeles, 1955), p. 67: "He would explain grammatical figures, rhetorical embellishment, and sophistical quibbling, as well as the relation of given passages to other studies."

2. *Ed.cit.*, p. 56; transl. McGarry, p. 68 "subject matter was presented to foster faith, to build up morals, and to inspire those present at this quasicollation to perform good works."

3. Migne, *PL.* 199, col. 949. "The student of grammar correctly sets out on the path of grammar, and proceeds along it, when after correct speech he pursues just living and conduct . . . he pursues the just way of dialectic, judging truly in word and deed, who shows discrimination by distinguishing the true from the false, the straight from the bent . . . in the footsteps of rhetoric he enters on the right way who can impress his audience with well turned criticism and instruct them by leading them from rigid interpretation of the law to justice . . . hence the trivium leads not only to eloquence but builds paths to the virtues."

4. See Ph. Delhaye, "L'enseignement de la philosophie morale au XIIe siècle," *Medieval Studies* II (1949), 77–99.

5. "Not on account of any usefulness, but for the delight of the style." See *Petri Abaelardi, Opera Theologica* II, CC Cont, med. XII, ed. E. M. Buytaert (Turnholti, 1969), pp. 190–91 (*Theologica Christiana* II, 125). See also J. Jolivet, *Arts du langage et théologie chez Abélard* (Paris, 1969) and T. Gregory, "Abelard et Platon" in E. M. Buytaert (ed.), *Peter Abelard* (Leuven / The Hague, 1974), pp. 38–64. For Augustine see R. J. O'Connell, *Art and the Christian Intelligence in St. Augustine* (Oxford, 1978) and Ch. Mohrmann, "Saint Augustine and the 'Eloquentia' " in *eadem, Etudes sur le latin des chrétiens* t. 1, 2me éd. (Roma, 1961), pp. 351–70.

6. See M. Pei, *French Precursors of the Chanson de Roland* (New York, 1948, repr. 1966) and J. W. B. Zaal, *'A lei francesca' (Sainte Foy, v. 20)* (Leiden, 1962).

7. P. Zumthor, *Langue et techniques poétiques à l'époque romane* (XIe–XIIIe siècles) (Paris, 1963), pp. 223–24. See also S. Kay, "The nature of rhetoric in the *chanson de geste*," Zeitschrift für Romanische Philologie, 94 (1978), 305–20.

8. See T. Hunt, "Aristotle, Dialectic and Courtly Literature," *Viator* 10 (1979), 95–129 and id., "The Dialectic of *Yvain*," *MLR* 72 (1977), 285–99. According to Mary Dickey, *The Teaching of Rhetoric in the Eleventh and Twelfth Centuries, with particular reference to the schools of Northern France* unpubl. B. Litt. thesis, Oxford, 1953, p. 154 the eleventh-century commentaries on the *De inventione* and *Rhetorica ad Herennium* "stress the logical rather than the stylistic interest of rhetoric." On the rhetoric of the *exordium* see Hunt in *Forum for Modern Language Studies* 6 (1970), 1–23 and ibid. 8 (1972), 320–44.

9. See the new critical edition in progress by B. B. Boyer and R. McKeon (Chicago / London, 1974–).

10. John of Salisbury, *Metalogicon* ed. Webb, pp. 154 f.

11. See now D. H. Green *Irony in the Medieval Romance* (Cambridge, 1979).

12. W. Brand, *Chrétien de Troyes. Zur Dichtungstechnik seiner Romane* (München, 1972).

13. See W. Wetherbee, *Platonism and Poetry in the Twelfth Century. The Literary Influence of the School of Chartres* (Princeton, 1972); P. Dronke, *Fabula. Explorations into the uses of myth in medieval Platonism* (Leiden, 1976); H. Brinkmann, "Verhüllung ("Integumentum") als literarische Darstellungsform im Mittelalter," in *Der Begriff der Repraesentatio im Mittelalter*, Miscellanea Medievalia Bd. 8 (Berlin / New York, 1971), pp. 314–39.

14. See the articles of E. Jeauneau reprinted in id., *Lectio Philosophorum* (Amsterdam, 1974).

15. F. J. E. Raby, "*Nuda Natura* and Twelfth-Century Cosmology," *Speculum* 43 (1968), 72–77.

16. See Dronke, *Fabula*, pp. 15 ff.

17. See M.-D. Chenu, *La théologie au XIIe siècle* (Paris, 1957), 159–90.

18. On the celebrated prologue to Marie's *Lais* see T. Hunt, "Glossing Marie de France," *Romanische Forschungen* 86 (1974), 396–418.

Rhetorical *Topoi* as "Clues"
In Chrétien de Troyes

MARIANTONIA LIBORIO
Istituto Universitario Orientale, Naples

Lᴇᴄᴛᴏʀ ɪɴ ꜰᴀʙᴜʟᴀ is the title of Umberto Eco's latest book. It studies the role of the reader as co-participant in the text, as directed and required by the author.[1]

This is, in a way, what I intend to do in this paper. Not that I am actually searching for the reader inside Chrétien de Troyes romances, at least not in the way it has been done up to now, that is by looking for direct addresses by the author to his audience as a sort of *captatio benevolentiae*. This kind of phatic communion with the public is typical of certain literary genres in the Middle Ages; mainly the epic and to a lesser extent narrative poems such as *dits, lais, contes, fabliaux* . . . It can be found in Beroul's *Tristan*[2] and in Chrétien too.[3] This is certainly one way of calling the reader into the text, but it is not what I am concerned with here.

I am interested instead in examining the way Chrétien involves his hearer or reader by giving him clues, setting strategies to direct his attention to the most important knots of his narrative. In other words, I am looking for the ground rules which Chrétien laid down for the very serious game he is playing with literature.

Rhetorical *topoi* are not only skilled exercises in rhetoric to impress a learned audience; they are—at least in Chrétien—technical devices, well known to the medieval audience. A full appreciation of their functioning is essential to reach an understanding of the *sens* of the text.

It is of course impossible to analyse all of Chrétien's *topoi*. I will limit my analysis to two of them: the *effictio* and the *locus amoenus*.

The need to give a full description of the characters who will play a role in the text is in itself of great interest. Very few and very limited *descriptiones personarum* are to be found in the epic. In the universe of the *chanson de geste* the *effictio* is implicit in the role of all the actants:[4] they are heroes or villains, one or the other. *Roland est proz et Oliviers est sage*: as description this is quite enough.[5] The heroes are known to the audience; they exist in their full stature before the text begins, the author needs only to name them. The ideological frame in which the epic characters move is likewise fixed once for all. It is quite familiar to the audience. There is no need of further clues within the body of the text.

The situation is different in the *roman courtois*. The frame of reference has to be built anew; values and behaviours are not previously set; the *fabula* is not always known to everybody; the ideology is not yet fixed. Erec, Lancelot, Yvain, Perceval and even Eneas and Brut do not exist as medieval heroes until the author gives them life, summoning them onto a scene which is unpredictable because it has its own new values to impose. The hearer or reader has to be taken by the hand and helped to understand rightly the complex new reality he faces. The cultural model is changing; disruptive forces are no longer relegated to the EX world; they are inside the IN world.[6] They are even inside the new type of hero who has to fight them under unsuspected forms. The recognition of heroes and heroines is no longer to be taken for granted. One of the functions of the *effictio* in the romances is to unmistakeably point them out to the reader.

A complete *effictio*, from top to toe, that calls onto the scene Nature or God or both of them, is the rhetorical marker that singles them out.[7]

The *effictio* — so we are often told — is always more or less the same: ladies and knights are stamped in the same mould. The explanation given is usually that "it is a *topos*." This explanation is tautological and misleading. The reason for this sameness is deeper. What the *courtois* author is trying to do is to create the model of a new hero. A model has to be a standard figure. So the *effictio* is not important for the variety of its elements, but for the completeness of the standard ideal. Its most important function is to tip off the reader, saying: "This is the hero, this is the heroine, let them be your courtly ideal." This function is evident in Chrétien. But Chrétien is not a passive echoer of rhetorical devices learned in school. He turns them to his own ends. Even in *Erec et Enide*, his first literary success, he has gone well beyond the bookishness of treatises and rules. The medieval hearer or reader, like the modern one, is surprised at the repeated *effictio* of Erec and of Enide as well. The first one serves the purpose of recognition:[8] hyperboles, the intervention of God and Nature leave no doubts about it. Still the reader schooled in medieval rhetoric should feel something strange, a sense of uneasiness; the *effictio* in both cases is provocatively incomplete: Erec is not fully armed, as a knight should be; Enide is in rags, which is quite atypical for a lady of verse romance.[9]

The incomplete *effictio* is a very important clue (*un indice*, in Barthes' terms) that is intended to unsettle expectations. The message expressed by the manipulation of the well known rhetorical *topos* can be framed in this way: "Here are the hero and the heroine, all right, but be careful; they are not what they should be, not yet; be alert and read the story well and think about it if you want to know why."

At each important stage of the romance, further uses of the *effictio* add something new to the growing portrait of both Erec and Enide. What Chrétien is doing, with his original use of an *effictio* in progress, is to underline the different stages Erec and Enide are going through in order to fulfill their role as perfect *chevalier* and real *dame*. The hearer or reader is aware of this development, the repeated *effictio* works in the text as a generative structure and as a clue to the right decoding of the narrative.

Let us take another example, *a contrariis*. If it is true that the *effictio* is the marker of the hero, be he a real one or a potential one, we should not be surprised to find no *effictio* at all in the *Chevalier de la charrete*. Lancelot, the anti-hero, doesn't deserve one.[10] He doesn't even have a name, which is still another hint for the reader. He is a non-existent knight (*un cavaliere inesistente*, as Italo Calvino would say). Love, an excessive and adulterous love, has completely destroyed his rationality and, hence, his personality, to the point where he doesn't know whether he exists or not:

> ne set s'il est, ou s'il n'est mie,
> ne ne li membre de son nom,
> ne set s'il est armez ou non,
> ne set ou va, ne set dou vient;
> de rien nule ne li sovient
> fors d'une seule, et por celi
> a mis les autres en obli;
> a cele seule panse tant
> qu'il n'ot, ne voit, ne rien n'antant.
> (vv. 716–724, ed. M. Roques)

This is a very good example of an *effictio à l'envers* and of Chrétien's freedom in handling common rhetorical stock.

Let us now see how Chrétien plays with the other *topos* I have chosen to analyse (of course the choice is not innocent): namely the *locus amoenus*. Leaving aside the history of this *topos*,[11] in medieval lyric and narrative the *locus amoenus* is the typical setting for love, not only in literature but also in manuscript illumination.[12] The Provençal *canso* had established it as an erotic stereotype, a *type-cadre* as Zumthor would call it;[13] thus, at its appearance in the text, the reader knows what to expect. The semantic markers connected with its appearance are "renewal of life," "natural beauty," "perfection of love," "happiness." They are in a reciprocal relationship of implication. The descriptive elements: season, greenery, flowers, birds, fountain and so forth are all supposed to work together to enhance the semantic meaning of the scene.

What happens in Chrétien de Troyes? I have chosen three occurences of the *topos*: the magic garden in *Erec et Enide*, the opening of *Perceval* and the episode of the *pucele* in the tent (again in *Perceval*).

The magic garden is the setting of part of the much discussed episode of *La Joie de la Cort*.[14] The vergier is every bit as beautiful as it should be: there are flowers and fruits, birds singing, precious and beneficial grass, at the same time certain details astutely scattered here and there give the reader a feeling of danger. The garden is closed within a wall of magic air: people around are weeping and expressing pity for Erec; inside the garden there is of course a beautiful lady, but she is ringed about with horrifying pikes surmounted by the severed heads of previous intruders. The semantic oppositions are clear: closed *versus* open, self-centeredness *versus* sociability (consider, for instance, the seemingly pointless remark that fruits can not be taken away), death *versus* life.

The *topos* is subtly exploited so as to overturn its meaning. This is not simply an aesthetic *tour de force*, a game to show off the author's skill; Chrétien is sending messages to his hearer or reader, who must interpret everything that happens in this topical garden as warning against the dangers of this kind of love. *Demezura* is signified in several details;[15] they are not mere descriptive indulgence (description is seldom mere indulgence); they are meaningful hints that generate the following action as a consequence of what they imply; they are supposed to help the reader to interpret what is going on inside the garden not on the surface level (another battle ending in still another victory for Erec) but on a deep structural level.

Let us turn to the opening lines of *Perceval*:

> Ce fu au tens qu'arbre foillissent,
> Que glai et bois et pre verdissent,
> Et cil oisel en lor latin
> Cantent doucement au matin
> Et tote riens de joie aflamme . . .
>   (vv. 69–73, ed. W. Roach)

The setting is immediately recognizable; the reader translates: *locus amoenus*, therefore "scene of love," therefore "happiness." But all his expectations will be frustrated: instead of an inspired lover, ready to sing his love there is a rude *vallès, li fix a la veve fame*, going to keep an eye on the *Herceors que sa mere avoit / Qui ses avaines li semoient* (vv. 82–83). The anti-climax is intentional and significant. In fact, in this beautiful setting, no scene of love will take place (Perceval is not ready for love; Chrétien's romances are always *Bildungsromane*), instead there will be the brutal if ambiguous entrance of fully armed warriors (vv. 112–124; 137–54).

The *Conte del Graal* is not, as Chrétien has forewarned his reader in the Prologue, a love story, a typical narrative elaboration of the *locus amoenus topos* as *Erec et Enide*, but something different, never yet attempted by anyone (vv. 63–64), such as will call into question not only this particular *topos* but the overall ideological frame as well.

Is Chrétien's hearer or reader perhaps not yet on the right path? He gives him another hint: Perceval is in the forest, awakened by birds singing; he finds himself near a tent:

> En une praerie bele
> Lez le rieu d'une fontenele.
>
> (vv. 639–40)

Within the tent there is of course a sleeping beauty. But what happens then has nothing to do with courtly love. The rude *vallès* (the scene is humorous, of course!) kisses the *pucele, volsist ele ou non*, takes away her ring, eats her food and leaves her in despair, well aware what fate will befall her.

Again, a well-known *topos* has been played on in a way which is typical of Chrétien.

But then—one might ask—why resort to these empty shells, these *loci communes* in the first place? Couldn't Chrétien have invented his own original settings and conventions?

Of course not. The *topoi* are necessary, not only to him, but to every writer, for at least two reasons. The first is to bring him into contact with the audience. If you want to be understood you had better use the language everybody speaks. Second, the *topoi* help to actualize a frame of reference (a literary encyclopedia) which is common to both author and reader. Then, when the reader relaxes, thinking he knows what is going to happen and feels he will be gratified by the usual, reassuring story, the author can start flashing his signals to deceive him, to unsettle his presuppositions, upset his faith, create anxiety, suspense and critical attention. The reader is, therefore, obliged to rethink the *topoi* that he feels he knows so well, to make an effort to investigate more deeply. He will pick up clues, set new frames,[16] collaborate and play the game. The author is there to guide him. The rhetorical *topoi* are the thread he offers to lead his audience through the labyrinth of the text.

In Chrétien's romances—but, I think, in all worthwhile literature—rhetorical *topoi* are never mere ornaments. Even the purely descriptive ones (I said my choice was not innocent!) are much more then that. As I have said elsewhere,[17] they generate the text because doing depends upon being (albeit the reverse is true too). But, still more important, they create a universe of discourse common to the audience and to the author and can be used then as clues that will orient the decoding of the text.

Through the rhetorical *topoi* (not only through them of course), the audience finds the keys to that special sort of puzzle which a literary text is. Apparently unconnected pieces will find their place in the *bele conjointure*, which is what a story should be not only for Chrétien de Troyes.

Notes

1. U. Eco, *Lector in fabula* (Milano, 1979).

2. A. Varvaro, *Il "Roman de Tristan" di Béroul*, (Torino, 1963), pp. 71–86.

3. To give few examples at random, cf. *Erec et Enide*, vv. 1238–39; 1668; 6420; *Le Chevalier au lion*, v. 28ss.; 2163–65; *Le Chevalier de la charrete*, v. 1446; 1480ss.; 1495; *Le Roman de Perceval ou Le Conte du Graal*, vv. 3248–52; 3577; 4815; 6216; 6516–18. I quote from the CFMA except for *Perceval*, [ed. W. Roach, Textes Littéraires Français (Paris, 1959)].

4. A. Greimas, *Sémantique structurale* (Paris, 1966); *Du sens* (Paris, 1970); *Maupassant. La sémiotique du texte: exercices pratiques* (Paris, 1976).

5. C. Segre, *Semiotica filologica* (Torino, 1979), pp. 5–21.

6. Ju. Lotman-B. A. Uspenskij, *Tipologia della cultura* (Milano, 1975); *Semiotica e cultura* (Milano-Napoli, 1975); "The Dynamic Model of a Semiotic System," in *Semiotica*, 21, 1977, pp. 193–210. M. Corti, "Modelli e antimodelli nella cultura medievale," in *Strumenti critici*, 35, 1978, pp. 3–30. C. Segre, *Semiotica filologica*, cit.

7. A. Faral, *Les Arts poétiques du XIIe et XIIIe siècle*, (Paris, 1971) (original ed. 1924). A. Colby, *The Portrait in Twelfth-Century French Literature* (Genève, 1965).

8. *Erec et Enide*, vv. 81–104; 401–410.

9. M. Liborio, "I luoghi privilegiati della descrizione," VI Convegno Interuniversitario di Bressanone, luglio 1978, to be published in the *Atti*.

10. M. Liborio, "Qui petit semme petit quelt." L'itinerario poetico di Chrétien de Troyes, in *Studi e ricerche di letteratura e linguistica francese*, 1, 1980, pp. 1–62.

11. E. R. Curtius, *Europäische Literatur und lateinisches Mittelalter* (Bern, 1948). D. Thoss, *Studien zum locus amoenus in Mittelalter* (Wien-Stuttgart, 1972).

12. G. Agamben, *Stanze. La parola e il fantasma nella cultura occidentale* (Torino, 1977).

13. P. Zumthor, *Essai de poétique médiévale* (Paris, 1972), pp. 92–94.

14. *Erec et Enide*, vv. 5689–5714.

15. For instance the *effictio* of Maboagrain, vv. 5848–55, cf. M. Liborio, "Qui petit semme petit quelt," cit., p. 21.

16. U. Eco, *Lector in fabula*, cit., pp. 79–80 and the bibliography he gives.

17. M. Liborio, "I luoghi privilegiati della descrizione," cit.

The Rhetorical Figure of Systrophe

SALOMON HEGNAUER
University of Zürich

I

I<small>N THIS ESSAY</small> I first make a definition and analysis of the figure of speech singled out for detailed study; I shall then give a brief survey of its history; and finally I shall discuss the function of systrophe in poetic contexts.[1]

Let me start with two examples. In *Richard III* the Duchess of York deplores and abuses her state using this rhetorical form:

> Dead life, blind sight, poor mortal-living ghost,
> Woe's scene, world's shame, grave's due by life usurped,
> Brief abstract and record of tedious days,
> Rest thy unrest on England's lawful earth,
> Unlawfully made drunk with innocents' blood.[2]

In the following sonnet Sidney's Astrophel fashions his declaration of love along a similar rhetorical pattern:

> Stella, the onely Planet of my light,
>   Light of my life, and life of my desire,
>   Chiefe good, whereto my hope doth only aspire,
> World of my wealth, and Heav'n of my delight.[3]

The classical definition of *systrophe* — and to my knowledge the only analysis of this particular rhetorical figure at all — is found in Peacham's *Garden of Eloquence*, where it is exemplified by another classical instance from Cicero:

> *Systrophe*, of some called *Conglobatio*, of others *convolutio*, and it is when the Orator bringeth in many definitions of one thing, yet not such definitions as do declare the substance of a thing by the general kind,

and the difference, which the art of reasoning doth prescribe, but others of another kind all heaped together: such as these definitions of *Cicero* be in the second booke of an Orator, where he amplifieth the dignitie of an hystory thus, An historie, saith he, is the testimony of times, the light of veritie, the maintenance of memorie, the schoolemistrisse of life, and messenger of antiquitie.[4]

From these examples *systrophe's* pertinent rhetorical features can be deduced: *Systrophe* is a chain of at least three tropes that amplify a given term of reference (life, Stella, or history), usually and most effectively without a predicative verb to conduct the comparison, and likewise without any connective *and's* or alternative *or's*. Its individual members are mostly set in *parison*, syntactical parallelism. Reduced to its briefest formula: *Systrophe* is an elliptical periphrasis of *one* tenor by three or more asyndetic and isocolical analogies. *Systrophe* is, then, on the one hand, a compound trope knit together by various subsidiary rhetorical links, such as, alliteration, *antimetabole, paronomasia*, and others; on the other hand it also belongs to the paradigm of implicit tropical substitution; its cluster of elliptically and asyndetically juxtaposed analogies sets a stream of consciousness flowing on various levels of association and interpretation. These facts may account for *systrophe's* conspicuous absence from almost all the available Classical and Renaissance handbooks. "Totalitarian" rhetoricians may have looked upon *systrophe* as on a particularly exigent form of periphrasis, or an especially patterned type of congeries; or else split it up into its basic tropical constituents, such as single metaphor, oxymoron, or hyperbole.

This, then, is the place for a digression on the curious history of both the term and the figure of *systrophe*. Among Peacham's predecessors only Trapezuntius includes a reference to what he calls *convolutio* in the fifth book of his *Rhetoricorum libri quinque* (1523),[5] and in Robert de Basevorn's medieval *Forma Praedicandi* (1322) *convolutio* is described and listed as the thirteenth of the twenty-two "ornaments employed in the most carefully contrived sermons;"[6] whereas Hermogenes of Tharsos was apparently the first to speak of *to kata systrophen schema* in a more or less definite stylistic context.[7] However, in all these three instances *systrophe / convolutio* refers to a rather vague stylistic concept of ellipsis and compression, and has nothing in common with the strict rhetorical figure which – according to and after Peacham – we have come to call by this name. After so much (or so little) evidence I am very much inclined to give Peacham all the honour in the rhetorical parentage of *systrophe*. He seems to have adapted the unspecific term *systrophe / convolutio*, as he found it in Hermogenes and Trapezuntius, respectively, to a highly specialized and differentiated figure of speech that was as yet without a name, having been covered variously by *translatio, expolitio, periphrasis, synonymia*, et al.[8]

It would mean jumping to a rash conclusion to argue that the birth of a new rhetorical figure was designed to meet the needs for virtuoso ornamentation, ecstatic exultation and heady deprecation as encouraged by the Catholic Baroque. This claim, however tempting to the abstracting scholar, cannot be maintained in the face of classical Greek and Roman, and medieval evidence. It is obvious that wherever people swear, make love, or pray, they needs avail themselves of *systrophe*. My card-index files instances from Classical Greece (the Homeric Hymn to Ares, and Klytaimnestra's equivocal welcome of Agamemnon are among the earliest recorded examples); to Cicero, and Seneca, and medieval Latin hymns; Dante and Shakespeare used it; later occurrences include Musset and Rimbaud, Rilke and Borchardt, among others.[9] The only conclusion that this sudden appearance of a newly described figure and redefined term in Peacham allows us safely to draw is that the *Zeitgeist* heightened the sensibility and increased the awareness of the metaphorical implications dormant in the hitherto barely recognized rhetorical structure, in concord with the vast re-systematization of rhetoric in the Renaissance.

II

LET US NOW CONSIDER the rhetorical function of *systrophe* in the poetic context.

Rhetoric in general, and *systrophe* here in particular, provide the abstract formulas for various feelings and thoughts; formulas distilled from actual speech; formulas that therefore can be re-filled with varying semantic contents, just as mathematical formulae supply the abstract laws for actual physical phenomena; they yield concrete results when applied to practical problems.

To the phonologist *sytrophe* might appear as the stammering and staggering attempt to say the same thing over and over again; the psychologist may root this halting and stumbling approach in a heightened emotion, originating in either awe or fear, admiration or intellectual wonder; the sociologist could place such feelings in the distance between the speaker and the addressed which – by these attempts – is to be bridged somehow. Thus in rhetoric, finally, *systrophe* provides the abstract formula for the literary endeavours to stress the gap between tenor, i.e. the term of reference, and the writer.

Even Peacham had something to say on "The use of this figure," and he also added a "Caution," realising its inherent danger:

> This figure is an ornament of singular grace and eloquence, serving most aptly and eligantly to commend vertues and dispraise vices. – It is not good to affect this ornament too much, nor to use it too oft, nor in using it to make too many definitions of one thing.[10]

Consequently, in the traditional division of rhetoric, *systrophe* is firmly rooted in *demonstrative oratory*, and deploys its fullest persuasive force nowhere better but where somebody is to be exalted or "debunked," where its effect is increased by making ample use of hyperbole and by being set in direct apostrophe. By definition, Greek *systrephein* meaning *to turn back to, to revolve around, systrophe* seems to be excluded from the subtly logical argument, which might shed a light on the curious fact that neither Donne nor Marvell ever used this figure. Its volley-technique does not promote an argument, but rather strikes home *one* particular point of reference. The fireworks of witty comparisons tend to blur the more complex levels of analogy and to anneal just the most obvious correspondence. Indeed, *systrophe* moves into its very own in *laus* and *vituperatio*, in such literary forms as the dedication, the prayer, the spell, the curse, eulogy, and invective.

Let me only recall the famous seventeenth-century poetic contro-versy *On Hope*, on which Cowley and Crashaw wrote matching and opposed poems. Both the accusing party, represented by Cowley, and the counsel for the defence, a role taken up by Crashaw, avail themselves of the same systrophic technique to make their respective points with almost equal success and conviction:

> Brother of Feare! more gaily clad,
> The merrier Foole o'th'two, yet quite as mad,
> Sire of Repentance! Child of fond desire . . .   (Cowley)

> Deare Hope! Earth's dowry, and Heaven's debt,
> The Entity of things that are not yet.
> Subt'lest, but surest being! Thou by whom
> Our Nothing hath a definition.   (Crashaw)[11]

Technique and intention are apparent: the entire stanza revolves around *one* subject, a metaphorical cocoon is spun round the same term in order to raise or deflate its importance and standing.

Such a figure of heightened sensibility and rarefied *préciosité* must have been gladly embraced by a time that was both partly Catholic and wholly Baroque, and indeed *systrophe* flourished at no time more preciously. By its means Crashaw and his mystical contemporaries worked themselves up into a state of rapturous ecstasis, while Herbert, Vaughan, Gryphius and Hofmannswaldau used it to bid an equally ostentatious farewell to the bitter-sweet world and its tempting and corrupting riches.[12]

Of more interest and greater consequence is the fact that in the same period Herbert and others started to realise the deeper valence of what had hitherto appeared as a merely decorative figure. They evolved its argumentative force by adapting it to an intellectual process and thus moved it into *deliberative oratory*.

What I mean to say can be most clearly demonstrated in Herbert's sonnet *Prayer*:

> Prayer the Churches banquet, Angels age,
>   Gods breath in man returning to his birth,
>   The soul in paraphrase, heart in pilgrimage,
> The Christian plummet sounding heav'n and earth;
> Engine against th'Almightie, sinners towre,
>   Reversed thunder, Christ-side-piercing spear,
>   The six-daies world transposing in an houre,
> A kinde of tune, which all things heare and fear;
> Softnesse, and peace, and joy, and love, and blisse,
>   Exalted Manna, gladnesse of the best,
>   Heaven in ordinarie, man well drest,
> The milkie way, the bird of Paradise,
>   Church-bels beyond the starres heard, the souls bloud,
>   The land of spices; something understood.

What might strike us on a first reading as a pretty butterfly-collection of analogies on prayer, is, in fact, the traditional device of *systrophe*. What is truly original and imaginative, indeed is that *systrophe* in this instance serves no longer epideictic, i.e. laudatory purposes — at least not exclusively so — but that it is employed in a cognitive process of interpretation and definition, as it were. Among the figures necessary to articulate the Catholic or any other faith, such as metaphor, paradox, or self-referential tautology, *systrophe* takes a conspicuous place.[13] It approaches the unknown X, that is prayer, in a technique of continuous translation similar to the one used in the approximation of the circle by way of super-imposed polygons. By this process that ideally can go on for ever, one can get infinitely close to the infinite without reaching it ever.[14]

In deliberative *systrophe*, used for definition, the metaphorical process undergoes a strange transformation. The single metaphor is no longer the self-important "Key that opens to all Mystery,"[15] but just *one* of many attempts at fencing in the absolute. In its excessive use of analogies *systrophe* in effect devalues the currency of the single metaphor. Realising and admitting the inadequacy of one metaphor, it rushes on to the next, and again to a third, and so on; when it stops, it is not because it has attained to the truth, but because it despairs of the possibility of ever attaining it. Each subsequent translation makes the preceding one appear relative, and at the same time adds a new angle to the total picture. A *systrophe* of such dimension (27 cola in the case of *Prayer*) is both a demonstration of poetic stamina and metaphorical virtuosity, as well as an admittance of the helplessness of metaphor when confronted with the divine. There is no earthly reason why twenty-seven analogies — or come to that, fifty or a hundred—should explain the mystery, any more than say three or even a single one. Neither is there a reason why Herbert should stop after twenty-seven translations and not go on, if not for ever, at least for some time longer. Or rather, the only reason for stopping there (or earlier) is the recognition and admittance of the inadequacy of the analogical method in pursuit of the unnameable. This is implied in the enigmatic "something understood," with which Herbert closes his systrophic meandering.

This systrophic attempt at the divine transcendence is dramatised in an untitled German poem by Angelus Silesius (ca. 1657):

> Du allerschönstes Bild, wem soll ich dich vergleichen?
> Den weissen Lilien? dem bunten Tausendschön?
> Den roten Rosen? Nein, ach, nein, denn sie vergehn,
> Verdorren und verbleichen.
>
> Vielleichte soll ich dich die goldene Sonne nennen?
> Den silberfarbnen Mond? den schönen Morgenstern?
> Vielleicht die Morgenröte? Ach nein, es fehlet fern:
> Ich müsste dich verkennen.
>
> Die Sonne borgt von dir ihr Licht und alle Strahlen,
> Der Monde seinen Schein, die Sterne ihren Glanz,
> Die Rötin ihre Zier: Der Himmel muss sich ganz
> Von deiner Schönheit malen.
>
> Vielleichte gleichst du dich dem Blitz der Seraphinen?
> Dem Thronenkönige? dem schönsten Engelein?
> Dem Cherubinen-Fürst? Ach nein, es kann nicht sein:
> Sie müssen dich bedienen.
>
> Nun schau, ich finde nichts. Weil ichs doch an soll zeigen,
> So sag ich klar und frei, dass du, o Jesus Christ,
> Die ewige Schönheit selbst und unvergleichlich bist:
> Drum ist es besser: schweigen.

The poet tentatively suggests analogies of what—in the final stanza—turns out to be Jesus Christ. Yet, after every handful of metaphors he recognises the inadequacy of his comparisons, because they fall so much short of their purported end. They are subsequently replaced by a string of new analogies, which then are discarded again for the same reasons. Since this movement could go on indefinitely, but—within the poetic framework—must be brought to an end, Silesius concludes in the only positive statement about Christ, that He is incomparable. This is the obvious message of any *systrophe* that approaches the divine. There only remains to draw the philosophical consequence: "Drum ist es besser: schweigen."

Systrophe thus becomes the ultimate analogy, and at once the annihilation of all analogy. It uses nothing but analogies, but by the sheer number of them the weight and significance of the individual metaphor is reduced, or at least moved into a wider perspective. The subtle system of rhetoric accommodates even the aporia of language in the rhetorical figure of *systrophe*.

Notes

1. For further discussion see my doctoral dissertation, *Systrophe: The Background of Herbert's Sonnet "Prayer"* (Berne, Frankfurt, Las Vegas, 1981).

2. *Richard III* IV. 4. 26–30.

3. Sir Philip Sidney *Astrophel and Stella*, Sonnet 68, lines 1–4.

4. Peacham, Henry *The Garden of Eloquence* (1593) ed. W. G. Crane (New York, 1977).

5. He writes in the section on the stylistic feature *circumductio*: "Convolutio est oratio ita verbis composita, ut tota in se contineri videatur, neque eius pars aliqua comprehendi possit, nisi totam absolveris, haec et rotundam et pulchram facit orationem. Circumducit vero quatenus omnia inter se membra adeo complicantur, ut nullum sine aliis intellegi possit, et in unius membri corpus convenire videantur." The example cited to illustrate this figure does not, however, correspond at all with what we have come to think of as systrophe: "Cicero in epistola ad Curionem. Te rogo, ut memineris quantaecunque tibi accessiones fient, et fortunae, et dignitatis, eas te non potuisse consequi, nisi meis puer olim fidelissimus atque amatissimus consiliis paruisses. Item si hoc statueris, quarum laudum gloriam adamaris, quibus artibus hae laudes comparantur, in his esse elaborandum."

6. "The thirteenth ornament is called Convolutio, in which any part of a statement corresponds to every part of every other statement. It is called Convolutio because there is not the determined application of one part to one part, but of all parts to all parts. One cannot easily use this ornament." Quoted from J. J. Murphy *Rhetoric in the Middle Ages* (Berkeley and Los Angeles, 1974), p. 354.

7. *Peri ideon*, ed. Rabe, p. 294, lines 6–10; as Professor J. Monfasani has pointed out to me in a personal letter. Translated into English the passage runs approximately thus: "And also the scheme that we call systrophe is completely heaped / thrown together, as for instance 'for if then when we succoured the people of Euboea . . .' etc., and likewise 'for he who prepares the things with which I shall be tied up . . .' etc."

8. Crane has noted such an adaptation and assimilation in other figures; cf. pp. 14 & 20 of his introduction to the Scholars Facsimiles & Reprints edition cited above.

Richard A. Lanham, the only "modern" Anglo-American rhetorician to list the figure at all, avowedly depends on Peacham, from whom he also takes the examples. The French type of *conglobation* follows a different line of tradition. Pierre Fontanier, for example, by explicitly relating *conglobation* with *énumération* and *accumulation*, clearly goes back to Trapezuntius' / Hermogenes' stylistic notion of *convolutio* / *circumductio*: "La *Conglobation*, que l'on appelle encore *Enumération, Accumulation*, est une figure par laquelle, au lieu d'un trait simple et unique sur le même sujet, on en réunit, sous un seul point de vue, un plus ou moins grand nombre, d'où résulte un tableau plus ou moins riche, plus ou moins étendu." *Les Figures du discours* (Repr. Paris, 1968), p. 363.

"*Conglobation*. Accumulation de preuves. La conglobation combat la partie adverse par une sorte de feu roulant d'arguments." Similarly Henri Morier *Dictionnaire de Poétique et de Rhétorique* (Paris, 1961).

9. Aeschylus *Agamemnon*, lines 895–902–3; Cicero *de Oratore* II.ix.36; Seneca *Hercules Furens*, lines 1065–1076; *Veni Creator Spiritus; Ave Maris Stella*; certain passages from the *Gloria*, the *Credo*, and the *Salve Regina*; St. Bernard's prayer to the Virgin in Dante's *Paradiso*, xxxiii, lines 1–21; Shakespeare *The Rape of Lucrece*, lines 764–70; lines 925–29; *Macbeth* II.ii.36–40; *Hamlet* II.ii.295–300; III.i.150–54; *Othello* II.i.109–12. et al.

10. Ibid.

11. *On Hope. By way of Question and Answer, betweene A. Cowley, and R. Crashaw*. lines 61–63 (Cowley); lines 11–14 (Crashaw).

12. In *The Temple* the following poems are partly or—as in the case of *Prayer I*—completely systrophic: *Prayer I, Frailtie, Sunday, To all Angels and Saints, Miserie, Dotage*. In the *Silex Scintillans* of Vaughan numerous examples of systrophe can be found: *The Incarnation and Passion, The Morning-watch, H. Scriptures, Son-dayes, The Proffer, Joy, The Garland, The Rainbow, Fair and yong light!, The Night, Quickness*. In the *Carmen Deo Nostro* of Crashaw *systrophes* can be found in the following poems: *Nativity Hymn, Epiphany Hymn, In the Glorious Assumption of Our Blessed Lady, The Weeper, On Hope*. et al. to cite just some metaphysical examples.

13. Cf. Austin Warren, *Richard Crashaw. A Study in Baroque Sensibility*. (Baton Rouge, La., 1939), p. 192 f.: "Oxymoron, paradox, and hyperbole are figures necessary to the articulation of the Catholic faith."

14. I am indebted to E. B. Greenwood's article "George Herbert's Sonnet *Prayer*: A Stylistic Study" in *Essays in Criticism*. XV (1965), pp. 27–45.

15. Vaughan *H. Scriptures*. l. 7.

Argumentative Aspects of Rhetoric and their Impact on the Poetry of Joost van den Vondel (1587–1679)

MARIJKE SPIES
University of Amsterdam

In this paper I wish to discuss the role of argument in rhetoric as it concerns the poetry of the *poeta laureatus* Joost van den Vondel.[1] I will illustrate my proposition by way of an analysis of Vondel's poem celebrating the new Amsterdam town hall, which today is the Royal Palace, on the Dam Square, a majestic and sumptuously decorated building, a triumph of seventeenth-century Dutch architecture and art.

At the end of the sixteenth and the beginning of the seventeenth century the most progressive Dutch poets were drawn to the Pleiadic, Neo-Platonic conception of poetry, according to which "true" literature distinguishes itself by an innate quality that may perhaps best be described as "inspired imagination." This is, certainly in the first resort, a specifically *lyrical* conception, which regards freedom of mind and a multiplicity and diversity of imaginative ideas as the pre-eminent poetic qualities. This conception was theoretically elaborated by no less a person than Daniel Heinsius, notably in his inaugural speech at Leyden University in 1603: *De poetis et eorum interpretibus*, which marks a moment of crucial importance for the whole development of vernacular literature.[2]

Although clearly Neo-Platonic in origin and initially also in content, in the course of time this lyrical conception of *literature* narrowed to a conception of *lyrical poetry*, and appeared to run parallel to Aristotle's ideas about tragedy and the epic. We may infer this for Heinsius himself, and in midcentury we find it explicitly in Gerardus Joannes Vossius' *De artis poeticae natura ac constitutione liber* of 1647.[3]

According to Vossius it is at its most recent and optimum stage of development that literature is characterized by inspiration and imagination. In an earlier phase of history literature did not exist in this sense, and poems were nothing more than metrical orations in rhyme.[4] In his *Poeticarum institutionum, libri tres* (likewise of 1647) he again draws attention to this, in his opinion older, form of literature. In reference to this Vossius mentions his *Commentariorum rhetoricorum, sive oratorium institutionum libri sex*, which first appeared in 1606 and of which in 1643 a fourth elaborated new edition had been published.[5] But in his literary text-book he wants to present only what he considers the optimum form of literature.

When Vossius speaks of the development of poetry, he alludes to developments that are alleged to have taken place in Roman antiquity. Yet — whether or not this is coincidence — it tallies with what we may observe in the sixteenth and seventeenth century. Graham Castor has already pointed out that in France the Pleiadic conceptions replaced those of the *seconde rhétorique*, which emphasized rhetorically structured argumentation.[6] Elsewhere I have tried to prove that we not only come across a similar conception in Julius Ceasar Scaliger's *Poetices libri septem* of 1561, but that it also underlies, in any case in the Netherlands, a whole tradition of sixteenth-century Neo-Latin poetry.[7] Though Vossius may, almost a century later, consider the rhetorical conception outdated, and though not wanting to disapprove of the *docere* as such he rejects its rhetorical realisation for poetry in the strictest sense of the word, the question remains whether everyone agreed with him in that respect. Which brings me to Joost van den Vondel. Practically untouched by lyrical fashion, Vondel wrote long poems in the humanistic vein of the sixteenth century, always aiming at the instruction of the audience through rhetorical means.

I have begun with this sketch of some literary-historical lines of development in order to make clear that even in the sixteenth and seventeenth century the relation between rhetoric and literature is not a firmly-established one. On the contrary, different interpretations may be assigned to this relation, depending on which view one supports about the object and function of literature. On the one hand, when the specific literary quality is located in the sphere of inspiration and imagination, a relation with rhetoric exists in point of *elocutio* and in point of *loci* and *argumenta*. Vossius indicates this clearly in the first paragraph of his *De artis poeticae natura ac consitutione liber*, referring for these aspects to his rhetorical handbook.[8] But what the poet, given this conception, *cannot* obtain from the *ars oratoria*, are the conditions which determine the coherence, the structure of his work. Whereas for epic and tragedy this is the unity of action defined by fictional reality (the *imitatio*), in the case of lyric poetry it is the ungoverned inspiration of the author.[9]

On the other hand, when the education of the public through rhetorical means is regarded as a function of literature as well, the poet is just as much concerned with the more dialectical aspects of rhetoric, that is to say the argumentation- and discussion-patterns that rhetoric is also and often mainly concerned with, in so far as it is an argumentative theory. In relation to poetry the importance of these aspects is emphasized by Scaliger, again in the first paragraph of his work.[10]

Rather unjustly, at least in the Netherlands, hardly any attention has been paid by literary-historical studies to these argumentative aspects of the *ars oratoria*. In my opinion one of the main reasons lies in the fact that in his famous *Handbuch der literarischen Rhetorik* Lausberg connects poetry rather strictly with too one-sided a conception of the *genus demonstrativum*.

Now, as we all know, the epideictic genre occupies a special place within classical rhetoric, in that its main function does not lie in the argumentative treatment of a point at issue, but in the *amplificatio* of established facts, with a view to pleasing the public rather than convincing it. This view, notably advanced by Aristotle, reappears for example in Cicero's *De partitione oratoria*, and Vossius argues along the same lines: in his study *De rhetoricae natura ac constitutione liber unus*, first published in 1621, he asserts that the panegyric serves mainly to exhibit the eloquence of the orator to the satisfaction of the public.[11] Lausberg's infatuation with the *l'art pour l'art* aspect of the epideictic genre—an infatuation culminating in the italicized sentence "Das Lob der Schönheit ist die Hauptfunktion der epideiktischen Rhetorik"[12]—is probably connected with his twentieth-century conception of poetry. It induces him to print in small type everything relating to the ethical aspect of the genre, reducing it to notes,[13] and to neglect the argumentative aspects altogether.

Yet this was most certainly not intended by Aristotle and even less so by Vossius. Aristotle even emphasizes the ethical aspects of the genre,[14] and in his *Commentariorum rhetoricorum libri sex* Vossius says in so many words that in the *genus demonstrativum* it is not only excellent and fluent speech but also an excellent and virtuous way of life that matters. Since because of this, the orator is concerned with vices and virtues, Vossius claims that the genre comes close to the *genus deliberativum*.[15] This implies that the argumentative aspects of rhetoric are of equal importance to the *genus demonstrativum*. In fact Vossius assigns the epideictic together with both other genres to that group of truly rhetorical discourses that consider a finite question, on the basis of evidence and argumentation. He distinguishes this group from the *orationes* intended to appeal merely to the emotions, such as, for instance, congratulations and plaints.[16]

It is not immaterial to our argument to point out that Vossius, as a theorist of rhetoric, went so far as to emphasize the specifically argumentative character of this *ars*. In the *Commentariorum rhetoricorum libri sex*, his successful handbook of rhetoric, he dedicates by far the greatest part of the first three books to argumentative issues, and his philosophical discourse *De rhetoricae natura ac constitutione liber unus* may for the greater part be regarded as an elaboration of the thesis which Aristotle postulated in the opening pages of his treatise on rhetoric: "Rhetoric is a counterpart of Dialectic."[17] With this Vossius continues the fifteenth- and sixteenth-century tendency to emphasize the similarities between dialectic and rhetoric. This tendency had led Ramus to the revolutionary step of relegating the whole of argumentation-theory to logic, curtailing rhetoric to a mere theory of style and recitation.[18] About half a century later, what has been called the Neo-Ciceronian Contrareformation[19] leads in Vossius' case to an analysis which, on the basis of their similarities, specifies the differences between both disciplines on the level of argumentation. On account of the specific content, purpose and function of rhetoric, namely to persuade the audience to adopt a certain kind of behaviour concerning a particular question, rhetorical argumentation has its own specific characteristics, not only in the sphere of emotionally-appealing means of persuasion but also in the rational sphere.[20]

Vossius' rather abstract reflections in this respect need not concern us further, since in his *Commentariorum rhetoricorum libri sex* the principles of rhetorical argumentation are dealt with concretely. Of these principles the rhetorical forms of the syllogism: the *enthymema* and the *epicheirema,* are of importance where the structure of a rhetorical discourse is concerned, and the same goes for the theory of the different *status* which Vossius elaborated in detail, following in the footsteps of Hermogenes.

As regards the former, Quintilian points out the possibility of building up entire rational discourses on the model of the simple or complex *epicheirema.*[21] This *epicheirema* consists at the most of a *propositio,* its supporting arguments, an *assumptio,* again with supporting arguments, and finally a conclusion.[22] The fact that Vossius wants to split up the central section of an oration into two main parts — a *propositio,* which sets out the problem and provides the premises for the conclusion, and a *contentio,* the argumentation of the concrete case[23] — is closely bound up with the form of this *epicheirema.* The force with which he — following Aristotle[24] — propagates this division as the most essential, and the minimal importance he attaches to the *narratio* as an independent structural component, implies a positive preference for the argumentative character of an oration rather than for its narrative value, which after all determined the attractiveness of the rhetorical model for a great many *poetae.*[25]

As regards the different *status,* the distinct levels involved in the dispute between supporters and opponents — the *status conjecturalis,* the *status finitionis,* the *status qualitatis,* and the *status quantitatis,*[26] to confine ourselves to four — of these Vossius maintains, in imitation of Cicero's *Topica,* that they are also directly involved in the *genus demonstrativum.* For even in a eulogy it may be open to question whether something has actually been done by someone (*status conjecturalis*). Likewise the precise definition (*status finitionis*) or the moral evaluation (*status qualitatis*) of the action may be questionable. Vossius adds that even if these things are not actually called in question, they might be potentially.[27]

The latter implies that in the *genus demonstrativum*, which hardly ever explicitly formulates a *dubium*, and hence has no means of determining a certain central *quaestio* with a specific *status*, all these different discussion-levels must be considered, in order to meet all potential objections.

So, where Vossius is concerned, there is no question of even the least trace of a Lausbergian equation of poetry with a display-platform-conception of the *genus demonstrativum*. On the contrary, compared with the sixteenth-century humanistic tradition, Vossius seems to present the different disciplines with a more explicit division of labour, assigning imagination and narration to poetry and argumentation to rhetoric, and defining in turn the rhetorical way of argumentation more clearly in contrast to dialectic.

It is this argumentative aspect of rhetoric that particularly appeals to Vondel as a *poet*. His seventeenth-century biographer Geeraardt Brandt bears witness to Vondel's interest when he informs us of the fact that in about 1625 Vondel took lessons in "logic or the art of dialectic, in order to write better poetry."[28] The fact that several at least of his panegyrics are built according to the argumentative principles mentioned above, shows how he benefitted from these lessons. He follows the principles so ardently propagated by Vossius-*rhetor*, namely: the division of the middle part of an oration into a *propositio* and a *contentio*, and the construction of the latter according to the *status*-theory. This applies not only to *Het Lof der Zee-vaert* ('In Praise of Navigation') of 1623, but also to his *Inwydinge van het Stadthuis t' Amsterdam* ('Inauguration of Amsterdam Town Hall') of 1655, and his *Zeemagazyn* ('Marine-Arsenal') of 1658.[29] That is, it applies to poems that were written after Vossius had come up with his view on the division of labour between poetry and rhetoric in his literary-theoretical works, published in 1647, and this in spite of the fact that Vondel and he were personal acquaintances.

For the purpose of demonstration I will now give a survey of the argumentative construction of the *Inwydinge van het Stadthuis t' Amsterdam*, the 1378-line poem written by Vondel when the new Amsterdam town hall came into use, and which appeared on that occasion in the form of a booklet of 44 pages.[30]

To start with the most general division: Vondel's poem consists indeed of an *exordium*, a *propositio*, a *contentio* and a *peroratio*, the parts that Vossius considers to be essential.

I will not go into all the ethical and emotional arguments adduced in the *exordium*, in order to render the public *attentum* and above all *benevolum*, because they do not immediately contribute towards a better understanding of the rational argumentation. One rational function of the *exordium*, though, does concern us, namely the *docilem parare*, informing the public what the poem will be about. Vondel indicates that his subject will be the town hall, civil authority and the annual fair, and all this in praise of Amsterdam. Thus he presents, as I will demonstrate in what follows, the different subjects that constitute the material of his argumentation.

In fact all three subjects return *in abstracto* in the following *propositio.* This *propositio* presents a general thesis, as is the case in all of Vondel's panegyrics that I have analysed. In this particular case it is a compound thesis which postulates that: (a) human weakness necessitates authority, and that therefore a town hall as seat of the government exists for the good of the community; and (b) that people may continue practising their trade and conducting their business, if the government is on the alert for enemies from without, and that a town hall may therefore be regarded as a house enclosing a thousand other houses. Thus two items that form the components of the argument, propagate, in the form of a syllogism, the necessity for a town hall, namely: public authority, and the community defined in terms of economic activity. Hence the conclusion that the town hall may be regarded as the town's heart. Five instances of other *republicae* are adduced as the inductive proofs of this proposition.[31]

This leaves Vondel to demonstrate that the concrete instance: the Amsterdam town hall, meets the above-argued criteria, namely: that it is an adequate seat of a reliable civil authority, and that it is the stimulating centre of community life. The *contentio* which now follows is entirely dedicated to this argumentation, and apart from eight lines forming the *peroratio*, it monopolizes the rest of the poem. Thus the argumentative middle part of Vondel's poem does indeed display the construction of an *epicheirema*, be it one of an extremely complex structure.

Vossius in particular emphasizes that one of the reasons for making a distinction between rhetoric and dialectic, is the fact that rhetoric deals with individual concrete, instead of general abstract issues.[32] For the sake of argumentation of such an individual issue, the rhetoricians have in fact derived specific rhetorical *loci* from the dialectical *loci communes.*[33] As examples of *loci speciales* belonging to the eulogy of buildings, Quintilian mentions honour, utility, beauty, and the makers or founders, whereas Vossius in his survey of these *loci* emphasizes in particular the architectonic qualities.[34] All these *loci* may be found in the *contentio* of Vondel's *Inwydinge.* But the striking thing is that besides these *loci*, we also come across *loci* belonging to the eulogy of cities. These *loci*: the history, the situation and geography of the city of Amsterdam — mentioned by both Quintilian and Vossius as the specific *loci* belonging to the city-*laus*[35] — are the ones that constitute the lion's share of the poem, especially early in the argumentation.

In this Vondel may have followed an example. For in one of the most familiar Latin translations of Aphthonius' *Progymnasmata*, there figures a poem that bears a clear resemblance to the *Inwydinge*, as far as its structure according to the *loci* belonging to the eulogy of cities and buildings is concerned. I have in mind the sixteenth-century translation of Rodolphus Agricola and Johannis Maria Catanaeus which, annotated by R. Lorichius, was published in Amsterdam no less than seven times between 1642 and 1665. In this translation a great many examples have been added to Aphthonius' text, one of them a panegyric in praise of Marburg University, entitled *Encomium Marpurgensis Academiae*, in which the construction according to *loci* is indicated in the margin.[36] But the very resemblance between the *Encomium* and the *Inwydinge* makes the differences all the more significant. The structure of the *Encomium* is dictated by not much more than the order in which these *loci speciales* are presented by Quintilian. By means of the eulogistic arguments derived from these *loci*, we are presented with an enumeration of the moral and material qualities of town and academy, while there is no question of an argumentative structure in terms of 'since . . . therefore'. Thus this sixteenth-century *Encomium* is indeed one long *amplificatio*, conforming to the precepts of the non-argumentative *genus demonstrativum.*[37] The absence of something like a universal *thesis* presented in a *propositio*, against the background of which all these *argumenta* might be given an argumentative function, is also indicative of the non-argumentative character of this poem.

In Vondel's case, on the other hand, these same *loci* do follow the order of a certain argumentative structure, so that his *contentio* indeed represents an argumentation. This structure is in fact that of the different *status*.

Argumentation is called for when there is a *quaestio*, that is to say in this case when the praiseworthiness of the object may be called in question. This holds good most certainly in the case of the Amsterdam town hall, an enormous and expensive object of prestige.[38] Vondel comes forward with the objections that could be made against the building only towards the end of his poem: the size and splendour of the building supposedly bear witness to too much confidence in the favours of changeable fortune. But all 1194 preceding verses anticipate the refutation of this proposition, so that when the objections are actually raised, the reader or listener is sufficiently indoctrinated to discredit these statements and to go along with the ensuing positive proposition.[39]

The gist of the argument is that the municipal authority of Amsterdam, as the representative of God on earth, is itself best qualified to consider what degree of sumptuousness (the *locus* of beauty) befits the venerability of its own seat of government, and subsequently it is argued that the many tasks that have to be accomplished by the authorities for the benefit of the community necessitate such an enormous building (the *locus* of utility). Although expressed only towards the end of the poem, it is necessary for the argumentative analysis to keep in mind that this is what has to be proved: the *assumptio* of the *epicheirema*. Two lines of argumentation may be derived,[40] in terms of which it has to be demonstrated that the Amsterdam town hall is indeed an adequate seat of the municipal government of Amsterdam.

Only after this has been proved, can the praiseworthiness of the municipal government of Amsterdam be brought forward in order to demonstrate also the *honor* of its seat. The criteria for this praiseworthiness are set down in the *propositio.* They are the maintenance of order within the community, and the outward defence of the community.

Concerning the praiseworthiness of the Amsterdam town hall itself, the first compound question that may be raised by a critical mind is: is the town hall indeed the functional centre of the town, and is it indeed the result of a correct decision of the municipal authorities. These questions belong to the level of the *status conjecturalis*, and each has its own *sub-status*.

The question whether the Amsterdam town hall is indeed the functional centre of the town, immediately invites the counter-question just how the functional centre of the town should be defined. Thus Vondel's *contentio* begins with a bird's-eye view of the history of Amsterdam (a *locus* belonging to the city-*laus*), demonstrating how the situation of the different historical town halls was functionally changed in accordance with the economic development of the town from fishing-village, via centre of regional trade, to trading metropolis. At present, anno 1655, the new town hall is situated on the Dam Square, the great market-place, centre of the international trading empire (the *locus* of the situation of a town, belonging to the city-*laus*).

A similar procedure is followed where the second part of the question is concerned. The question whether the building of the town hall is indeed the result of a correct decision of the authorities, invites the counter-question as to just how that decision was effected and carried through. In answer to this Vondel traces briefly the course of events during the planning-stage, and demonstrates how, due to the steadfastness of the municipal authorities, and despite a great many setbacks, the building of the town hall proceeded. It is a highly-coloured account, evidently doing violence to the true course of events,[41] but not to such an extent that for a more general public the story deserves no credit at all.

So here we are with the town hall on the Dam Square. Nevertheless this does not mean that Vondel considers the subject closed, because a critical reader might object that the Dam Square is not the centre of the town as defined above, and that the building of the town hall does not adequately reflect the decision and perseverance of the municipal government. In answer to these potential objections Vondel starts with a description of the Dam Square as both architectonic and functional centre of the town (again a *locus* belonging to the city-*laus*), and continues with a description of the building activities, under the inspiring guidance of the architects. It is an answer on the level of the *status finitionis*, concerned with the precise definition, and for which Cicero recommends the description as an adequate means.[42] Only when these potential objections have been answered have both parts of the issue been settled. And only now is the discussion of the town hall on the level of the *status conjecturalis* brought to a satisfactory conclusion: everything indicates that is is indeed both the functional centre of the town, and the result of a correct decision on the part of the municipal authorities. Although by now we have reached verse 612, we have not yet even glimpsed the town hall itself. The lines of argumentation followed meant that first all kinds of other matters had to come up for discussion, so that for those who do not see through the argumentative structure, the poem may create the impression of a rambling chaos. The needs of the trading town (the annual fair of the *exordium*), and the capacities of the city-council (the civil authorities of the *exordium*), are indeed the qualities that determine the praiseworthiness of the town hall.

Here Vondel arrives at a kind of intermediate conclusion, anticipating the *status qualitatis*. In this conclusion, on the basis of utility, beauty and venerability (the *loci* belonging to the *laus* of buildings) both lines of argumentation come together at the same point, the issue at stake: the town hall itself.

But . . . there is a 'but'. For at this point the critical reader or listener might object that this is all very well, but that the town hall itself proves that all has come to nought. Vondel also has to justify the hitherto formulated pretensions with regard to the town hall itself, which means that here again the burden of proof at the level of the *status finitionis* rests on the poet. The problem is again solved by means of a description, passing in review exterior and interior of the town hall, and the main decorations in the form of paintings and sculpture.

Thus Vondel finally and definitely arrives at the *status qualitatis*, the level to which the special *loci* in praise of buildings belong.[43] After all that has gone before the beauty and utility may quickly be settled. Having also finally raised the objections against the building *expressis verbis*, now all further emphasis is placed on the venerability of the building, the *honor*. Entirely according to the criteria laid down in the *propositio*, by means of a detailed eulogy of the Amsterdam municipal authorities, Vondel proves the respectability of the seat of government.

Regarding this municipal government: in the rest of the Republic of the United Provinces opinions varied on the moral qualities of those in power in Amsterdam. In the *peroratio* Vondel calls upon the antagonists to acknowledge at last that the welfare of the entire country depends on Amsterdam and its municipal authorities. Yet when he does so, the rational argumentation has already been completed.

Regarding this argumentation I hope I have demonstrated that Vondel's lessons in logic had a fruitful result. It would appear that Vossius' tendency to emphasize the argumentative character of rhetoric, leads in the case of some of Vondel's poetry to a more distinctly argumentative framework, compared with sixteenth-century literary texts. At the same time he seems in this respect to be running counter to the seventeenth-century literary trend, codified by the same Vossius, which wanted to liberate poetry precisely from the dictates of rhetorical argumentation.

Notes

1. I should like to thank Mrs. Patricia van Hees for translating this, and Mr. Paul Vincent for some editorial corrections.

2. J. H. Meter, *De literaire theorieën van Daniël Heinsius. Een onderzoek naar de klassieke en humanistische bronnen van De Tragoediae Constitutione en andere geschriften* (Amsterdam, 1975), p. 86, pp. 95–105, pp. 108–18, pp. 186–94. Marijke Spies, "Het epos in de 17e eeuw in Nederland; een literatuurhistorisch probleem. II," *Spektator* 7 (1977–78), pp. 562–94, notably pp. 578–80. Cf. also P. Tuynman, "Petrus Scriverius. 12 January 1576–30 April 1660," *Quaerendo* 7 (1977), pp. 5–45, notably p. 13.

3. Spies, "Het epos in de 17e eeuw. II.", pp. 580–81.

4. Gerardi Joannis Vossii *De artis poeticae natura ac constitutione liber* (Amsterodami, 1647), III. 10, 11 and 17, pp. 15–19. See also Marijke Spies, "Het epos in de 17e eeuw in Nederland: een literatuurhistorisch probleem. I" *Spektator* 7 (1977–78), pp. 379–411, notably p. 390.

5. Gerardi Joannis Vossii *Poeticarum institutionum, libri tres* (Amsterodami, 1647), III. xiii. 5, p. 69, and 9, p. 72. For the dates of the editions of the *Commentariorum rhetoricorum, sive oratorium institutionum libri sex* see C. S. M. Rademaker, *Gerardus Joannes Vossius (1577–1649)*. Diss. Nijmegen (Zwolle, 1967), "Bibliografie," no. 3, p. 276. See also: Spies, "Het epos in de 17e eeuw. II," p. 565.

6. Grahame Castor, *Pléiade Poetics. A Study in Sixteenth-Century Thought and Terminology* (Cambridge, 1964), chap. 1 and 2.

7. Spies, "Het epos in de 17e eeuw. I," pp. 396–97, and "Het epos in de 17e eeuw. II," pp. 566–69 and pp. 572–73.

8. Vossius, *De artis poeticae natura ac constitutione liber,* I. 1, pp. 2–3.

9. Vossius, *De artis poeticae natura ac constitutione liber,* VI. 8, pp. 34–35. Vossius, *Poeticarum institutionum, libri tres,* I. i. 1, p. 6 and II, xiv. 4–5. p. 75. See also Vossius, *De artis poeticae natura ac constitutione liber,* XI. 6, pp. 66–67. In more detail: Spies, "Het epos in de 17e eeuw. I and II," respectively pp. 390–91 and pp. 564–65.

10. Julius Caesar Scaliger, *Poetices libri septem*. Faksimile-Neudruck der Ausgabe von Lyon 1561 mit einer Einleitung von August Buck (Stuttgart etc. 1964), I. 1, p. 3, col. 1 C. In more detail: Spies, "Het epos in de 17e eeuw. I and II," pp. 396–97 and pp. 566–69 respectively.

11. Aristotle, *The 'Art' of Rhetoric*. With an English translation by John Henry Freese (London etc. 1967), I. ix. 40. Cicero, *De partitione oratoria,* 21. 71. Gerardi Joannis Vossii *De rhetoricae natura ac constitutione, et antiquis rhetoribus, sophistis, ac oratoribus, liber unus,* 5. I have used the edition enlarged by Vossius himself which appeared posthumously in 1658 in Gerardi Ioh. Vossii *De logicis et rhetoricae natura ac constitutione libri II* (Hagae-Comitis, 1658). The expression referred to may be found on pp. 45–46. For the dating of the first edition see Rademaker, *Vossius,* "Bibliografie," no. 8, p. 277. See also Vossius *Commentariorum rhetoricorum libri sex,* I. iii. 1, p. 17.

12. Heinrich Lausberg, *Handbuch der literarischen Rhetorik. Eine Grundlegung der Literaturwissenschaft.* 2 vols. (München, 1960), t.1, par. 239, p. 130. See also par. 241, p. 131.

13. See e.g. Lausberg, *Handbuch,* t.1, par. 240, p. 131, note 1, and par. 253,

p. 138. Cf. also par. 1163, pp. 555–56, and par. 1165, pp. 557–58.

14. Aristotle, *The 'Art' of Rhetoric*, I. ix. 1–37.

15. Vossius, *Commentariorum rhetoricorum libri sex*, I. v. 1, pp. 43–44.

16. Vossius, *Commentariorum rhetoricorum libri sex*, I. iii. 2, pp. 23–24.

17. Aristotle, *The 'Art' of Rhetoric*, I. i. 1; cf. also I. ii. 7.

18. On this see W. S. Howell, *Logic and Rhetoric in England, 1500–1700* (Princeton, 1956), pp. 148–65.

19. Howell, chap. 4 "Counter Reform: Systematics and Neo-Ciceronians."

20. Vossius, *De rhetoricae natura ac constitutione liber unus*, 4, 5 and 6, pp. 27–49.

21. Quintilianus, *Institutio oratoria*, V. xiv. 10.

22. Vossius, *Commentariorum rhetoricorum libri sex*, III pars. prior. v.4, p. 374.

23. Vossius, *Commentariorum rhetoricorum libri sex*, III pars. prior i.2, pp. 322–23, and iv.2 pp. 365–66.

24. Aristotle, *The 'Art' of Rhetoric*, II. xiii. 1–3.

25. On Ant. Seb. Minturno, *De poeta* (Venice, 1559) see e.g. S. F. Witstein, *Funeraire poëzie in de Nederlandse renaissance. Enkele funeraire gedichten van Heinsius, Hooft, Huygens en Vondel, bezien tegen de achtergrond van de theorie betreffende het genre*. Diss. Utrecht. (Assen, 1969), pp. 55–58 and p. 72. Cf. also Scaliger, *Poetices libri septem*, I.1, p. 3, col. 1 CD and III. 108. p.159–109. p.160.

26. Vossius, *Commentariorum rhetoricorum libri sex*, I. vi. 7, pp. 120–21.

27. Vossius, *Commentariorum rhetoricorum libri sex*, I. vi.8. pp. 121–22. Cf. Cicero, *Topica*, 25.93.

28. Geeraardt Brandt, *Het leven van Joost van den Vondel*, Ed. by P. Leendertz jr. ('s-Gravenhage, 1932, orig. 1682), p. 19.

29. Printed in: *De werken van Vondel* ed. J. F. M. Sterck e.a. 10 tomes + reg. (Amsterdam, 1927–40), respectively t.2, pp. 431–55, t.5, pp. 859–904 and t.8, pp. 654–55. My detailed rhetorical analysis of *Het Lof der Zee-vaert* is published in *Vondel bij gelegenheid*, ed. L. Roose en K. Porteman (Middleburg, 1979), pp. 63–91. A similar analysis of the *Inwydinge van het Stadthuis t' Amsterdam* has been published in *Visies op Vondel na driehonderd jaar* ed. S. F. Witstein and E. K. Grootes (The Hague, 1979), pp. 165–217. Marjonne M. van Randwijk gives an analysis of the *Zeemagazyn* in her master's thesis, a copy of which may be found at the Institute for Dutch Studies of the University of Amsterdam.

30. See: J. H. W. Unger, *Bibliographie van Vondels Werken* (Amsterdam, 1888), no. 549, p. 107.

31. That the *exemplum* is the rhetorical form of logical induction is argued by Vossius in his *Commentariorum rhetoricorum libri sex*, III pars. prior. v.6, p. 376.

32. Vossius, *De rhetoricae natura ac constitutione liber unus*, 4, pp. 37–39.

33. Vossius, *De rhetoricae natura ac constitutione liber unus*, 18, pp. 119–20.

34. Quintilianus, *Institutio oratoria*, III. vii. 27. Vossius, *Commentariorum rhetoricorum libri sex*, I. v. 39, p. 105.

35. Quintilianus, *Institutio oratoria*, III. vii. 26. Vossius, *Commentariorum rhetoricorum libri sex*, I. v. 39. p. 104.

36. See E. J. Kuiper, *De Hollandsche "schoolordre" van 1625* (Groningen, 1958), p. 137 and p. 211. I have used the edition Aphthonii *Progymnasmata*, partim à Rodolpho Agricola, partim à Johanne Maria Catanaeo, Latinitate donata; cum scholiis R. Lorichii (Amsterodami, 1655). The poem referred to is on pp. 217–41.

37. See e.g. Quintilianus, *Institutio oratoria*, III. vii. 6. See also Aristotle, *The 'Art' of Rhetoric*, I. ix. 40.

38. See Katharine Fremantle, *The Baroque Town Hall of Amsterdam* (Utrecht, 1959).

39. We are here dealing with a shift in the logical order of argumentation for reasons of manipulation, one of the issues that constitute the differences between rhetorical argumentation and dialectic. Cf. Vossius, *De rhetoricae natura ac constitutione liber unus*, 18, p. 122.

40. On this see Cicero, *De oratore*, II. xxx. 132. Cicero, *De inventione*, I. xiii. 18. Quintilianus, *Institutio oratoria*, III. x.5-xi.20. See also Vossius, *Commentariorum rhetoricorum libri sex*, I. vi. 6, p. 118.

41. See I. van Vondels *Inwydinge van 't Stadthuis t' Amsterdam*, 1655, ed. by M. E. Kronenberg. (Deventer, 1913), pp. 8-14.

42. Cicero, *De partitione oratoria*, 12. 41.

43. Vossius, *Commentariorum rhetoricorum libri sex*, I. vi. 7, p. 121.

Part III

Rhetoric and Philosophy

Rhétorique et Philosophie: Introduction

ALAIN MICHEL
University of Paris–Sorbonne

Seule la sagesse a sa fin en soi. Nous ne saurions considérer qu'il en va de même pour la rhétorique et cette erreur est la première que nous devions éviter. Ceci constitue du même coup la raison fondamentale pour laquelle nous devons confronter rhétorique et philosophie. Elle explique les autres raisons, qui sont historiques. Les deux disciplines n'ont cessé de se rencontrer. Nous comprenons pourquoi et cela nous dicte la méthode du présent exposé: d'une part, notre enquête sera historique, mais d'autre part la question que nous poserons d'abord sera la suivante: quelles sont, au plan des principes, les dettes mutuelles qui existent entre la rhétorique et la philosophie?

I

Il faut chercher en premier lieu ce que la rhétorique se doit à elle-même. Disons que c'est tout l'apport de la sophistique, avec laquelle elle s'est d'abord confondue. Celle-ci a conduit la pratique oratoire à peu de choses près jusqu'à sa perfection. Protagoras et d'autres ont enseigné l'art de la discussion selon le pour et le contre. Gorgias a mis au point une esthétique des figures. On a commencé à réfléchir sur les parties et les genres du discours.

Tout se passe comme si la rhétorique se devait tout à elle-même. Elle doit pourtant quelque chose à la philosophie et c'est peut-être le plus important: il s'agit de sa propre mise en question, accomplie par Platon: celui-ci s'opposait à la fois à une *mimésis* trompeuse et à des méthodes de persuasion qui n'hésitaient pas à noyer le vrai dans le vraisemblable.

Cependant, à l'issue de cette mise en question, la philosophie s'est efforcée de se réconcilier avec la rhétorique et de l'intégrer dans son enseignement. Tel fut le rôle d'Aristote, qui, suivi par de nombreux disciples, assura la naissance d'une terminologie rigoureuse en accord avec le vrai. On peut énumérer brièvement ses apports à cet égard. Il cherche à réconcilier le vrai et le vraisemblable en définissant leurs rapports exacts et le bon usage du second; pour cela, il fait intervenir sa logique, c'est-à-dire une théorie des idées générales, et l'on arrive ainsi à la doctrine des lieux communs, des "thèses," des enthymèmes. D'autre part, Aristote, qui veut conserver dans sa philosophie ce qu'il y avait d'utile chez Gorgias, propose dans la *Rhétorique* III et la *Poétique* tout un système de concepts esthétiques: clarté, nature, grandeur, grâce.

Ainsi, selon les leçons de l'école péripatéticienne, l'enseignement de la sophistique reprend place dans une philosophie d'ensemble et on peut dire cette fois que la rhétorique, critiquée par Platon, remise en ordre par Aristote, doit presque tout à la philosophie. Mais il faut aller plus loin et se demander ce que la philosophie peut devoir à la rhétorique.

L'évolution ultérieure de l'une et de l'autre nous renseignera. Nous constaterons d'abord que la rhétorique a beaucoup favorisé certains choix philosophiques, le succès de certaines écoles. C'est en grande partie à cause d'elle que Cicéron s'est attaché à la tradition platonico-aristotélicienne et a pris ainsi une voie où l'humanisme devait le suivre. Il s'agit, dans la sagesse antique, de la tendance la plus ouverte au dialogue, qui accepte le pluralisme et qui rejette les dogmatismes sans renoncer (comme le feront les purs sceptiques) à croire dans l'existence du vrai.

D'autre part, la rhétorique favorise une approche du réel. Le *Phèdre* nous disait que celle-ci se fait par l'amour. Chez les orateurs de la tradition latine, *pectus* et *natura* viennent entourer *ratio*. Cette tradition se prolongera à travers le moyen âge et, en passant par les notions d'*intellectus* et de *sensus*, on arrivera jusqu'à Pascal et aux textes sur l'*Art de persuader*, qui mettent bien en lumière, face à la "géométrie" cartésienne, ce que cette discipline a de spécifique. D'autre part, comme l'ont montré, après les travaux de Dupréel, ceux de M. Perelman, la rhétorique rend à la dialectique toute sa place par rapport à la logique: la dialectique est une manière rationnelle d'aborder l'irrationnel dans le langage et dans l'action. Comme l'atteste le modèle cicéronien, cette doctrine ne nie pas l'existence du vrai; mais elle montre que toute une partie de l'existence humaine se situe en deçà du vrai dans le monde du probable, de la discussion, de l'indétermination, du doute.

C'est qu'en effet la pratique de l'éloquence, l'art ou la faculté de la parole suppose une intégration du savoir à la vie. Cicéron, après Aristote et les Sophistes, s'est bien aperçu que l'homme qui parle se trouvait pratiquement obligé de parler de tout. Cela pose la question de la culture générale, qui a été formulée avec une force particulière dans le *De oratore*. D'autre part, pour atteindre à la plénitude, l'éloquence doit réunir des vertus ou des disciplines apparemment opposées: par exemple, chez un Cicéron, on voit, dans les discours ou dans les dialogues, se réconcilier les langages parlé et écrit. La culture et la pédagogie interfèrent plus ou moins chez Rabelais et chez Montaigne. Plus largement dans les "questions politiques" qui forment depuis Aristote la matière de tout discours, il se produit une rencontre nécessaire de l'action et de la contemplation. C'est par la rhétorique surtout, par la parole, que les intellectuels trouvent prise sur la politique.

En conclusion, nous avons à nous demander ceci: faut-il subordonner la rhétorique à la philosophie? Beaucoup de philosophes l'ont cru après Platon. Je pense surtout à la *Lettre 88* de Sénèque, mais aussi aux exposés plus nuancés de Philon d'Alexandrie, dans le *De congressu eruditionis causa*, et d'Augustin, dans le *De doctrina christiana*: dans le meilleur des cas, la rhétorique est présentée comme une servante de la philosophie. On comprend les raisons de cette position. Mais sans doute faut-il redouter qu'il ne s'agisse d'une servante maîtresse.

Aussi préférons-nous peut-être l'attitude que prenait Cicéron dans le *De oratore*, III, 55 sqq.: depuis Socrate, les philosophes ont eu selon lui le tort de briser l'unité de la culture, de séparer *cor* et *lingua*, les mots et les choses, le fond et la forme, la philosophie et son langage. Il faut au contraire maintenir cette unité de la parole. La véritable rhétorique n'est que l'art ou la faculté d'exprimer la sagesse; elle traite de la forme donnée à la philosophie. C'est dans cet esprit que s'est développée, à partir du IIe siècle, la *Seconde sophistique*. Les discours célèbres d'Aelius Aristide ne constituent nullement une condamnation de la philosophie. Mais la sophistique qui s'y exprime apparaît au contraire comme un moyen de réconcilier rhétorique et philosophie: elle est la philosophie dans le langage ou le langage dans la philosophie, l'action dans la contemplation, la recherche de l'être dans les mots, de l'être ou de l'idéal.

On voit que la rhétorique, ainsi comprise, se confond avec la méditation sur la parole dans ce qu'elle a de plus exigeant. Il n'y a pas lieu de s'étonner si, au IVe siècle, c'est précisément, la culture issue de la seconde sophistique qui est venue inspirer les premiers chefs d'oeuvre de l'hymnodie chrétienne savante. Voici par exemple un chant de Grégoire de Nazianze:

> O Toi, l'au-delà de tout,
>   comment t'appeler d'un autre nom?
> Quelle hymne peut te chanter?
>   Aucun mot ne t'exprime.
> Quel esprit te saisir?
>   Nulle intelligence ne te conçoit.
> Seul, tu es ineffable;
>   tout ce qui se dit est sorti de toi.
> Tous les êtres te célèbrent,
>   ceux qui parlent et ceux qui sont muets.
> Tous les êtres te rendent hommage,
>   ceux qui pensent
>   comme ceux qui ne pensent pas.

L'universel désir, le gémissement de tous
aspire vers toi.
Tout ce qui existe te prie
et vers toi, tout être qui sait lire ton univers
fait monter un hymne de silence.
(Trad. A. Hamman)

On voit que tout ce texte constitue une méditation sur la parole. Mais il ne peut faire moins que de la mettre en rapport avec son absolu, avec le Verbe divin. C'est jusque là que conduit nécessairement une réflexion véritable sur la rhétorique. On ne peut traiter de la parole sans poser la question de l'ineffable. Ici aboutit et se résout l'opposition entre rhétorique et philosophie. Tout le moyen âge l'a su, aussi bien chez les Byzantins que chez les Catholiques, et la Renaissance également. Nous ne devons jamais l'oublier.

II

IL EXISTE AINSI un lien fondamental entre la parole, beauté et vérité, action et contemplation, et la culture philosophique ou même théologique. C'est cette idée qui domine les oeuvres que Cicéron et après lui Philon d'Alexandrie et Augustin ont consacrées à la rhétorique et aux *artes*. Une telle doctrine, qui s'appuyait sur une analyse rigoureuse des exigences du réel, ne pouvait manquer de trouver dans l'histoire de fortes applications. Nous allons le montrer, par une brève esquisse, en dessinant, suivant une ligne approximativement chronologique, les grands domaines de la culture humaine où la rhétorique s'est trouvée mise en oeuvre.

Cela s'est produit, bien sûr, dans le langage. Comme nous venons de l'indiquer, il s'agissait de découvrir l'être dans les mots. En gros, c'était toute la philosophie de la référence qui se trouvait en cause. Cela conduisait par exemple à une théorie de la métaphore: je pense à Jean Scot Erigène. Celui-ci dit que Dieu est, mais aussi qu'il n'est pas puisqu'il est différent de tout ce qui est. Comment surmonter cette contradiction? En recourant, précisément, à la rhétorique de la métaphore, en disant qu'il sur-est, *superest*. On sait combien ces problèmes de langage garderont d'importance. Cette question des *res et uerba* se prolongera jusqu'au réalisme, au nominalisme, au débat sur les universaux. De Jean Scot à Jean Duns Scot, on ira de la ténèbre à l'univocité de l'être. On suivra ainsi un chemin qui partait d'Aristote, qui aboutit à Heidegger et à la linguistique moderne: aujourd'hui encore, comme à la fin du moyen âge, on se demande à la fois ce que signifient les mots et ce qu'ils "supposent."

La rhétorique intervient aussi dans l'histoire de la science. Cela est manifeste au temps de la Renaissance chez un Ramus. Comme l'ont montré en particulier les travaux de M. Vasoli, celui-ci oppose une logique du réel (qu'il trouve dans l'invention dialectique) à la logique de la forme. On peut, on doit suivre les règles du formalisme aristotélicien pour aboutir à la conclusion que Socrate est mortel puisque tous les hommes le sont. Mais, pour pouvoir se servir de ce syllogisme, il faut d'abord *définir* l'homme. La définition, bien avant Aristote, était préconisée par la dialectique platonicienne. Ramus en trouve aussi l'exigence dans les *Topiques* ou dans les *Académiques* de Cicéron. Ainsi la théorie de l'invention, dans la mesure où la rhétorique y rencontre la dialectique, tient une place importante dans la genèse de la science moderne. Pour résoudre un problème, il faut chaque fois que l'imagination du savant, comme celle de l'orateur, ait à se disposition tous les "lieux" de l'argumentation et des idées, qu'elle combinera au mieux. Déjà Raymond Lulle avait tenté d'esquisser une telle combinatoire. Il a été, dans une large mesure, suivi par Leibniz et même par la science moderne. Il faut s'attendre à ce que l'épistémologie insiste de plus en plus sur cette rhétorique des "formes symboliques," qui intervient dans la science comme dans tout langage.

Bien entendu, cela nous conduit à parler de la métaphysique et nous le ferons à propos de la philosophie la plus récente et du conflit qui oppose aujourd'hui ce qu'on appelle le matérialisme et l'idéalisme. Ce débat se reflète à travers l'histoire dans l'organisation même des traités de rhétorique, dans leur plan. Chez Aristote, Cicéron, Scaliger, on commence par l'étude de l'invention, c'est-à-dire des idées, puis on passe à la forme, c'est-à-dire aux mots et notamment à leur agencement en tropes et figures. Mais, après Locke et la méditation sensualiste sur l'expérience, les points de vue se modifient. On admet alors que l'idée naît de la rencontre et de la combinaison des sensations matérielles. Dans l'*Art d'écrire* de Condillac (qui constitue en fait un manuel philosophique de rhétorique), l'auteur adopte une ordre inverse: le mot, la phrase, le discours. A travers Fontanier, l'on va ainsi jusqu'à Derrida. Ricoeur tend à montrer (après Richards) que le texte, en tant que tel, peut fournir une médiation entre les deux doctrines. C'est bien à lui qu'on aboutit, mais on part de l'idée et non seulement du mot.

Enfin (et quoiqu'il puisse sembler), un autre domaine où la rhétorique trouve une place importante est celui de la morale. On pourrait croire que celle-ci est récusée aujourd'hui. Mais elle subsiste au moins sous le nom de sociologie ou d'anthropologie. Elle reste, au sens antique, la science des moeurs. Ce sont régions où la persuasion garde son rôle. L'exégèse des lieux communs n'est pas la moindre des tâches qui s'offrent au chercheur en notre époque vouée aux *media*, aux propagandes, à la publicité.

D'une manière plus profonde, la rhétorique apparaît comme la médiation de la sagesse dans les créations du langage. Mais, du point de vue qui est actuellement le nôtre, elle revêt ainsi deux aspects. Elle peut être un langage commun qui rend compte des pluralismes si frappants aujourd'hui dans les sciences et les arts. Entre les disciplines ou les époques, elle établit les moyens d'une *traduction*: elle aboutit ainsi, dans la pluralité, à la possibilité des rapprochements ou des synthèses. Mais elle peut être aussi affirmation de la *différence*, contre toutes les entreprises de "récupération" ou d'assimilation réductrice. Au nom du soupçon, qui intervient si souvent et si fort dans notre temps, elle prend alors la forme de la dénonciation.

On peut en finissant méditer sur ce choix, qui existe entre traduction ou dénonciation. A la nouvelle éloquence, il est donné de trouver sa voie entre de tels maîtres: Heidegger ou Nietzsche, Munteano ou Meschonnic.

The Case for Sophistry

ROGER MOSS
University of Essex

"the only arms I allow myself to use . . ."

I

THE CASE AGAINST SOPHISTRY is well-known. It is that sophistry diverts language towards performance and paradox, with the aim of impressing or—even more vulgarly—simply of vanquishing the auditor, its criterion being what may be *said* regardless of whether it may be said *truthfully* or whether it should be said.

It is perverted logic, perverted philosophy—logic and philosophy in the service of rhetoric. But it is also perverted rhetoric, a mutation of the reliable system, and its appropriate slogan might adapt that of a more recent decadence: *artes* for *artes'* sake.

The historians of rhetoric, from Dionysius of Halicarnassus to J. J. Murphy, have always been in the forefront of attacks upon sophistry's claims on rhetoric. To Dionysius, writing in the first century B.C., a new rhetoric "from some Asiatic death-hole" has sprung up and replaced the old Attic philosophical rhetoric. It is just like what happens in "the houses of the profligate and abandoned":

> there sits the lawful wife, freeborn and chaste, but with no authority over her domain, while an insensate harlot, bent on destroying her livelihood, claims control of the whole estate. . . .[1]

Murphy, in a history of mediaeval rhetoric published in 1974, is only a little more restrained. To him the phrase "sophistic rhetoric," as applied to the "Second Sophistic" of the first four Christian centuries, is "almost a contradiction in terms," for:

sophistry—that linguistic heresy which denies communication as an end
of language—is by its very definition anti-rhetorical.[2]

Though the metaphor shifts from the sexual to the theological sphere, the emphasis on sin remains; and as with sin the advisable attitude towards sophistry
is to be against it.

But as these attacks also inadvertently confirm, the tendency with sophistry,
as with sin, is for it to keep cropping up. What C. S. Baldwin writes of the
"Second Sophistic":

> The theory of rhetoric as the energizing of knowledge and the humaniz-
> ing of truth is explicitly the philosophy of Aristotle and implicitly that
> of Cicero, Tacitus, Quintilian. What the later professors of rhetoric had
> rather in mind is the training of immediate personal effectiveness; and
> this theory of rhetoric as an art of the speaker is at once as old as the
> other and as permanent. Its name is sophistic. . . .[3]

is broadly right, particularly to the extent that it defines the contrast in terms
of precept versus practice. The fifth-century sophists teach by example, in action, and it is this which distinguishes sophistry from rhetoric down the ages:
the reality of third-century Asianism from the Attic ideals of Dionysius; the
suasoriae and *controversiae* of Augustan Rome from the demand for moral effectiveness made by Quintilian; the thirteenth-century Parisian achievements with
the divisional sermon from the initial programme for a Christian use of rhetoric
laid down by Augustine in *De doctrina christiana*; the mediaeval use of *amplificatio*
to mean greater length from the Ciceronian idea of a figure of intensification;
the use of *similiter desinens* and *similiter cadens* in English Euphuistic prose style
from Thomas Wilson's plea in his, the first, English *Art of Rhetoric* in 1553:

> my talk is to this end, that they should neither only, nor chiefly be used,
> as I know some in this our time do overmuch use them in their writings.
> And overmuch (as all men know) was never good yet.[4]

In fact, the treatment that Euphuism has received at the hands of the historians
of rhetoric is a good example of the need for a re-assessment of sophistry. It
used to be that the Euphuistic style was traced back to the precedent of Gorgias;[5]
Croll later traced the same features in mediaeval religious prose.[6] But the search
for sources only arises out of the belief that the occurrence is bizarre and needs,
as it were, the excuse of history. Instead we should recognise, in recognising
the prevalence of sophistry, three separate instances of the impulse towards
sophistry—which we may define as the call for language to face the world by
facing first its own reality in the world—resulting in an intensity of patterned
and figured language that is in each instance similar.

The first case for sophistry, then, is an historical and scholarly one: that there is in sophistry a field worth studying, and a fertility in that field, constantly productive of new "sophistries," worth understanding. History and theory here are more than usually interdependent. To recognise the importance of sophistry in the history of rhetorical practice, it is necessary to clear away the assumption that sophistry is worthless, negligible, even dangerous. Equally, to understand why sophistry is important, why it takes the forms it does, and what it signifies for the perception of language—to develop, in other words, a theory of sophistry, which I now intend to do—it is necessary to distrust the limits that conventional theory has placed on the historical development of rhetoric, and to re-assess the sources of that power in language which rhetoric claims to channel and augment.

II

EVEN THE OFFICIAL HISTORIES of the preceptive tradition recognise that rhetoric emerges amidst a profusion of counter-claims. There is a story told of the first writer of a rhetorical handbook, the fifth-century Sicilian Corax, that he sued his pupil Tisias for unpaid fees. Tisias replied that even if he lost the case he should not have to pay, since it would be evidence of Corax's inadequate teaching; Corax answered that, on the contrary, even if Tisias won the case he should have to pay, since it would be evidence of Corax's good teaching. The judge is reputed to have dismissed the case with the proverbial remark: "a bad egg from a bad crow (*korax*)." The story is probably apocryphal, but that only serves to emphasize the way in which rhetoric's ability to "make the worse case appear the better," its dealings in paradox, its determination to seek victory, and its inner assumption that effective speaking can only be the product of training and not of innate ability or access to the truth—in short, its propensity to sophistry—are a cause for concern and for grudging admiration from the very beginning.

The example of Thoas, son of Andraimon, in Book 15 of the *Iliad*, however, tells us that training in speech was established long before the sophists. We are told first that Thoas is a skilful spear-thrower and wrestler. Then that:

> . . . In assembly few of the Achaians
> when the young men contended in debate could outdo him.[7]

It must be educational; why else would it be "young men"? It must be competitive; why else would it be "outdo"? And it must also be a skill as essential to a man in public life as fighting-skill, and in some ways analogous to that skill; why else couple spear-throwing and wrestling with speech-making? It is hard to believe that such competitive disputation would have had truth rather than effectiveness as its aim in the Homeric age any more than in the Roman – when it became a public entertainment to vie with gladiatorial contests and the like. Thoas, it seems, is as much a sophist as Protagoras, whose collection of model arguments entitled *On Truth*, changed its name in the course of time to one equivalent to the wrestling term "throws"[8] – strategies with which to floor your opponent.

If we are to observe in some detail an ancient sophist at work, we can do no better than consider Sinon at the gates of Troy. No other Greek does more to defeat the Trojans, and he does it in a manner as properly heroic as Diomedes or Achilles – alone, and without any defences other than his skills. The difference is that these are skills of language. It is not enough to say that he does it by lying. The first thing he says is true, and makes him vulnerable: "I admit I am a Greek." After that all he does is to offer the Trojans interpretations of what they have seen with their own eyes: the departure of the ships, the presence of the horse, and his own appearance amongst them. Sinon weaves these things into a plausible whole, a tale which plays on the Trojans' piety – and into a net which traps them. But we should not mistake the role played by the gullibility of the Trojans; the demand for coherence in response to Sinon's words is civilised and humane, not a sign of weakness. And it is a fact that the events related by Sinon are connected. They are connected by the very trickery to which the Trojans succumb: the ships are in hiding, not in retreat; the horse is a concealed personnel-carrier, not an offering; and Sinon is a sophist, not a refugee. What Sinon does is to offer the wrong coherence, not a coherence maintained through language, but a coherence made possible by the fact of language, by its ability to create a separate reality. But it runs counter to the purposes we set aside for language to say that the events cohere only in the denial of language, and in this sense it is no good saying that the Trojans should simply have distrusted Sinon's words. It is easier to believe a language that takes no account of itself than to believe one that does. Perhaps more successful kinds of piety have learnt to hold onto silence as a dependable medium of truth, but the Trojans' piety inheres in their trust in language, their innocence of rhetoric. The wooden horse is an exact image of such a view of language: a supposedly sacred object, which we willingly take in though it contains the means of our destruction. The defeat of the Trojans is therefore the defeat of language-based piety, and with it of the primitive world. Belief in language loses; language wins.

Sinon explores a region where direct violence has failed for ten long years and where the obliquities of language can succeed in a moment. In doing so, he offers a significant contrast to that commonplace of the apologists for rhetoric: the orator, like Cineas the pupil of Demosthenes, sent by Pyrrhus against the Romans,[9] who pacifies an enemy by persuasion. Sinon offers the power of language, not as a substitute for action, but as action in its own right. Whilst a moral defence for him may be that he saves both the Trojans and the Greeks from prolonged violence, in fact his speech is directly in the service of violence – and is in any case more likely to suffer moral obloquy for the violence that it does to language, and to its assumed relationship with truth. Where the later rhetoric tries to define a persuasive power that will violate neither the integrity of the truth nor of the auditor, Sinon's sophistry reveals language itself as a kind of violence.

Any evaluation of the role that Sinon plays in the fall of Troy is considerably complicated by the fact that Homer does not deal with the story in its chronological place at all, and omits any mention of Sinon from Demodokos' account in Book 8 of the *Odyssey* (presumably in order to highlight the irony of Odysseus' own tricksy role), so that we have to rely on the account put into the mouth of Aeneas by Vergil. The effect of this is that the case of Sinon becomes a case against sophistry,[10] exposing the danger of the Greeks that lies not only in the gifts they bear but also in the language with which such gifts are likely to be wrapped, and ceases to be an account of the nature of language in any way at all. One irony of this is that, in writing the *Aeneid*, Vergil himself is conspiring with tradition to be another Sinon – to make things cohere by telling a tale that is not true – and that the great and abiding untruth of Vergil's poem is this: that the Romans owe their status and their culture to the pious Trojans and not to the deceitful Greeks.

But the fall of Troy remains an undoubted watershed in Greek culture – before it, a sense of communal value and the open commitment to violence in defence of honour; after it, dispersal and wandering, and its great hero the man of resource and guile – and it is hard to believe that the lesson taught by Sinon has not contributed to this. *Metis* – the kind of deceitful intelligence shown by Antilochus in the chariot race in Book 23 of the *Iliad* – we know to have been treated by the Greeks with a respect that has since been overruled by the insistence on ordered and analytical intelligence. It is the flexibility that animals display, that the hunter must learn, and the fighter from him. But *metis* in language, which is Sinon's brand of intelligence, takes away from language in the *Odyssey* the directness it had possessed – in speeches, oaths, vaunts – in the *Iliad*.

It has been shown that the same words and their cognates that gather around *metis* – indicative of a multi-colored, fast-moving, intricate appearance (the skin of a slippery snake or the motion of a wily octopus) – are also used to describe the language and effects of the sophists.[11] In colloquial English today a similar metaphor takes us from the connotations of "intelligent" and "clever" to those of "brilliant" and "flashy," and shows us that we still do not necessarily trust what we approve of. When *polymetis* Odysseus tells Polyphemus that his name is Nobody – so that the giant is left abandoned crying "Nobody is killing me" – he succinctly demonstrates the paradoxical nature of language that in naming nothing it is still offering the substantiality of language. This ability to use language to create rather than to reveal identity, whether it is telling the fantastic truth to the court of Alcinous, or humdrum lies to Eumaeus, is what makes Odysseus a forerunner of the sophists.[12]

The tradition has seen to it that his reputation has gone the same way as Sinon's. Comparison with Penelope is all that is needed to see the incompatibility of this with the morality of the original. She, the type of the faithful wife to later tradition, is just as much a trickster: literally a "rhapsode" (*rhapsodos*, weaver or stitcher) alongside her husband, in the daily ravelling and unravelling of her cloth—a story and net with which she catches the suitors *out*.[13]

This multiplication of rhapsodes and sophists inside the legend may remind us that the watershed in political culture represented by the fall of Troy coincides with a watershed in poetic culture: the change from the *Iliad*'s inexplicably preserved orality to the *Odyssey*'s fully-exploited literacy.[14] It is more than just a change in technique; it is a loss of directness, issuing from the loss of an occasion, perhaps also a "fall." But we have not, I think, really understood the nature of this occasion until we have understood Plato's disgust at bardic culture and its effects on people.[15] The phonic repertoire of the bards, mnemonic though it may have been in cause, must have had the effect on its audience of pushing language as a pulsing reality to the fore at the expense of any abstractable meaning or narrative thread. Add an insistent musical rhythm, and we have not just a device to enable the poet to recall and perform the poem, but an intensity and totality that must have disabled the audience from maintaining any awareness that they were being persuaded; not just a neutral "encyclopaedia," but an ideology more or less literally drummed into its hearers. Language's power to "move" or "sway" people would have lost none of its physical connotations. Directness, for the bard as for his subject-matter, is the directness of violence: the affirmation of community against otherness, of authority within that community, and of the insistent language-kinship that re-affirms the bondedness of such a community. In this violence lies what we attenuatedly call the power of language; in its heightening of the people's language, into phrases and rhythms within which are locked a vision of the world that is indistinguishable from reality, it reaches a socially and psychologically determined sparking-point that we weakly define as "memorable." You can hear something of it today from those who have grown up alongside the twinned violences of Welsh mining and Welsh pulpit oratory. It relates physique to thought in a way that makes language an instinct alongside aggression or sexual desire. This is the violence, the seductiveness, of language that Sinon reveals, and it is, I suggest, the original condition of rhetoric.

It is surely not enough to respond to the passing away of such a language with nostalgia for lost notions of community, of the unity of thought and word, content and form, or of the centrality of poetry to its people. The distance that writing puts between the poet and both his material and his audience is also the distance of contemplation. It frees language from involvement in the direct coercion that bardic culture imposed, whilst at the same time leaving it with the possibility that it may have lost any power, any reliability. It is this condition of language that sophistry addresses, and whose changes Homer both advances and expresses. No story is more faithful to the overwhelming sense of loss that comes out of victory than the Trojan story, and no poet writes more lucidly of the death of heroes than the poet of the *Iliad*. Might this not be because of the awareness that this monumental undertaking–to write down in something approaching its entirety the collected history and wisdom of tradition–was at the same time bringing that tradition to an unprecedented degree of life, and freezing it to death?[16] When Shakespeare causes Hamlet to speak of Hecuba and the death of Priam, it is as if literary culture is still mourning the loss of directness that went with the fall of Troy. Might it not be that the *Odyssey*'s image of the resourceful individual and his distance from home is what it has since become, a perennial metaphor for the writer? Odysseus may get home, and in a concluding act of violence defend the same code of sexual honour that was defended at Troy. But in getting there he has discovered means that may or may not be justified by the end, and revealed that the alternative to violence or to a language compromised by violence is a language that compromises itself by violating the truth. The *Odyssey* and its hero in this way uncover the roots of sophistry: the recognition that whilst the power of language may be a distorting and a violent power, there is no potency in language to be found elsewhere, and that the truest use of language may be the one that is true to its inherent capacity for distortion.

III

I HAVE SPENT this much time establishing the close relationship between sophistry and epic, not to give it a respectable pedigree so much as to define sophistry as a practical exploration of what can be done in language after the loss of the Homeric world. In their habits of public performance; in the highly-wrought use of alliteration, assonance, rhyme and other parisonic devices, parallelisms of all kinds, that identifies their language; in their dual role as creators and as teachers; even in their espousal of a pragmatic rather than a theoretical approach to what they teach–in all these ways the classical sophists echo their bardic predecessors. In the case of Gorgias, who for our purposes is the most accessible and the arch-sophist (not least in his diminution of the role assigned to *arete* in teaching, and his pre-occupation with the arts of language), two of the three extant works use the residue of epic subject-matter–an encomium of Helen and a defence of Palamedes.

But the echo of the epic world is an empty one, registering loss and not continuity, and registering also (in contrast to the radical Socrates) that there is nowhere else to go. Performance is no more than that, a virtuoso appeal for recognition and applause, not a necessary condition of communication. Patterned language is ornament not mnemonic technique. Teaching is combative and individual not communal, and what is taught is aimed at the discrediting of absolute values rather than the invocation of shared ones. The heroes of epic are used against themselves: language is no longer there to agree on the nature of Helen's or Palamedes' wrongdoing, but to show that even they can be made out to be praiseworthy or defensible. There is no air of nostalgic revival about sophistry. Rather the irony, uncertainty, even the despair, of men looking back at lost certainties with a wry and antagonistic attitude towards them, and forward with no sense of security in a future language.

Out of such an attitude arises parody. Two uses of the term, contemporary with the period in which the sophists emerge, suggest the same condition of dependence upon, and criticism of, epic that applies to sophistry—the amateur *parodoi* who performed brief, locally topical, mock-epics after the itinerant professionals had finished their serious work; and the attempt through "parody" (comparable to the Jewish *midrash*) to fit the authoritative words of the bards to the realities of everyday life.[17] We may indeed see special significance in the prefix "para" with its connotations both of distance and attachment. Discourse in the post-Homeric world was perhaps inevitably para-discourse.

Not only do we find parody ("para"-poems/songs) but also parado("para"-thoughts/opinion) in this transitional phase; and in a last excursion into the pre-sophistic world I want to touch on Heraclitus and his tradition.[18] The Ionian philosophers have generally been viewed as the forerunners of empiricism and scientific enquiry, the very opposite of sophistry. But their assertion of a basic universal substance is necessarily a statement of the paradoxical nature of appearance, and in each of its successive forms (Thales' water, Anaximander's unnamed Ur-substance, Anaximenes' air, Heraclitus' fire) it moves away from the stable and obvious earth towards the fluid and ambiguous.[19] This sounds less like an attempt to look at the world than an attempt to find out what language is capable of substantiating, drawn along by the very qualities of variety and imagination that characterise the linguistic culture of the time. Heraclitus offers fire as a principle of changeableness rather than a material basis, and the famous dictum that you cannot step into the same river twice is an example of this principle. But where it is usually taken as a contribution to the philosophy of perception, it should perhaps be seen as a criticism of language, of the way the word "river" falsely arrests and confines what is essentially in motion. Perhaps the sophists should be recognised as successors to the Ionian philosophers, identifying in language itself the next most logical basic substance. Like them, Heraclitus is less concerned to play with restrictions in logic, which after all had not by then been fully formulated, than he is to use paradox and fragmentation to proclaim the freedom of the world from its appropriation by the word—and the corollary of this, which is the freedom of language. It is in this atmosphere and against this essentially poetic view that Aristotle pronounces the founding principle of logic, that something cannot both be and not-be at the same time. But by then the bards had long since stopped proving powerfully that it could.

The treatises of Gorgias,[20] with their fondness for paradox, have rhetoric emphatically at their centre, rather than being assaults on logic or sceptical assaults on the world. Language is built up to the full pitch of its powers, and in the next moment it is denied that anything has been said or done at all. The ambivalence of language experienced by Gorgias and his contemporaries— close to and yet severed from its roots—makes language itself a paradox, rather than merely the vehicle of paradoxes.

Even, for instance, from a bare summary of the treatise *On Nature* or *On the Non-Existent*—which argues that nothing exists; that even if it did it would be incomprehensible; and that even if it were comprehensible it would be incommunicable—it is clear that the rhetorical strategy of the "even if" formula, which concedes each stage of the argument without denying anything, is more important than strict logical progression. Only the last step is left unconceded, and the case for that is argued in terms of language's self-restricting substantiality—speech is a thing different from, say, colour and therefore cannot render it; speech is a thing existing in the speaker and therefore cannot at the same time exist in the hearer without losing its identity—which themselves make a paradox out of the conflict between their ability to communicate and their communicated denial of that ability. This critical demonstration of rhetoric's capabilities and its limits is surely more nearly what the treatise is about than a philosophical interpretation, which must take some part of the argument, probably the opening, unquestioningly.

In a more direct way, when Gorgias says in the *Palamedes*:

> If by means of words, it were possible for the truth of actions to become free of doubt [and] clear to hearers, judgement would now be easy from what has been said . . .

the temptation is in one large gesture opened up and laid aside. And when, at the end of the *Helen*, he says with chilling clarity: "I have by means of speech removed disgrace from a woman . . . ," he chills precisely because he is in the same moment saying: I have done nothing, neither to the force of tradition nor to the reader's moral sense. One argument he uses to free Helen from guilt is that persuasion would have had the same power over her as violent abduction. But for the reader to acknowledge himself persuaded by this, he must yield up his freedom to language's irresistible force, and as soon as he does that language ceases to be capable of communicating knowledge.

Even Gorgias' genres are paradoxical: a praise of the unpraiseworthy, a defence of the indefensible, a proof of the unprovable. The temptation to give them the labels of a definite genre ("mock-epideictic," for example) should be balanced against the need to see the space of language in each of them extended to its possible infinity by breaking through the restrictions within which language conventionally operates. Substantiality of language is, therefore, not just an extra attraction of their diction, but an integral part of their meaning. That this possible infinity is always ready to collapse into an equally possible nullity is part of it too: language is not allowed to rest in the fixed proportion of utterance to sense that logic and official rhetoric prefer.

The violence that I suggested lay at the heart of the power of bardic language has not disappeared from the language of the sophists. Parody wrests words out of their accustomed forms; paradox violates the sacred relationship between words and thoughts. Barely suppressed aggression is a real part of sophistic verbal display, in its content and in the desire to win even at the cost of truth— *arete*, like Latin *vir-tus*, is not in origin a moral quality. But it is not possible to create a language that simply *states* its own appropriation of reality and the link between this and the instinct towards violence. Such a language will have lost the capacity for this innocent vision. Sophistry, as we have seen with Sinon, substitutes violence-in-words for violence-in-action; it provides a kind of literary vaccination against the actuality of violence in the world and against the inevitability of its effect on language.

The other side of this is play and pleasure. That euphoria with which we greet the excesses, the twists and the leaps of sophistic writing—and which we probably respond to with the bared teeth of a smile—is, of course, the result of our awareness both of the violence that is being done to language and of the violence that is therefore spared us at that moment in other, more immediate, departments of our life. These forms of gratification are probably a great deal closer to the underlying nature of literature's ability to give pleasure than we are accustomed to recognise.

One familiar explanation for Gorgias' works is that they were training toys for his pupils, and he himself says of the *Helen* that it is *paignion*, an amusement or plaything. The objection to this must be that it is impossible to single this one statement out for straightforward reading in such a reflexive text. Like the paradoxes of language examined earlier, this statement has the quality of the paradox of the Cretan liar. But it reminds us, that in making out a case for sophistry, there is a danger of forcing Gorgias into too theoretical a mould, and discarding with the playfulness the practicality of his exploration of the possibilities (and impossibilities) of language. When the *Helen* is described as "an essay on the nature and power of *logos*,"[21] the time to re-instate frivolity is long past. This need not be restricted to the educational needs of the young. For when an adult audience hears language—rather than hearing about it—in its ability to deflect messages with its own force-field, the seriousness of the enterprise of language falls in question. Persuasion ceases to be directed at a point beyond language, but becomes in-grown, persuasive of the capability— perhaps simply of the presence—of the writer and his words. At that point it becomes sophistry.

IV

THE GREAT CASE against sophistry is that pursued by Socrates and recorded by Plato, especially in the *Gorgias, Protagoras,* and *Phaedrus.* The earlier dialogues argue that rhetoric is a skill and not, as the sophists claim, the art of all arts. Like cookery or cosmetics it dresses up things more fundamental; but it is philosophy—like dietetics or physical training—which deals in the fundamentals, and it is only from philosophical enquiry that true and effective speaking will come.

The clarity of this argument, and the completeness of the split of truth from rhetoric, has become blurred by the time we get to the *Phaedrus.* Plato uses the last part of the dialogue to establish the conditions for what he calls a "philosophical rhetoric." This has led to the *Phaedrus* being given a pivotal role in the process of rapprochement that takes place over three generations between what Socrates (presumably) said and what Aristotle is able to write in the *Rhetoric.* Plato's "philosophical rhetor," however, is a dubious entity when imagined in any real civic, or even educational, setting: he must acquire divine wisdom, which is avowedly a lifetime's work, before he speaks, so that the gap between human need and Plato's idealism remains as great as ever. It is this same uncertainty about what the dialogue is saying that has enabled critics who agree that the *Phaedrus* concludes a series of exchanges on the subject of rhetoric, including Plato's earlier dialogues and the encomiums of Helen by Gorgias and Isocrates, nevertheless to disagree fundamentally on the attitude towards Isocrates in the closing remarks: one taking the recantatory spirit seriously and seeing an olive-branch offered to the chief rhetorical teacher of the day;[22] the other seeing Plato lash out in ever more damaging sarcasm at the moment when the Academy is about to go into competition with him.[23] Similar indecisiveness is shown in the dialogue towards poets, those other Socratic *bêtes noires:* they are given a typically churlish place between soothsayers and artisans in the hierarchy of souls, and later on placed alongside logographers and clerks as "pullers and pasters of words"; but they are also included with other types of divine madness, and placed first in the same hierarchy of souls, as "followers of the Muses," with philosophers and lovers.[24] Writing is subject to the most blatant ambiguity of this kind. In a famous digression it is rejected as being inferior to words "written on the soul of the hearer,"[25] whilst being of course the medium of Plato's expression.

I want to suggest that there is a significance to this pattern of acknowledgement and disavowal of the means of communication which goes beyond any transitional status we may ascribe to the dialogue. It is there in the fact that the very subject-matter of the dialogue is in dispute. Partly, of course, the way that we turn from the subject of speech-making to the myth of the charioteer in Socrates' second speech can be put down to the success of the Socratic/Platonic exercise against rhetoric. It is they more than anyone who have defined rhetoric as marginal, and created the philosophical terms within which the soul and love are self-evidently important. But this is also a specific response to the different natures of the three speeches. The first two—Lysias' speech and Socrates' reply—stand as examples of speech-making because of their brevity, and because their choice of subject-matter, that it is preferable for a boy to have an admirer who is not in love to one who is, is a standard paradox of the epideictic type. But Socrates' second speech reverses the proposition and disregards proportion, relishing its own ability to demonstrate that the self-regarding business of talking about talking must give way to serious questions of definition, because any speech has to be a speech about something, and because the truth of what it is about outweighs any value it may have as a speech.

In short, the disproportion of the speech—like Beethoven's *Grosse fuge* in the Op. 130 Quartet in its passionate rejection of formal constraints—is a "message" to be noticed, along with the overt subject-matter of the speech, and not a problem to be smoothed over in the search for a desirable "unity."[26] The positive achievement of the dialogue does, therefore, lie in what it has to say about love and the soul; and unity—which is, after all, a rhetorical demand—is one victim of its negation of rhetoric.

In the long run, though, Plato puts the lover and the rhetorician back together again, at least as an analogy. Each speech is imagined as the speech of a suitor addressing a boy; seduction is offered as a special case of persuasion, arguably as the extreme relationship of an orator to his auditor. In his speech, Lysias connects his freedom from the irrational passion of love with his command of the powers of persuasion; Plato implies parity at a different level, between a speech that is stylish but without content and a love based on the attractions of physical beauty but without regard for the boy's well-being. Both the rhetorical and the emotional bases of Socrates' reply are equally corrupt—thus the need for the palinode and Socrates' final speech—except that it moderates the predatory character of the suitor somewhat, and reflects this rhetorically in its willingness to lay before the boy a clear, albeit false, definition of love.

In Socrates' main speech love and rhetoric find a common set of principles in an idealist psychology of aesthetics. "Beauty"—what the beloved has to offer the lover—and "knowledge"—what the lover, as an older man, has to offer the boy—are shown to be interchangeable terms. The good speaker, like the good lover, cares for the well-being of his auditor and has an aim beyond immediate gratification. More than this, the willingness of the good lover to "persuade and train" his beloved in the acquisition of wisdom[27]—the sophists' aim, of course—will be motivated and matched by the beloved's ability to offer a direct insight into the divine world through the unique quality of his beauty. In this sense, love is no longer an analogy to persuasion, but rather defines it as redundant. Rhetoric is replaced by love as the only true ground for the relationship between teacher and pupil, orator and auditor. Even before his impractical programme is outlined, the "philosopical rhetor" is a chimera, his validity pre-empted by the silent contemplation of true lovers.

What exactly has happened? Socrates has set out to show that he can beat the sophists at their own game. He ends up transcending that game, asserting love as the only proper rhetoric, and therefore the real subject of the dialogue. On the way he steals many of the sophists' most distinctive clothes—paradox, parody, the denial of the means of communication within the discourse, an attachment to practical rather than theoretical demonstrations. And in fact, the ingenuity of the *Phaedrus*, as well as its real importance, lies in the way it rejects the rhetorical half-way house of Aristotle, and establishes human instinct, albeit of an idealised kind, as the true basis of power in human communication, both of which, as we have seen, are perceptions whose origin is to be found in sophistry. Out of the profundity of its rejection of sophistry, the *Phaedrus* is able to give great insight into its nature and an unwitting testimony to its influence.

V

To COMPARE the simplicities of the *Gorgias* with the subtleties of the *Phaedrus* is to see that sophistry was not simply put down in the fourth century. Its survival depends on language being intensely and freely used to explore man's fundamental nature, and this leads us to the third case for sophistry, the literary one. A single example must suffice.

James Joyce's *Ulysses* uses Homer, even in the twentieth century, to measure the gap between true heroism and the modern hero's loss of grandeur, between powerful language and the depleted language of the present. In the "Aeolus" chapter Joyce shows intimate familiarity with the devices of classical rhetoric in order to play them off against the modern civic discourse of journalism. At the end of that chapter he can have his autobiographical hero, Stephen Dedalus, who has just told a tongue-in-cheek tale headed with the title of Joyce's own first book *Dubliners*, spoken of in these terms:

> You remind me of Antisthenes . . . , a disciple of Gorgias, the sophist.
> It is said of him that none could tell if he were bitterer against others
> or against himself.[28]

It is not entirely a measurement of loss. When he finishes his account of
Antisthenes with this: "he wrote a book in which he took away the palm of
beauty from Argive Helen and handed it to poor Penelope," Professor MacHugh
obliquely reminds us that Joyce himself is engaged on a work that will take
the values and aspirations of epic and transfer them to the provincial, domestic
milieu of an uneventful Dublin day—mock-epic, certainly, but also epic mocked
for its lack of ordinary reality.

It is not the overt resemblances that make sophistry relevant to Joyce's writing,
though. Within all this there is a bitterness, a self-consciousness and an air
of parody—a sense of the loss and power entailed in language—that spreads
far wider than reference to the classics, and which I think we have good reason
to call sophistic.[29]

Towards the end of the *Portrait*, Stephen speaks of the freedom and integrity of his art, and of using for his defence "the only arms I allow myself to
use—silence, exile, and cunning."[30] The silence of the writer behind his own
work; exile as a theme and as a metaphor—these have been much discussed
in Joyce's work. It is perhaps not entirely surprising that the elements that
add up most clearly to a sophistic intent, "arms" and "cunning," have been paid
the least attention. But they are there, even in the strategy of using the name
Stephen Dedalus. It is cunning of two kinds: "conning," erudition, in the
hybridisation of martyrs to Christian and classical ideals; and low cunning in
the (non-autobiographical) quirk that makes the unusual name worthy of comment. Meaning is proffered and ironically withdrawn in a single gesture: the
name attacks the pretence to autobiography, and then attacks its own symbolic content.

Language is a weapon in Stephen's hand, whether it is the blow-by-blow
account given to the rector with which the young Stephen returns the insult
of the pandybat, or the scalpel which an older Stephen inserts into the gap
that has grown up between the English priest's language and his own in the
single word "tundish." But it is a weapon also to be used against itself, against
the temptation to fix an absolute language, or any position of priority, from
which more direct kinds of violence might be justified. Stephen recognises early
on that God is prayed to whether he is called "God" or "Dieu," and it is this
lesson he applies when he refuses to follow the path of linguistic nationalism.
Exile in Europe is Stephen's political response to English domination. A book
that re-visits the city of his homeland in terms of the broadest European tradi-

tion, cast in the oppressor's language, is Joyce's literary response.

The monocular vision of the discourse of nationalism is exposed in the "Cyclops" chapter of *Ulysses*. But this is the first of three chapters that intensify the use of parody, and expose language itself—in its capacity for gigantic over-flow, in its prostitution to the commercial considerations of women's jour-nalism, in the entirety of literary tradition—as capable of a kind of aggression, locking the world into a vision created by the words. Silence, exile and cun-ning, suggest the fluid, self-denying ways by which Joyce seeks to unlock this capacity. Partly he makes it harmless by making it funny; partly he emphasises the distortions it imposes, so that nothing, not even a tin of sardines,[31] can escape the language it is made to speak. The line between play and fighting is, as always, an indistinct one.

The great invention, and the great act of cunning in *Ulysses* is the creation of Leopold Bloom. It is the one thing that does most to turn the book away from the conventions of narrative point-of-view and narrative voice towards a multifocal and polyphonic mode. But Bloom the sensualist, the analyst, the man of experience, also offers the possibility of a degree of realism which Stephen, the aesthete, the synthesiser, the theorist, had ruled out. What Joyce does is to make language an insistent part of this reality. In the first of Bloom's chapters the criteria of realism—ordinariness, inclusiveness and plain-speaking—are parodically extended to the point at which conventional narrative, con-ventional decorum and conventional syntax, are all overthrown. As we go along, the chapter incorporates Bloom's fantasies on a piece of newspaper he picks up in the butcher's, his wife's commission for the purchase of a pornographic novel, her mistaken (and meaningless) pronunciation of the difficult word "metempsychosis," and Bloom's use of a page from *Titbits* to wipe himself in the lavatory. Each of these demands language beyond the conventions of nar-rative realism; each of them also shows language/writing debased in the world of action. Realism is the victim, not the result, of this. The real result is a language which frees itself from the normal constraints, and reveals language in its most base—and most basic—uses: the parody, fragmentation and self-substantiating play with words, which Hugh Kenner has identified as the "se-cond voice" of rhetoric in the book, and from whose point of view the realistic "denotative plain style [is] one of its departments merely."[32] Against realism, Joyce offers sophistry, insisting in the face of the world's inaction or corrupt action (one recalls the importance of the word "paralysis" throughout his writing) on the act of writing and the active creation of language.

Notes

This essay is a considerably revised and expanded version of a paper given at the inaugural conference of the International Society for the History of Rhetoric in Zürich in June 1977. It also includes material from another paper, "Phaedrus Ancient and Modern," presented to the Society's third conference in Madison, Wisc., in April 1981. I would particularly like to thank Peter France, Brian Vickers and Walter J. Ong for their comments on the early stages.

1. Dionysius of Halicarnassus, *On the Ancient Orators*, trans. S. Usher (Loeb, 1974), p. 5 f.
2. J. J. Murphy, *Rhetoric in the Middle Ages* (Berkeley, 1974), p. 35.
3. C. S. Baldwin, *Ancient Rhetoric and Poetic* (reprinted Gloucester, Mass., 1959), p. 247.
4. Thomas Wilson, *The Arte of Rhetorique*, facsimile with intro. by R. H. Bowers (Gainesville, Fa., 1962), p. 228 (my modernisation).
5. By Landmann, *Der Euphuismus* (1881). See also Theodor Gomperz, *Greek Thinkers*, trans. L. Magnus (London, 1901), vol. I, pp. 477–80.
6. Morris Croll, intro. to Croll and Clemons, ed. John Lyly, *Euphues: The Anatomy of Wit* and *Euphues and His England* (London, 1916).
7. *The Iliad of Homer*, trans. R. Lattimore (Chicago, 1974), Book 15, p. 316.
8. W. K. C. Guthrie, *A History of Greek Philosophy* (Cambridge, 1969), vol. III, p. 264.
9. Wilson, *The Arte of Rhetorique*, uses this example in his preface.
10. *The Eclogues, Georgics and Aeneid of Virgil*, trans. C. Day Lewis (London, 1966), Book 2, p. 166:

> Such was the artful, treacherous perjury Sinon used
> To impose on us. We were tricked by cunning and crocodile tears—
> We whom neither Diomed nor Larissaean Achilles
> Could conquer, not in ten years, not with a thousand warships.

11. Marcel Detienne and Jean-Pierre Vernant, *Les ruses d'intelligence: la Metis des grecs* (Paris, 1974); trans. J. Lloyd, *Cunning Intelligence in Greek Culture and Society* (Hassocks, 1978), pp. 33, 39, 41.
12. At the beginning of Sophocles' *Philoctetes*, Odysseus persuades Achilles' son, Neoptolemus, to use a stratagem identical to Sinon's—and in the same cause, the defeat of Troy:

> Trick Philoctetes by a tale . . . , When he asks who you are
> And where you come from, say you're the son of Achilles—
> No need to lie so far . . .

(trans. E. F. Watling, Penguin Classics, 1953, p. 165), the initial truth of which is to be followed by the claim that he is now an enemy of the Greeks.

In the brief but instructive debate which follows, Odysseus argues for sophistry against Neoptolemus' alternatives: violence ("I'd rather beat this man by force than by deception") and, as a second best, persuasion, rhetoric.

13. Detienne and Vernant, *Cunning Intelligence*, refer to the associations of the image of the net with *metis* (pp. 42, 294–97). If such a metaphorical interpretation of Penelope seems far-fetched consider the fifth-century one by Anaxagoras, where the cloth is an emblem of dialectic, the warps being the premises, the woof the conclusion, and the torches by which she worked the light of reason. See J. E. Sandys, *A History of Classical Scholarship* (reprinted New York, 1958), vol. I, p. 30.

14. The proximity of domestic detail in the *Odyssey* to that of its first audience, as well as the play with narrative and language, has led one critic to claim that "the poet of the *Odyssey* is, among other things, the first great critic of the *Iliad*." See J. M. Redfield, *Nature and Culture in the Iliad* (Chicago and London, 1975), p. 39. There is a sense in which all epic after the *Iliad* must be mock-epic, and this arises not merely from its supremacy as a record of heroic action, but also from the immediacy with which it carries over the sense of oral creation.

Perhaps it is worth adding that Greek legend has it that Palamedes, a trickster second only to Odysseus, was responsible for the invention of the alphabet during the years of the Trojan War. Like Corax, Palamedes is hoist with his own petard: Odysseus betrays him with a forged letter.

15. See especially E. A. Havelock, *Preface to Plato* (Oxford, 1963). My account of oral culture also owes a great deal to Albert Lord, *The Singer of Tales* (Harvard, 1960), and to the writings of Walter J. Ong.

16. Vergil's intuition, that in order to re-create the spirit of epic one has to turn to the losing side, and to its cadet branch, was surely right.

17. See F. J. Lelièvre, "The Basis of Ancient Parody," *Greece and Rome* n.s. (1954), pp. 66–81.

18. I am indebted to Philip Wheelwright, *Heraclitus* (Princeton, 1959).

19. Gomperz, *Greek Thinkers*, vol. I, p. 48, refers to the scepticism that must have been brought about by the Ionian philosophers.

20. Quotations from Gorgias have been based on the following translations of Diels-Kranz: R. K. Sprague, ed. *The Older Sophists* (U. of South Carolina, 1972), "Gorgias," trans. G. A. Kennedy; Kathleen Freeman, *Ancilla to the Pre-Socratic Philosophers* (Oxford, 1971); and on LaRue Van Hook, "The Encomium on Helen," *Classical Weekly* (15 February, 1913).

21. L. Verséyni, *Socratic Humanism* (New Haven, 1963), p. 44. The most important recent 'philosophical' interpretation of sophistry is that by Mario Untersteiner, *The Sophists*, trans. K. Freeman (Oxford, 1954). But there is a nineteenth-century tradition of defending the sophists against Socrates that is similar in tendency and as important; it is briefly outlined in Guthrie, *History of Greek Philosophy*, vol. III, pp. 10–13. George Grote and Theodor Gomperz are its chief proponents, and the attack on Grote by Nietzsche is of great sigificance for this essay, suggesting as it does the grounds for an entirely different defence of sophistry:

> . . . he would like to raise them to the rank of men of honour and moralisers — but it was their honour that they refused to cheat with big words and phrases, and had the courage, which all strong spirits have, to recognise their own unmorality.

(*The Will to Power*, Para. 429). See E. R. Dodds, "Socrates, Callicles and Nietzsche" in his edition of Plato's *Gorgias* (Oxford, 1959).

22. Gilbert Ryle, *Plato's Progress* (Cambridge, 1966), pp. 259–72. Ryle concludes that the *Phaedrus* contributes to, and can be dated by, the shift from "eristic" to rhetoric in the Academy's teaching.

23. R. L. Howland, "The Attack on Isocrates in the *Phaedrus*," *Classical Quarterly* 31 (1937).

24. *Phaedrus* (trans. W. Hamilton, Penguin Classics, 1973), 245A, 248D, 278D.

25. *Phaedrus*, 278A.

26. See e.g. W. C. Helmbold and W. B. Holther, "The Unity of the *Phaedrus*," *University of California Publications in Classical Philology*, vol. 14, 9 (1952); G. E. Mueller, "The Unity of the *Phaedrus*," *Classical Bulletin*, vol. 33 (March-April, 1957); R. M. Weaver, "The *Phaedrus* and the Nature of Rhetoric," *Philosophy, Rhetoric and Argumentation*, eds. Natanson and Johnstone (U. of Pennsylvania, 1965).

27. *Phaedrus*, 253B.

28. James Joyce, *Ulysses* (Penguin Modern Classics, 1969), p. 149.

29. *Ulysses* is also partly a product of Zürich—a point I mention not merely because this was the location for the Rhetoric Society's founding, but also because it provides an economical way of pointing to twentieth-century "sophists" who do not depend on overt reference to epic or rhetoric. Tristan Tzara was in Zürich at the same time, exploring along with other Dadaists the self-substantiality of language, and the possibility of turning it towards violence in order to protest obscurely against the larger violence raging outside Switzerland. Both have been the subject of a recent play, *Travesties*, by Tom Stoppard, whose title alone suggests that delight in using language to generate realities of its own, which Stoppard has popularised more than any recent playwright, and which is one of the roots of sophistry. His interlude, *New-found-land*, exploits the clichés of America to praise America in a virtuoso manner that warrants consideration under the heading of mock-epideictic rhetoric. It is, however, to Beckett's Lucky that we should turn for a dramatic presentation of the *horror vacui* underlying such play with language.

30. James Joyce, *A Portrait of the Artist as a Young Man* (Penguin Modern Classics, 1966), p. 247.

31. Joyce, *Ulysses*, p. 384.

32. Hugh Kenner, *Joyce's Voices* (London, 1978), p. 95. It is encouraging that Kenner should have spent a chapter of this book identifying Joyce as a "Pyrrhonist"—that is, as a sceptic reliant on language alone. Pyrrhonism is a third-century form of the phenomenon I have generally identified as sophistry.

Retorica e "Studia humanitatis"
nella cultura del Quattrocento

EUGENIO GARIN
Scuola Normale Superiore di Pisa

I

D<small>I JACOB BURCKHARDT</small> sono debitori, senza eccezione, quanti si occupano di storia della cultura del Rinascimento, e in particolare del Rinascimento italiano. È infatti nell'opera sua che si definì nettamente, a livello storiografico, quel tema di un rinnovamento radicale come rinascita, che paradossalmente faceva appello al passato per rompere con il passato. Sorto in Italia come programma di riscossa nazionale, e trasformatosi in un mito, dette origine a un'epoca ben caratterizzata della civiltà occidentale. "Gli antichi," fattisi ben presto "modernissimi"—sono parole di uno dei suoi *Frammenti storici* più felici—soppiantarono completamente una tradizionale visione del mondo, mentre "l'intero firmamento spirituale *veniva* orientato in una nuova direzione," e si affermava "un'arte che ben presto travolse . . . quella dell'intera Europa." Così, in Burckhardt per la prima volta, è possibile leggere "la trascrizione concettuale abbreviata" di tutta la ricchezza di un tempo.[1]

A lui però possono richiamarsi in modo legittimo solo quanti, magari rifiutandone tesi ed analisi, ne accettano tuttavia la premessa di fondo: che il Rinascimento ha espresso in forme originali, nei vari campi della vita e della cultura, una unità d'ispirazione. Arti figurative e attività politiche, letteratura e scienza, costumi e religione, attestano una svolta radicale; le loro variazioni sono fra loro interdipendenti e, insieme, inscindibili: per ripetere l'espressione burckhardtiana, fu "l'intero firmamento spirituale che venne orientato in una nuova direzione."

Orbene, su due punti è necessario insistere ancora affrontando i problemi dell'età della Rinascita: 1. sulla chiarezza programmatica che fino dalle origini caratterizzò il rinnovamento degli *studia humanitatis:* e cioè sulla scoperta che gli antichi autori, anche se spesso già noti, potevano divenire strumenti di liberazione umana attraverso una lettura diversa che li collocasse criticamente in una loro dimensione autentica; 2. sulla comune consapevolezza che la svolta realizzata col ritorno all'antico investiva ogni aspetto del sapere e dell'operare, perché investiva l'uomo nella sua totalità, quale si esprime nel suo linguaggio. In un testo molto eloquente Enea Silvio Piccolomini proclamò una volta con lucidità estrema la corrispondenza esatta fra lettere ed arti: Giotto come Petrarca; *dum viguit eloquentia viguit pictura*. Quando si rinnovarono le lettere, riemersero anche le arti: *post Petrarcham emerserunt litterae, post Jotum surrexere pictorum manus*. Quando la *facundia* decadde e la *rhetorica* giacque inefficace, tutte le cose furono *rudia, inepta, incompta*,[2] Altrove, proprio Pio II loda la Signoria di Firenze per l'uso politico delle epistole del Salutati, più pericolose per il duca di Milano di schiere di cavalieri in campo.[3] Ma per tornare alle arti, nella unità della cultura, nel 1957 John K. Spencer intitolava un suo saggio molto interessante *Ut rhetorica pictura*, in voluto parallelismo con l'oraziano *ut pictura poesis*, richiamandosi, oltre che al luogo ora citato del Piccolomini, a Leon Battista Alberti e alla sua insistenza sul rapporto di corrispondenza fra discorso pittorico e discorso 'retorico': "in omni nostra oratione spectari illud vehementer peto: . . . me . . . veluti pictorem hisce de rebus loqui." L'Alberti si compiace, per un verso, di distinguere il discorso 'matematico' — ossia rigidamente tecnico e formalizzato — dal discorso naturale (*non ut mathematicum, sed veluti pictorem*), mentre, per un altro verso, sembra divertirsi a trasferire alla pittura le virtù comunemente attribuite alla parola e allo scritto.[4] È un *topos* degli umanisti, la cultura come dialogo, il colloquio con gli autori antichi, la società dei morti e dei vivi, la scuola in cui insegnano attraverso il recupero storico-filologico i maestri di ogni tempo. L'Alberti batte sulla corrispondenza dei vari mezzi espressivi: "tiene in sé la pittura forza divina . . . , piangiamo con chi piange, e ridiamo con chi ride, e dogliamoci con chi si duole . . . ; fa gli uomini assenti essere presenti, ma più i morti dopo molti secoli essere quasi vivi." E in quest'ultima immagine non è difficile riconoscere il motivo reso celebre dal Machiavelli nella famosa lettera a Francesco Vettori del 10 dicembre 1513, che ha fissato in termini indimenticabili il concetto umanistico della cultura come società ideale che si struttura nella comunicazione, nel linguaggio, nel discorso. Meno noto, che già l'Alberti, in un testo forse del 1440, del *Theogenius*, avesse svolto con singolare efficacia il paradosso della solitudine che la cultura, ossia la lettura degli autori, gli *studia humanitatis*, trasforma in società, anzi nella società per eccellenza, per una specie di politicità trascendentale. E l'Alberti, non dimentichiamolo, è uno scienziato, un architetto, un pensatore di grande statura, non un qualsiasi povero maestro di retorica. Per questo la sua prosa, così simile e diversa rispetto a quella di Machiavelli, è degna di essere tenuta ben presente. Scrive:

> io mai men solo che quando me truovo in solitudine. Sempre meco stanno uomini periti, eloquentissimi, appresso di quali io posso tradurmi a sera e occuparmi a molta notte ragionando; ché se forse mi dilettano e' iocosi

e festivi, tutti e' comici, Plauto, Terenzio, . . . e simili facetissimi eccitano
in me quanto io voglio riso. Se a me piace intendere cose utilissime a
satisfare alle domestiche necessità, . . . molti dotti, quanto io gli richieg-
gio, mi raccontano della agricultura, e della educazione de' figliuoli, e
del costumare e reggere la famiglia, e della raggion delle amicizie, e della
amministrazione della repubblica, cose ottime e approvatissime. Se
m'agrada conoscere le cagioni e principi di quanto io vedo vari effetti
prodotti della natura, s'io desidero modo a discernere il vero dal falso,
il bene dal male, s'io cerco conoscere me stesso e insieme intendere le
cose prodotte in vita per indi riconoscere e riverire il padre, ottimo e
primo maestro e procuratore di tante maraviglie, non a me mancano i
santissimi filosofi, appresso de' quali io d'ora in ora a me stessi satisfacen-
do me senta divenire più dotto anche e migliore.[5]

La pagina è esemplare per intendere la funzione assegnata agli *studia
humanitatis*, e cioè la scoperta della funzione mediatrice che gli 'autori,' restau-
rati nella loro autenticità, hanno per l'accesso alla realtà: il metodo, dirà
Machiavelli, di dialettizzare la lezione delle cose, ossia l'esperienza, e la lettura
degli *auctores*, ossia la storia. Che era, a metà del Quattrocento, una conquista
comune, se Valla poteva, quasi nello stesso giro d'anni, costruire una nuova
teologia sulla filologia e sulla critica neotestamentaria, dopo avere propugnato
in scontri memorabili un analogo accesso ai testi giuridici. Con Valla come
con Alberti ci muoviamo a un alto livello di consapevolezza teorica. A livello
umile, ma sul delicato terreno della fede, in una predica di San Bernardino
del 1425 possiamo leggere, a proposito degli studi: "non aresti tu gran piacere
se tu vedessi e udissi predicare Gesù Cristo? . . . San Paolo, Santo Agostino,
Santo Gregorio, Santo Geronimo e Santo Ambrogio? orsù va, leggi i loro libri,
qual più ti piace . . . e parlerai con loro, ed eglino parleranno teco; udiranno
te e tu udirai loro."[6] Un umanista che fu anche maestro di teologia—perchè
non è vero, come eminenti studiosi vanno ripetendo, che vi fosse assoluta divarica-
zione fra discipline teoriche e lettere—Bartolomeo della Fonte sul cadere del
secolo dirà che il linguaggio *viribus eloquentiae* fonda le società, le struttura nel
diritto, e le cementa nella cultura.

Ma per tornare all'Alberti, ciò che forse ora importa di più è la ricorrente
connessione fra retorica e pittura nel richiamo a una più profonda unità che
si esprime nei vari linguaggi. Non a caso, negli anni cinquanta (forse nel 1458),
nel suo celebre trattato d'architettura il Filarete sottolineava la corrispondenza
fra architettura e retorica: "io ne do questo exemplo allo edificare antico al
moderno come proprio le lettere, cioè come il dire di Tullio . . . . E così questa
similitudine vi do l'edificare".[7] Né si tratta, si badi, di una mera analogia ester-
na: ossia del richiamo all'antico, comune ai letterati e agli architetti. Il riferimento
è ben più profondo, alla struttura dell'uomo e delle sue forme espressive, che
seguono ritmi corrispondenti così nel discorso letterario come negli edifici

Nella famosa biografia di Filippo Brunelleschi, composta da Antonio di Tuccio Manetti, architetto egli stesso e scienziato, che con l'artista aveva avuto rapporti diretti, il nesso retorica-architettura, e la mediazione degli antichi, si approfondiscono e si precisano perfino nel voluto trasferimento all'architettura del linguaggio proprio della retorica. Dicendo del viaggio a Roma del Brunelleschi, dopo avere notato che "vide el modo del murare degli antichi e le loro simitrie," aggiunge che "parvegli conoscere un ordine di membri e d'ossa molto evidentemente."[8] E sui termini *ordine, invenzione, ornamento*, batte con intento preciso. L'Alberti e il Filarete, infatti, come il Brunelleschi, quando si richiamano a Tullio, ossia alla retorica classica, lo fanno per indicare quelle simmetrie, ordini e proporzioni, che hanno mutuato dallo studio degli antichi. D'altra parte non nascondono la piena consapevolezza che il convergere di retorica e architettura è fondato sul carattere umano di ogni opera dell'uomo: nella casa e nella città, come nell'istituzione e nell'orazione, si manifesta l'uomo, e cioè la sua costituzione fisica e la sua misura mentale. Scrive Filarete: "quello che sia, el circulo, e 'l quadro e ogni altra misura è dirivata da l'uomo." E soggiunge: "Hai veduto e inteso donde è dirivata la prima origine dello edificare, ora intenderai come la forma dello edificio è dirivata dalla forma e misura de l'uomo: sì come per necessità e bisogno de l'uomo da lui fu trovato l'edificio, così quasi ogni forma e natura ha de l'uomo esso edificio. Come per ragioni e figure ti mostrerrò, essi edifici sono proprio fatti sotto questi modi e similitudini, e così ordinati e dirivati. E che sia vero, tu sai come l'uomo ha in sé misura, forma e membri (così l'edificio vuole avere forma, misura e membri)." Simmetrico in tutto all'uomo è l'edificio, "s'amala quando non mangia . . . e viene scadendo a poco a poco, . . . e poi si casca morto." La sua costruzione ha radice nell'intelletto, che lo progetta per poi realizzarlo a propria immagine, in individualità come l'uomo irriducibili l'una all'altra. Scrive ancora Filarete: "volse dunque Idio che l'uomo, come che in forma la immagine sua fece a sua similitudine, così e' partecipasse in fare qualche cosa a sua similitudine mediante lo'ntelletto."[9]

In questo senso l'edificio e il discorso, il palazzo e l'orazione, obbediscono agli stessi principi di invenzione, di ordine, di proporzione, di simmetria—e la stessa misura si ritrova come sigillo nell'opera: " io ne do questo essempio all'edificare . . . come proprio le lettere, cioè come dire di Tullio e di Virgilio . . . , cioè delle lettere tulliane e virgiliane." L'autore del primo scritto importante 'sulla dignità e l'eccellenza dell'uomo,' Giannozzo Manetti, nel 1436, in una orazione composta per la consacrazione del Duomo di Firenze, non esita ad affermare: "admirabile huius sacrae basilicae aedificium mihi diligentius saepenumero intuenti prope instar humani corporis esse videtur."[10] L'orazione intendeva celebrare il compimento della cupola del Brunelleschi, nella cui opera concordemente si ravvisò il più bel frutto dell'architettura dell'età umanistica, ossia della sostituzione della 'praticaccia'—per usare la forte espressione del

Filarete—con la razionale riflessione realizzata alla scuola degli antichi: insomma il resultato del progresso teorico determinato dagli *studia humanitatis* (dalla filologia e dalla storia) nel campo dell'architettura. Che era quanto l'Alberti esaltava nel Brunelleschi che aveva guardato a quei "virtuosissimi passati antiqui" per poi trovare, "senza precettori, senza essemplo alcuno, . . . arti e scienze non udite e mai vedute." Con accenti commossi Filarete esclama: "benedico l'anima di Filippo di ser Brunellesco, cittadino fiorentino, famoso e degnissimo architetto e sottilissimo imitatore di Dedalo, il quale risuscitò nella città nostra di Firenze questo modo antico dello edificare, per modo che oggi dì in altra maniera non s'usa se none all'antica, tanto in edificii di chiese, quanto ne' pubblici e privati casamenti."[11]

Che cosa fosse l'imitazione del Brunelleschi aveva colto l'Alberti con tutt'altra penetrazione: "senza precettori, senza essemplo alcuno, . . . arti e scienze non udite e mai vedute," anche se Filarete intuiva la funzione determinante della scoperta dell'antico. Alla fine del secolo, il 'grammatico' Poliziano, sottile studioso di dialettica, fine esegeta d'Aristotele e primo chiosatore della *Poetica*, affronterà con grande acume il problema dell'imitazione in splendide pagine polemiche, le cui argomentazioni troveranno un'eco europea attraverso il filtro del *Ciceronianus* di Erasmo. L'imitazione era tutt'altra cosa dalla copia servile di un modello: era stimolo a una creazione del tutto originale; era la scoperta di nuovi strumenti espressivi. Ai tempi di Poliziano, probabilmente, l'imitazione si caricava anche di toni derivati dalla teurgia, di moda nei circoli ficiniani. La somiglianza dell'immagine artificiale col modello vivente, o divino, magicamente strappava al modello la vita, o la divinità, e la imprigionava ad animare la materia plasmata con arte dedalea—e le statue dedalee vivevano e si muovevano. Gli storici odierni hanno torto a non ricercare l'atmosfera dell'ultimo Quattrocento carica di suggestioni magiche, quando sentono parlare delle immagini spiranti vita.

Comunque, fra il Brunelleschi e l'Alberti si imponeva a Firenze anche lo studio della prospettiva, con le sue tecniche e i suoi giuochi sempre più raffinati, con la sua razionalizzazione dello spazio e i suoi virtuosismi squisiti. Santo Spirito e San Lorenzo sono lì, e così la struttura architettonica della Trinità del Masaccio. Non è certo il caso di ricostruire qui i complessi studi di ottica geometrica che le produzioni dei pittori e degli architetti presuppongono, o di tentare di delineare l'attività delle scuole che se ne vennero moltiplicando in città. In un saggio molto acuto, Wittkower, proprio riferendosi a Brunelleschi e a Masaccio, ebbe a dire dell'illusionismo della Rinascenza ("la Trinità del Masaccio—scrisse—è la prima grande opera dell'illusionismo rinascimentale, compiuta sotto l'impressione delle idee del Brunelleschi").[12] Siamo, nel discorso pittorico o architettonico, di fronte alle tecniche della nuova 'retorica'. Platone che è, non dimentichiamolo mai, la grande scoperta teorica della nuova cultura, nel decimo libro della *Repubblica* (ma anche nel *Sofista*), parla della pittura in 'prospettiva' (σκιαγραφία) come di una tecnica che usa l'inganno (γοητεία), puntando sulle emozioni, sugli affetti (πάθημα). Siamo, cioè, nell'ambito, non della visione vera della verità, ma del discorso 'retorico', con tutto quello che la retorica significa in Platone, soprattutto se si tenga conto delle precisazioni del *Fedro*. La prospettiva, ha precisato Bianchi Bandinelli, segue alla scenografia, alle tecniche teatrali, e come la retorica si giustifica bene sul piano pratico, persuasivo, pedagogico.[13] Può trovare il proprio posto nella 'vita civile' di Firenze al tempo delle grandi scelte che ne agitarono il corso lungo il secolo XV.

In ogni caso, quello che conviene sottolineare è che nel Quattrocento, soprattutto intorno alla metà del secolo, il ritorno all'antico e la lezione degli *studia humanitatis*, non riguardano aspetti particolari della cultura, ma investono con le loro conseguenze tutti i settori della vita. Quello che da ogni parte si vuole sottolineare è l'unità di fondo del nuovo corso della civiltà cittadina, e il carattere non marginale nè settoriale del 'ritorno all'antico'. In un testo celebre, dalla forte carica ideologica, e che per molti aspetti ha il sapore di un manifesto, la *Laudatio Florentinae Urbis* – stesa nel 1403 ma ancora al centro dell'attenzione, e delle polemiche politiche, nel 1436 – Leonardo Bruni, repubblicano sincero, batterà proprio sul significato di una esatta corrispondenza fra strutture architettoniche urbane, strutture istituzionali della città, e strutture fisiche e intellettuali dei cittadini. La *convenientia* della *urbs cum suis civibus* è paragonata alla *similitudo* dei figli *cum suis parentibus*.[14]

Non può sfuggire l'importanza di un testo modellato sulla *Panathenaica oratio* di Elio Aristide, volutamente inteso a sottolineare il parallelo fra Firenze e Atene, e dovuto alla penna di un moralista, di un filosofo, traduttore impegnato di Platone, e traduttore e illustratore delle opere morali e politiche di Aristotele, biografo dei grandi trecentisti, magistrato e futuro cancelliere di Firenze. Si potrà parlare di lui come di un retore, ma a condizione di dare un rilievo e un senso tutto particolare alla retorica. Non questo, per altro, è ciò che importa ora, ma l'insistenza sull'armonioso corrispondere e convergere, nella città, degli ideali etici e politici, del fiorire economico, delle magistrature e degli edifici: la città, insomma, come una perfetta unità, per l'unità della sua vita morale e materiale. L'uguaglianza dei diritti (*ius equum in omnibus*), l'uguaglianza delle condizioni (*maiorum cum minoribus exequata condicio*), l'equilibrata coesistenza delle classi (*ex diversis ordinibus . . . quaedam equabilitas*), la libertà (*nusquam viget tanta libertas*): tutto questo si rispecchia in un'amministrazione che nelle proprie dimore, che ne simboleggiano le funzioni, opera sotto gli occhi di tutti: "parata semper iudicia, parati magistratus, patet curia, patet summum tribunal."[15] Senonché ciò che più colpisce è la simmetria fra queste immagini e le costruzioni del Brunelleschi, dall'Ospedale degli Innocenti al Palagio di Parte Guelfa, ove "l'aula del consiglio . . . totalmente aperta alla luce" doveva indicare che "la vita politica è identificata con l'evidenza, la chiarezza," la razionalità: *parata, patet*. Per non dire dell'Ospedale degli Innocenti e del suo rapporto con la piazza della SS.ma Annunziata, così manifestamente destinata all'incontro sociale, alla conversazione civile, a cominciare dalla scalinata dell'Ospedale. Viene fatto di leggere in parallelo le pietre e le prospettive brunelleschiane, i capitoli dell'*Architettura* dell'Alberti e le pagine pedagogiche della *Vita civile* in cui lo speziale Matteo Palmieri venne trascrivendo in volgare fiorentino Cicerone, Quintiliano e Plutarco. "La città non è fatta di pietre—leggiamo—ma di uomini: gli uomini si debbono coltivare e drizzare a produrre i frutti." In verità, e su questo si vuole battere, nella città uomini e pietre si incontrano nello sforzo cosciente di far coincidere città ideale e città reale, ordinamenti giusti e costruzioni. Guardando all'Ospedale degli Innocenti, a quell'antichissimo brefotrofio, nelle strutture disegnate per l'avvenire dal Brunelleschi su commissione dell'Arte della seta è difficile non pensare alla volontà di trasfigurare le colpe e le sventure della società di oggi in un sogno platonico di perfetta repubblica. Collocato in un centro vivo d'incontro cittadino, lo splendido edificio, chiuso e isolato nei confronti della piazza, è tutto aperto e luminoso all'interno, quasi a simboleggiare che i bimbi abbandonati, i figli di genitori ignoti, allevati in uno spazio insieme partecipe e separato, sono destinati a diventare gl'incontaminati abitatori di una città futura più giusta. D'altra parte non dobbiamo dimenticare che Platone era, a Firenze, il maestro a lungo desiderato, da quando sulle orme di Petrarca Coluccio Salutati lo era andato curiosamente ricercando. Crisolora, chiamato alla cattedra di greco in città, aveva aperto il secolo traducendo la *Repubblica*. Leonardo Bruni aveva continuato rendendo in latino molti dei grandi dialoghi, fra cui, giova sottolinearlo, il *Gorgia* e il *Fedro*. Per non dire, soprattutto dal Concilio in poi, dell'evidente sogno di attuare, in quella che si sentiva la nuova Atene, la città ideale di Platone "solo che è piacesse a chi tutto governa (sono parole del 'platonico' Palmieri), per grazia dare lunga e tranquillissima pace all'umile nostra Italia." A Platone sappiamo che pensa Cosimo il Vecchio nei suoi colloqui col filosofo riformatore Giorgio Gemisto Pletone, mentre senza dubbio Lorenzo ebbe innanzi l'immagine platonica del reggitore dotto, esperto di filosofia, difensore della giustizia, dell'equilibrio e della pace. Ma, ciò che più conta, proprio ser Filippo Brunelleschi fece pubblica professione di politica platonica in quella vivacissima intervista concessa forse intorno al '40 all'ingegnere senese Mariano di Jacobo detto il Taccola, a cui confessò di desiderare una repubblica governata dai dotti, dai competenti.[16]

È stato facile, ovviamente, osservare che non di politica, o di filosofia, si tratta ma di retorica; non di libertà o di giustizia per tutti, ma di minoranze ricche e potenti; non di spinte progressive, ma di difesa di privilegi; non di rinnovamento, ma di conservazione. Retore illuso il Bruni; aristocratico conservatore l'Alberti. Le Arti che finanziavano le opere pubbliche costruite dal Brunelleschi erano in mano di una oligarchia che sarebbe stata presto soppiantata da un tiranno. Gli stessi termini di "popolo", "libertà" e "uguaglianza" indicavano tutt'altra cosa da quel che si intenderà dopo la Rivoluzione francese.

Tutto vero, certo. Eppure non bisognerebbe dimenticare mai le differenze reali che separavano dalle varie tirannidi e monarchie feudali le libere repubbliche cittadine come Firenze, ricca di una tensione politica non a caso destinata a concludere il secolo col tragico esperimento popolare del Savonarola, per riemergere ancora, a difesa della libertà contro le soldatesche straniere nell'assedio del '30. Proprio Burckhardt, in un frammento, scrisse con grande lucidità del travagliato reggimento di Firenze: "ciò che qui percepiamo in generale è una suprema consapevolezza politica, e poi la partecipazione di una grossa quota di cittadini alla vita pubblica e alle questioni costituzionali." È "quella *società*, che doveva divenire il substrato, il fondamento vitale della civiltà e dell'arte. È una pluralità di forze tollerate che se ne fanno portatrici."[17] Ed è proprio lì, in quelle lotte cittadine, che si alimenta quella passione per il pubblico confronto, quell'arte del disputare e del persuadere, appunto quella sempre più raffinata retorica civile, che è il nerbo di tanta parte della vita fiorentina nell'età dell'Umanesimo. D'altro lato, "nonostante ogni riserva, una cosa è innegabile: ogni fiorentino aveva la salda convinzione di poter dire la propria opinione nella sua città, come uomo libero, con la coscienza della possibilità di governare egli stesso un giorno, sia pure all'ombra di capi più potenti. E su tale coscienza, per quanto esigua fosse la realtà che effettivamente copriva, non sarà mai esagerato insistere."

Comunque una cosa risulta chiara in quel Quattrocento cittadino, che a Burckhardt dava l'impressione "della freschezza e del vigore spontaneo di una generazione veramente eccezionale": che sotto il segno dell'antico, e alla sua scuola, si venne determinando una svolta in tutte le forme dell'attività umana, e che il rinnovamento prese corpo insieme nelle arti figurative come nell'urbanistica, nel linguaggio come nella letteratura, nei progetti di città come nel costume, nell'educazione come nelle tecniche. Era dovunque un richiamo all'uomo, una riflessione sul suo operare e sulla società, un modo nuovo di vedere i suoi rapporti con le cose e con Dio, in uno sforzo di umanizzare il mondo, che sboccava a volte – il Filarete ne è un esempio cospicuo – in un antropomorfismo ossessivo fino all'assurdo. È certo però che nei monumenti come nelle scritture si esprime una nuova concezione del mondo. Nella luce e nelle armonie simmetriche di Santo Spirito si prega Dio in modo diverso, come la Trinità di Masaccio o gli affreschi del Carmine sottintendono una lettura nuova del dramma del Cristo. E usare, per interpretare la struttura del reale, i dialoghi di Platone e le *Enneadi* di Plotino, o, addirittura, Lucrezio e Epicuro, al posto della *Fisica* e della *Metafisica* di Aristotele, non è solo un cambiamento di libri di testo nelle scuole. Platone leggono e traducono, e confrontano con un nuovo Aristotele, non professori allo Studio ma Cancellieri nei Palazzi del popolo, e grandi mercanti, ambasciatori e magistrati, e studiosi riuniti da astuti banchieri.

II

PROPRIO QUESTA unità di fondo di tutta una cultura, che muta volto a una città, se è reale—come a me par reale—e se si è alimentata—come a me sembra si sia alimentata—di un nuovo rapporto con la civiltà antica, proprio questa unità smentisce la tesi che il rinnovamento umanistico possa ridursi a puro fatto di scuola, accentuato da contrasti e da gelosie di maestri di grammatica, a una riforma, e neppur essa profonda, dell'*ars dictandi*, e non implichi invece un modo nuovo di concepire il rapporto dell'uomo con la sua storia e con la realtà. Il contrasto non potrebbe essere più radicale, né è facile a superarsi, come quello che implica divergenze di metodo, di modi di concepire talune discipline—dalla retorica alla filosofia. La distanza delle posizioni è tale, e il linguaggio delle parti a volte tanto disforme, che l'unica cosa proficua da fare è, forse, chiarire i termini del dissenso. E nel farlo mi riferirò soprattutto a un grande studioso, a cui quanti si occupano di studi sul Rinascimento si sentono debitori per il mirabile censimento di materiale manoscritto consegnato ai preziosi volumi dell'*Iter Italicum:* voglio dire Paul Oscar Kristeller.[18] E scelgo il Kristeller non solo perché alla sua autorità si rifanno quanti rifiutano le vedute che sono venuto esponendo, ma perché è colui che con più misura ha condotto la discussione, e con più solidi argomenti, via via riconoscendo almeno in parte le ragioni degli altri. Vorrei aggiungere ancora due osservazioni: quando il Kristeller parla di filosofia contrapponendola alla retorica egli pensa soprattutto alla filosofia teorica e sistematica, quella, per esemplificare, incarnatasi in Aristotele e in S. Tommaso; e nella storia egli è incline a cogliere piuttosto la continuità che la rottura. In fondo, per una strana contraddizione, questo studioso insigne del Rinascimento, che fu età di fermenti e di crisi, guarda con simpatia alle ordinate sistemazioni.

Egli comincia con il contestare già l'uso di termini come 'umanesimo,' 'umanistia,' *studia humanitatis*. La parola umanista, ricorda, entrata nell'uso alla fine del Quattrocento e soprattutto nel Cinquecento, a simiglianza di *legista, jurista, artista*, indica un maestro di scuola che insegna discipline umanistiche, ossia grammaticali, letterarie, retoriche: non filosofia, dunque, non concezioni del mondo, non rinnovamento della cultura, ma "una fase caratteristica" della "tradizione retorica della cultura occidentale." Non la retorica di Vico, in quanto filosofia del linguaggio e della storia, ma se mai Cicerone, ossia, come dice testualmente, "quel modo eclettico di pensare che era pronto a raccogliere briciole di conoscenza ovunque potesse trovarne, a che caratterizza anche molti trattati umanistici."

Non insisterò sugli aspetti più vivacemente polemici del Kristeller, sia a proposito della continuità col Medioevo, sia a proposito dei supposti limiti degli umanisti, e degli artisti. Accentuati dai suoi seguaci, sono stati invece spesso attenuati dal Kristeller, il quale ha pur riconosciuto i contributi indiretti dell'umanesimo rinascimentale, "non filosofico, ma che ebbe importanti implicazioni e conseguenze filosofiche," addirittura "enorme immagazzinamento di nozioni e idee nuove" decisivo per "il processo di fermento intellettuale" anche se il giudizio finale su Petrarca, Valla, Alberti resta questo: "opera dilettantesca," priva "non solo di originalità, ma anche di coerenza, di metodo e di sostanza," che ci lascia "spesso a mani quasi vuote."

Non chiederò al Kristeller, come conciliare queste mani quasi vuote con l'enorme immagazzinamento di nozioni e di idee nuove che anch'egli ammette, e neppure osserverò che a taluni sembrano grandi pensatori Erasmo, Montaigne, Pascal e Rousseau, e che l'umanità deve alla meditazione di Petrarca e di Alberti pagine indimenticabili. Il problema e la discussione devono rimanere sul terreno rigorosamente storico. Su questo terreno si pongono subito alcune questioni di metodo. E, prima di tutto, la mancanza, in questa prospettiva, di una rigorosa periodizzazione, e l'uso troppo generico del termine di umanesimo rinascimentale, e anche di *studia humanitatis* e di discipline umanistiche. Ora in un fenomeno che si estende almeno dalla metà del Trecento al Cinquecento avanzato, andranno pur fatte numerose distinzioni, perchè non giova alla chiarezza mettere insieme, e mescolare, la trattatistica di Petrarca, del Valla, di Giannozzo Manetti, di Leon Battista Alberti e di Angelo Poliziano. Dialoghi, certo, orazioni e trattati, ma ricchi di contenuti diversi, e in cui la forma dialogata non si ispira solo a modelli ciceroniani (non è un ciceroniano Valla), ma anche al dialogo socratico-platonico che non è tanto facile espungere dalla filosofia.

Ora se si distinguono, come è necessario distinguere, i vari momenti di un fenomeno culturale durato oltre due secoli, ci si accorge subito che la situazione dei tempi di Petrarca è ben diversa da quella maturata fra la fine del Quattrocento e il primo Cinquecento, in cui emerge la parola *humanista*, e in cui si consolida quella figura del "grammatico," di cui si fa forte il Kristeller, connettendola alla sostenuta continuità fra *dictatores* medievali e primi umanisti. In quei due secoli, a chi ben guardi, muta l'immagine dell'antico da restaurare, mutano e si accrescono gli *auctores*, mutano i barbari da respingere, mutano i miti. I secoli bui che all'origine costituivano una parentesi di due secoli, alla fine sono una tenebra di un millennio. Firenze, che ai tempi del Salutati guardava alla Roma dei Cesari, con Leonardo Bruni guarda alla repubblica e alle città etrusche, per idealizzare successivamente prima Atene e poi Gerusalemme. Né significa la stessa cosa l'ammirazione di Petrarca per Cicerone, quella di Valla per Quintiliano, e la misurata ma ferma critica al ciceronianismo del Poliziano. Così come varia il modo di vedere il latino, e i suoi rapporti col greco per un verso e col volgare per l'altro.

Comunque, se vogliamo rifarci all'uomo che nei secoli, e non a torto, fu considerato il padre del nuovo corso di studi, e cioè a Petrarca, dobbiamo rilevare che le sue motivazioni teoriche furono due, e molto precise, e chiaramente formulate: la polemica contro il logicismo e lo scientismo da un lato, l'appello per una ripresa platonica dall'altro. Col che ci muoviamo in un campo un po' diverso dall'*ars dictandi*. Si aggiunga che Petrarca non fu maestro di scuola, non ne apprezzò la funzione, e rifiutò la cattedra fiorentina. Del resto non furono maestri di scuola Cola di Rienzo, Coluccio Salutati, Leonardo Bruni, Matteo Palmieri, Giannozzo Manetti, Leon Battista Alberti—come non lo saranno, per chiamare in causa gli esponenti della nuova filosofia, né Cusano, né Marsilio Ficino, né Pico della Mirandola. Il nuovo corso, che è poi innanzitutto un modo diverso di leggere testi antichi e nuovi, entra nelle scuole e diventa programma solo dopo un lungo periodo di contrasti e di lotte, dentro e fuori della scuola, fra discipline e maestri. Quando vi penetra, fa veramente scoppiare le vecchie strutture. Poliziano, per prendere un "grammatico," è il primo a utilizzare nell'originale la *Poetica* d'Aristotele, nota solo nella versione latina del compendio d'Averroè. Poliziano ne traduce alcune parti e la discute come introduzione al suo corso sul teatro classico, così come nei corsi di logica si serve di commenti greci dell'*Organo,* e nelle discussioni filologiche analizza l'origine di termini come "entelechia," "endelechia," o "sinderesi," in un tipo di esegesi storico-critica che sembrò filosoficamente assai rilevante a un pensatore come Pico della Mirandola che impostò la polemica forse più penetrante del secolo su linguaggio tecnico dei filosofi e linguaggio retorico dei letterati.

In realtà il nodo della questione è proprio nella rivendicazione del valore delle discipline logiche, politiche ed estetiche, esse pure filosofiche—se filosofia è non solo fisica ma anche psicologia e antropologia. Gli 'umanisti'—e questo anche il Kristeller deve ammettere—leggono e commentano i testi dialettici e morali, sono maestri delle discipline che riguardano l'uomo e la società, a cominciare dal linguaggio, dai mezzi espressivi, da quel tessuto che cementa le città umane che, come amano ripetere, non sono fatte solo di pietre. Così attraverso il loro insegnamento viene emergendo l'egemonia di una filosofia dell'uomo, morale e politica, retorica e poetica, che assume un rilievo tutto particolare in una vita cittadina dalle forti tensioni sociali e politiche. Le altre discipline non si rifiutano, né si combattono; se ne sottolinea il fine e il significato nei confronti dell'uomo. Non a caso l'umanesimo rinascimentale fiorisce nella città-stato, in un momento di crisi, di trasformazione strutturale, quando sembra incrinarsi tutto un mondo di valori. Non a caso ad alimentare il nuovo corso culturale sono i mercanti letterati che ha studiato Christian Bec, o i magistrati e gli uomini di legge messi a fuoco da Myron Gilmore e da Lauro Martines. Non a caso la forma letteraria cara agli umanisti è il dialogo, o l'epistola che è dialogo anch'essa, o l'orazione che è colloquio con un uditorio sempre più numeroso: la verità non è un dogma, è una ricerca collettiva e un confronto, un coro dove ogni voce ha diritto di manifestarsi. Il suo luogo è una piazza, un arengo, un consiglio, una scuola. Il suo scopo un nuovo modo di costruire la città degli uomini: un nuovo linguaggio. Quello che è sembrato scetticismo, l'inizio di una nuova teoria del sapere.

In questo contesto la polemica di Petrarca ritrova tutta la sua importanza: sul piano politico, nel travaglio della Chiesa avignonese e delle città italiane; sul piano filosofico, nel dibattito europeo sulla logica terministica e sulla nuova fisica, mentre urgeva dovunque un bisogno di valori. Petrarca combatte su più fronti: in logica, contro il formalismo dei logici inglesi, in difesa del linguaggio naturale e della poesia; in fisica, in difesa dell'uomo, della vita interiore, della vita morale e spirituale in genere: della vita con le sue passioni, e della morte. Sono d'accordo col Kristeller nel negare che l'*Ignoranza* sia antiaverroistica.[19] Non credo invece che ci lasci un pugno di mosche in mano: è la battaglia di sempre contro lo scientismo e il tecnicismo in nome della vita morale e dell'interiorità, della libertà e dell'umanità. Allora era la fisica parigina che si stava diffondendo negli Studi italiani, e la 'barbarie' del Merton College che divenne un *topos* della letteratura del Quattrocento.[20]

Senonché Petrarca individuò un altro punto cruciale della discussione: si rese conto che il problema concerneva il rapporto fra le discipline, e come tale investiva il cuore stesso del filosofare: la relazione fra scienze della natura e scienze dell'uomo, fra azione e contemplazione, fra intelletto e volontà. Si sono spesso letti, in questi ultimi anni, giudizi singolarmente sfocati a proposito della fitta polemica contro i medici, avviata da Petrarca, ma dilagata poi nel confronto fra *civilis* e *naturalis justitia*, fra leggi e medicina—ove non sempre gli umanisti difendono il diritto, ma sempre sono coscienti che il nodo del problema è il fondamento della conoscenza dell'uomo e della natura, delle leggi naturali, umane e divine. Probabilmente è nella miriade di testi che affrontano questo contrasto, e nell'altra grande polemica su poesia e teologia, sulla teologia poetica, sulla poesia teologica degli antichi, e sulla metafisica poetica: è proprio in tutta questa ricca produzione che deve cercarsi il prologo del più originale pensiero tardo quattrocentesco e cinquecentesco di Ficino e di Pico, di Leone Ebreo e di Giordano Bruno, delle loro teologie platoniche ed ermetiche, e della loro filosofia dell'amore e della natura.

Certo se misuriamo Petrarca e Leon Battista Alberti (ma anche Erasmo o Montaigne) sul modello delle *summe* tomistiche, dobbiamo espungerli dalla filosofia; ma se si pensa a quell'altra filosofia, che gli umanisti dicevano essere la *nostra* filosofia, e che un grande moralista inglese del Settecento chiamava filosofia di casa,[21] e cioè la filosofia della nostra dimora umana, allora è difficile non apprezzare quella prima impostazione del rapporto fra *Naturwissenschaft* e *Geisteswissenschaft*, e quel vichiano ricercare la logica delle scienze morali entro il linguaggio naturale degli uomini.

Naturalmente per rendersene conto bisogna sfruttare i risultati della paziente esplorazione degli scrittoi degli umanisti compiuta dal Kristeller, e leggere gli autori—e non solo gli inediti, ma anche le opere stampate—non giudicare, come tutti fanno, Salutati, Bruni, Alberti o Valla, da alcune pagine. L'*Ercole* del Salutati, il *De fato*, il *De nobilitate legum et medicinae*; l'introduzione all'etica del Bruni accolta nel grande *corpus* giuntino di Aristotele e Averroè, non sono esercizi di scuola da trascurarsi. Di Valla e Alberti non è lecito isolare un'opera, o una battuta. È strano che chi parla tanto di retorica, si lasci poi sfuggire la verità elementare che tutte le opere di questi autori sono un gran dialogo, dove ogni testo è la battuta di un interlocutore da integrarsi nel tutto. Staccare i dialoghi della *Famiglia* dal processo di una meditazione veramente drammatica ha portato a un'incomprensione opaca e convenzionale. Staccare le opere italiane dell'Alberti dalle latine, inquietanti e mirabili, significa non rendersi conto innanzitutto di una originalissima impostazione del problema linguistico—significa anche precludersi la comprensione di una dialettica ricca e feconda. Chi cerchi la filosofia, non nei manuali scolastici, ma nella autentica riflessione sulla umana esperienza, saluterà nell'Alberti uno dei pensatori più ricchi delle origini del pensiero moderno. Quanto a Valla, la sua dialettica come i suoi dialoghi sul bene, le sue "eleganze" come le sue note di filologia testamentaria, hanno costituito uno degli stimoli più efficaci della riflessione in un'età di crisi. Al *De libero arbitrio* tornerà ancora Leibniz per citarlo lungamente nella *Teodicea*.

Da Petrarca a Ficino, pur fra contrasti e differenze profonde, e con limiti a volte vistosi, è un discorso unitario che si sviluppa, ed è un discorso "filosofico": di una filosofia, per riprendere un grande tema del *Fedro* platonico, che non è solo dialettica delle idee ma, innanzitutto, psicagogia: riflessione sull'uomo per la formazione dell'uomo: educazione per una società in trasformazione. Come si ricostruiscono le città secondo modelli più razionali, così si formano gli uomini e le istituzioni, e cioè il linguaggio, il diritto, le leggi, la religione. Alla radice la coscienza, conquistata attraverso la filologia, della complessità e ricchezza dello sforzo umano verso la verità e il bene: non solo Aristotele, ma Platone, Plotino, Epicuro, e poi Parmenide ed Empedocle; non solo Cristo, ma Mosè e Maometto—la pace della fede di Cusano, la pace della filosofia di Pico.

Questo non vuol significare un giudizio tutto in positivo; tutt'altro! Vuol dire che la tematica dibattuta fra Petrarca e Machiavelli, e, perchè no?, fra Giotto e Michelangelo, importa una nuova concezione del mondo, non a caso destinata a tradursi in una nuova educazione dell'uomo. La retorica in tal caso, non indica l'altro dalla filosofia, ma un'altra filosofia, umana e mondana, una *saggezza* nuova: e chiamiamola pure retorica, se con Perelman intendiamo *une philosophie réthorique* avversa a tutti i dogmatismi e gli assolutismi, rivolta agli uomini di buona volontà perchè operando trasformino la società. Francesco Patrizi da Cherso la faceva fiorire nelle repubbliche dove vive la libertà. Alcuni secoli dopo Tocqueville scriverà: "nelle discussioni politiche di un popolo democratico emerge un carattere di universalità che le rende importanti per tutto il genere umano. Tutti gli uomini vi si interessano, perchè vi si tratta dell'uomo che è uomo dovunque." Appunto questo ideale di una cultura non divisa, per una umanità non lacerata, che discuta *in pace* e in libertà, costituì lo spirito degli *studia humanitatis,* della educazione liberale, la forza di un programma educativo e politico, l'ispirazione unitaria di una concezione del mondo.

Note

1. J. Burckhardt, *Lezioni sulla storia d'Europa* [*Historische Fragmente aus dem Nachlass,* gesammelt von Emil Dürr, Stuttgart 1929], tr. it. M. Carpitella (Torino, 1959), p. 113.

2. Aeneae Sylvii Piccolominei *Opera quae extant omnia* (Basileae, 1551), pp. 646–47 (ed. Wolkan, Wien, 1918, II, p. 100 n.).

3. Aeneae Sylivii Piccolominei *Opera omnia,* p. 454.

4. L. B. Alberti, *De pictura,* ed. C. Grayson, (Bari-Roma, 1975), pp. 10–11 (cfr. J. R. Spencer, " 'Ut rhetorica pictura.' A study in Quattrocento Theory of Painting." *Journal of the Warburg and Courtauld Institutes* 20, (1957), pp. 26–44.

5. L. B. Alberti, *Theogenius,* in *Opere volgari,* ed. C. Grayson, vol. II (Bari, 1966), pp. 73–74. Cfr. Ch. Bec, "De Pétrarque à Machiavel: à propos d'un 'topos' humaniste (le dialogue lecteur/livre)," *Rinascimento,* serie II, vol. XVI (1976), pp. 3–18.

6. S. Bernardino da Siena, *Le prediche volgari,* a cura di C. Cannarozzi, (Firenze, 1940), vol. III, pp. 297 e sgg.

7. Antonio Averlino Detto Il Filarete, *Trattato di architettura,* a cura di A. M. Finoli e L. Grassi (Milano, 1972), vol. I, p. 229.

8. Antonio Manetti, *Vita di Filippo Brunelleschi,* ed. D. De Robertis (Milano, 1976), pp. 64–66.

9. Filarete, *Trattato,* vol. I, pp. 13 esgg.

10. Giannozzo Manetti, *Oratio,* ed. E. Battisti, "Umanesimo e esoterismo" (a cura di E. Castelli), (Padova, 1960), pp. 310–20.

11. Filarete, *Trattato,* vol. I, p. 227; vol. II, p. 657.

12. R. Wittkower, "Brunelleschi and 'proportion in perspective' ", *Journal of the Warburg and Courtauld Institutes,* XVI (1953), pp. 275–91. Cfr. G. C. Argan, "The architecture of Brunelleschi and the origins of perspective theory in the fifteenth century," ibid., IX (1946), pp. 96–121; R. Beltrame, "Gli esperimenti prospettici del Brunelleschi," *Rendiconti dell'Acc. Naz. dei Lincei,* Scienze morali, serie VIII, vol. 28 (1973), pp. 417–68.

13. R. Bianchi Bandinelli, *Archeologia e cultura,* (Roma, 1979), pp. 146–63.

14. H. Baron, *From Petrarch to Leonardo Bruni. Studies in Humanistic and Political Literature* (Chicago and London, 1968), pp. 232–63; L. Bruni, *Panegirico della città di Firenze* (Firenze, 1974).

15. L. Bruni, *Panegirico,* p. 92.

16. Per il testo del Taccola (ma anche per alcune osservazioni sulla prospettiva e il 'platonismo'), cfr. E. Battisti, *Filippo Brunelleschi* (Milano, 1976), pp. 20–21, 48, 58. I testi del Palmieri sono tratti dal *Della vita civile,* ed. F. Battaglia (Bologna, 1944).

17. J. Burckhardt, *Lezioni*, pp. 132–33, 140–42.

18. Fra i molti scritti del Kristeller sugli argomenti qui toccati rinvio in modo particolare alle due raccolte: *Concetti rinascimentali dell'uomo e altri saggi*, (Firenze, 1978), che riunisce materiali tratti da più volumi precedenti); *Renaissance Thought and its Sources*, ed. by M. Mooney (New York, 1979). Per il complesso della produzione del Kristeller, cfr. *Bibliography of the publications of P. O. Kristeller for the years 1929–1974*, in *Philosophy and Humanism. Renaissance Essays in Honor of P. O. Kristeller*, ed. by E. P. Mahoney (Leiden, 1976), pp. 545–89.

Per alcune osservazioni sulle *artes dictaminis*, cfr. anche M. Baxandall, *Giotto and the Orators*, (Oxford, 1971), pp. 5 e sgg.

19. P. O. Kristeller, "Petrarch's 'Averroists': A note on the history of Aristotelianism in Venice, Padua and Bologna," *Mélanges Augustin Renaudet. Bibliothèque d'Humanisme Renaissance*, 14, (1952), pp. 59–65.

20. E. Garin, "La cultura fiorentina nella seconda metà del '300 e i 'barbari Britanni'," *Rassegna della Letteratura Italiana*, s. VII, vol. 64 (1960), pp. 181–95.

21. *Honest home-philosophy* è espressione di Shaftesbury, nella conclusione del *Soliloquy or Advice to an Author* (cfr. *Characteristics*, ed. J. M. Robertson, London, 1900, vol. I, p. 234). Benedetto Croce tradusse *home-philosophy* con *filosofia casalinga*, contrapposta a *mock-science* (*La Critica XXIII* [1925], p. 3).

Rhétorique contre philosophie?
Un inédit de Martin Le Franc

MARC-RENE JUNG
University of Zürich

Le point d'interrogation après le titre de ma communication "rhétorique contre philosophie?" voudrait simplement souligner le poids très relatif que représente le petit texte dont je vais vous parler, dans le débat séculaire entre la rhétorique et la philosophie.

Si le texte de Martin Le Franc n'a rien de métaphysique, il a cependant son importance dans l'histoire de l'humanisme français, puisqu'il s'insère, fort opportunément, dans le vide documentaire que représente le deuxième quart du XVe siècle, entre ce qu'on a appelé le premier humanisme français, avec les Jean Gerson, Nicolas de Clamanges, les frères Col et Jean de Montreuil, et les activités en faveur de la rhétorique des Guillaume Fichet et Robert Gaguin. C'est dans cette perspective historique que certaines idées de Martin Le Franc, banales aux yeux du connaisseur de la rhétorique de l'antiquité ou des premiers humanistes italiens, acquièrent leur véritable dimension.

Martin Le Franc est l'auteur de deux textes français, du *Champion des dames*, écrit en 1440/42, et de l'*Estrif de Fortune et de Vertu*, composé en 1447/48, dont on a montré récemment, les rapports avec le *De remediis utriusque fortunae* de Pétrarque.[1] Or, Le Franc, comme bien d'autres écrivains de son époque, a aussi écrit en latin, mais les francistes (je dirais presque: comme d'habitude ...) n'ont pas jugé bon de déchiffrer ces textes, malgré le principe méthodologique que M. Garin a fort justement rappelé, à savoir que toute enquête doit tenir compte aussi bien des écrits en langue maternelle que de ceux qui sont en latin.

Dans un manuscrit de Wolfenbüttel on trouve, au milieu de textes du Pogge, d'Isota Nogarola, de Guarino da Verona et de bien d'autres, deux épîtres latines de Martin Le Franc.[2] Dans la première, adressée au duc Amédée de Savoie, le futur pape Félix V, Le Franc, qui se qualifie de disciple d'Arcésilas, pose, après bien des éloges hyperboliques du *divus princeps*, sa candidature à un poste de secrétaire. Nous savons que cette démarche a été couronnée de succès.

La deuxième épître, dont j'aimerais vous parler plus particulièrement, est adressée aux secrétaires de la chancellerie de Savoie. Après un début filandreux, dont les allusions biographiques, qui gardent encore leur secret, nous font comprendre que l'auteur avait séjourné à la chancellerie ducale, qu'il qualifie d'Hélicon et de source pégaséique, Le Franc lance aux secrétaires très éloquents une question de rhétorique: *pars modo mea sit vos inter eloquentissimos rethoricam iacere questionem.* Nous nous trouvons donc dans une situation de dialogue, si caractéristique de l'époque, comme l'a encore rappelé M. Garin. Voici la question que pose Le Franc: Dans l'art de bien dire, quel est l'élément le plus important, de l'*ars*, de l'*exercitatio*, ou de l'*imitatio?*

Pour chacun de ces termes, Le Franc fournit des arguments susceptibles de militer en sa faveur.

L'*ars* garantit l'ordre, de sorte que sans l'art rien ne saurait durer ni plaire. Chez les poètes, ce sont Orphée, Musée, Homère, Hésiode et Esope, qui trouvèrent les *poesis precepta*, tandis que chez les orateurs, cet honneur revient à Hermagoras, Aristote, Gorgias Leontinus, *noster Cicero* et Quintilien. Tout *artifex* doit connaître l'*ars*, témoins le peintre ou le *scriptor*, qui sont appelés ainsi non parce qu'ils font de la peinture ou parce qu'ils écrivent, mais parce qu'ils connaissent la théorie de la peinture et de l'écriture: *pingendi scribendique rationes.* Il faut donc donner la prééminence à l'*ars*.

Quant à l'*exercitatio*, on pourrait la préférer parce que, sans elle, l'*ars* ne saurait se manifester rapidement. Bien des gens peuvent porter des jugements valables *de lineamentis corporumque figuris*, mais sans l'exercice de la peinture ils ne sauraient représenter *quod intus effigiatum est*. Même remarque à propos des musiciens, qui auraient beau disserter longuement des proportions musicales: sans la pratique, ils ne passeraient jamais pour des *suaves armonici*. Ils est donc évident qu'il n'y a aucun art sans l'exercice correspondant. Les *prisci oratores* nous en fournissent la preuve. Démosthène par exemple, *quod non habuit, usu comparavit*; ou encore Gracchus, qui fit ses exercices de *pronuntiatio* au son d'un cor d'ivoire, dans lequel soufflait un de ses serviteurs chaque fois que l'orateur baissait la voix ou que son débit se ralentissait.[3]

L'*imitatio* enfin devrait l'emporter sur les deux autres, parce qu'aujourd'hui, affirme Le Franc, on n'estime que la *facundia* qui sent son Cicéron ou son Tite-Live (*nisi Ciceroniano vel Tituliviano balsamo fuerit circumlota*), tout comme le poète doit imiter Homère et Virgile. Cicéron lui-même étudia à fond les orateurs grecs et romains et Virgile inséra dans ses poèmes des vers d'Homère. Ceux qui vinrent après, Lucain, Stace et *Galtherus* (qui doit être Gautier de Châtillon), imitèrent les *priores oratores: Posteri quoque Lucanus Statius Galtherus, quoad potuerunt, visi sunt priorum actorum dictis sua dicta confirmare.* On notera ici ce terme bien français d'*actor*, acteur dans le français du XVe siècle, et la mention de Gautier de Châtillon, du XIIe siècle, auteur français d'expression latine, déjà allégué par Nicolas de Clamanges, dans sa polémique contre Pétrarque, pour prouver la qualité et la continuité des *bonae litterae* en France.[4] Le Franc continue: Sénèque prit pour modèle Socrate, tout comme Phidias et Praxitèle, *quorum Rome adhuc extant opera,*[5] imitèrent Zeuxis et Appelles.

Et à notre époque, *nunc quoque,* pour être un bon musicien, il faut imiter Guillaume du Fay et Binchois,[6] et pour bien dire et bien faire, il faut imiter Guillaume Bolomier, le vice-chancelier de la cour de Savoie! Jugez donc, écrit Le Franc aux secrétaires de la chancellerie, s'il ne faut pas préférer l'imitation aux deux autres. Quant à moi, je suis un serviteur zélé de l'imitation que les modernes, *moderni,* semblent préférer,[7] et j'imite Carnéade, qui, après avoir parlé *in utramque partem* devant le Sénat romain, prit congé de Rome dans une *ornatissima oratio.*

J'ignore où Le Franc a trouvé que Carnéade, chassé de Rome, aurait encore fait un magnifique discours d'adieu. Y a-t-il là une allusion à des différends qui auraient surgi au sein de la chancellerie de Savoie à propos de l'éloquence, de sorte que l'allusion à Guillaume Bolomier, qui finira noyé (1446) dans le lac Léman pour affaires politiques, serait une allusion ironique? et que le discours d'adieu de Carnéade serait la propre épître de Martin Le Franc?

Quoi qu'il en soit, la citation d'Arcésilas et de Carnéade me semble jeter une lumière neuve sur l'*Estrif de Fortune et de Vertu* dont on a toujours dit qu'il se situait dans la plus pure tradition du débat médiéval. Ceci peut être vrai quant à la forme de cette *altercatio,* mais le fondement théorique de la démarche de Le Franc paraît bien être le principe académique du *in utramque partem dicere.* Ainsi la réflexion théorique serait en avance sur la mise en pratique.

La fin de l'épître de Le Franc est consacrée à l'éloge de l'éloquence, laquelle, certes, a besoin d'être fondée sur la *sapientia,* mais qui est ce qu'il y a de plus approprié pour donner du lustre au genre humain. Suivent des arguments bien connus: c'est l'éloquence qui a conduit l'homme de l'état sauvage à l'état civilisé; c'est elle qui a instauré les lois, elle qui, enfin, fait toute la beauté de la vie humaine. Or ceux qui possèdent cette éloquence sont peu nombreux: des philosophes, des géomètres, des experts dans les autres arts—il y en a en profusion, mais on trouve difficilement un homme éloquent: *multi philosophi sunt, multi geometri sunt, multi ceterarum artium sunt, pene quidem una in plebe cernimus eloquentem.*[8] Et Le Franc d'énumérer toutes les situations dans la vie, où l'éloquence est la chose la plus agréable ou la plus féconde. On a besoin d' elle dans les affaires privées et dans celles de l'état (*res publica*); on l'utilise pour s'adresser à Dieu. C'est elle qui te tient joyeuse compagnie aussi bien lorsque tu es seul chez toi que lorsque tu te trouves à la campagne: *si rus eas, tecum rusticatur.* Pour Martin Le Franc, l'éloquence dépasse de loin l'activité de l'orateur: *ubi non viderit audientes, pro verbis utitur litteris.* La fin de l'épître énumère encore une fois tous les domaines de l'éloquence: elle adoucit nos peines, elle nous fortifie dans la désolation, elle éteint la fureur du peuple, elle est indispensable aux princes, elle sert à chanter les louanges de Dieu, bref, c'est l'éloquence qui nous permet de mener une vie bonne et heureuse.

Voilà l'éloquent plaidoyer pour l'éloquence, écrit autour de 1435. J'en tirerai rapidement quelques conclusions.

1. Le Franc connaît son Cicéron, et utilise notamment les dernières découvertes, le *de oratore* et le *pro Archia*, mais dans la triade des fondements de la rhétorique, *natura* est absente.[9] Le Franc, avec les *moderni* (et avec la *Rhét. à Herennius*), préfère l'*imitatio*.

2. L'éloquence est le fondement de la civilisation humaine; c'est l'éloquence qui distingue l'homme civilisé (le terme *educere* revient plusieurs fois sous la plume de Le Franc) de l'homme qui n'a pour lui que la nature. Et cette éloquence englobe l'orateur, le poète et tous les autres arts.

3. Dans cette perspective, l'imitation n'est plus la seule imitation de Cicéron ou de Tite-Live. Chaque art ou mieux: chaque éloquence a ses modèles. Il faut souligner ici que Le Franc propose des modèles contemporains: du Fay et Binchois pour la musique, ce qui amènera notre auteur, dans le *Champion des dames*, à faire l'éloge des arts contemporains: musiciens, enlumineurs, peintres, entailleurs, sont au sommet de leur art. Quant à la littérature française, Le Franc est plus réservé, mais il énumère les grands auteurs du passé, de Jean de Meun à Machaut, à Christine de Pisan, voire à Dante. Ne les propose-t-il pas comme modèles a imiter?

4. Aux clercs, c'est-à-dire aux gens du discours rationnel, dit Le Franc encore dans le *Champion des dames*, il ne reste qu'à gloser les textes déjà existants. Voilà pourquoi Le Franc, lorsqu'il parle de la *vita solitaria* à la fin de son épître aux secrétaires du duc de Savoie, se console non pas avec la philosophie, mais avec ce qu'il appelle éloquence. Pétrarque n'aurait pas dit cela, ni Nicolas de Clamanges.

5. Pour un futur protonotaire apostolique et traducteur de la Bible, Le Franc demeure plutôt laconique quant aux rapports de la théologie et de l'éloquence. Là encore, il se sépare des humanistes français du début du XVe siècle.

Je crois donc, pour conclure, que Martin Le Franc occupe une place non négligeable dans l'histoire de l'humanisme français, humanisme latin ou français, et que son attitude vis-à-vis de l'éloquence, même si elle peut en grande partie être ramenée à des sources, est significative par son éclectisme même.[10]

Notes

1. Le meilleur connaisseur de l'oeuvre de Martin Le Franc est actuellement Oskar Roth; voir ses *Studien zum 'Estrif de Fortune et de Vertu' des Martin Le Franc* (Bern, 1970); du même, "Martin Le Franc et le 'De remediis' de Pétrarque," *Studi Francesi*, 45 (1971) 401-19; du même, "Martin Le Franc et les débuts de l'humanisme italien. Analyse des emprunts faits à Pétrarque," in *Il Petrarca ad Arquà* (= vol. 2 des Studi sul Petrarca) (Padova, 1975) p. 241-56.

2. MS 2859, f. 62-65v; cf. Otto von Heinemann, *Die Handschriften der herzoglichen Bibliothek zu Wolfenbüttel*. 2. Abteilung. Die Augusteischen Handschriften, Bd. IV, Wolfenbüttel, 1900, p. 67-69. Un autre texte latin de Le Franc, également inédit, se trouve aux p. 265-88 du ms. 55-57 de la Bibliothèque municipale de Dole. Il s'agit d'un dialogue *de bono mortis* entre Le Franc et un certain Johannes (probablement Jean Servion); ce texte est dédié à Pierre Heronchel. Le Franc et Heronchel (ou Aronchel) seront les collaborateurs de Jean Servion pour la traduction de la Bible.

3. Je me demande comment la *fistula* dont parle Cicéron dans le *de oratore* 3.225 à propos de Gracchus, a pu se transformer en cor d'ivoire, en un véritable olifant. Cette transformation de l'instrument destiné à scander le rythme des péroraisons de Gracchus, montre combien la situation de l'*orator* romain demeurait incompréhensible à notre auteur du XVe siècle.

4. Nicolas de Clamanges, épître *Quod in superiori*, écrite en 1394. C'est l'épître V de l'édition des *Opera omnia* de I. M. Lydius, Louvain, 1613, t.II, p. 24 et suiv. Le nom de Gautier manque dans l'édition Lydius, mais il se trouve dans les manuscrits. On attend toujours une édition critique des épîtres de Clamanges! Notons que Pétrarque, dans son invective contre Jean de Hesdin, s'était moqué de l'auteur de l'*Alexandreis*. Martin Le Franc est donc bien "français".

5. D'où Le Franc tient-il cela? Je lis chez Pétrarque, *Fam*. VI, 2, 13: Hoc Praxitelis Phidieque extans in lapide tot iam seculis de ingenio et arte certamen.

6. Nunc quoque, qui celestibus armoniis nostri superegregii et omnium modestissimi musice professoris G. Du Fay aut carminibus suavissimis Binchois sua similifacit, dicitur in arte prestare.

7. Sed ut imitacioni paulisper deserviam, quam magnopere moderni probare videntur. . . .

8. Cette déclaration de Martin Le Franc rappelle le début du *de oratore*, où Cicéron insiste sur la rareté, *paucitas*, du vrai orateur, qu'il oppose au grand nombre des "techniciens," philosophes, mathématiciens, musiciens, grammairiens; même les poètes sont plus nombreux que les orateurs. Dans son épître V, citée ci-dessus, à la note 4, Clamanges exprime une idée analogue: nemo mirabitur, rarissimos semper in mundo fuisse dignos istarum disciplinarum [sc. oratoria et poetica] artifices.

9. Cf. *de inv.* I 2 ars, studium, exercitatio et, en plus, facultas ab natura profecta; *de orat.* II 232 natura, studium, exercitatio; Quintilien, *inst. orat.* III 5, 1 natura, ars, imitatio — et surtout tous les textes qui prennent la défense de la poésie à la fin du XIVe siècle, où natura ne manque jamais.

10. Certaines réflexions de Le Franc sont d'ailleurs loin d'être banales. Ainsi cette défense du "langage quotidien," qui annonce les "papiers journaux" de Joachim Du Bellay: "Et aussy ne nieray je avoir dit pluseurs choses par aventure et despourveument, ainsy

qu'il advient en langage quotidien et familier, lesquelles trouvé n'eusse en longue muserie. Car mainte chose est faicte par cas aventureux a laquelle art ne sçaveroit attaindre."
Le Champion des Dames, éd. A. Piaget (Lausanne, 1968), pp. 4–5.

Territorial Disputes:
Philosophy *versus* Rhetoric

BRIAN VICKERS
Eidgenössische Technische Hochschule Zürich

Anyone involved with the study and teaching of rhetoric must be aware that the subject continues to be misunderstood and misrepresented. That "rhetoric" or "rhetorical" persist as pejorative terms need not surprise us very much when we consider that the same fate has overtaken other important concepts in art: "prosaic" became a term of abuse in the English eighteenth and nineteenth centuries, ironically when much of the major creative work in English literature was taking place in a prose genre, the novel; while many pejorative terms have been derived from the theatre, indeed most terminology and imagery from that source has been negative.[1] No one thinks the worse of drama today because of this, yet rhetoric continues to be distrusted. Probably nothing will ever dislodge the use of "rhetorical" to mean "false" or "over-elaborate, insincere"; all the same, while attempting to purify these terms of their negative associations by using them as neutral descriptive tools, we ought also to keep an eye on the large-scale pejorative movements, those attacks on rhetoric from Plato to St. Augustine (in the *Confessions*), Locke, Kant, and Croce, to name only the most celebrated. Among the defenders of rhetoric we can list Isocrates, Cicero, Quintilian, Augustine (in the *De Doctrina Christiana*), Valla, Nizolius, Ramus, Vico, Kenneth Burke, and Chaim Perelman.

This dispute has attracted some attention in our time,[2] yet rather in terms of content than in method: of the issues at stake rather than the ways in which those issues were formulated. I am concerned with the categories used to evaluate rhetoric, and my starting point is the observation by Sir Isaiah Berlin that

> the task of philosophy, often a difficult and painful one, is to extricate and bring to light the hidden categories and models in terms of which human beings think (that is, their use of words, images and other symbols),

to reveal what is obscure or contradictory in them, to discern the conflicts between them that prevent the construction of more adequate ways of organising and describing and explaining experience. . . .

Since these often unexamined and unconscious categories and concepts cause disagreement when they clash with one another, the philosopher's task is to construct "other, less internally contradictory, and (though this can never be fully attained) less pervertible metaphors, images, symbols and systems of categories."[3] I shall be concerned here with some conceptions of rhetoric, especially those used to pervert and dismiss the art.

I

THE INITIAL PROBLEM, from which many attacks have taken rise, concerns the nature of rhetoric, whether it is a discipline with a formal content proper to itself, not shared with other disciplines. The short answer to that question would be that it is not autotelic or self-sufficient, that it does not have a body of knowledge peculiar to itself, in the way that physics does, or music, or architecture. Since its field is human communication and human behaviour it links up with ethics, psychology, sociology, anthropology, politics, law. It is concerned with the methods of communication, expression, comprehension, persuasion, dissuasion—all the ways in which men and women interpret the experience of living. It is the science of language, which includes semiotics, gesture, memory. It is a process rather than a self-contained subject;[4] I should prefer to call it a service-industry, capable of almost endless application. So many other disciplines have made use of rhetoric to organize their techniques of invention, discovery, expression: logic, philosophy (especially moral and political philosophy), the sciences (I am thinking in particular of Francis Bacon's awareness of rhetoric's role in communication within and without the sciences), painting, architecture, music, and so on. As Omer Talon, the colleague of Peter Ramus put it, rhetoric, not having a definite domain, could spread through all the arts: *in immenso rerum omnium atque artium campo libere vagari.*[5] For over two thousand years rhetoric controlled a hard-to-define territory, existing on several planes and in more than one mode—no single metaphor is going to be able to capture it—which other disciplines visited frequently, taking away with them knowledge and insight into how men speak and think, how they persuade, how they can be persuaded. In a sense, whoever wishes to communicate must use rhetoric in one form or another. "Whenever there is persuasion," Kenneth Burke wrote, "there is rhetoric, and wherever there is 'meaning', there is 'persuasion'."[6] Human communication is seldom that ideal of neutral performance which some opponents of rhetoric espouse, whereby one person addresses another without any thought of persuading, or convincing, or moving them, with no concern whether understanding or agreement take place. The neutral transmission of information – perception without judgment or evaluation – is a myth, as Gregory Bateson has shown: "the logician's dream that men should communicate only by unambiguous digital signals has not come true and is unlikely to."[7] One of the charges against rhetoric, that it fostered ambiguity and confusion, is in fact a charge against language itself. Where seventeenth-century theorists wished to abolish language and replace it by ciphers, we now know enough about the functioning of all sign-systems to be aware of the inevitable complexities inherent in the act of interpretation. Words, like other signs, have an arbitrary meaning conferred on them by a language, or society, or social group, or family, or individual; the act of de-coding is both pluralistic and individualistic, subject to conventions well or badly understood, subject to the moods or emotions of speaker(s) and hearer(s). It seems futile to accuse the arts of speech of not having remedied the deficiencies inherent in the very nature of language. Our awareness of the inter-subjectivity of communication, as of all other modes of interpreting the world, must make us sceptical of those who attack rhetoric in the name of some system or category that claims a monopoly on truth.

In examining three famous attacks on rhetoric, by Plato, Kant, and Croce, I want to draw attention to the categories used in their discussion, especially what I call excluding categories. These are often dichotomies, binary categories in which one side is right, the other wrong; one side is privileged as authentic, legitimate, true, while the other receives the negatives of those concepts and is dismissed from serious consideration. The enunciation of these categories is often arbitrary, and works less by rigorous analytical deduction than by analogy, association, insinuation, manoeuvres performed with a polemical and destructive intent, sometimes openly.

The first, and most influential of these attacks, is the *Gorgias*,[8] a masterpiece of rhetorical and argumentative strategy. In this polemical dialogue Socrates hunts the Sophists down remorselessly, taking their claim that rhetoric "brings freedom to mankind in general and to each man dominion over others in his own country" through "the power to convince by your words" (452d–e), and denying rhetoric any inherent subject-matter, any monopoly over persuasion (453–54), and any ability to tell right from wrong (455a). Socratic dialectic begins to drive in a series of wedges, binary categories, that effectively separate rhetoric from any serious or worth-while human activity. Socrates – so less diffident or "ignorant" here than elsewhere – claims to know the difference between "the true" and "the false" (458a), and asserts that rhetoric "has no need to know the truth about things but merely to discover a technique of persuasion, so as to appear among the ignorant to have more knowledge than the expert" (459c). Gorgias assents to these statements, but one cannot help feeling that Plato has destroyed the potential of the dialogue form by making the opponent such a dummy: the result resembles more the hunting of the Snark than of Leviathan. Gorgias' young friend Polus is brought into the action, only to be put down by Socrates, told to "restrain his exuberance," speak briefly and to the point (461–62).

Having confirmed his dominance over his opponents, Socrates proceeds to deliver the kernel of his argument (462–66), a passage so famous, or notorious, that one barely needs quote it. Yet it may be good to be reminded that Socrates does not work by an open-minded evaluation of the whole art, allowing both good and bad sides to appear, but rams home a series of dichotomies, or excluding categories, in which rhetoric is dismissed by analogy. It is said to be not an art but "only a routine and a knack," which "produces gratification and pleasure" rather than knowledge or truth, and is part of the same activity— "an activity that is not very reputable"—as cookery and medicine. These arts deal with the outer rather than the inner man, yet Socrates trivializes them (since both preparing food and curing disease help to keep even philosophers alive) by dismissing them as forms of "flattery". Flattery, the genus, "having no thought for what is best, . . . regularly uses pleasure as a bait to catch folly and deceives it into believing that she is of supreme worth." Rhetoric, too, as one of the species of flattery, comes under the condemnation of being "bad . . . because it aims at what is pleasant, ignoring the good," so that Socrates feels justified in refusing "the name of art to anything irrational." The whole discussion is based on a series of simple binary models: rhetoric is equated with the arts of appearance rather than reality; rhetoric deals with surfaces, philosophy with depths. It has no real knowledge (*episteme*), but only urges on us convictions or opinions (*doxa*).

It is rather late in the day to become indignant about this brilliant and unscrupulous performance. Elsewhere, in the *Phaedrus*, Plato will allow more value to rhetoric, provided that it is integrated, or subordinated, to his philosophic system. But the *Gorgias* resembles too much a jealous and one-sided contest for superiority in which the proponent does not hesitate to travesty the arguments of the other side, and to deny them any coherent or rational case. It may well be, as Nietzsche thought,[9] that Plato was envious of the rhetoricians: he certainly makes Gorgias deliver some megalomaniac claims for the domain of rhetoric, for instance that it "includes practically all other faculties under her control" (456b). It may be true, as Gerald Else has argued, that he thought he could do better at rhetoric than the rhetoricians.[10] At all events, it was a brilliant performance by Plato, and one must agree with Cicero's paradox that "it was when making fun of orators that he himself seemed to be the consummate orator."[11] Yet, if it is rhetoric, it is rhetoric of a highly dubious sort, manoeuvring categories and analogies by sleight-of-hand to effect an arbitrary identification of rhetoric with ignoble and disreputable arts, and seeking to arouse in the listener or reader emotions of disgust and contempt. Certainly, if rhetoric were concerned with nothing more significant than pleasure or power at any price then it would be properly dismissed. Yet its function, even then, was much more valuable, and I am left with the feeling that if it had not seemed necessary to assert territorial rights Plato and Socrates could have produced far more convincing arguments for the other side. Between them they embodied a remarkable union of philosophy and rhetoric.

Immanuel Kant, in his *Critique of Aesthetic Judgement*, also combined formidable intellectual resources with great expressive power. Here, too, excluding categories are used to privilege one discipline and dismiss another: only, here, the favoured discipline is not philosophy (which Kant would probably have thought too valuable to put in the same scales with rhetoric), but poetry. While poetry had, from the time of Aristotle, been regarded as essentially identical with rhetoric (having metrics as an additional resource),[12] an autonomous poetic began to emerge only in the eighteenth century. In Kant's work, and for the first time in history, to my knowledge, poetry is used as a stick to beat rhetoric. The arts of speech are said to be rhetoric and poetry:

> *Rhetoric* is the art of transacting a serious business of the understanding as if it were a free play of the imagination; poetry that of conducting a free play of the imagination as if it were a serious business of the understanding.[13]

Every reader notes the antithesis: yet the distinction is more elaborate than antithesis, is in fact made by the rhetorical figure *antimetabole*, or repetition with inversion ("eat to live, not live to eat"). The function of this "sharp and witty figure," according to one rhetorician, is to "show out of the same words a pithy distinction of meaning."[14] Kant is cunningly using rhetoric against itself.

But as he develops his paradox Kant breaks up the coherence of rhetoric. Whereas both rhetoric and poetry had been given the triple functions of *docere*, *movere*, and *delectare*, Kant fractures this triad to privilege the poet and handicap the orator. Poetry is defined as "a free play of the imagination," which promises no intellectual or cognitive function, but in fact performs one. The orator, by contrast, "announces a serious business, and for the purpose of entertaining his audience conducts it as if it were a mere *play* with ideas" (p. 185). The orator is denied the power of *movere*, an odd and arbitrary gesture given the remarkable growth in the seventeenth and eighteenth centuries—above all in Germany, ironically enough—of detailed analysis of rhetoric's power to move the feelings, an analytical psychology of language of remarkable richness.[15] Kant does not enquire how the orator works: he just denies him seriousness or understanding, reducing him to the level of an ineffectual entertainer. Continuing his demolition without examining rhetorical theory, and without analysing a single text, he pronounces that the orator totally "fails to come up to his promise, and a thing, too, which is his avowed business, namely, the engagement of the understanding to some end." This point, unsupported by rational arguments, is achieved by the manipulation of a binary category in the manner of a conjurer, or a card-sharper. Give with one hand, take away with the other, and rely on the audience not noticing the subterfuge.

When he comes to talk about rhetoric on its own, in section 53, Kant expresses his animus openly:

> Rhetoric, so far as this is taken to mean the art of persuasion, i.e. the art of deluding by means of a fair semblance . . . is a dialectic, which borrows from poetry only so much as is necessary to win over men's minds to the side of the speaker before they have weighed the matter, and to rob their verdict of its freedom. Hence it can be recommended neither for the bar nor the pulpit.

For such serious activities it would be "below the dignity" of their existence to know "the art of talking men round and prejudicing them in favour of any one" (p. 192). Kant rejects "the machinery of persuasion, which, being equally available for the purpose of putting a fine gloss or a cloak upon vice and error, fails to rid one completely of the lurking suspicion that one is being artfully hoodwinked" (p. 193). Almost as an afterthought, he reverts to his binary model, claiming that "In poetry everything is straight and above board. It shows its hand . . . it does not seek to steal upon and ensnare the understanding with a sensuous presentation" (ibid.).

These are the arguments of Plato, re-stated with more violence. Again the conception is totally negative; no contrary evidence is brought in. Persuasion is identified with violence, deception, imprisonment, exploitation. Kant apparently concedes the orator total effectiveness—he seems to succeed automatically in his goal. This is to accept the claim made by rhetoricians for the practical efficacy of their discipline while then turning it round against them. Yet Kant's re-formulation of the power of rhetoric would deprive men of the power to resist, deny them reason, or free will. Kant makes men into automata in order to stigmatise rhetoric. His antipathy to the discipline leads him to make a false conception of man. So, more explicitly, he adds a footnote to express his

> disapproval of an insidious art that knows how, in matters of moment, to move men like machines to a judgment that must lose all its weight with them upon calm reflection. Force and elegance of speech (which together constitute rhetoric) belong to fine art; but oratory (*ars oratoria*), being the art of playing for one's own purpose upon the weaknesses of

men (let this purpose be ever so good in intention or even in fact) merits no *respect* whatever ["ist gar keiner Achtung würdig"]. (ibid.)

Bent on driving the last nails into the coffin of rhetoric, Kant even falsifies history, claiming that "Besides, both at Athens and at Rome, it only attained its greatest height at a time when the state was hastening to its decay, and genuine patriotic sentiment was a thing of the past" (ibid.). The truth is quite the opposite, of course. He who is willing to distort historical record in this way barely deserves serious attention.

The significance of Kant's attack on rhetoric is three-fold. First, it consists of a mere rejection, unargued, using tactics of smear and insinuation. Secondly, like Plato's attack it devalues rhetoric by putting it in the inferior position in a binary category. Thirdly, it is itself rhetorical, using a number of strategies to confuse and alarm the reader. He is to be stampeded into a judgment against rhetoric by being told that otherwise rhetoric will stampede *him* to judgment, manipulate him like a machine over which some other person has total control— an early premonition of Dr. Frankenstein!—to a decision which he will certainly regret on consideration. Rhetoric will force you to a wrong or evil decision. Kant rejects persuasion, yet is willing to accept "Force and elegance of speech": but you cannot drive a wedge into rhetoric like this, especially since persuasion (forbidden) derives from force (accepted). Samuel IJsseling has commented that Kant not only provides "no critical justification for the use of such opinions but he even attempts quite inadvertently to force them upon his readers" (op. cit., p. 86). If Kant can claim that the orator deprives man of the freedom to think for himself, then he would be guilty of the same failing, except for the fact that in his formulation he has left out man's constant possession of free-will, reason, and judgment.

Any mere modern student of rhetoric must feel temerarious criticizing one of the greatest of philosophers, but I cannot believe that Kant even attempted to do justice to rhetoric. His attempt to bully the reader lacks subtlety, coherence, and persuasiveness. It is another example of bad rhetoric.

A hundred years after Kant, and writing from a quite different standpoint, Benedetto Croce also eliminated rhetoric from an aesthetic system. Since Croce's whole *Aesthetic* is committed to a holistic or monist concept of art, which refuses to make any distinction between style and content, idea and expression, it is not surprising that he should have rejected rhetoric. In an earlier theoretical chapter, with the title "Indivisibility of expression into modes or degrees,"[16] he operates a whole series of excluding categories of the right/wrong model. Rhetoric's "division of expression into various grades" is simply "illegitimate" (Croce is the law-maker, it seems); the distinctions of various types of trope and figure "reveal their philosophic nullity when the attempt is made to develop them in precise definitions, because they either grasp the void or fall into the absurd" (pp. 68f.). The emotive use of such words as "nullity," "void," "absurd" should not obscure the point that, contrary to Croce's claims, rhetoric (alone!) is able to offer "precise definitions" of all these devices. Croce takes as an example the "very common" definition of metaphor as consisting "of another word used in place of the proper word." He has manipulated the definition by introducing the concept "proper" – metaphor is *translatio* or transference of any appropriate word – and then he indulges in sarcasm:

> Now why give oneself this trouble? Why substitute the improper word for the proper word? Why take the worse and longer road when you know the shorter and better road?

A tyro in logic could see how Croce has loaded his argument by slipping in the terms "improper," "worse," and "longer". There would be many ways of discovering why we use metaphor, but they will not be discovered by such methods.

For Croce there is one terminology that is "fixed as correct" for each writer or context, after which "all other uses of it become improper or tropical" (p. 72). This yes/no, right/wrong model reappears in a later section of the *Aesthetic*, where Croce gives a series of what he calls "Historical Sketches" of particular doctrines, which are introduced by an allegory – a well-known rhetorical figure, of course. The birth of a science is said to be "like that of a living being: its later development consists, like every life, in fighting the difficulties and errors, general and particular, which lurk in its path on every side" (pp. 420–21). The "forms of error" are numerous, mingle with "the truth," and are not easily uprooted. It goes without saying, by now, that rhetoric is one of these "errors," one of these "negations of the concept of art itself," and Croce calls for "scientific criticism" to be perpetually on the alert, not to rest content with mere statement of the truth, for it is a sad fact that

> a simple affirmation of the truth has not always been accompanied by any considerable recapture of enemy territory (p. 421).

Croce sees the role of his new discipline, aesthetics, as being aggressive, combating rhetoric; indeed earlier he recommended that, despite all his criticism of them,

> the rhetorical categories should continue to appear in schools: to be criticized there. The errors of the past must not be forgotten and no more said, and truth cannot be kept alive save by making them combat errors. Unless an account of the rhetorical categories be given, accompanied by a criticism of them, there is a risk of their springing up again . . . (p. 72-73).

Rhetoric is to be kept on as a tame Hydra for the budding aesthetician to decapitate from time to time.

Croce's militant attitude is clearly visible, and colours every part of his supposedly historical survey. Classical rhetoric is said to have consisted of "a manual or *vademecum* for advocates and politicians," giving advice "to those striving to produce certain effects by means of speech" (p. 422). Rhetoric's organic function in the state is here minimized, its power to develop human expressiveness passed over, and its relevance to literature and education in every form ignored. Croce is a master of the rhetorical figure known as *meoisis* or belittling, and he immediately passes on to Plato's criticism of the Sophists— so much for the history of rhetoric! After these two pages Croce gives two pages to its history down to Kant, with whose "gar keiner Achtung würdig" he naturally identifies himself. The Middle Ages is passed over for an account of the Renaissance which is another travesty of history. Where one might have stressed the rediscovery of rhetoric for the *vita activa* in Florence, or its central role in the revival of education, the vast number of treatises in Latin and all the vernaculars, its great and demonstrable influence on literature, law, politics, the fine arts—instead of all this, Croce singles out three writers who supposedly criticized rhetoric for failing to be a systematic science: Vives, Ramus, and Patrizzi (pp. 424f.). Certainly these writers—like so many rhetoricians before or since—attacked the weaknesses of other rhetoric-books while recommending their own (if rhetoricians had not been so ready to criticize their predecessors they might not have given so many weapons to the enemies of rhetoric). But what Croce does not go on to show is the very great contribution that they made to rhetoric. Vives' *De ratione dicendi* is the first modern treatise to be devoted to the anatomy and physiognomy of style, perhaps the first modern stylistics. His *De Tradendis Disciplinis* (nowhere mentioned by Croce) is one of the most thorough and intelligent accounts of the role of rhetoric in education. The reforms of Ramus and Talon may indeed have separated rhetoric from dialectic, but in their systematic development of *elocutio* and their espousal of the vernaculars, the Ramists had a great and beneficial influence in applying rhetoric to literature.

Having given such a misleading account of this trio, Croce perverts history further by casting them as reformers "held up to odium by the traditionalists" and swept away by them. In fact Vives' rhetorical works won much recognition and were widely used, while the Ramist reforms were absorbed by many writers, not all of them obviously Ramistic. The rhetorical tradition was much more flexible than this historian could conceive. And, despite the weaknesses that he diagnoses, rhetoric persisted, for Croce can list treatises appearing up to the 1880s. Yet he declares it dead.

Turning from history to analysis, Croce levels the standard criticism of the systematic philosopher, that

> Rhetoric can never be considered a regular science, being formed of a congeries of widely dissimilar cognitions. It included descriptions of passions and affections, comparisons of political and judicial institutions, theories of the abbreviated syllogism or enthymeme and of proof leading to a probable conclusion, pedagogic and popular exposition, literary elocution, declamation and mimicry, mnemonic, and so forth (pp. 423 ff.).

Croce's sarcasm has the subtlety of the early novels of Dickens; yet, in reply, we note that he has lumped together the diverse social, political, and cultural roles of rhetoric with its teachings on psychology and with its internal processes: *inventio, dispositio, elocutio, pronuntiatio,* and *memoria.* These are all perfectly relevant in their contexts, but arranged higgledy-piggledy like this cannot but seem incoherent. The same trick could be played with the philosophy of Aristotle, or Descartes, or Hegel, or any thinker with rich and diverse interests. The fact is that Croce nowhere tries to take rhetoric seriously, being content to score easy debating points. Thus he takes the concept of ornament in its degraded modern sense of "something additional superimposed" upon ordinary speech (p. 427), before subjecting it to mockery. Yet traditional beliefs held that the language of art is the language of nature heightened and intensified. The stress in rhetorical theory on the orator or poet having to feel deeply the emotions he wishes to represent or arouse proves that rhetoric conceived of a continuum of speech and feelings, a coherence between inner and outer states, rather than the outer being draped over the inner like some garment. To get at the truth it is necessary to reverse his terms: in rhetoric "beautiful form" is not "an addition or embroidery" but a "spontaneous thing"—and its spontaneity, we would add, is the result of art, imitation, and exercise.

When he comes to discuss the classifications of tropes and figures Croce heaps up lists in a throw-away manner ("Figures of speech amounted to a score or so . . . ," "figures of thought to about the same number") before dismissing them all: "considered rationally they are simply capricious." The fact that "many classes of the ornate" appear as tropes in some systems and figures in others—this is another exaggeration: the number of devices appearing in both lists is very small—supposedly proves that it is "the arbitrary caprice of an individual rhetorician" that determines it. We can concede that rhetoric, attempting to cope with all linguistic phenomena, proliferated instances at the expense of tidy schematization; yet we note that while Croce has seized on, and exaggerated this weakness, he has totally failed to notice the stress given by classical and Renaissance rhetoricians to the *functions* of the figures and tropes, in representing or arousing the feelings, in giving imaginative unity and coherence, and so on. He claims that Longinus is alone in discussing the function of a figure (metaphor), yet one reading of the classic texts will show how much he has ignored.

His travesty of the doctrine of *elocutio* is the more surprising in that in a later section, separated from this by four more pages of mockery and abuse ("the fallacies of school doctrine," "its inherent absurdity") Croce comes to discuss those modern writers who revived traditional rhetorical theory about the functional nature of the figures. When Vico stated that figures and tropes "are not 'caprices of pleasure' but 'necessities of the human mind'," Croce claims that he was "framing his new concept of poetical imagination," necessitating a "wholesale reconstruction of the theory of rhetoric" (p. 432): yet the idea is as old as Aristotle. Du Marsais is given credit for attacking "the theory of rhetorical ornament" in 1730 when he wrote that the schemes or tropes derive from life:

> nothing is more natural, ordinary and common than figures: more figures of speech are used in the town square on a market-day than in many days of academical discussion.

Yet this idea can be found in Aristotle, Quintilian, Longinus, Puttenham, Abraham Fraunce, Sidney, and no doubt others.[17] Croce imagines that by referring to Du Marsais giving "instances of quite obvious and spontaneous expressions in which Rhetoric cannot refuse to recognize the figures of apostrophe, congeries, interrogation, ellipsis, prosopopoeia" (p. 433), he is somehow disproving the theory of rhetorical ornament. But he is in fact proving another point, the organic relationship between the figures and the feelings, that unity formed by the "natural language of the passions."

At this point in his argument Croce seems to have gotten his historical perspective reversed. Whereas he has been arguing for the progressive decline of rhetoric from the time of Plato's criticism of the Sophists—a decline, if so, that had all the opposite features—he now begins to write in terms of an evolution or welcome advance. After Du Marsais, he says,

> the psychological interpretation of figures of speech, the first stage towards their aesthetic criticism, was not allowed to drop.

Although the psychological interpretation of the figures had been going on for two thousand years (in addition to Aristotle and Quintilian we should mention Longinus and Demetrius), for Croce it gets under way with the *Elements of Criticism* (1762) of Henry Home, Lord Kames, who discovered that the rationale of the figures consists "in the passional element," analysing them "in the light of the passional faculty." This supposedly new movement is continued with Blair's *Lectures on Rhetoric and belles lettres* (1783), which defines the figures as "language suggested by imagination or passion," and it finds analogous expressions in France (Marmontel) and Italy (Cesarotti), while in Germany "an effort was made by Herder to interpret tropes and metaphors as Vico had done, that is to say as essential to primitive language and poetry" – an attempt of which Croce naturally approves.

With Herder we have reached Romanticism, which, Croce happily notes, "was the ruin of the theory of ornament, and caused it practically to be thrown on the scrap-heap." But accuracy makes him record that the Hydra has not yet been wiped out, for even Herder ("whose knowledge of art," Croce observes contemptuously, "seems to have been confined to a little music and a great deal of rhetoric"), even Schelling, Solger, Hegel and others, still retained discussions "devoted to metaphor, trope and allegory" – "for tradition's sake," he adds apologetically, "without severe scrutiny." Croce heaps odium on other writers who retain rhetoric, recommends De Sanctis and his "anti-rhetoric," and closes with another invocation of what he claims to be

> the very nature of aesthetic activity, which does not lend itself to partition; there is no such thing as activity of type *a* or type *b*, nor can the same concept be expressed now in one way, now in another (p. 436).

One wonders what Croce would have made of modern discussions of the *topos* as a kernel of associations, used and varied by poets across several centuries and in many languages; or of our rediscovery of the force of literary conventions. As two modern historians of literary criticism put it, in his monistic system

> no distinction can be made between state of mind and linguistic expression. Croce consistently denies the validity of all stylistic and rhetorical categories, the distinction between style and form, between form and content, and ultimately, between word and soul, expression and intuition. In Croce, this series of identifications leads to a theoretical paralysis: an initially genuine insight into the implications of the poetical process is pushed so far that no distinctions are possible.[18]

Whatever result it might have on his criticism in general, it seems clear that Croce's particular aesthetic theories denied him any possibility of understanding rhetoric. We might, then, simply dismiss him as an idiosyncrasy, were it not for his influence on several generations, and for the fact that he was able to ally his own theory to a much wider tradition of hostility to rhetoric. He did his best to "recapture enemy territory."

II

I AM NOT WISHING to argue that all these attacks on rhetoric were misplaced: Plato's exposure of the moral relativism of rhetoric was entirely correct, since the existence of a *vir malus peritus dicendi* is an obvious possibility.[19] Only we would add that other disciplines can also be perverted to the service of evil: think of what Nazi ideology did to philosophy, law, biology, and medicine. My point is that many of the anti-rhetorical treatises are territorial disputes which use what I have called excluding categories, dichotomies that reject rhetoric by simply juxtaposing it with some other discipline in the form of positive against negative. The defenders of rhetoric could either deny the negative accusations, or they could simply turn the antithesis round against philosophy. While Cicero answered Plato's attack by proposing a peace-treaty between rhetoric and philosophy, in which certain gifted individuals (such as himself) should master both disciplines, Quintilian took direct issue with the philosophers, urging that "the principles of upright and honourable living" should not be the prerogative of philosophy alone.[20] Rhetoric and philosophy were once one discipline, but due to the great demand for rhetoric in public affairs the rhetoricians "ceased to study moral philosophy, and ethics, thus abandoned by the orators, became the prey of weaker intellects," namely the philosophers (I, pr. 13 ff.).

So, under Quintilian's leadership rhetoric will approach those authors who "usurped the better part of the art of oratory," and "demand back what is ours by right" (I, pr. 17). Quintilian does not have a great deal to say about philosophy, but he allows himself some scathing remarks about those "who make ostentatious professions . . . of being philosophers" (XI, i. 33); he argues that the orator must know philosophy, but not that form practiced in theoretical isolation from society. In reclaiming their own, orators must turn it to "the actual practice and experience of life" (XII, ii. 6–9; 4.385 f.), above all cultivating moral philosophy or ethics (XII, ii. 15–20; 4.389 ff.). His parting crack is against those arrogant and slothful men who desert oratory for the philosophers' schools and there pretend a "moral superiority, while leading a life of debauchery at home." These are pretenders in a way that an orator could never be: *Philosophia enim simulari potest, eloquentia non potest* (XII. iii. 12): but, we must reply, everything can be simulated.

If even Quintilian was not above answering abuse with abuse, later defenders of rhetoric went to more violent lengths. Marius Nizolius wanted to "throw out all dialecticians and metaphysicians, and put in their place grammarians and rhetoricians," rejecting the logical works of Aristotle as "vicious."[21] Ramus' violence against Aristotle is only too well known, and in the Humanists' response in general we seem to move from one extreme to the other. Ermolao Barbaro attacks the scholastics from the stock Humanist viewpoints of their uncouth language, and their non-involvement with the *vita activa*: without "practical knowledge . . . a man as man is not a philosopher, but a monster" (Breen, p. 35). Melanchthon opposes Pico on similar grounds, and draws attention to his polemical use of binary categories (Breen, p. 55). Yet in turn he subordinates philosophy to rhetoric, placing philosophy, as Quirinus Breen puts it, "in a kind of beggarly position, for he does not leave it free to be itself" (p. 50). One of the constant features of the disputes among the Liberal Arts, indeed, is the lack of any longer view: the opponent of a discipline does his best to annihilate it as quickly and comprehensively as possible, not asking whether he or his mother-discipline might ever need it again. If some of the more extreme defenders of rhetoric had been given the other Liberal Arts together with a destruct button, I fear that they might have wiped them out altogether. At times they remind me of Puritan soldiers smashing stained glass windows and religious statues.

The moral to be deduced from this survey concerns the attitude that we, as defenders of rhetoric, should take towards its opponents. My belief is that while we should do everything possible towards establishing the right historical context, we are not bound to endorse rhetoricians in their swinging attacks. The spirit in which we ought to approach these disputes is exemplified by Mr. Breen when he attacks Melanchthon for indiscriminately identifying rhetoric and philosophy: it is all very well to assert the primacy of rhetoric,

> But if Homer, Demosthenes, Caesar, and Octavian are to be equated with Plato and Aristotle as philosophers one may as well say that words have lost their meanings (p. 45).

An example of how not to handle this issue is provided, in my opinion, by J. E. Seigel. In what remains a useful and valuable book he falls into the common error of not only explicating his authors but also of taking their part: he identifies with their view-points, and if he does not always explicitly endorse them he almost never criticizes them, either. The issue at stake is the Florentine Humanists' tendency to defend rhetoric by attacking and despising philosophy. Salutati and Leonard Bruni do so rather mildly, but Lorenzo Valla in *De Voluptate* (ca. 1431) gives philosophy the inferior role, claiming that rhetoricians have excelled them even at their own game: "Orators treated the questions of ethics 'much more clearly, weightily, magnificently' than did 'the obscure, squalid, and anemic philosophers'." Valla revives Quintilian's claim that the philosophers originally stole from the orators, and wishes that Cicero " 'would have attacked the thieving philosophers with the sword of eloquence—queen of all things— entrusted to him, and had punished the malefactors'."[22] Carrying the attack ino the enemy's camp, Valla claims that the moral ideas which the philosophers have discovered (especially *honestas*) are worthless: " 'Part of the philosophers' throats we shall cut with their own sword, the other part we shall incite to an internal war and a mutual destruction' " (Seigel, p. 148).

The quarrel between rhetoric and philosophy is an old one, and Valla does not mind reviving old weapons, attacking all classical philosophy, since it was produced by pagans, whom Jerome called "fomenters of heresy" (pp. 154–56), making what Mr. Seigel neutrally describes as a "total indictment" of Boethius for having preferred philosophy to both Christianity and rhetoric (p. 157 f.). Given the Florentine Humanists' need to validate their own existence we must not expect from them a balanced account of medieval philosophy, but there are limits, and when Valla tries to show that " 'the major part of Latin logic is false' " (pp. 161 ff.), I lose all sympathy with him. Mr. Seigel, however, can, with a straight face, summarize Valla as having declared "all traditional philosophy to be outside the pale of true learning" (p. 168), without seeing how absurd that proposition is. One word in his summary may, however, be a criticism — but it may also be an endorsement:

> Valla's redefinition of philosophy had the primary effect of making philosophy a part of rhetoric, and thus of helping to accomplish that revenge on behalf of Oratory which Valla criticized Cicero for not having carried far enough (p. 167).

"Revenge": is it fitting that discussions of philosophy should be conducted according to the code of the vendetta? Two quotations from Shakespeare come to mind: one from *Troilus and Cressida*, where Hector says that

> pleasure and revenge
> Have ears more deaf than adders to the voice
> Of any true decision.   (II.ii.171ff.)

The other is from *The Tempest*, where Prospero says that

> The rarer action is
> In virtue than in vengeance.   (V.i.27f.)

To turn the tables, gently, on the rhetoricians who attack philosophy, I would say that they need to use more reason, and more virtue. To answer abuse with abuse is to answer one blinding with another: in the end the Liberal Arts will be unable to see anything, least of all each other. It is distressing to observe disciplines which are meant to help, to complement each other, fall out. To adapt Alexander Pope's couplet about the quarrels between Wit and Judgment, so too, Rhetoric and Philosophy

> often are at strife,
> Tho' meant each other's Aid, like *Man* and *Wife*.[23]

III

THE POLEMICS for and against rhetoric may clarify some issues, but they obscure many more. All too often the defence of rhetoric merely takes the form of an answer to Plato: the defender accepts the terms and issues defined by Plato and hotly rejects them. He does not think the issue out afresh, nor conceive of it in other categories, or on a new time-scale. Like much controversy, his answer is determined by, becomes parasitic on, the original attack. Samuel IJsseling has argued that the attack on rhetoric was beneficial to Plato, aiding the development of his own ideas and the establishment of metaphysics as a philosophical discipline, above and beyond words.[24] We are glad that Plato, at least, profited from the encounter: rhetoric and its defenders did not!

The terms and issues defined by Plato are still with us. One of the greatest scholars of our time in the field of Renaissance studies, Paul Oskar Kristeller, has recently surveyed the history of rhetoric.[25] In his account of its Greek origins he writes that Plato "was a bitter critic of the Sophists and of their rhetoric, and branded it as a fake knowledge that produced opinions but no firm knowledge" (p. 218). That is a fair summary of the *Gorgias*, and it is followed by an account of the *Phaedrus*, with its partial rehabilitation of a "rhetoric disciplined by philosophical and ethical considerations and thus capable of serving as an instrument of truth." That is, of course, the function given to rhetoric in its epideictic form, which from Plato himself down to the eighteenth century stressed the duty of poet and orator to celebrate virtue and attack vice,[26] and Professor Kristeller gives sympathetic attention to those writers who linked philosophy (especially ethics) with rhetoric, such as Isocrates, Aristotle, and Cicero. Yet at the end of his survey he reveals his fundamental allegiance:

> I am at heart a Platonist, on the issue of rhetoric as on many, though not on all, others. Rhetoric in all its forms is based on mere opinion, and therefore it should be subordinated to philosophy, that is, to all forms of valid knowledge where such knowledge is available (p. 258).

Rhetoric is useful "for expressing and conveying knowledge and insight": but only as a servant.

> Yet in our universe of discourse, and in our system of education that should reflect this universe, rhetoric should not occupy the center, but be subordinated, not only to philosophy, but also to the sciences as well as to poetry and the other arts (p. 259).

That is a fairly comprehensive subordination, coming as it does as the last paragraph of the book (one recalls Aristotle's teaching that the end of an oration is its most important part, leaving the strongest impression on the listener). Yet it merely returns us to Plato's binary category, setting real knowledge (*episteme*) against opinion (*doxa*). Further, Professor Kristeller aligns himself "with many respectable philosophers" in holding that "our true intellectual and moral freedom" consists in "the submission to truth and to valid norms" (p. 258). What disturbs me about this discussion is his declaration of a single category, "truth" or "knowledge," as being the sole province of philosophy. Surely the history of philosophy, sociology, anthropology, and linguistics over the last hundred years has taught us how problematic such concepts as "truth" or "reality" really are, and how equally problematic is the language in which we formulate them. Given any such monistic conception of truth one is tempted to reply, in the words of the hero—a failed and disappointed hero—of a poem by Clough, that in future

> I will look straight out, see things, not try to evade them;
> Fact shall be fact for me; and the Truth the Truth as ever,
> Flexible, changeable, vague, and multiform, and doubtful.[27]

By which I do not deny the concept of truth, but suggest that it is not an absolute, nor the prerogative of one group of scholars rather than another. Truth is relative, as all important concepts and values are relative, their exact nature being the individual's task to discover or ratify for himself. Our whole act of experiencing reality is subjective, our use of language is inter-subjective, and any one in search of objective truths in a world after Nietzsche, Husserl and Popper, say, is doomed to a dusty answer. Plato attacked the Sophists for their ethical relativism, and while many scholars would agree that the attack was unfair, we have now reached a stage in which relativism can be defended—not cynicism, not amorality, not indifference, but an honest admission that, in phenomenological terms, the acts of perceiving the world, interpreting its signs, evaluating its actions, are all irremediably personal. They are not solipsistic, since individual interpretations can be shared, and in language as an exchange-system we can watch the process of individual experience accumulating into group experiences, of a constant reciprocal movement between the person and larger social units. There can be no single, absolute, eternally valid truth.

With the disappearance of a monist or categorical concept of the truth the way is open, it seems to me, for rhetoric to achieve respectability, at least, with philosophers for its ability to present all that may be said on a topic, and for its encouragement to take part in dialogue.[28] A distinguished historian of Greek rhetoric has explained that "Gorgias' fondness for antithesis is a direct reflection of his belief that truth is relative and requires the clear expression of contrasts and alternatives as the basis of definition and choice."[29] In larger stylistic forms and genres, such as the thesis, in which students argued on either side of a topic, or the dialogue, which could present many differentiated view-points, rhetoric had a positive influence on the process of discussion, analysis, and judgment.

In a sense, the dispute is an unreal one: thought cannot do without expression, any more than language can exist without ideas. At all events, it now seems pointless to dismiss rhetoric for not discovering "the truth," and it seems unhelpful to continue to rank the arts and sciences in some form of hierarchy: each has its own role, and the totality of human knowledge requires cooperation rather than aggression.

Our task as students of rhetoric in a time when more information about rhetoric, philosophy, education, and related disciplines is available than ever before in world history, is to see rhetoric in her terms, and in our own. We must understand rhetoric synchronically, as a discipline or system in its own right; also diachronically, as a way of writing, thinking, seeing, and teaching which had an incalculable influence on Western culture for over 2,000 years. Our position is rooted simultaneously in the past and present: we are ancients in a world of moderns; and moderns in a world of ancients. I do not regard this dual perspective as disabling, but it means that we must be able to move between the two points with sympathy for, and understanding of, both.

Notes

1. Cf. Jonas Barish, "The Antitheatrical Prejudice," *Critical Quarterly* 8 (1966): 329–48, and Brian Vickers, "Francis Bacon's Use of Theatrical Imagery," *Studies in the Literary Imagination* 4 (1971): 189–226.

2. For modern studies see Samuel IJsseling, *Rhetoric and Philosophy in Conflict. An Historical Survey* (The Hague, 1976); Jerrold Seigel, *Rhetoric and Philosophy in Renaissance Humanism. The Union of Eloquence and Wisdom, Petrarch to Valla* (Princeton, 1968); Quirinus Breen, *Christianity and Humanism. Studies in the History of Ideas* (Grand Rapids, Michigan, 1968), ed. N. P. Ross, pp. 1–68, which collects Breen's essays and translations of the dispute between Pico della Mirandola, Barbaro, and Melanchthon, first published in *Journal of the History of Ideas* 13 (1952), 384–426; (however it must be noted that Breen's interpretation of Pico's part in this debate as a straightforward attack on rhetoric—rather than a mock-attack, parodying the extreme position of the logicians—is too simple, as any reader with a knowledge of Renaissance techniques in epideictic and mock-epideictic will recognize. A valuable corrective by Letizia Panizza, "Pico's 1485 Defence of Philosophy vs. Eloquence and Socratic Irony" was presented

at the 1979 conference of the International Society for Neo-Latin Studies, and is forthcoming in the *Acta*); Alain Michel, *Rhétorique et Philosophie chez Cicéron* (Paris, 1960); Hanna Barbara Gerl, *Rhetorik als Philosophie. Lorenzo Valla* (München, 1974).

3. Isaiah Berlin, *Concepts and Categories* (Oxford, 1980), pp. 10–11.

4. See the paper by Michael Leff, above page 71.

5. Talon (or Talaeus), *Institutiones oratoriae* (1545), p. 8; cit. Basil Muntéano, *Constantes Dialectiques en Littérature et en Histoire* (Paris, 1967), pp. 151 f. The essays on rhetoric in this volume remain some of the most lucid and intelligent analyses of the rhetorical tradition, especially in France.

6. Kenneth Burke, *A Rhetoric of Motives* (New York, 1950), p. 172.

7. Bateson, "Redundancy and coding," in *Steps to an Ecology of Mind* (London, 1973), p. 388. For further comment on the fallacies of value-free, emotion-free communication, as manifested in the histories of rhetoric by W. S. Howell, see my "Rhetorical and anti-rhetorical tropes: On writing the history of *elocutio*," *Comparative Criticism* 3 (1981): 105–32, at pp. 111–13.

8. *Gorgias*, tr. W. D. Woodhead in *The Collected Dialogues of Plato*, ed. E. Hamilton and H. Cairns (New York, 1963), pp. 229–307.

9. IJsseling, pp. 9, 107, citing Nietzsche, *Werke*, 3 vols, ed. K. Schlechta (München, 1956), III, 337.

10. Else, *Aristotle's "Poetics": the Argument* (Cambridge, Mass., 1957).

11. *De Oratore*, I.xi.47; tr. E. W. Sutton and H. Rackham (Loeb Library: London, 1959) p. 35 f.

12. See, for instance, Bernard Weinberg, *A History of Literary Criticism in the Italian Renaissance*, 2 vols. (Chicago, 1961), I, 109, 152, 804–5; Brian Vickers, *Francis Bacon and Renaissance Prose* (Cambridge, 1968), pp. 96 ff., 141 f., 281 ff., 288 f.; and M. H. Abrams, *The Mirror and the Lamp: Romantic Theory and the Critical Tradition* (New York, 1953).

13. *The Critique of Judgement*, tr. J. C. Meredith (Oxford, 1928, 1973), p. 184.

14. John Hoskins, *Directions for Speech and Style*, ed. H. Hudson (Princeton, 1935), p. 15.

15. See my essay above, p. 136 and note 12.

16. Croce, *Aesthetic*, tr. D. Ainslie (London, 1906; 1959), p. 67.

17. I have collected some of these pronouncements on the figures being the "natural language of the passions" in *Classical Rhetoric in English Poetry* (London, 1970), pp. 87, 94, 100, 103, 109 f., 114.

18. R. Wellek and A. Warren, *A Theory of Literature* (1949; quoted from Penguin edition, 1963), p. 184.

19. For an analysis of the naiveté of many Renaissance rhetoricians, who see rhetoric and persuasion as automatic prerogatives of virtue, contrasted with Shakespeare's view of persuasion as the tool of unscrupulous manipulators, see my essay, " 'The power of persuasion': Images of the Orator, Elyot to Shakespeare," in James J. Murphy (ed.) *Renaissance Eloquence. Studies in the Theory and Practice of Renaissance Rhetoric* (Berkeley and Los Angeles, 1982).

20. Quintilian, *Institutes of Oratory*, tr. H. E. Butler, 4 vols. Loeb Library: (London, 1963), vol. I, p. 11.

21. Breen, p. 44. On Nizolius see Breen's edition of his *De veris principiis et vera ratione philosophandi contra pseudo-philosophos*, 2 vols. (Rome, 1956), and R. P. McKeon,

"The Transformation of the Liberal Arts in the Renaissance," in *Developments in the Early Renaissance,* ed. B. S. Levy (Albany, N.Y., 1972), pp. 158–223, at pp. 217–19. In Nizolius' treatise rhetoric becomes the truly universal art, its subject matter being everything in human knowledge: Cicero's injunctions were at last taken seriously, thus finally demonstrating their impractibility.

22. Seigel, op. cit., p. 142; quoting from Valla's *Scritti Filosofici e Religiosi,* ed. G. Radetti (Firenze, 1953), pp. 30–31. On Valla see also Hanna-Barbara Gerl's book (above, note 2). While more scholarly, and more balanced than Seigel's, it makes the same error of treating Valla's polemics with uncritical respect, accepting his claim that rhetoric is "the true philosophy" (p. 74), and saying of his attack on Aristotle that "Diesen Kampf bestreitet die Rhetorik . . . in einem unerhörten Totalitätsanspruch," to replace or transcend all other arts and sciences (p. 78). Valla seems to me, at any rate in his polemical works, to have been well-meaning but hysterical and unbalanced. Such attacks ultimately bring rhetoric into disrespect.

23. Pope, *An Essay on Criticism,* lines 82 f.

24. IJsseling, op. cit., pp. 5, 14 f.

25. *Renaissance Thought and Its Sources,* ed. M. Mooney (New York, 1979), Part V (consisting of lectures delivered in 1975): "Philosophy and Rhetoric from Antiquity to the Renaissance," pp. 213–59.

26. See the Introduction above, pp. 19.

27. *Amours de Voyage* (1858), Canto V, lines 100 ff.

28. See the contributions to this volume by Eugenio Garin and Chaim Perelman.

29. George Kennedy, *The Art of Persuasion in Greece* (London, 1963), p. 65.

C. S. Peirce's Philosophy of Rhetoric

JOHN R. LYNE
University of Iowa

C. S. PEIRCE (1839–1914) contributed voluminously to philosophy, mathematics, and the empirical sciences, and the range and substance of that contribution will undoubtedly occupy scholarly attention for generations to come.[1] From the perspective of the rhetorical tradition, one cannot help being intrigued by Peirce's desire to reconstruct the ancient trivium in light of the new methods of science and logic that had so influenced him. That trivium would consist of Speculative Grammar, Critical Logic, and Speculative Rhetoric, and would be understood as a complete logic of signs, or semiotic. Although Peirce's work in elaborating this grand semiotic theory occurs in episodes spanning several decades and presents considerable problems of interpretation, one finds in it a consistent devotion to systematization. Hence, while there is much we do not know about the Speculative Rhetoric Peirce foresaw, one can find within his theory of signs and in his phenomenological categories a well grounded philosophy of rhetoric, and a set of principles by which that rhetoric should proceed.[2]

Peirce provides various definitions of Speculative Rhetoric, or methodeutic,[3] but they seem to have in common a concern with the constructive use of signs in methodical application. Speculative Rhetoric differs from Critical Logic, or logic in the narrower sense, in its concern with the actual life and function of signs. Peirce's remarks on Speculative Rhetoric are scattered and incomplete, but it is clear that he envisioned a bright future for this branch of his trivium.[4] I want to consider some of the work that is implied in the project of generating a complete Speculative Rhetoric, drawing what clues I can of Peirce's intentions, but also by speculating a bit as to what work is justified by Peircian principles. I especially want to explore how the traditional notion of audience fits within this scheme that often seems centrally concerned with abstract logical relations.[5]

The clearest outline of what Peirce considered the tasks of the third branch of semiotic appears in MS 774, dated about 1904, "Ideas, Stray or Stolen, about Scientific Writing, No.1."[6] Here he makes clear that the context for Speculative Rhetoric is the entire semiotic milieu within which sign-users operate. This is important, I think, for it shows that the work of Speculative Rhetoric cannot be completed solely by the abstract consideration of method. Rather, the particular modes of sign construction present to a community will have to be systematically studied, and in human sign usage (semiosis) at least, so will the psychological processes that bear on the translation of signs into other signs.[7] This should not be thought inconsistent with Peirce's usually strong insistence that semiotic must not be reduced to psychology—there is no reason to suppose that he has here given up the attempt to account logically for the nature of signs. It does indicate, however, that a logical account of Speculative Rhetoric requires consideration of how human cultural factors may bear on interpretation. The special character of sign vehicles and the special character of interpreters are conditions of semiosis, as are the structure of "ideas to be conveyed." Just how these elements are concocted in any concrete case will be a largely accidental matter; but that they must somehow be concocted is a logical requirement of semiosis.

To say that Speculative Rhetoric accounts for an entire semiotic milieu is to suggest that it cannot be elaborated entirely within a realm of perfect Third-ness, Peirce's category of regularity or habit. Instead it faces the ongoing task of analyzing different sorts of interpretive habits as they arise in actual fact or Secondness. The logic of signs, that is to say, must be supplemented by the dynamics of signs as they engage different sorts of interpreting intelligences. I believe Peirce must have had this in mind when he employed the term "rhetoric" for this branch of semiotic. He was well acquainted with the tradition of the term,[8] and it is unlikely that his ethics of terminology would permit him to invoke that tradition without good reason. Rhetoric, in its several traditions, has sought the mechanisms by which minds are effectively engaged in sign pro-cesses. By chance or by design, the major traditions of rhetoric—the Aristotelian, belletristic, and scientific—are all represented in Peirce's first "mode of specializa-tion"(see diagram). And like traditional rhetorics, Speculative Rhetoric presup-poses a grammar and logic.

Peirce attributes three components to any sign: a "representamen" is a ver-bal or nonverbal token which stands in some respect for an "object" to some "interpretant," the notion of "object" not being limited to material objects, and the interpretant not defining a person as such, but only an interpretive func-tion.[9] This irreducible triadic relation has implications for grammar, logic, and rhetoric. If a grammar and logic of signs study interpretants in the abstract, then a rhetoric of signs, if I am interpreting MS 774 correctly, would study how interpretants are embodied in interpreters. Such a view accentuates the interplay between the formal and material elements in semiosis. As a transla-

Diagram 1: Peirce's Proposed Speculative Rhetoric
(Abstracted from MSS 774 and 777)

Modes of Specialization	Leading Divisions
Nature of ideas to be conveyed	*Rhetoric of fine arts (principal subject matter: feelings)*
	Rhetoric of practical persuasion (principal subject matter: resolves)
	Rhetoric of science (principal subject matter: knowledge)
	Communication of discoveries *Mathematics* *Philosophy* *Special Sciences*
	Scientific digests and surveys
	Application of science to special purposes
Class of signs to be interpreted	*Rhetoric of speech and languages Rhetoric of words, sentences, paragraphs, sections to be read at one sitting, separate works, collections of works, short publications, long publications, etc.*
	Dialects
	Languages
	Families of Languages
Nature of signs into which interpretation is to take place	*Rhetoric of signs to be translated into human thought*
	Processes whereby an idea can be conveyed to a human mind and become embedded in its habits

tion of interpretants into further interpretants, semiosis is not logically conditioned by the fact that one interpretant may occur in one mind and the next in another mind (inhabiting another body). When one considers the processes whereby signs may become effective in the world, however, the discontinuities among persons and their respective belief-habits become highly pertinent. For semiosis to generalize from one mind to another, it is necessary that signs be taken up by each mind in relation to what it already knows. The process is therefore a dialectical one which cannot accurately be projected from the standpoint of the sign-user alone. Each mind (or "quasi-mind") comes to a given sign from a different semiotic ancestry, and thus renders its interpretant in a different way. Whether we should say each renders a different interpretant for the same sign is another question; suffice it to say for now that each yields an interpretant from a different perspective or in a different semiotic context or history.

That each interpreting mechanism brings to the process its own web of semiotic relations must be an irreducible condition of semiosis, since, as Peirce has demonstrated, there are no immediate cognitions.[10] One consequence, I believe, is that in addition to understanding the kinds of interpretants that any given sign can yield, Speculative Rhetoric requires a full account of interpreting minds (or quasi-minds). Put another way, Peirce's theory of interpretants usefully describes the kinds of sign effects that are possible; but it offers no clue as to which effects will be probable. Such clues are available only as we supplement what we know about signs generally with knowledge of the constellations in which they occur, and even the psycho-cultural mechanisms through which they operate. In other words, the Secondness of Thirds—the interaction and collision of habits—must be given its due.

The notion that interpretive habits come in separate bundles—occupy separate minds or domains—is a recognition of the place of Secondness in the elaboration of Speculative Rhetoric. Thus, while it must cultivate its methods at the highest level of generality, a universal rhetoric would have to account for sign processes that are effective only in certain universes of discourse. Thus, for example, "The rhetoric naturally adapted to a Shemitic tongue must be very different from a rhetoric well suited to Aryan speech."[11] Such differences constitute interpretive clusters that define communities, scientific, artistic, or practical. One clear implication of the program defined in MS 774 is that Speculative Rhetoric involves a study of such interpretive clusters, whose analogue in traditional rhetoric is the audience.

Peirce does not seem especially concerned with audiences in the usual sense, and because he is generally suspicious of public oratory, it would be unlike him to say much about the ways that popular audiences can be swayed, as did so many of the traditional rhetoricians. Speculative Rhetoric, he says, is a study of a purely scientific kind, not a practical science.[12] Despite his disdain for sophistry, however, Peirce recognizes as Bacon did before him that even in communicating scientifically to scientific minds one must present the truth in different ways to achieve the understanding of different people. Thus we do find him concerned with audiences in some sense. In connection with his "universal rhetoric," for instance, he writes that "Every question of rhetoric turns upon the question to what sort of reader is the writing addressed; that is the reason that to writing of different purposes different codes of rules are applicable" (MS 777). Restated from a more general semiotic viewpoint, the question becomes "To what sort of interpreter is the sign addressed?," and this provides a starting point for the semiotic analysis of audience.

Peirce discusses at various places the character of different sorts of interpreters. A crude categorization of these interpreters, I believe, would acknowledge three different kinds, which I will describe as the divided self, concrete others, and the community.[13] There are strong similarities in the norms of address prescribed for these different sorts of audiences. At the same time, there are differences dictated by their different degrees of independence. That is to say, one's own thoughts are more under one's control than are the thoughts of another person, while the thought of a community is even less under such control. Let us consider the divided self. While Peirce eschews talk of the individual, he puts some emphasis on the "intramural" rhetorical process that engages the different "parts" of the self.[14] Now, first of all we must ask how he conceived of these so-called parts of the self. One's suspicion, of course, is that something like a faculty psychology underlies this kind of talk, although Peirce has been said to have repudiated faculty psychology.[15] His repudiation, however, appears to be more of the particular kind of faculty psychology that had preceded him than of the notion that there could be faculties. In MS 650 (p. 24), for instance, Peirce writes that the notion that there are three "parts of the soul," or three departments or elements of thought, "is substantially true, although the lines were never accurately drawn between the three." Drawing those lines, apparently, has to do with discerning certain habits of mind (MS 659, p. 12). While Peirce unfortunately does not elaborate the point, these evidently correspond to the Categories, which are sometimes approached in terms of phenomenological faculties (5.42).[16]

There is another sense in which the self divides, however, and that is along the lines of the temporal modalities. Hence the self of one moment must address the self of the next through the medium of signs. A person's thoughts, Peirce maintains, ". . . are what he is 'saying to himself'; that is, is saying to that other self that one is trying to persuade; and all thought whatsoever is a sign, and is mostly of the nature of language" (5.421). The self of the next moment is not just a dialogical collaborator in thought, therefore, but a quasi-mind that must somehow be moved or influenced by persuasion. Reference to this dialogue as a specifically persuasive, or rhetorical, process recurs in MS

498. Another variation on the theme appears at 6.336: "All thinking is dialogic in form. Your self of one instant appeals to your deeper self for his assent."

This picture of a process whereby one part offers a line of reasoning and another part passes critical judgment is maintained in other contexts as well. It is also presupposed, for instance, when Peirce maintains a distinction between the inventional and justificatory moments in internal "discourse." This distinction is described as that between "reasoning" and "argument" at 2.27 and "argument" and "argumentation" at 6.456. The reasoning self, that is, becomes an arguing self in order to justify what it believes. Seen in this way, that "other" part of the self presents the same sort of problems to the sign-user as a truly external audience would. The similarity, in fact, shows up in several ways. First, as the self is sprawled over the temporal modalities of past, present, and future, it is always partly opaque and "other" to itself. Second, one knows "his own mind" only through signs, in much the same way that he knows the contents of another's mind (MS 612). Thus self-deception and self-ignorance are not only possible but real and present problems (MS 443, p. 26). Finally, one internalizes certain "norms of right reasoning" (1.606), such that the inner voice meets with a critical standard even before it addresses other persons. What we call a person, in short, is a plurality of critical and interpretive habits. The notion of audience-as-other, therefore, is already at work at this level. Thus when we look at our chart of the functions of Speculative Rhetoric we should be reminded that Peirce saw the creation of "resolves," the arousal of "feelings," and the generation of habits as procedures to be practiced on the self as well as on others.[17]

When it comes to communicating with other persons, Peirce applies the relational principle. A completely "new" sign cannot successfully be communicated; the communicative process depends on "filling out and correcting" signs already understood by the audience (MS 774 and 613). The relational nature of signs makes it possible (in the extreme case which reveals the rule) for a blind man to be an optical investigator, or a color blind person to understand what scarlet is like, to use two of Peirce's examples. One need not have experiences identical to those of another person, in other words, for the nature of that experience to be shared in some respect—in respect, that is, to certain of its relations.[18] This implies that communication is partly a "drawing from" the audience in addition to a "giving to": Tell a man where a diamond mine is, writes Peirce, and you tell him nothing unless you map it against those paths and places he already knows.[19]

The relational nature of signs also makes it necessary to recognize the elasticity that can be exercised in the construction of premises for an argument. Logical inference from any point A to any conclusion C is a continuous movement that may be broken down infinitesimally (5.329). A syllogism, for instance, can only represent a relationship of judgments made at points in this process. All the unstated premises and inferential principles necessary to the completion of the argument function enthymematically, and depend on "common knowledge as defining a sphere of possibility" (2.449). Different audiences, particularly when different universes of discourse are involved, are in a position to supply different "leading principles" and different premises. For instance, when a mathematician speaks to another mathematician, the working enthymemes in that situation make it unnecessary for him to fill in every trivial step of a proof—it is neither more nor less *logical* for him to do so. It would seem to be the same for two biologists or, for that matter, two friends. The different premises and inference habits that may be in the repertoire of different audiences may all provide equally logical means of moving to a conclusion.

To account for any inference habit given in culture is to enter the realm of the rhetorical—to the separate "codes of rules" which govern rational argument and other forms of communication in different universes of discourse. Scientific intelligences, taken either categorically or individually, may be classified according to their characteristic modes of reasoning (2.644). Part of Peirce's skill as a critic, one finds, lay in his ability to identify and hold up to scrutiny the leading principles of his opponents. It would be a mistake to reduce such leading principles to psychology, perhaps, but at the point where relevant inference patterns are effected only in certain groups or individuals, it becomes practically useless to maintain any meaningful distinction between pure semiotic relations and psychological habits.

There is one further point I wish to make concerning concrete audiences. Speculative Rhetoric is intended to further inquiry, and it is Peirce's position that inquiry is always moved forward by some intellectual discomfort or irritation, which he calls doubt. Every inquiry, he writes, takes rise in the observation of some phenomenon that "breaks in on some habit of expectation" (6.469). There is no reason to suppose that such phenomena are restricted to brute facts, however. What I want to suggest here is that an important part of what moves inquiry along is the tension occasioned by differences of judgment, such as might occur from different points of view or frames of reference. Such differences can create a felt need to interpret, correct, translate— to further the semiotic process of relating this interpretant to that one. Hence confrontation with another mind can be one of the primary sources of constructive doubt. The need to address is implied in the very definition of a sign, and it is one reason we can never completely lose sight of the notion of an interpreting intelligence as we look to the various aspects of Peirce's trivium.

The audience that Peirce most favors and urges us to address is the community, since truth cannot be merely for us individually. Thus we find ourselves judged by "a vague personification of the community" (1.586) in ethical matters, and judged in matters of knowledge by the community of "scientific intelligences." Since "no mind can take one step without the aid of other minds," (2.220) the community is a dialogical collaborator with the individual investigator. Another of its functions, however, is teleological. Since there are no self-certifying epistemic episodes, we must look toward a consensus over time as validation for our beliefs.[20] We must anticipate an audience that will continue to respond to new doubts as they arise.

The necessity of incorporating an idealized element in the audience, which is to say the need to invest the concept with sufficient potential, led Peirce to speak of a "final opinion," conceived as the goal toward which the investigating community is aimed. He foresaw an ideal convergence of opinion on any given issue in the scientific community.[21] Such a convergence, he went so far as to say, is "fated," though the precise process or time required to reach it is by no means determined. Truth will out through an unpredictable combination of chance, reason, and brute experience. This process must be consciously expedited, however, and part of what enables us to do that is the belief that there really can be progress toward understanding. Thus, even if the final opinion is *purely* an ideal, it functions teleologically as the goal of inquiry.

Because the community is partly unrealized, it cannot be approached as a finite, determinate thing. It must be approached as a sign: vague, and waiting to be interpreted. When we address it, therefore, we are participating in defining the community, a public "quasi-mind." "Two minds can communicate," Peirce writes in MS 498, "only by becoming in so far one mind." Scientific intelligences may communicate only insofar as they stand upon a common substratum of presuppositions and move according to common inference habits—which is to say they must share a common rhetoric.

I believe that the concept of audience, while it in no way serves to specify the particular methods to be found in methodeutic, does provide an important element in a satisfactory account of how inquiry moves forward. In a sense, the audience provides the standards that inquiry must meet to be successful[22] — standards that Critical Logic alone cannot provide, because it does not take account of the various purposes of inquiry nor the variety of intelligences to which proof (and indeed meaning) must be made manifest, nor the diverse materials and media through which signs may become efficacious. Speculative Rhetoric must account for all of these, and it must account to judging intelligences, which are to be found in different types of audiences.

Notes

1. Recent estimates put the number of published essays at more than 800, with perhaps several times that many unpublished ones. See Max H. Fisch, Kenneth L. Ketner, and Christian J. W. Kloesel, "New Tools of Peirce Scholarship, With Particular Reference to Semiotic," paper presented to the 1977 meeting of the Semiotic Society of America. The best source of primary literature generally available is *Collected Papers of Charles Sanders Peirce*, vols. 1–6, ed. Charles Hartshorne and Paul Weiss (Cambridge, Mass. 1931–35) and vols. 7–8, ed. Arthur Burks (Cambridge, Mass.). Other important materials appear in Carolyn Eisele's *The New Elements of Mathematics by Charles S. Peirce*, 4 vols. (The Hague and Atlantic Highlands; 1976), and Charles S. Hardwick, *Semiotic and Significs: The Correspondence between Charles S. Peirce and Victoria Lady Welby* (Bloomington, Ind., 1977).

2. That Peirce, uniquely among metaphysical thinkers, grounds his overall philosophy in a conception of signification is argued by Josiah Lee Auspitz, "The Metaphysical Adequacy of Peirce's Semiotic," paper presented to the 1979 World Congress of International Association for Semiotic Studies, Vienna. For more detailed treatment of the relationship between Peirce's semiotic and rhetoric, see John R. Lyne, "Rhetoric and Semiotic in C. S. Peirce," *Quarterly Journal of Speech* 66 (1980), 155–68.

3. Speculative Rhetoric, variously referred to as methodeutic, universal rhetoric, and formal rhetoric, is called the "general doctrine of methods of attaining purposes, in general" (2.108) and the "doctrine of the general conditions of the reference of Symbols and signs to the Interpretants which they aim to determine" (2.93). It is said to "ascertain the laws by which in every scientific intelligence one sign gives birth to another, and especially one thought brings forth another" (2.299). In MS 774 Peirce speaks of a "universal rhetoric," defined as "the secret of rendering signs effective."

4. He believed it was "destined to grow into a colossal doctrine" (3.454).

5. John E. Braun argues that Speculative Rhetoric has little to do with discourse as traditionally conceived, in "The 'Speculative Rhetoric' of Charles Sanders Peirce," *Philosophy and Rhetoric*, vol. 14, no. 1 (1981), pp. 1–15.

6. MS 774 has been published, with a bibliographic note by John Michael Krois, in *Philosophy & Rhetoric* 11 (1978), 147–55. Page numbers cited in this essay refer to that publication. Manuscript numbers cited in this text are taken from Richard S. Robin, *Annotated Catalogue of the Papers of Charles S. Peirce* (Amherst, Mass., 1967).

7. In "Ideas, Stray or Stolen," Peirce writes: ". . . One inevitable result of basing rhetoric upon the abstract science that looks on human thought as a special kind of sign would be to bring into high relief the principle that in order to address the human mind effectively, one ought, in theory, to erect one's art upon the immediate base of a profound study of human physiology and psychology. One ought to know just what the processes are whereby an idea can be conveyed to a human mind and become embedded in its habits" (pp. 154–55).

8. See Max H. Fisch, "Peirce's General Theory of Signs," *Sight, Sound, and Sense*, Thomas A. Sebeok, ed. (Bloomington, Ind., 1978), p. 60 ff. Peirce mentions the desirability of preserving the old associations of the term "rhetoric" at 2.229 and 1.444.

9. The object may be a thing, a class, or a collection of things, existing or not, or

"something of a general nature desired, required, or invariably found under certain general circumstances" (2.232).

10. Peirce's most famous arguments against immediate or intuitive knowledge appear in "Questions Concerning Certain Faculties Claimed for Man," *Journal of Speculative Philosophy* 2, no. 2 (1868), 103–14; and "Some Consequences of Four Incapacities," *Journal of Speculative Philosophy* 2, no. 3 (1868), 140–57.

11. "Ideas, Stray or Stolen," p. 154.

12. Ibid., p. 152.

13. I have elaborated a similar tripartite conception of the audience elsewhere. See John R. Lyne, "Rhetoric Mediation," *Rhetoric 78*, ed. Robert L. Brown and Martin Steinmann (Minneapolis, Minn., 1979), 251–57.

14. Two helpful analyses of the dialectical nature of Peirce's semiotic appear in Joseph Ransdell, "Another Interpretation of Peirce's Semiotic," *Transactions of the Charles S. Peirce Society* 12 (1976), and Jarrett Brock, "Peirce's Conception of Semiotic," *Semiotica* 14, no. 2 (1975), 126.

15. James K. Feibleman, *An Introduction to the Philosophy of Charles S. Peirce: Interpreted as a System* (Cambridge, Mass., 1969), p. 460.

16. I follow the standard practice here of citing volume and section number from Hartshorne and Weiss, *Collected Papers*.

17. In MS 674, Peirce sketches a program of habit-formation essential to liberal education, defined as "learning to govern [oneself] so as to attain the ends that will prove satisfactory to him."

18. The paradox of how communication is possible (since I cannot know that anyone has precisely the same experiences as I do) dissolves when one applies this relational view.

19. "Ideas, Stray or Stolen," p. 152.

20. Cf. Chaim Perelman's conception of the "universal audience," *The New Rhetoric: A Treatise on Argumentation*, trans. John Wilkinson and Purcell Weaver (Notre Dame, Ind., 1969). An explicitly Peircian view of justification, based on the ongoing criticism of the community, is formulated by Carl Wellman, *Challenge and Response: Justification in Ethics* (Carbondale, Ill., 1967).

21. That the "final opinion" is an ideal is made clear in Peirce's "Reply to the Necessitarians," *The Monist* 3 (1893), 526–70.

22. Peirce defines proof as that removing of all real doubt from those minds that might apprehend it (2.782).

Rhétorique, dialectique, et philosophie

CH. PERELMAN
Université de Bruxelles

Les notions fondamentales de la philosophie sont presque toutes des notions confuses, qui ne prennent leur sens et leur portée que par rapport au système dans lequel elles sont élaborées et précisées. Cette affirmation d'ordre général vaut plus particulièrement pour des notions telles que "rhétorique" et "dialectique," dont nous verrons qu'elles varient selon le système philosophique dans lequel elles sont intégrées.

Pour illustrer ce fait, indiquons, très brièvement, comment ces notions sont comprises chez Platon, chez Aristote et chez Ramus (Pierre de la Ramée), qui a exercé une grande influence en Europe occidentale jusqu'aux environs de 1700.

Pour Platon, à la suite de Zénon d'Elée, la dialectique est une technique essentiellement purgatoire qui, en révélant les contradictions qu'entraîne une opinion (souvent une définition) avancée par l'interlocuteur, oblige ce dernier à se rétracter, à admettre que sa thèse n'est pas défendable. Le but de la dialectique n'est pas de livrer une thèse positive, conforme à la vérité, mais de préparer l'esprit pour une intuition, une *réminiscence*, une évidence, qui garantirait la vérité grâce à la vision retrouvée de telle ou telle partie du monde des idées.

Une fois assuré de la vérité d'une thèse, le philosophe doit la communiquer à d'autres, la faire admettre. Dans ce but, il devra se servir de la rhétorique, conçue comme psychagogie, que Platon condamne dans le *Gorgias* et dans le *Protagoras*, quand elle est utilisée sans vergogne par les sophistes et les démagogues, mais dont il fait l'éloge dans le *Phèdre* quand elle est un instrument de propagation de la vérité.

Pour réussir dans son entreprise de persuasion, le philosophe devra connaître les espèces d'âmes auxquelles il adresse son discours, les variétés d'auditoires qu'il veut convaincre et auxquelles il doit adapter son propos. Il faut, par ailleurs, que son discours ait des qualités esthétiques, qu'il soit construit d'une façon organique, les différentes parties du discours s'adaptant les unes aux autres comme les organes d'un être vivant: la valeur artistique aura également un effet de persuasion indéniable. Ce qui caractérise la dialectique et la rhétorique chez Platon, c'est que ni l'une ni l'autre ne suffisent au philosophe, la première préparant le terrain pour l'appréhension de la vérité (retrouvée grâce à la réminiscence), la seconde servant uniquement à la communiquer à autrui.

Contrairement à la philosophie de Platon, qui est unitaire et entièrement dominée par la recherche de la vérité, celle d'Aristote est pluraliste et distingue, à part l'*Organon*, qui réunit les oeuvres consacrées à la logique et aux questions de méthods, les disciplines théorétiques, pratiques et poétiques. Alors que les disciplines théorétiques visent la recherche de la vérité, les disciplines pratiques (telles que la rhétorique, l'éthique, la politique) nous fournissent des techniques d'action sur autrui (l'action sur les choses étant curieusement négligée), les disciplines poétiques ayant pour but la création d'une oeuvre ayant une valeur artistique.

Contrairement à Platon, pour Aristote toute matière n'est pas objet de science, de savoir démonstratif. Ne peut être objet de science que ce qui est nécessaire et invariable, l'intuition portant sur les éléments simples et les premiers principes. Par contre, ce qui est contingent et variable, tout objet de délibération et d'action, ne peut donner lieu qu'à des opinions plus ou moins raisonnables, plus ou moins plausibles.

Aristote distingue deux espèces de raisonnements, les raisonnements analytiques, démonstratifs, dont les conclusions sont nécessaires ou du moins vraies, et les raisonnements dialectiques dont les conclusions sont plus ou moins défendables, plus ou moins acceptables. Les raisonnements analytiques sont les seuls admissibles pour exposer et démontrer les propositions scientifiques, les raisonnements dialectiques sont ceux que l'on utilise dans les délibérations, les controverses, et dans toutes les assemblées publiques, chaque fois qu'il y a lieu de critiquer, de justifier une opinion. Il n'existe pas de méthode unitaire universellement applicable: "il serait également absurde, cela saute aux yeux, d'accepter d'un mathématicien des raisonnements plausibles et de réclamer d'un orateur des démonstrations" (*Ethique à Nicomaque*, 1094b).

On voit que, pour Aristote, un champ énorme, celui de la pratique, en tout cas, de la morale, du droit et de la politique, ne peut recourir qu'aux raisonnements dialectiques, qu'il étudie dans la *Rhétorique* et les *Topiques*. Alors qu'il analyse, dans les *Topiques*, les techniques de la controverse, celles où il s'agit d'attaquer et de défendre des opinions, dans la *rhétorique*, il développe celles permettant de persuader, d'influencer un auditoire par des discours.

Aristote n'hésite pas à affirmer que le recours aux topiques est indispensable quand il s'agit d'examiner les premiers principes de toute science (*Topiques* 101a–b), de les faire admettre par tous ceux auxquels ils ne s'imposent pas comme évidents. C'est ainsi que celui qui nie le principe de non-contradiction pourrait être convaincu par le recours à la rétorsion, qui est un argument *ad hominem*.

Nous voyons ainsi l'affirmation par Aristote de deux domaines, celui de la science et celui de l'opinion, l'un régi par les preuves analytiques, l'autre par les preuves dialectiques, avec une restriction, c'est que les premiers principes dépendent également de preuves dialectiques, quand le recours à l'intuition ne suffit pas pour les fonder.

Sous l'influence des stoïciens et des néoplatoniciens, la logique a été identifiée à la dialectique, au Moyen âge et à la Renaissance, ce qui avait pour conséquence de négliger la distinction essentielle établie par Aristote entre les raisonnements analytiques et dialectiques. Mais, alors que les scolastiques tardifs, les "terministes," s'attachaient surtout, sous le nom de dialectique, à la logique formelle et à l'étude de la structure du discours, une orientation opposée se développe chez les humanistes de la Renaissance, sous l'influence de Lorenzo Valla, de Rodolphe Agricola et de Jean Sturm. Ils ont plutôt tendance à abandonner la logique formelle au profit des topiques et de la rhétorique. Ce n'est pas le cas de Pierre de la Ramée (Ramus). Dans sa dialectique, il examine tant les raisonnements analytiques nécessaires, que les raisonnements dialectiques qui ne sont que probables; en outre, il y développe la théorie de l'invention et de la disposition, qu'il soustrait à la rhétorique traditionnelle, le tout faisant partie, d'après lui, de l'*ars disserendi*. La rhétorique se limite, dans cette conception à l'art de bien parler, à l'étude du discours orné, des figures de style et de l'action oratoire: une "Rhétorique" ainsi conçue sera publiée par son ami et collègue Omer Talon.

Le résultat le plus clair de cette conception ramiste, c'est que la notion d'auditoire n'occupe plus la place centrale que lui accordait la rhétorique d'Aristote. Dans sa dialectique, Ramus ne fait intervenir l'auditoire que quand il traite de la "méthode de prudence" opposée à la "méthode de nature". Celle-ci présente l'ordre du discours conformément à l'évidence et à la nature des choses. La méthode de prudence, par contre, est recommandée quand il s'agit de surprendre l'interlocuteur "fascheux et rétif" en ne lui montrant pas immédiatement où l'on veut en venir. Elle ne convient nullement au développement d'une science, mais uniquement quand il s'agit d'opinion; c'est pourqoui d'ailleurs, Descartes la néglige dans son "Discours de la Méthode". Quant à la rhétorique, qui ne traite que des ornements, des figures de style, qui peuvent dans certains cas exciter les émotions et les passions, elle est entièrement étrangère à la preuve et à la persuasion qui était le centre de la rhétorique aristotélicienne.

Cette dernière conception de la rhétorique—qui pourrait avoir quelque intérêt pour l'historien de la littérature,—mais n'en a aucun pour le philosophe—a conduit au mépris de cette discipline chez les romantiques, à sa dégénérescence et à l'oubli dans lequel elle est tombée. Par opposition à cette rhétorique réduite, je voudrais présenter mes propres vues en la matière.

Signalons, pour commencer, que logicien de carrière, ayant obtenu un doctorat en philosophie avec un thèse sur Gottlob Frege, le fondateur de la logique moderne, j'étais formé dans la perspective du positivisme, de l'empirisme logique, qui voulait limiter les méthodes de la philosophie à celles des sciences déductives et naturelles, celles-ci n'étant conçues que comme mise en forme systématique de l'expérience. Le point faible de l'empirisme logique, c'était son scepticisme, son subjectivisme et son irrationalisme dans le domaine des valeurs, qui entraînait ses adhérents à nier la possibilité d'une raison pratique, le monde de l'action restant complètement sous l'emprise des intérêts, des passions et de la violence. C'est cette façon de voir que j'avais adoptée encore dans ma première étude sur la justice, rédigée en 1944.

Mais mon tempérament philosophique allait à l'encontre de cette attitude de renoncement. M'étant mis en quête d'une logique des jugements de valeur, je me suis inspiré des analyses entreprises par Frege pour mettre à jour la théorie de la déduction. Mais alors que lui s'était proposé d'analyser les raisonnements des mathématiciens, je me suis donné la tâche d'analyser les raisonnements de ceux qui raisonnent sur des valeurs, pour montrer que telle valeur, tel choix, telle action sont préférables.

Un long travail d'analyse, entrepris en commun avec Mme. L. Olbrechts-Tyteca, nous a menés, à notre grande surprise, à la conclusion inattendue qu'il n'existe pas de logique spécifique des jugements de valeur, mais que l'on utilise, dans ce domaine, comme dans tous ceux où il s'agit d'opinions, de techniques visant à persuader et á convaincre, longuement étudiées par les Anciens dans les ouvrages intitulés "Rhétorique," et "Topiques." Alors que la logique moderne était limitée à l'étude des raisonnements démonstratifs — les raisonnements analytiques d'Aristote — elle avait oublié l'existence de raisonnements dialectiques, ceux où l'on argumente en vue de persuader et de convaincre. Or, il est indéniable qu'il existe un domaine énorme qui échappe au calcul et à la démonstration, celui où l'on délibère et l'on discute, où l'on critique et où l'on justifie, et où l'on se sert de toute sorte d'arguments pour obtenir l'adhésion d'un auditoire.

Cet immense domaine, est-ce celui de la dialectique ou celui de la rhétorique? Nous avons hésité, au début, sur la manière de le qualifier, mais à la réflexion, nous avons opté pour le terme rhétorique: notre *Traité de l'argumentation* a été intitulé également *La nouvelle rhétorique*, pour l'opposer à la rhétorique des figures. L'avantage de cette option, c'est d'attirer l'attention sur le fait que *toute* argumentation se développe en fonction d'un auditoire et que le "vraisemblable" dont il est question dans les raisonnements dialectiques doit être conçu comme l'acceptable, le raisonnable qui ne peut être défini à l'aide de critères impersonnels, indépendants des esprits qui le jugent. Les figures de rhétorique ne doivent plus être étudiées isolément, en dehors de leur contexte, en n'examinant que leur structure, mais doivent être envisagées en fonction de leur action sur l'auditoire. Il en sera de même pour l'ordre du discours quand il s'agira de présenter "la méthode" ou l'arrangement des arguments en vue d'obtenir le meilleur effet de persuasion. Comme, d'autre part, l'argumentation est conçue dans toute sa généralité, d'une façon complémentaire à la logique formelle, à la démonstration et au calcul, tout discours non-formel visant à persuader, relève d'une façon ou de l'autre, de la nouvelle rhétorique.

Cette façon d'envisager la rhétorique fait de la dialectique et de la philosophie des variantes de l'argumentation. On dira qu'est dialectique le discours s'adressant à un seul auditeur: un tel discours se présente, sauf dans des cas pathologiques, comme un dialogue, une délibération ou une controverse. Le discours philosophique, par contre, qui est un appel à la raison, s'adresse par excellence à l'auditoire universel: il se veut acceptable par tous les hommes qualifiés pour en juger. Le discours philosophique prétend valoir pour tous, comme l'action morale conforme à l'impératif catégorique de Kant.

Les discours scientifiques ne seraient que des cas particuliers d'un tel discours universel, à partir de conventions et de méthodes admises et d'un ensemble de faits qui n'est pas en question.

Nous constations l'existence d'une multiplicité de discours philosophiques, souvent opposés et même incompatibles. Dans la mesure où ils s'adressent tous à un auditoire universel, ils ne peuvent négliger aucun des auditeurs qu'ils voudraient convaincre; à moins de le disqualifier pour l'une ou l'autre raison, comme incompétent ou déraisonnable, ils doivent prendre en considération ses objections. Un philosophe, par vocation, doit être ouvert au dialogue. Le prophète, celui qui n'écoute que son Dieu, qui ne connaît qu'une seule vérité, une vérité absolue indépendante de tout esprit humain, pourrait, à la rigueur, ne tenir compte d'aucune objection. Il n'en est pas de même de ceux qui visent le raisonnable, qui s'élabore dans la recherche d'une adhésion de l'auditoire universel. On voit comment la nouvelle rhétorique, devenue l'instrument indispensable du discours philosophique[1], devrait occuper, à côté du discours formel, tant logique que mathématique, une place centrale dans la formation de notre pensée et de notre culture.

Notes

1. Cf. ma communication "Philosophie, rhétorique, lieux communs," *Bulletin de la Classe des Sciences morales et politiques de l'Académie Royale de Belgique*, 1972, 5e série, t. LVIII, pp. 144–56.

Rhetoric Revalued is a selection of the best papers given at the first two conferences held by the International Society for the History of Rhetoric. This body, which has over 400 members around the world, includes all the distinguished critics and historians of rhetoric of our time. The papers selected here encompass fundamental work on classical, medieval, and Renaissance rhetoric, together with challenging re-evaluations of relationships between rhetoric and philosophy, rhetoric and literature, and the rhetorical tradition.

Brian Vickers, Professor of English and Renaissance Literature, holds the Chair of English at the Swiss Federal Institute of Technology, Zurich, and is University Lecturer in English at Cambridge University. Among his many books and articles are *Francis Bacon* (1978), *Shakespeare's Coriolanus* (1976), *Classical Rhetoric in English Poetry* (1970), and "A Bibliography of Rhetoric Studies, 1970–1980" (*Comparative Criticism* 3: 1981). He has written extensively on Bacon, Shakespeare, Renaissance poetry, and the rhetorical tradition.

mRts

meðieval & Renaissance texts & stuðies
is the publishing program of the
Center for Medieval & Early Renaissance Studies
at the State University of New York at Binghamton.

mRts emphasizes books that are needed —
texts, translations, and major research tools.

mRts aims to publish the highest quality scholarship
in attractive and durable format at modest cost.